Privatization and Regulation with Special Reference to Insurance Regulatory and Development Authority of India

Privatization and Regulation with Special Reference to Insurance Regulatory and Development Authority of India

Ranjeet Singh
Department of Public Administration, Panjab University
Chandigarh

ADROIT

Adroit Publishers

NEW DELHI • KATHMANDU

ISBN : 978-81-87393-62-7

2019

Published by
ADROIT PUBLISHERS 4675/21, Ganpati Bhawan, Ansari Road,
Daryaganj, New Delhi-110 002 Phone : 011 23266030
adroitpublishers@gmail.com
C/O Vajra books, Thamel, Jyatha,
Kathmandu, Nepal l KTM: +977-9808357451

Typeset in Garamond Premier Pro by Arun Sharma,
Akriti Graphic Solution, Delhi-110081 E-mail: arun263923@gmail.com
Ph: 9999414390

Foreword

Government of India adopted Liberalization, Privatization and Globalization (LPG) reforms during the early 1990s in consonance with neo liberalism adopted worldwide. Under LPG reforms many sectors of Indian economy including telecom, infrastructure, capital market, insurance, electricity which were hitherto monopoly of government were opened up to private sector. With a view to protect the interests of the consumers during deregulation period, sector specific regulatory authorities were set up. In the insurance sector Insurance Regulatory and Development Authority of India (IRDAI) was set up in 2000. The major mandate of the IRDAI is to protect the interests of and secure fair treatment to policyholders and bring about speedy and orderly growth of the insurance industry. Now the question arises whether IRDAI has successfully achieved its mandate or not. The answer of this question can be found by undertaking systemic research on the role of IRDAI. The present book is an attempt in that direction. No doubt researchers have examined the performance of IRDAI earlier. The present work, however, is different from other studies on account of formulation of research problem, theoretical framework, formulation of hypotheses, research methodology, data analysis, testing of hypotheses and identification of relevant policy prescriptions.

The book contains seven chapters dealing with introduction, theoretical foundations of regulation, insurance sector de-regulation in India and select countries, organization and working of IRDAI, role of IRDAI and Concluding observations. The book brings out interesting findings by soliciting the perceptions of primary stakeholders, namely, policyholders, agents, officials of life insurance firms, Insurance Ombudsman and official of IRDAI and analyzing the data by using diverse methodology in the form counterfactual analysis, regression analysis, data envelopment analysis.

The important findings of the book are that IRDAI has been effective in promoting growth in insurance sector, spreading insurance to the rural sector, regulating investments of life insurance firms and protecting interests of policyholders. However, IRDAI has been ineffective in promoting efficiency in the conduct of life insurance business in India. The other findings revealed that score card of IRDAI in not satisfactory on account of insurance density and insurance penetration as compared with world average. The agents of insurance firms tend to conceal information from the prospective buyers in matters such as free look period and existing grievance redressal mechanisms. The Insurance Ombudsman Centres are overburdened with complaints.

In the light of above findings the study suggested policy prescriptions for improving the working of IRDAI. The study recommends that IRDAI should organize information dissemination workshops and campaigns for making policy holders aware about grievance redressal mechanism for protecting their interests. NGOs and civil society should also be involved in insurance literacy and also providing feed back to the regulator. Insurance firms should tap new customers instead of indulging in recycling business for improving insurance density and penetration. Insurance firms should minimize their inputs and maximize their outputs for improving efficiency. At Insurance Ombudsman Centres where pendency of complaints is high additional Ombudsman may be appointed. Insurance firms should shun target-centric approach and follow customer-centric approach on ethical grounds. IRDAI should have its independent personnel policy so as to recruit and train officials and build their capacities to achieve its objectives. Lastly, IRDAI should be subjected to periodic assessment by independent agency for social cost-benefit analysis.

The findings of the book are of immense importance to policy makers, regulators, officials of IRDAI and life insurance firms, policyholders, academicians and researchers.

Prof. B.S. Ghuman,
Vice-Chancellor,
Punjabi University, Patiala.

Contents

1

Introduction

1.1 Relationship Between Market and State

Both Inter-Related:

The doctrine of Laissez-faire propagated by Adam Smith during 17th and 18th century, limits the role of government in matters relating to law and order, essential public utilities and defense of the country. Due to the limited role played by the state, public spending remained around 10 percent of the Gross Domestic Product in most of the industrial countries of the world[1].

Gradually, in the early 20th century, the doctrine of Laissez-faire lost in JNU its so-called influence. During and after Great Depressions (i.e. between 1924–1934 C.E.,) the demand for government regulation and intervention in economic affairs was propagated by economists such as J.M. Keynes, Paul Samuelson, Richard Musgrave, etc. had grown up due to market failure, welfare state concept and demand for public good. Market failure was considered as the main reason for government intervention[2]. Economists were of the view that sources of market failure were natural monopoly and externalities[3]. Apart for this, the Marxist and socialist thinking had also stimulated the debate over income inequalities due to Laissez-faire and suggested income re-distribution by state intervention. The prime focus of this era was to build a market structure which is least affected by fluctuations. Regulatory bodies were established to lessen inefficiencies engendered by the market failure. This paved way for the state

1. Vito Tanzi (1997), "The Changing Role of the State in the Economy: A Historical Perspective", *International Monetary Fund Working Paper*, paper presented at conference on, 'Decentralization, Inter-Governmental Fiscal Relations and Macroeconomic Governance' Organized by Advanced School of Public Administration (ESAF), Ministry of Finance of Brazil and OECD Development Centre,16-17 June, 1997Brasilia, p.9.
2. Kieron Walsh (1997), *Public Services and Market Mechanisms: Competition, Contracting and the New Management*, Hampshire, Macmillan, pp.6-11.
3. Sam Peltzman (1989), "The Economic Theory of Regulation after a Decade of Deregulation" *Brookings Papers: Microeconomics*, University of Chicago, p.4.

intervention where and when the public enterprises enhanced public employment. Furthermore, welfare schemes were launched for the poor and marginalized[4].

In the 1970s, state failure paved way for deregulation of economy influenced by contemporary economists i.e. Ludwig Von Mises, Friedrich von Hayek and Milton Friedman. During that phase, instead of minimal role of state –a complementarity between market and state was advocated and termed by Joseph Stiglitz as 'third way'[5]. Thus, the state had adopted the approaches of deregulation and re-regulation with the demand of hour to discharge its functions efficiently and to overcome its earlier inadequacies.

Market Grown Phenomenon

In nutshell, with the ever increasing population, development in technology, social complexity and diversification of economic activities, the role of State has witnessed a sea change from a doer of public activities to a distributor of public benefits and facilitator of change. In order to provide services to the masses, the pendulum of the economy has swung from regulatory to free market, re-regulation and thus, with emerging challenges and fallacies, it adjusts its position back and forth[6].

Emergency of Twin Theories of Regulation

The changing role of State in economic affairs specially in the form of regulation has led to two theories of regulation, namely, public interest theories of regulation and private interest theories of regulation. Public interest theories assume that regulators have sufficient information and enforcement powers to promote public interest. Market failure and government intervention to promote public interest are fundamental to public interest theories. Thus, public interest theories regard regulator as benevolent or to promote public interest at large while private interest theories assume that information asymmetry with respect to cost, demand, quality and other dimensions of firm behavior exists on the part of regulator. Due to existence of information asymmetry, the economic agents such as legislators, voters or consumers tend to pursue their private interest even at the cost of public interest[7].

The regulations in the deregulated era were introduced to prevent market failure, promote competition and protection of consumers interest.

1.2 Significance of the Area of the Study

Due to worldwide changes in global economy, Indian economy was deregulated in form of privatization, liberalization and globalization in the early 1990s. In the wake of these reforms, necessary changes in public policies were introduced to streamline

4. Tanzi, *op.cit.*, P.10
5. Joseph Stiglitz (2003), "Globalization and the economic role of the State in the new Millennium", *Industrial and Corporate Change*, Volume 12, Number 1, pp.9-10.
6. David H. Rosenbloom (1989), *Public Administration: Understanding Management, Politics and Law in the Public Sector*, McGraw-Hill Book Company, New York, p. 355.
7. Johan den Hertog (2010), "Review Of Economic Theories of Regulation", *Discussion Paper Series nr: 10-18*, Tjalling C. Koopmans Research Institute, Utrecht University, The Netherlands, pp. 2-5.

the economy vis-à-vis protect the interest of consumers and promote fair competition among the players. In this backdrop, this study focuses on the mechanisms adopted by the government in the form of Regulatory Commissions to regulate various sectors of economy.

1.3 Selection of the Research Problem

Deregulation of economy and introduction of liberalization, privatization and globalization reforms various sectors such as telecom, infrastructure, capital market, insurance, electricity, etc, were unshackled from government monopoly by opening them to private sector accompanied by establishing sector specific regulatory bodies. The present study confines only to regulatory mechanism in insurance sector. This is dues because of time and resource constrations.

Insurance sector was deregulated in 1999 with the passage of Insurance Regulatory and Development Authority Bill in December, 1999. Present study covers the deregulation of insurance sector. Prior to the deregulation era there were six firms, namely, Life Insurance Corporation, National Insurance Company Ltd., the New India Assurance Company Ltd., the Oriental Insurance Company Ltd and the United India Insurance Company Ltd and General Insurance Corporation catering to insurance needs of the country. After deregulation, 53 players, comprising 6 public and 47 private are in the fray. Two legislations govern the insurance sector: The Insurance Act 1938 and Insurance Regulatory and Development Authority Act 1999. Under the current guidelines, there is 49% equity cap for foreign partners in an insurance company. IRDAI established by IRDAI Act, 1999 with a view to promote the interest of policy-holders. It started functioning on 19 April, 2000 with one chairperson, with four full time and two part time members.

1.4 Insurance Regulatory and Development Authority of India: An Introduction

The key objectives of the IRDAI (supra) are to promote competition for enhancing customer satisfaction through increased consumer choice and lower premiums along with ensuring the financial security of the insurance market.

IRDAI as a regulator performs functions such as regulation, promotion and ensuring orderly growth of the insurance business and re-insurance business; issuance to the applicant a certificate of registration, renew, modify, withdraw, suspend or cancel such registration; protection of the interests of the policy holders; specifying requisite qualifications, code of conduct and practical training for intermediary or insurance intermediaries and agents; specifying the code of conduct for surveyors and loss assessors; promoting efficiency in the conduct of insurance business; promoting and regulating professional organisations connected with the insurance and re-insurance business; levying fees and other charges for carrying out the purposes of this Act; calling for information from, undertaking inspection of, conducting enquiries and investigations including audit of the insurers, intermediaries, insurance intermediaries and other organisations connected with the insurance business; control and regulation of the rates, advantages, terms and conditions that may be offered by insurers in respect of general insurance business not so controlled and regulated by the Tariff Advisory Committee under section 64U of the Insurance Act, 1938 (4 of 1938); specifying the form and manner in which books of account shall be maintained and statement of accounts shall be rendered by insurers and other insurance intermediaries; regulating investment of funds by insurance companies; regulating maintenance of margin of solvency; adjudication of disputes between insurers and intermediaries or insurance intermediaries; supervising the functioning of the Tariff Advisory Committee; specifying the percentage of premium income of the insurer to finance schemes for promoting and regulating professional organizations referred to in clause (f); specifying the percentage of life insurance business and general insurance business to be undertaken by the insurer in the rural or social sector.

Keeping in mind the broad spectrum of functioning of IRDAI it is difficult to undertake and evaluate each function of the IRDAI in this study. The study is only confined to life insurance sector thus functions having ramifications with non-life and re-insurance are not covered. Specifically, the study deals with functions such as role of IRDAI in promoting the growth of life insurance business in India; role of IRDAI in promoting efficiency in conduct of insurance business; role of IRDAI in spreading the life insurance business in rural areas; effectiveness of IRDAI in protection of interests of policy holders; efficacy of grievance redressal mechanisms of IRDAI and effectiveness of IRDAI in regulating investment of funds by insurance companies.

1.5 Review of Literature

Review of literature has been categorized into three sub-themes, namely, Regulation, Deregulation and Re-regulation in deregulated environment.

(a) Studies on Regulation Views of Exports & Economics:

1. **Rossenbloom (1989)**[8] opines that due to increase in economic, technological and social complexity of life during past century, regulatory administration emerged. Regulatory administration is to assure safety of products, services, processes and technologies and promoting proper functioning of market. It fosters reliability and predictability which is essential for maintaining proper economic dependency. Regulations are essential for preventing environmental degradation through the use of 'environmental impact statements'. Regulation promotes healthy employment practices and thus it prohibits undesirable economic production and employment practices, such as child labour. He further explains that regulation suffers on account of being expensive, incompetent, dampening economic performance, causing delays and red tapism and creeping corruption.
2. **Butcher (1995)**[9] emphasizes the involvement of central government in the regulation of the new public sector management arrangements. He cites that

8. Rosenbloom, *op.cit.*, pp. 351-393.
9. Tony Butcher (1995), "Managing The Welfare State: The Politics of Public Sector Management", *Public Administration*, Volume. 73, Number. 3, pp. 494-495.

internal market of National Health Service is managed by the Department of Health and also Centre plays an important role in regulating the tendering processes in local government and the National Service.

3. **Stoker (1995)**[10] finds that regulation has distinctive role to play. State intervention in the economy is essential to manage and sustain demand and provide the infrastructure necessary for mass production. The role of state has also increased through the collective provision of education, health, housing and income support. He further states that working class demands for better social condition and in the process it helps to sustain the norm of consumption, providing the social stability and security.

4. **Cherunilam (2000)**[11] states that Welfare State concept, necessarily lays emphasis on State intervention. He cites R.A. Musgrave and P.B. Musgrave: "Public Finance in Theory and Practice", that so called capitalist economies are in fact 'mixed' economies, as substantial part of business activity is regulated by State. He opines that a State performs four different roles i.e. regulatory, promotional, entrepreneurial and planning role. In regulatory role, the government determines conditions under which the persons or associations may enter in business by granting them charter, franchise, or license. It regulates the conduct of economic ventures thereby lays down standards and prohibitions. According to him, it is Government that regulates relationships between various segments of economy and a settles disputes between various players or participates.

5. **Meier and Rauch (2000)**[12] opine a goal a benevolent State to maximize social development. They cite Nicholas Stern who puts forth five arguments for state intervention, namely, (i) market failure, (ii) income distribution, (iii) rights to certain facilities, (iv) rights to education, paternalism (relating to drugs) and (v) rights of future generations. They further state that a necessary (but not sufficient) condition for a state to be 'developmental' is professionalization of the state bureaucracy.

6. **Shafritz and Russel (2000)**[13] opine existence of more regulation proportionate to crowded and economically developed place. They opine that regulation has its origin in legislation. Since legislations are not comprehensive, the details of rules are specified by administrative agencies and they have full force of law. Agencies begin with some form of legislative mandate and lend to interpret that mandate into policy decisions, specifications of regulations, statements of penalties and enforcement provisions.

---

10. Gerry Stoker (1995), "Intergovernmental Relations", *Public Administration*, Volume 73, Number 1, pp. 101-122.
11. Francis Cherunilam (2000), *Business and Government*, Himalaya Publishing House, Mumbai, pp. 1-11.
12. Gerald M. Meier & James E. Rauch (2000), *Leading issues in Economic Development*, Oxford University Press, New Delhi, pp. 421-425.
13. Shafritz and Russel, *op.cit.*, pp. 11-14.

7. **Dasgupta and Sengupta (2001)**[14] argue that objectives of regulations are to curb the evils of private enterprise and to make it confirm to the overall goals of social and economic justice laid down by the government.

8. **Devas and Kelly (2001)**[15] opine that regulating businesses can be justified where there are market failures of one sort or another such as monopoly, imperfect information or significant externalities. They further opine that licensing is often a crude form of regulation, however, it may be less effective than other instruments such as codes of practice, producers' insurance and liability assignment or targeted taxes and subsidies. Due to globalization of trade, regulatory mechanism has become complex and there has been shift from blanket regulation to targeted interventions related to particular industry.

9. **Mishra & Bhat (2002)**[16] opine that regulations promote competition by minimizing the abuse of monopoly power. It enables enterprises to pursue their commercial objectives along with maintaining some kind of competitive environment to expand the scope of yielding efficiency. They cite World Bank Consultancy Report on the Telecom in Korea, Malaysia, Indonesia, U.S. & Australia, which found that regulatory success depends on a well defined, clear legal mandate, separate from government ministry having policy responsibilities for the sector, complete autonomy for a regulatory body with formal mechanism for all stakeholders to make their views known and without day to day interference from the government or the operator.

10. **Rehman (2007)**[17] studies the regulatory mechanism of Bangladesh Health Care Sector and came across certain inadequacies. The regulatory mechanism suffers from nepotism, the regulator is influenced by political parties and social networks etc. Sometimes, obstacles arise in the way of regulators from unofficial influences, including the "unholy" behaviour of administrative colleagues, professional colleagues, peers, etc. Thus, he opines that in order to make regulatory function efficiently, goals and structure of regulatory system need to be clarified and designed equitably. There should be plurality of regulatory practices, to be achieved through the involvement of consumers, community representatives, providers and professionals, civil society and also that of the State.

11. **Hertog** (2010)[18] explains that there are two broad theories of economic regulations namely, public interest theories of regulation and private interest

14. A. Dasgupta & N.K. Sengupta (2001), *Government and Business*, Vikas Publishing House, New Delhi, pp. 91-103.
15. Nick Devas and Roy Kelly (2001), "Regulation or Revenues? An Analysis of local business licenses with A Case Study of the Single Business Permit Reform in Kenya", *Public Administration and Development*, Volume 21, Number 5, pp. 381–392.
16. R.K. Mishra and K.S. Bhatt, *Privatization,* Vikas Publishing House Pvt. Ltd., New Delhi, pp.1-19.
17. Redwanur Rehman (2007), "The State, the Private Health Care Sector and Regulation in Bangladesh", *The Asia Pacific Journal of Public Administration*, Volume 24, Number 2, pp. 191-206.
18. Hertog, *op.cit.*, pp. 2-5.

theories of regulation. Public interest theories of regulation assume that the regulator have full information and benevolent to promote public interest. While private interest theories of regulations believe that the regulator suffers on account of information asymmetry in aspects of cost, demand, quality and other dimensions of firm behavior consequent to which the economic agents exploits the situation and tends to promote private interest at the cost of public interest. He further classified regulations into economic regulations and social regulations. Economic regulations are further classified into Structural as also conduct regulations. Structural regulations primarily concerns regulations of market structure in the form of restrictions on entry or exit and rules for firms to provide professional services. Conduct regulations on the other hand are used to regulate market behavior of producers and consumers in the form of price controls, labeling of products, rules against advertising and maintaining minimum quality standards. On the other hand-social regulation is regulation in areas of environment protection, occupational health and safety, consumer protection and equal opportunities to all.

12. **Government of Victoria (2011)**[19] states that regulation is necessary as in some instances, the market cannot promote public interest because of market failure. Thus government regulation is justified on the grounds that outcomes of the market may be improved. Market failure occurs due to externalities, information asymmetry, public goods and overwhelming market power resulting in monopoly.

13. **Chortareas, Girardone and Ventouri (2012)**[20] state that regulation hampers efficient operations of banks as whenever regulations are implemented with aim to restrict the activities of banks, the operational efficiency and conduct of business of banks are the most affected. The banks in spate of strict regulatory mechanisms, react by engaging in riskier activities and tends to invest in ways and means that help in circumventing the stipulated regulatory mechanism. Thus, it could have adverse impact on economic performance of banks. On the basis of DEA tests, they further retorted that interventionist approaches in the form of supervision, monitoring and restricting bank activities had resulted in fall in banking efficiency.

14. **Barth, et. al., (2013)**[21] opine that there are two conflicting views regarding banking regulations. These are (i) public interest view and (ii) private interest view. Public interest view emphasized that government regulates banks in public interest and promotes efficient banking and thus, prevents market failure. While private interests view retorts that regulation in banking sector

---

19. Government of Victoria, (2011), *Victorian Guide to Regulation*, Department of Treasury and Finance, Melbourne, pp.1-5.
20. Georgios E. Chortareas; Claudia Girardone and Alexia Ventouri (2012), "Bank supervision, regulation, and efficiency: Evidence from the European Union", *Journal of Financial Stability*, Volume 8, pp. 292-302.
21. James R. Barth, Chen Lin, Yue Ma, Jesús Seade and Frank M. Song (2013), "Do bank regulation, supervision and monitoring enhance or impede bank efficiency?" *Journal of Banking & Finance*, Volume 37, pp. 2879–2892

tends to promote special interests of few and thereby impacts banking efficiency.

15. **OECD (2014)**[22] highlights that regulation is a tool for achieving policy objectives of governments. Not only implementing regulations but ensuring compliance is also necessary for well functioning of society and government. Thus, to improve regulatory compliance governments tends to enforceability and inspections. But in most of the countries, very less attention is paid towards the process of regulatory enforcement and inspections. If inspections are conducted efficiently and effectively then regulatory costs involved - can be reduced significantly. Thus, government mechanisms for regulation are desired to be based on sound principles of regulatory management.

16. **Jong and Witteloostuijn (2015)**[23] expresses that regulation is double edged sword as it may benefit society and may also have negative effects on individual firms. Regulation affects the competitive capabilities of firms as it raises costs and decreases the flexible operating mechanisms. Regulation also tends to divert attention of management away from strategic issues and in the process capital investment decision are worst hit. Small and medium sized enterprises are more prone to such problems as they are not well equipped to deal with regulatory issues as compared to large scale firms.

(b) Studies on De-regulation:

17. **Grey and Jenkins (1995)**[24] raise questions on the failure of State due to its monopolistic nature. The solutions to the problems include creating markets, charging for services, liberalizing administrative regimes and even privatizing. Thus, motivation and incentive systems of traditional public organizations (incremental pay scales, career systems, job security) were also attacked and reforms were advocated which focused on performance related reward systems and management against targets. They, conclude that the progressive and attractive aspects of Public Management Theory therefore, stress decentralization, deregulation and delegation within a framework of executive models of centralization, coordination and control.

18. **Lane (2000)**[25] emphasises that it is very difficult to determine output and price by means of regulation because regulator has erroneous information provided by the regulated. Those who are regulated act within the confines of bounded rationality and they are opportunistic. He further opines that due to regulations, capture model emerges which means special interest of both the regulator and the regulated will dominate over the public interest. Thus,

22. OECD (2014), *Regulatory Enforcement and Inspection: OECD Best Practice Principles for Regulatory Policy*, OECD Publishing, pp. 4- 40.
23. Gjalt De Jong and Arjen Van Witteloostuijn (2015), "Regulatory Red Tape And Private Firm performance", *Public Administration*, Volume 93, Number 1, pp. 34-51.
24. Andrew Grey and Bill Jenkins (1995), "From Public Administration to Public Management: Reassessing a Revolution", *Public Administration*, Volume 73, Number 1, pp. 75-100.
25. Lane, *op.cit.*, pp. 118-142.

he suggests that instead of regulations, market should be de-regulated and degree of competition between actors must be enhanced. Government should search competitive forms such as bidding, contracting, franchising, separation between transmission, production and distribution to enhance competition.

19. **Cohen (2001)**[26] highlights that inefficiency of public enterprises due to absence of profit motive, problems of over–formality in public sector, political influence in the process of managing activities are apt arguments in favour of privatization. He further opines that in this complex economic society, no organization is purely private. All firms are regulated and must be sensitive to legal, social, cultural and political constraints. Conversely government organizations are not immune to the considerations of efficiency. He further highlights that privatization is not well suited in the areas of criminal and civil justice and areas with no obvious customers to provide resources to the organization that performs the work (e.g. homeless individuals).

20. **Breausc, Duncan, Keller and Morriss (2002)**[27] study the effects of privatization through Principle-Agent relationship. These authors opine that due to privatization, the relationship between the citizens and governments become more complex thereby forcing the government entity into the dual role of principle and agent. Due to duality, problems of accountability and monitoring become evident and it ultimately leads to dilution of responsibility and accountability. Thus, social contract between citizen and government is compromised and accountability mechanism is weakened.

21. **Prakash, Rao and Shukla (2002)**[28] state that due to poor performance of public sector enterprises in the nationalized era, the option of privatizing these enterprises is best sought world over. Thus, privatization is the most pragmatic answer to the economic constraints created by fiscal and budgetary pressures. Countries reinforce productive efficiency through reducing the relative importance of the State in economic activity.

22. **Savas (2002)**[29] studies the role of local governments in providing social welfare benefits in the United States. He opines that Vouchers are emerging as the preferred privatization method for many social welfare services. They can be used for food, housing, education, health care, child care, home care, elder care, job training and family services. They are advantageous because social services initially were monopolistic but vouchers had introduced both competition and user choice that improve services and minimize monopoly.

---

26. Steve Cohen (2001), "A Strategic framework for Developing Responsibility and functions from Government to the Private Sector", *Public Administration Review*, Volume 61, Number 4, pp. 432-440.
27. David A. Breausc, Christopher M.Duncan, C.Denise Keller and John C. Morriss (2002), "Welfare Style: Temporary Assistance for Needy families and the Search for Accountability", *Public Administration Review,* Volume 62, Number 4, pp. 415-422.
28. Jagdish Prakash, Nageshwar Rao and Mata Badal Shukla (2002), *Administration of Public Enterprises in India*, Himalaya Publishing House, Mumbai, pp. 377-403.
29. E.A. Savas (2002), "Competition and Choice in New York City Social Services", *Public Administration Review*, Volume 62, Number 1, pp. 82–91.

23. **Kaur (2003)**[30] cautions that mere change of ownership from public to private does not bring efficiency, but the sufficient competition is essential. Also productivity could be enhanced by granting greater degree of autonomy to managers of Public Enterprises and also making them more accountable through effective regulation policy.

24. **Narain (2003)**[31] opines that privatization is necessary for enhancing the performance of public enterprises, as it challenges the monopolistic tendency of public enterprises and thus provides competition and promote accountability. Private enterprises are free from political interference in day to day operations. He cautions by citing Human Development Report-1993 that private enterprises often tend to maximize short term revenue rather than building competitive markets for long term and also allegations of corruption are leveled against them. Market based capitalism may be destructive to the social stability and growth which will ultimately, affect vulnerable. He concludes that in order to achieve efficiency, there should be regulatory mechanism so that necessary market conditions for efficiency may prevail. He cites an International Monetary Fund (IMF) study that emphasises upon the appropriate regulatory framework so that privatization could become the most efficient.

25. **Brown (2004)**[32] highlights that deregulation issues continue to arise in transportation, energy, banking, broadcasting and cable. Recent competition in the cable and telephone industries has warranted a backtracking of deregulation efforts by the FCC as potentially counterproductive to the market's development. A chief concern with business legislation is the cost. That is, at what point does the cost of legislation outweigh the benefits? This cost-benefit question, first posed during the Reagan administration, is likely to persist. However, as products and services become more complex due to rapid technological change, various public constituencies are likely to ask for new regulations, and individual companies and industry groups will be required to maintain surveillance of current and pending legislation.

26. **Iacobucci, Trebilcock, and Winter (2005)**[33] opine that two kind of considerations should influence design of the deregulatory agenda. The first is economic. The desire for greater economic efficiency has undoubtedly, inspired the path of deregulation. The second kind of consideration is political. In their view, insufficient attention has been paid to political considerations in the deregulation of markets, which has in turn jeopardized the economic

30. Kaur, *op.cit.,* pp.1-18.
31. Narain, *op.cit.,* pp. 305-308.
32. Gene Brown (2004), *Deregulation,[Online] Available from* http://www.enotes.com/management-encyclopedia/deregulation [Accessed on 30 July 2008].
33. Edward M. Iacobucci, Michael J. Trebilcock and Ralph A. Winter (2005), "The Canadian Experience with Deregulation", *Queen's University Law & Economics* Working *Paper No. 2005-03,* Sauder School of Business, [Online] Available from http://ssrn.com/abstract [Accesses on 2 August 2008].

benefits of deregulation and suggested that future attempts at deregulation must do better in anticipating potential political obstacles to reform, even at the cost of departing from a "first-best" efficient regulatory reform, in order to keep the deregulation train on track.

27. **Demyanyk (2006)**[34] appreciates that in USA Interstate bank branching deregulation had a positive impact on self-employment for relatively poor women and minorities. There are on average fewer self-employed women and minorities—and they earn on average much less—than, correspondingly, men and white individuals possibly due to discrimination in the both labor and credit markets. Banking reform seems to have mitigated discrimination in lending and increased credit availability for the previously-discriminated groups. As a result, the growth rate of self-employment income for these groups increased. Importantly, it is deregulation and not direct government subsidies to banks for financing small businesses that positively influenced self-employment of previously discriminated women and minorities.

28. **Aulich and Flynn (2007)**[35] state that the private sector was the ultimate machine for promoting growth and economic recovery, and the public sector needed to be both smaller in size and restricted in its scope. In Australia, three modes of privatization were used. These are divestment, outsourcing and user pays and charging. Thus, they conclude that privatization has been one of the critical facilitators of a historic transition in the primary role of government from nation building to service delivery and from reliance on government as the primary service provider to a role as enabler or facilitator of community choice.

29. **Das and Abott (2008)**[36] highlight the objectives of Public sector reforms by postulating them as inputs of New Public Management world. The objectives are the delivery of collective welfare, to improve incentives and management decision making, to introduce superior private sector management principles and practices, to accommodate economic criticisms of public enterprises e.g. preventive abuse of the power of natural monopolies, to improve the availability of capital to public enterprises and to reduce public sector borrowing. They state that privatization in Malaysia mean not only the sale of public assets but also various forms of partial sale. Privatization encompassed corporatization and leasing of public sector goods and services by the government, management contracting and other activities such as Build–operation and

---

34. Yuliya Demyanyk (2006), "U.S. banking deregulation and self-employment: A differential impact on those in need," *Journal of Economics and Business*, Volume 60, Number 1-2, pp. 165-178.
35. Chris Aulich and Janine O' Flynn (2007), "From Public to Private: The Australian Experience of Privatisation", *The Asia Pacific Journal of Public Administration*, Volume 29, Number 2, pp. 153–172.
36. Mohan Das and Keith Abott (2008), "Modelling NPM in an Asian Context: Public Sector Reform in Malasiya", *The Asian Pacific Journal of Public Administration*, Volume 30, Number 1, pp. 59-80.

transfer. There were two phases of privatization–one from 1955 - 1990 known as "ad hoc privatization" and second from 1991 onwards known as "affirmative privatization".

30. **Coy, Pavlov and Wachter (2009)**[37] opine that large scale secondary markets for mortgage instruments have existed since the 1980s but in 1990s and 2000s, these markets were de-regulated which led to sub-prime crisis. The deregulation of these markets and feeble enforcement led to the crisis. It is viewed that markets could not have developed without a regulatory environment. In this way, lack of proper pricing control had culminated into market failure.

31. **Bassanini and Brunello (2010)**[38] suggest that an increase in product market, deregulation generates a sizeable increase in training incidence. The European countries which have undergone massive regulatory reforms in the form of deregulation have raised competition, which in turn, has increased investment in workplace training. Thus, the important link in the relationship between deregulation and productivity growth is the investment in human capital.

32. **Davis and Wolfram (2011)**[39] analyzes impacts of deregulation on US nuclear energy sector. The results revealed that deregulation and consolidation had increased ten percent operating efficiency in nuclear energy sector by decreasing the number of outage days per year and paving way for prudent investments in capacity. More over deregulation also led to increase in production of electricity and disinvestment had significant improvement in safety of nuclear reactor as prudent designs were used.

33. **Roy and Kemme (2012)**[40] find that banking crises were results of worsening capital adequacy ratio which were associated with financial liberalization and lack of regulatory control over banking institutions. Further rising income inequalities, excessive speculation in asset markets due to financial liberalization were also a cause of banking crisis.

34. **Timm (2013)**[41] states that deregulation in Georgia led to 10 percent annual

37. Patricia A.Mc. Coy, Andrew D.Pavlov and Susan M. Wachter (2009), "Systemic Risk Through Securitization: The result of Deregulation and Regulatory Failure", *Connecticut Law Review,* Volume 41, Number 4, pp. 495 to 501.
38. Andrea Bassanini and Giorgio Brunello (2010), "Barriers to Entry, Deregulation and Workplace Training: A Theoretical Model with Evidence from Europe", *CESfifo Working paper NO.2945, Category 4: Labour Markets* [Online] Available from: www.ssrn.com, [Accesses on 8 August 2013] pp. 2-23.
39. Lucas W. Davis and Catherine Wolfram (2011), "Deregulation, Consolidation, and Efficiency: Evidence From U.S. Nuclear Power", *National Bureau of Economic Research Working Paper 17341*, Massachusetts Avenue Cambridge, pp.1-40.
40. Saktinil Roy and David M. Kemme (2012), "Causes of banking crises: Deregulation, credit booms and asset bubbles, then and now", *International Review of Economics and Finance*, Volume 24, pp. 270–294.
41. Christial Timm (2013), "Economic regulation and State Intervention: Georgia's Move from Neo-liberalism to State Managed Capitalism", *Research Paper No. 2013/13*, Private University of Applied Science, pp. 1-27.

growth in GDP between 2005 and 2007 and FDI also consistently increased to USD 2 Billion in 2007 which was equivalent 0-20 percent of the GDP. Corruption also suffered a setback in the post deregulation era due to abolition of red-tapism. The reduction in corruption enhanced the ranking of the country in Ease of Doing Business Index.

35. **König (2014)**[42] opines that deregulation had adverse impact on employment. Deregulation of shop closing legislations had negative effect on retail sector employment in Germany as due to liberalization around 19,000 full time employed persons lost their jobs. Majority of job losses were among small establishments while medium and large establishments were relatively unaffected by change in law. Moreover job losses were borne by full time employees and part time employees were not affected.

36. **Walwei (2015)**[43] highlights that due to deregulation of labour market in Germany there was rise in number of unemployed workforce and also low-wage employment. Thus government re-regulated the labour market so as to strengthen the workforce rights and reverse the trend of unemployment. Due to regulation the situation in labour market improved significantly and unemployment declined from 5 million to 2 million or around 40 percent between 2005-2011. Currently, the unemployed are around 2.9 million which are 6.5 percent of the civilian labour force.

(c) Studies on Regulation in Deregulated Environment

1. **Economic and Political Weekly (1999)**[44] opines if Insurance Regulatory Development Authority (IRDA) successfully plays it's role, consumers can hope to get better insurance product and better service. Long term funds will be available to finance infrastructure that would benefit both from the additional premium income generated in the insurance sector and from the development of a market for long term debt. Opening of insurance market to private players will be generating competitive pressures for LIC and GIC and give them an outside chance to emerge as viable business organizations continuing to be government owned.

2. **Pant (2000)**[45] highlights that IRDA has a daunting task of establishing and promoting fair competition in the monopolistic insurance market. Insurance sector has not effectively tapped agriculture sector, thus IRDA must quickly

42. Charlotte Senftleben-König (2014), "Product Market Deregulation and Employment Outcomes: Evidence from the German Retail Sector", *SFB 649 Discussion Paper 2014-013*, Humboldt-Universität zu Berlin, Germany, pp. 2-15.
43. Ulrich Walwei (2015), "From deregulation to re-regulation: Trend reversal in German labour market institutions and its possible implications", *IAB Discussion Paper Articles on labour market issues 10/2015*, Institute For Employment Research, Germany, pp. 1-20.
44. Editorial, Dec (1999), "Ending the Insurance Monopoly", *Economic and Political Weekly* Volume 34, Number 49, p. 3403.
45. Niranjan Pant (2000), "Development Agenda for Insurance Regulation", *Economic and Political Weekly*, Volume 35, Number 10, pp. 762-764.

develop regulatory norms for addressing availability and affordability of appropriate agricultural and rural insurance products.

3. **Ranade and Ahuja (2000)**[46] both highlight the working of insurance regulators of China and suggest ways to strengthen insurance regulatory mechanisms in India in Insurance. They are of view that initial focus of IRDA must be on financial soundness and prior experience of entrants in insurance market. Development of competition issues would not be paramount in the early stages. Social consideration of serving relatively backward sections of society is best undertaken in form of entitlement vouchers or social obligations on all players, which can be tradable.

4. **Gupta (2002)**[47] points out at the issue of privatization of the health insurance business in India. She found that insurance schemes largely cover only the formal sector in India and most Indians (unemployed) remain uninsured. They spend large sum of money on health out of their pocket. Through public private partnerships insurance, major chunk of population could be provided health insurance facilities with quality and equity. It could be realized by creating a distinct body of health insurance that can go into planning as well as implementation of health insurance, taking into account the objectives of equity and efficiency.

5. **Mahal (2002)**[48] opines that even a well designed regulatory set up for private health insurance such as in the United States may not yield entirely satisfactory outcomes. There are high costs linked with private insurance but regulation can contain these costs by promoting financial solvency, large group insurance and managed care institutions such as Health Maintenance Organisation (H.M.O) combines the roles of provider and insurer. It is believed that health spending per capita is positively associated with the proportion of population covered by private insurance. Thus, he concludes that in an ideal world with well informed consumers, private insurance may be advantageous for cost and quality although it could have adverse impact from an equity point of view. He highlights that there is less regulatory focus, on the consumer of insurance products and on overall goals of health policy in the form of regulations. Regulatory regimes have little to say about quality of health care, as the aspect is presumably being taken care of, by other legislation or by market. In order to have uniform benefit packages to work and for competition to kick in among insurance companies, large buyer groups may have to be created on pattern of the U.S. and various European countries. There is need for better coordination between the activities of the IRDA and other bodies such as the Monopoly and Restrictive Trade Practices Commission.

46. Ajit Ranade and Rajiv Ahuja (2000), "Issues in Regulation of Insurance", *Economic and Political Weekly*, Volume 35, Number 5, pp. 331-336.
47. Indrani Gupta (2002), "Private Health Insurance & Health Cost", *Economic and Political Weekly*, Volume 37, Number 27, pp. 2795-2802.
48. Ajay Mahal (2002), "Assessing Private Health Insurance in India, Potential Impacts & Regulatory Issues", *Economic and Political Weekly*, Volume 37, Number 6, pp. 559-570.

6. **Mor and Nitsure (2002)**[49] state that economists and financial experts are stressing the need for a single or unitary regulator for whole financial market not only to achieve economies of scale, but to improve the financial market functioning by avoiding issues relating to jurisdiction. They cite the then RBI Deputy Governor, Y.V. Reddy's view while he proposed an umbrella regulatory legislation, creating an apex regulatory authority without disturbing the existing jurisdiction, with the Governor of RBI as its Chairman and three regulatory chiefs as its members. Thus, they conclude that by observing world over phenomena's and in order to make financial system to act as a true facilitator of economic growth and prosperity, there is need to seriously consider the possibilities of moving towards aggregated and consolidated supervision under one regulator.
7. **Nandraj and Khot (2003)**[50] argue that there is dismal performance by public health care facilities in India. The quality of private health care facilities is not upto the mark. There is absence of legislation for regulating private health care facilities, laboratories and various types of health centres. No standard of medical practice have been prescribed in terms of qualification of staff employed. Thus, in order to establish accreditation system for health facilities in India, there should be balanced representation of various stake holders such as hospital owners, administrators and professional bodies, alongside government, consumer body representatives and insurance companies. There is enduring need for strong regulations to bring quality health care within the reach of all.
8. **Ahuja (2004)**[51] appreciates the working of IRDA and says it had successfully regulated the insurance market but still more needs to be done. Pension and health insurance market is still under developed. Insurance industry should have strong self-regulation mechanism. FDI limit for insurance should be raised so that competition in insurance sector could blossom fully. Thus, insurance regulator needs to fine-tune the rules of the game according to the development of market.
9. **Bhat and Babbu (2004)**[52] criticize that IRDA place stringent conditions for licensing Third Party Administrator (TPA). TPA faces major challenge in bringing down settlement period as it is observed that lack of proper documents related to treatment often result in deferred or non-payment of claims. TPA increases accessibility to health care and cashless hospitalization facility, but, it reduces the choice of hospital on the part of consumer as one has

---

49. Nichiket Mor and Rupa Rege Nitsure (2002), "Organization of Regulatory Functions: A Single Regulator?", *Economic and Political Weekly*, Volume 37, Number 5, pp. 449-454.
50. Sunil Nandraj and Anagha Khot (2003), "Accreditation System for Health Facilities", *Economic and Political Weekly*, Volume 38, Number 50, pp. 5251-5255.
51. Rajiv Ahuja (2004), "Insurance: Over the Transition", *Economic and Political Weekly*, Volume 39, Number 32, pp. 3569-3571.
52. Ramesh Bhat & Sumesh K. Babbu (2004), "Health Insurance & Third Party Administrators: Issues & Challenges", *Economic and Political Weekly*, Volume 39, Number 28, pp. 3149-3157.

to go to the facility chosen by the TPA. The minimum standard of a health care are not defined, health care service providers have a much higher bargaining power in the system and could not be persuaded to follow standards and quality guidelines. There is lack of standardization or accreditation system for hospitals which causes concern over prices and billing.

10. **Gangopadhyay (2004)**[53] opines that the market solution in insurance for the small farmers demands payment of very high premium. Thus, he suggests that regulator should reduce the amount of paid up capital of Rs. 1 billion for NGOs, which can effectively tackle the insurance problems. As amount of premium would be less so poor farmers will also be able to insure their crops.

11. **Gupta, Roy and Trivedi (2004)**[54] criticize the working of TPAs, as some hospitals were not getting their payments on time and they were reluctant to work with them. Some of the hospitals have got TPA license, which is unethical and against the basic guidelines laid down by IRDA. Customers have to pay higher premium for the extra service being provided by TPA. IRDA must amend current regulations so that malpractices such as hospital backed TPAs could be rectified. IRDA must review the performance of each TPA objectively and also look into the matter of optimum number of TPAs in insurance sector.

12. **Mahapatra (2005)**[55] states that Third Party Administration plays a vital role as it forms bridge between a claimant, the medical service provider and the insurer in such a way that all parties are satisfied and nobody suffers due to loss. The regulations regarding TPAs has many flaws as there is no standard document that the three parties can swear by, thus, often their relationship come into conflicts. The customers' service expectations are often hampered due to billing format, pre-authorization for cashless admission disallowances, tariff per city/medical process coding, grievance redressal etc.

13. **In view of Rao (2005)**[56] the system of regulation or de-regulation has been abused by a few powerful market practitioners, thus, there has been legislative overdrive towards re-regulation. India is a strong votary of self-regulation but under the benign control of government. This gives a unique blend of 'controlled regulation'. According to the authority, self regulation has been a failure in non-life insurance in India.

14. **Ansari (2006)**[57] states that IRDA decision of disarraying of all non-life insurance is a welcome step to cope up with the true spirit of liberalization to minimize

---

53. Shubhashis Gangopadhyay (2004), "An Alternative to Crop Insurance", *Economic and Political Weekly*, Volume 39, Number 44, pp. 4763-4764.
54. Indrani Gupta, Abhijit Roy and Mayur Trivedi (2004), "Third Party Administrators: Theory & Practice", *Economic and Political Weekly*, Volume 39, Number 28, pp. 3160-3164.
55. S. K. Mahapatra (2005), "A Healthy Ground for TPA", *IRDA Journal*, Volume III, Number 6, pp. 19-20.
56. G. V. Rao (2005), "Ensured Success for Insurance Councils: What it Takes to Make Self-Regulation Tick", *IRDA Journal*, Volume III, Number 6, pp. 21-24.
57. H. Ansari (2006), "Marketing Opportunities & Challenges", *IRDA Journal*, Volume IV, Number 11, pp. 24-26.

impact on industry. It induces fair competition by continuous monitoring of new products and price change, gradual change of solvency regulation into RBC system, and more emphasis on "protection of policy holders"

15. **Jacob (2006)**[58] opines that detarrified market is fundamental component of liberalization i.e. free market and open market. IRDA cautiously treaded by opening the market after six years, as it felt that the players now have maturity and capacity. Detarrified market will have two implications - (i) it will lead to transition from 'administered pricing to risk based pricing", and - (ii) it will lead to "product differentiation".

16. **Chatterjee (2007)**[59] is of the opinion that with the sophistication of financial market due to liberalization, there is lack of knowledge on the part of consumer about various services available. Being financial literate, it helps consumer how to avoid becoming victims of fraud, how to exercise consumer protection, optimizing household budget. Thus, he suggests that strategy based on public private partnership model should be evolved so that people should be educated about financial market and its emerging trends.

17. **George (2007)**[60] opines that general insurers who have begin operations after the commencement of IRDA are excepted to raise 2 percent and 3 percent of their gross premium income in first and second year from rural areas. By fixing obligation of percentage of premium in rural areas, it may lead to an iniquitous spread of insurance in rural areas as a small number of large policies from well to do population can make up the necessary percentage without touching the rural population at all. He criticizes the current trend in India of private corporate hospital themselves starting TPAs and of TPAs starting health delivery networks which is unethical according to IRDA guideline.

18. **Mohan (2007)**[61] says that in the realm of liberalised economic policy, the Insurance Act 1938, needs a re-look to make it more vibrant and responsive to the emerging needs and challenges. He cites the Law Commission of India's 190th Report which recommended that period beyond which no repudiation of life insurance policy can be made be fixed five year from present two years. Law Commission also as recommended that penalties be levied after an inquiry by the adjucating officer to be appointed by IRDA. Commission also recommended that there should be a grievance redressal mechanism under the overall supervision of the IRDA. Similarly, instead of setting up of separate Insurance Appellate Tribunal to hear the appeals from the order of the IRDA, it would be desirable to make use of the existing Securities Appellate Tribunal.

---

58. Antony Jacob (2006), "Maturing Progressively: Indian Insurance Industry", *IRDA Journal,* Volume IV, Number 11, pp. 27-28.
59. Arup Chatterjee (2007), "Insurance Awareness: Where do We go from Here?", *IRDA Journal,* Volume V, Number 07, pp. 32-35.
60. Alex George (2007), "Critical Appraisal of Micro Health Insurance Laws", *Economic and Political Weekly,* Volume 42, Number 06, pp. 476-479.
61. S. V. Krishna Mohan (2007), "Insurance Legislation in India, Ancient yet Modern", *IRDA Journal,* Volume V, Number 11, pp. 21-22.

19. **Murty (2007)**[62] discusses KPMG report titled "Global Skills for Graduates in Financial Services" and finds that 58 percent of Indian financial services are facing difficulties in recruiting the people with the right set of skills. He advises that deteriorating standards in higher education can be raised up by public private partnership model. There is strong feeling in the market that growth in insurance business is likely to be impaired by lack of 'capital' and shortage of work force with right set of skills.

20. **Parekh (2007)**[63] highlights key supervision components as Market Analysis, Offsite Monitoring, Onsite Inspection, Preventive and Corrective Measures and Enforcement or Sanctions. Thus, depending upon the developments, markets are supervised. Some markets have one umbrella regulatory body for whole financial sector. While other have separate regulatory bodies for each sector. According to the author with the liberalization, de-tariffication, participation by retail investor, we will witness policy changes in India.

21. **Radhakrishna (2007)**[64] opines that in long run industry cannot be supervised or monitored closely by the regulator. The only solution is self-regulation and it could be done by some measures such as licencing of the new players should become stricter, track record and experience should be dominant parameters for eligibility and industry association should encourage exchange of information amongst members. Regulator could establish separate advisory body to discuss problems being faced and suggest best practices for industry to follow.

22. **Raju and Chand (2007)**[65] state that in order to have successful crop insurance scheme, public support is required. This could be in terms of subsidies on premium, meeting part of the administrative expenditure and reinsurance etc. Global experience shows that due to the special nature of agricultural production in several countries; premium payable by farmers is subsidized by the government.

23. **Vermani (2007)**[66] expresses that IRDA has significantly regulated the insurance market by issuing timely regulations, guidelines and keeping the industry in check. But with growth in economy and liberalization, more cautious approach is needed as insurance market in India is still in a nascent stage. He further opines that we are witnessing, a demographic change in the country and younger generation which is exposed and more favoured to the outside world

---

62. R. K. Murty (2007), "Insurance Literacy in India", *IRDA Journal*, Volume V, Number 07, pp. 21-24.
63. Ashvin Parekh (2007), "*Regulatory A*pproaches to Supervision and Inspection: A Look at Different Market", *IRDA Journal*, Volume V, Number 09, pp. 27-29.
64. Radhakrishna (2007), "Alternatives to Monitoring & Supervision: Difficult not Impossible", *IRDA Journal*, Volume V, Number 09, pp. 24-26.
65. S. S. Raju and Ramesh Chand (2007), "Progress & Problems in Agriculture Insurance", *Economic and Political Weekly,* Volume 42, Number 21, pp. 1905-1908.
66. Lalit Vermani (2007), "The Changing Pace of Insurance Laws: Going With Times", *IRDA Journal*, Volume V, Number 11, pp. 25-27.

demands - products and services which are at par with advanced countries. According to him thus, it is the biggest challenge for insurance market in India.

24. **Chandrasekharan (2008)**[67] states that major reason for policy lapsation is that the marketing and sales people don't look beyond the sale. Since there is no incentive offered in for conservation of policy, thus agents do not take interest in sustaining the policy. Some times misselling and also narrow interest of the agent leads to the lapsation of policy.

25. **Kakkar (2008)**[68] finds that Assets Liability Management (ALM) is an ongoing process of formulating, implementing, monitoring and revising strategies related to assets and liabilities in an attempt to achieve financial objectives for a given set of risk tolerances and constraints. The author opines that in order to overcome reinvestment risk one should enter into long term interest rate swap contracts where the insurer can exchange its market variable interest rate earnings with fixed interest rate earnings. IRDA should promulgate rule so that insurers could effectively counter this risk.

26. **Khandelwal (2008)**[69] opines that Indian Insurance Companies should integrate Environmental and Social criteria into their decision making process and join the movement of socially responsible investing. Insurance regulator should take lead role in creation of new sustainability indices like Dow Jones Sustainability Group Indices and the FTSE 4 Good Indices. The other SRI strategies include community investing and shareholder activism.

27. **Verma (2008)**[70] observes that persistency is essential for good health of insurance company. Lapsation adversely affects policy holder, the company, the agent and the industry in terms of forfeiture of premiums paid and cost of acquisition not fully recovered. He further suggests that for tackling lapsation, more robust sales should be made. Focus should be made on financial underwriting of the policy.

28. **Bhardwaj (2009)**[71] criticizes the role of agent who is mostly driven by the thought that disclosure of the facts of illness of the proposer in the form; could result in declination of the proposal by insurance company resulting in loss of commission to him. Thus, mostly it leads to the repudiation of the claims due to information asymmetry. He opines that had the proposer known about the importance of proper disclosures he could have offered to pay some extra premium and got the claim amount.

---

67. David Chandrasekhran (2008), "Policy Lapsation in Life Insurance: Role of Middle Man", *IRDA Journal*, Volume VI, Number 08, pp. 20-22.
68. Sunil Kakkar (2008), "Asset Liability Management (ALM) in Indian Insurance Companies", *IRDA Journal*, Volume VI, Number 06, pp. 11-13.
69. Rajesh Khandelwal (2008), "SRI and Relevance of ALM", *IRDA Journal*, Volume VI, Number 06, pp. 25-27.
70. Amitabh Verma (2008), "Life Insurance Business: Need for Improvement", *IRDA Journal*, Volume VI, Number 08, pp. 23-24.
71. C. L. Bhardwaj (2009), "Asymmetry in Life Insurance Selling: Bane for Poor Business Retention", *IRDA Journal*, Volume VII, Number 11, pp. 21-23.

29. **Chakraborty and Anita (2009)**[72] opine that in India, assessment of capital requirement for insurance companies follows a **formula approach** prescribed by IRDA. The principles of a risk based regulatory approach is to understand what the current risks to the operations of an insurance company are. Due to globalization, Indian markets have converged to many of the international practices, such as Economic Capital (EC), Market Consistent Embedded Value (MCEV) and international financial reporting standards. Thus, the challenge for actuaries lies in developing the skills required to implement robust RBC models and to communicate the results to various stakeholders.

30. **Chandrasekaran (2009)**[73] highlights that with less than 25% of the insurable population covered under life insurance, the potential for life insurance marketing is indeed huge. Thus, market sentiment is needed to be generated amongst masses in favor of purchasing the insurance product. According to him lack of customer education had hindered the growth of insurance sector.

31. **Chaudhary (2009)**[74] highlights that due to urgent need for environmental protection, insurance industry can support development of climate protection technologies. With new technology from solar, wind tidal and wave power, to geothermic and hydrogen technologies- investors and operators need the security provided by risk transfer solutions. An insurance company can be at the forefront of making innovative projects for its clients a reality by covering risks from new technologies that are very complex or involve high investments.

32. **Easwaran (2009)**[75] is of the view that the challenge faced by the Indian Insurance companies is that of disorientation and data fragmentation. Availability of accurate information at right time and the measure taken for non-existence of data are therefore, the major challenges. Another challenge are is that of volume of records/data that will have to be maintained by each insurance carrier. He opines that in a country like India, it's going to, become gigamic i.e. in billion of Gigabytes.

33. **Gopalakrishna (2009)**[76] cites Peter Drucker that purpose of business is to create a customer. The customer thus, reigns supreme in any business and insurance is no exception. In order to improve nature of service and its delivery in insurance sector, the agent must have adequate secretarial services and office facilities as a base for his sales and service functions. A mechanism for National Quality Award (NQA) as in U.S.A. and LIMRA (International) persistency Rater

---

72. S. P. Chakraborty and J. Anita (2009), "An Overview of RBC: Life Insurance Perspectives", *IRDA Journal*, Volume VII, Number 07, pp. 19-22.
73. David Chandersherkran (2009), "Marketing for Life Insurance Have Things Really Changed?", *IRDA Journal*, Volume VII, Number 05, pp.18-19.
74. Sanjib Chaudhari (2009), "The Cost of Climate Change: Urgent Need for Action", *IRDA Journal*, Volume VII, Number 02, pp. 26-27.
75. P R Easwaran (2009), "Data Driven Business: Key to Marketing Strategy", *IRDA Journal*, Volume VII, Number 05, pp. 20-24.
76. Gopalkrishna (2009), "Healthy Expansion of Insurance: Adopting Best Method", *IRDA Journal*, Volume VII, Number 10, pp. 19-21.

should be established to promote competition and boost the morale of insurer and agent.

34. **Goyal (2009)**[77] appreciates the reforms in Insurance sector in form of privatization, detariffication in the general insurance sector as also amendments in regulations for revolutionizing the insurance. He points out a still more need to be done e.g. use of technology to prevent fraud. Increased usage of mobile based platform would increase the accessibility for the consumer with premium payment remainder alerts. With use of derivatives life insurance companies can offer long term guaranteed products and variable annuity can also be product of the future.

35. **James (2009)**[78] is of the opinion that in order to join mainstream economic progress there is need for more sophisticated tools to sustain investments and increase prosperity, bringing in the modern forms of credit, savings and insurance which have exponential welfare effect on the people who rely on traditional mechanism. There is need to introduce insurance in new untapped areas and also in areas where already sub-optimal products exist so that unique needs of communities across geographical extent are satisfied. He further opines that various barriers which impede the spread of insurance. These are literacy and awareness barriers, distributional hurdles organizational difficulties, product limitations and choice options, service complexities, cost burdens, etc.

36. **Kapoor (2009)**[79] suggests that there is need for sustained consumer education programmes and various initiatives to inform consumers about how to seek redressal and also to ensure high-level service from insurance companies for customer satisfaction. According to the author, non-transparency and lack of empathy towards the policyholder on the part of the Insurer have been the main irritant factors, coupled with vague policy conditions. Ignorance of the rules and conditions of the policy contract on the part of the insured public is another major factor for grievance. The author further opines that the policy terms and conditions are not explicit and in simple language.

37. **Khandelwal (2009a)**[80] opines that reputation of insurance industry will improve through corporate social responsibility approach. Insurers need to improve the transparency of their business practices in order to win the trust of policy holders. There should be better disclosure of information about products in sales market. He further highlights that well written CSR reports, professionally monitored customer and public relation exercise will be best illustration.

---

77. Kamlesh Goyal (2009), "Defining Strategies for the Future Innovations and Development in Insurance", *IRDA Journal*, Volume VII, Number 09, pp. 15-17.
78. P. C. James (2009), "Going from Exclusion to Inclusion: Need for Facilitating the Exercise", *IRDA Journal*, Volume VII, Number 04, pp. 13-16.
79. Sheetal Kapoor (2009), "Insurance Ombudsman", *Yojana*, Volume 53, pp.62-65.
80. Rajesh Khandelwal (2009), "Fairness and Transparency through CSR Approach", *IRDA Journal*, Volume VII, Number 03, pp. 35-39.

38. **Khandelwal (2009b)**[81] opines that more than 80 insurance companies have signed statements with United Nation Environment Programme Finance Initiative (UNEP-FI). UNEP-FI plays important role by fostering international dialogue on the regulation of global risk and environment issues between the insurance industry, governmental bodies and financial regulators. He suggests that insurance companies must take proactive stance in the United Nation Global Compacts "Who Cares Wins" initiative and in the UNEP Finance Initiative's Working Group because a better consideration of environmental, social and governance factors will ultimately contribute to stronger and more resilient investment markets.

39. **Krishnamurthy (2009)**[82] states that IRDA issued guidelines to the insurer and the intermediaries that full information should be imparted to the customer during sale of the policy. According to him, information about the insurer are not given adequately to the customer. He reports about a seminar conducted on 29th July, 2009 by the Consumer Association of Indian at Chennai, in which it was suggested that material information on the insurance company including its performance in claims' lapses, grievance redresser should be made available to the proposer even at the time of solicitation, along with the proposal form, as is being done in the case of the other financial investments.

40. **Mishra (2009)**[83] is of the view that fundamental hazard in insurance is not being able to meet claims because of their variability. The hazard is known as "the risk of ruin". The insurer can bring the chance of ruin under control by holding appropriate amount of capital. Capital is essential for the ongoing solvency and viability of an insurer. Premiums need to be calculated not just on the basis of meeting expected claims and expenses, but also to provide an economic return on the appropriate level of solvency capital.

41. **Parasnis (2009)**[84] highlights that establishment of IRDA has played significant role in promoting business in insurance sector and it has also provided protection to policy holders. However, customer retention is the key concern of insurance sector. He says that Rs. 12,000 crore has leaked out of the life insurance industry where the customers have existed without reaping the benefit of a long term policy. Thus, improving customer education and awareness by adopting sustainable business practices, customer retention could be utilized for the growth of insurance business.

---

81. Rajesh Khandelwal (2009), "Best Practises in SRI: Venturing Beyond the Bottom Line", *IRDA Journal,* Volume VII, Number 10, pp. 22-23.
82. Gnanasundaram Krishnamurthy (2009), "Symmetry in Information: A Two Way Process", *IRDA Journal,* Volume VII, Number 11, pp. 19-20.
83. K. C. Mishra (2009), "Hazards in Insurance: Essential Factors in Underwriting", *IRDA Journal,* Volume VII, Number 01, pp. 29-31.
84. Paresh Parasnis (2009), "Creating Multi Prolonged Strategies in Tune With Innovations & Development", *IRDA Journal,* Volume VII, Number 09, pp. 21-23.

42. **Parekh (2009)**[85] appreciates the after effects of de-tariff market as customer have good number of choices of product without confusion. He notes that the insurance industry is still growing. The insurance regulator has achieved a successful de-tariff regime by insuring continued healthy solvency of the insurance companies and at the same time new ventures are being announced regularly. Thus it has resulted in significant stability of the market.

43. **Prasad (2009)**[86] states that there is need to look at rural sector, as a commercially profitable sector in insurance instead of obligatory requirement imposed by IRDA. The production system of agriculture, wage labour, micro enterprise and animal husbandry all have associated risk which may lead to income and revenue loss. Thus, insurance could mitigate the effect of loss and lead to stabilization of income and reduced poverty. In order to effectively penetrate in rural insurance sector, organizations need to develop an independent group, focusing on this sector and use technology to enthuse efficiency in delivery mechanism.

44. **Priyadarshi (2009)**[87] opines that the underwriting in the health sector for majority of the insurers is based on the 'accept or decline' method. i.e. the propose is either accepted or declined, based on whatever information is made available to the insurers. The process of 'Medical Underwriting' has just about started and needs more improvements. There are high claim ratios which hamper pro-active steps.

45. **Ramachandran (2009)**[88] emphasizes that the concept of treating customer fairly (TCF) is an attempt to align company's interest with that of its customers through various cultural and procedural initiatives. The insurance sector is at nascent stage in India then also it is adopter of TCF, as it is evident from governing statute as well as the guidelines issued by the IRDA. Insurance sector has expedited an unprecedented decline in persistency from 95% in financial year 2003 to 75% in financial year 2008. The way forward is proactively adopting TCF through need based selling, aligning the product portfolio with customer's needs, increasing customer education as well as transparency and robust redressal mechanism.

46. **Ramakrishnan (2009)**[89] criticizes the recent amendment being made to the Insurance Act, which has been referred to the standing committee. According to him, amendment of Sec 44, provides protection in the form of hereditary

---

85. Ashwin Parekh (2009), "Tariff Abolition: Advantages of A calibrated Approach", *IRDA Journal,* Volume VII, Number 02, pp. 15-16.
86. Parnav Parsad (2009), "Catalyst for Financial Inclusion: Insurance in the Rural & Social Sector", *IRDA Journal,* Volume VII, Number 04, pp. 20-21.
87. Partik Priyadarshi (2009), "Hazards in Health Insurance: Need for a Closer Look", *IRDA Journal,* Volume VII, Number 01, pp. 32-33.
88. T. R. Ramachandran (2009), "Indian Banking & Insurance Industry: Treating Customers Fairly", *IRDA Journal,* Volume VII, Number 03, pp. 15-18.
89. R. Ramakrishnan (2009), "Insurance Bill: Ill Conceived Changes", *The Hindu,* New Delhi, November 9, Business Review, p. 15.

commission to the agent's family. Now it will take away this protection. If Sec 63 is amended, which is regarding foreign insurers, it would mean that foreign insurer can freely operate in Special Economic Zones (SEZ) and need not file any periodic returns with IRDA. Thus, he opines that many amendments are quite minor in nature and some may result in far reaching changes - not always good for the insurance industry.

47. **Rao (2009)**[90] criticizes the post insurance behaviourial changes in the insured which are referred as moral hazards. While insurer's underwriters are trained to price risks, based on the physical features of the risk, they lack a lot more information, at the underwriter or the acceptance stage to discover the extent of moral hazard that usually gets associated with it. He further opines that insurers currently don't have a standardized mechanism to evaluate these issues.

48. **Rittershaus (2009)**[91] observes that to optimize a business and achieve the best possible profitability, an integrated system incorporating strategic planning, value based management and risk management is necessary. The system should be linked to pricing, to allow proper management of risk and to cover the risk capital costs of an insurer. Financial crisis has highlighted the need for sound risk and capital management. Thus, there should be a shift from traditional accounting based approach to an integrated risk management approach. Projects such as Pillar One (www.pillar one.org.) which are supported in Europe should be transferred to Asia. Pillar One focuses on risk management, Contracts, portfolios and organization. It is driven by new requirements of solvency II, and thus addresses all of the faces of risk.

49. **Singh (2009)**[92] opines that in India, a gradual approach towards implementing Risk Based Capital (RBC) framework would be ideal. The regulator, insurers and other industry experts should work closely while developing the framework. IRDA should organize training programs and conferences to enhance the senior management's understanding. Further it should also ask insurers to identify existing gaps in their risk capital management plans. **IRDA must involve actuaries to have best estimates of risks margins.**

50. **Sridhar (2009)**[93] notes that IRDA indicated that it was against implementing a mark-to-market regime for the valuation of investments of insurance companies. Mr.J.Hari Narayan, Chairman IRDA stated that current climate of volatility in the markets is not conducive to implement the Basle-II norms governing investment valuations. The regulators' nervousness stems from the

---

90. G. V. Rao (2009), "Risk Acceptance Criteria", *IRDA Journal,* Volume VII, Number 01, pp. 22-24.
91. Annet Rittershaus (2009), "Integrated Risk Management Safety Back in Fashion", *IRDA Journal,* Volume VII, Number 10, pp. 29-30.
92. Alam Singh (2009), "Collaborative Approaches in Implementation Risk Based Capital Regime", *IRDA Journal,* Volume VII, Number 07, pp. 10-13.
93. V.Sridhar (2009), "IRDA against Basle II norms for Insurance Industry", *The Hindu,* New Delhi, November 24, p.16.

fact that 60 per cent of the policies were unitlinked, which were affected by the vagaries of the stock markets.

51. **Sud (2009)**[94] is of view that strong relationships derive loyalty and loyal customers are the best source for new customer. He advises that proper need analysis should be done prior to product proposition to inculcate a "solution selling" culture within the field rather than "product selling" culture. Life insurers should consistently engage in continuous employee training and should aim at being widely known in the industry for importing life insurance knowledge. Regular process audits are required to ensure responsible behavior.

52. **The Hindu (2009a)**[95] reports that IRDA is in discussion with SEBI regarding guidelines for Initial Public offer (IPO) by insurance companies. Chairman IRDA J Hari Narayan said that transparency, accuracy, and access to information were essential to address the concerns of customers/investors and prepare them to detect "bubble" phenomena.

53. **The Hindu (2009b)**[96] retorts that IRDA has constituted a group to advise it on introducing new annuity products which will have exposure to stock market and give variable income. At present annuity provides fixed income at regular intervals, but the proposed new products could provide variable incomes to subscribers. The group will examine the current annuity product and see what steps are needed to strengthen the same.

54. **Jaiswal (2010)**[97] opines that payment of claims through physical cheques is an outdated and efficient practice. New methods of payment like electronic fund transfer should be implemented. She further opines that controlling fraud and leakage is an important part of claim adjudication. Methods to plug fraud and leakage should be implemented with the help of IT enabled solutions and focussed efforts by trained staff. Random verification and investigation, predictive modelling and trend watch, concurrent audit, in built red flag alert, business intelligence tools should be used to detect the fraud.

55. **The Hindu (2010)**[98] reports that stand-off between third party administrators and the health sector seems to have intensified with various associations of doctors claiming that the stance taken by the TPAs is unreasonable and illogical. TPA's unfair approach to cut down the cost of surgeries, ultimately causes down gradation of the quality of health care. This cost-cutting approach-affects the use of latest technology for medical purposes and thus, ultimately affects the quality.

---

94. Rajesh Sud (2009), "Customer Relationship Your Most Important Asset", *IRDA Journal*, 2009, Volume VII, Number 04, pp. 30-32.
95. *The Hindu* (2009), New Delhi, November 7, p. 15.
96. *The Hindu* (2009), New Delhi, November 7, pp. 15.
97. Malti Jaswal (2010), "Understanding TPA", *IRDA Journal*, Volume VIII, Number 8, pp. 20-22.
98. *The Hindu* (2010), New Delhi, August 26, p. 4

56. **Chaudhary and Kiran (2011)**[99] states that life insurance industry in India had witnessed phenomenal growth in post deregulation era. The variables, namely number of offices, number of agents, new business policies, products, premium income etc. has shown tremendous expansion from 2000 onwards.

57. **Gulati and Jain (2011)**[100] analyze various business figures in life insurance sector and concluded that the public life insurer i.e. Life Insurance Corporation is still the dominant market player even after the entry of various private players. The performance of LIC has not witnessed downfall in post deregulation era.

58. **Malik (2011)**[101] determines the relationship of profitability and internal factors of insurance companies in Pakistan by using multiple regression model. In the model, by taking profitability as dependent variable and age, size of company, volume of capital, leverage and loss ratio as independent variables it was concluded that age of an insurance firm and profitability are not related while size and volume of capital are positively related with profitability.

59. **Charumathi (2012)**[102] studies the factors that determine the profitability of life insurers operating in India by using regression analysis. The results showed that profitability of life insurers in India are positively influenced by size and liquidity. On the other hand profitability is negatively influenced by leverage, premium growth and equity capital.

60. **Gour and Gupta (2012)**[103] opine that solvency of life insurers in India depends on returns received from total investible funds and interest rate. During period 2009-10 to 2011-12 amongst the life insurer in India ICICI was found to be best in terms of performance of solvency ratio followed by firms such as Birla Sun Life, SBI, HDFC and LIC.

61. **Bawa and Chatha (2013)**[104] reveal that Life Insurance Corporation a state insurance player has good liquidity position among all life insurers. In case of private players insurance firms, namely, Future Generali, IDBI, Sahara, Shri Ram and SBI life have sound liquidity position. Life Insurance firms such as Aviva, Bajaj Allianz, IDBI, Max Life, Sahara and SBI life insurance have higher solvency ratio as compared to others.

---

99. S. Chaudhary and P. Kiran, (2011) "Life Insurance Industry in India- Current Scenario" *International Journal of Management & Business Studies*, Volume 1, Issue 3, pp 146-150.
100. N.C. Gulati and C. M. Jain (2011) "Comparative Analysis of the Performance of All the Players of the Indian Life Insurance Industry" *VSRD International Journal of Business & Management Research*, Volume 1, Number 8, pp 561- 569.
101. H. Malik (2011) "Determinants of Insurance Companies Profitability: An Analysis of Insurance Sector of Pakistan" *Academic Research International*, Volume 1, Issue 3, pp. 315-321.
102. B. Charumathi, (2012) "On the Determinants of Profitability of Indian Life Insurers – An Empirical Study" *Proceedings of the World Congress on Engineering*, London, U.K.
103. B. Gour and M.C. Gupta (2012), "A Review on Solvency Margin in Indian Insurance Companies" *International Journal of Recent Research and Review*, Volume II, pp 43-47.
104. Sumninder Kaur Bawa and Samiya Chattha (2013), "Financial Performance of Life Insurers in Indian Insurance Industry" *Pacific Business Review International*, Volume 6, Issue 5, pp. 44-52.

62. **Kumari (2013)**[105] analyses the financial performance of both public and private life insurance industry. For this purpose various parameters such as number of life insurance companies, private sector offices, insurance penetration and density, growth in premium income, size of insurance market were discussed. The study reveals that there had been a significant increase in the overall business performance of Indian life insurance industry after privatization.

63. **Gupta and Aggarwal (2014)**[106] opines that as in India, insurance penetration is around 4.1 percent which is below world average of 6.6 percent in 2011. Insurance penetration is below penetration level of Asian countries such as Hong-Kong, Japan, Taiwan, South Korea, Malaysia and Singapore. This shows that gestation period for insurance development post deregulation is quite long. Regulatory regime should encourage risk-based pricing and government should act as a promoter and facilitator of insurance services with privatization and liberalization of insurance services so that the level of insurance in the country could improve vis-à-vis the standards in the international market.

64. **Kumar (2015)**[107] discusses the future growth trend of insurance industry and reveals that by 2020 the insurance industry will touch the mark of US$ 350–400 billion in premium income, thereby; placing India amongst the top three life insurance markets and top 15 non–life insurance markets. The growth in insurance sector will be complemented by the recent amendments in the Insurance Laws (Amendment) Act by IRDAI.

65. **Venkatesan (2015)**[108] argues that many insurance companies have used television advertisements to make the consumer aware about the mis-selling of insurance products and to become vigilant by paying attention to basic guidelines while buying insurance products. The regulator has also instituted reforms measures to curb mis-selling. These efforts have improved the sale practices but mis-selling still prevails. He opines that two questions which remain unanswered even now are: What a citizen can do to protect himself/herself and how the mis-selling can be detected?

66. **Hedge (2015)**[109] while discussing the nature of the Indian economy opines that informal sector constitutes 50% of the Indian economy. The type of employment in informal sector is not permanent and it does lack any social security measures thus necessitating life insurance in this sector. The author

---

105. T.H. Kumari (2013), "Performance Evaluation of Indian Life Insurance Industry in Post Liberalization", *International Journal of Social Sciences Arts and Humanities*, Volume 1, Number 1, pp.7-14.
106. Priyanka Gupta and Vani Aggarwal (2014), "An Analysis of Insurance Sector: Penetration Perspective in India" *Working Paper No: 14,* Centre for WTO Studies (CWS) Indian Institute of Foreign Trade, New Delhi, pp.2-10.
107. Jagendra Kumar (2015), "New Insurance Regulations are more Transparent & Customer-friendly", *IRDAI Journal*, Volume 13, Number 3, pp. 18-26.
108. R. Venkatesan (2015), "Mis-selling of Insurance Products", *IRDAI Journal*, Volume 14, Number 5, pp. 2-8.
109. Ashay Ravi Hegde (2015), "Increasing Insurance Penetration to Rural & Informal Sector of the Economy", *IRDAI Journal*, Volume 14, Number 6, pp.15-17.

discusses ways and means to improve life insurance penetration in the informal sector which include:

(i) utilization of the Common Service Centre Network,

(ii) Increasing penetration of telephony and internet services in the rural economy and

(iii) tie-ups with banks and nonbanking financial companies as they expand into rural India. The author further argues that however concerted efforts had been made to improve penetration of life insurance in urban India by the life insurers in the form of spreading awareness about the importance and benefits of life insurance through print and electronic media, the informal sector and rural areas have remained neglected in the process. Spreading awareness about the importance and benefits of life-insurance in rural areas and informal sector can help a long way in improving the life insurance penetration in the concerned areas.

1.6 Summing-Up the Review of Literature:

The works of various authors reviewed in literature are summed up in Matrix 1.1 below:-

Matrix 1.1: Matrix Summing up the Review of literature

Theme	Author/Publication	Gist of Analysis
Regulation	Rossenbloom (1989), Butcher (1995), Stoker (1995), Cherunilam (2000), Meier and Rauch (2000), Shafritz and Russel (2000), Dasgupta and Sengupta (2001), Devas and Kelly (2001), Mishra & Bhat (2002), Rehman (2007), Hertog (2010), Government of Victoria (2011), Chortareas, Girardone and Ventouri (2012), Barth, et. al., (2013), OECD (2014), Jong and Witteloostuijn (2015)	Regulation promotes proper functioning of markets and forbids monopolistic tendencies, it assures safety of products, services and promotes social security thus Welfaristic Administration. Regulation emerges to cope with market failure situations. Regulation reduces fear, anxiety and risk factor amongst masses. Regulation suffers on account of being expensive, incompetent, dampening economic performance, causing delays and red tapism and creeping corruption.
De-regulation	Grey and Jenkins (1995), Lane (2000), Cohen (2001), Breausc, Duncan, Keller, Morriss (2002), Prakash, Rao and Shukla (2002), Savas (2002), Kaur (2003), Narain (2003), Brown (2004), Iacobucci, Trebilcock, and Winter (2005)· Demyanyk (2006), Aulich and Flynn (2007), Das and Abott (2008), Coy, Pavlov and Watcher (2009), Bassanini and Brunello (2010), Davis and Wolfram (2011), Roy and Kemme (2012), Timm (2013), König (2014), Walwei (2015).	It challenges the monopolistic role of state and promotes competition and accountability. It is antithetic to the capture model in which regulator and regulated dominates over public interest. Through competition domain of user choice is enlarged.

Theme	Author/Publication	Gist of Analysis
Regulation in the De-regulated Environ-ment	Economic and Political Weekly (1999), Ranade and Ahuja (2000), Pant (2000),Gupta (2002), Mahal (2002), Mor and Nitsure (2002), Nandraj and Khot (2003), Ahuja (2004), Bhatand Babbu (2004), Gangopadhyay (2004), Gupta, Roy and Trivedi (2004), Mohapatra (2005), Rao (2005), Ansari (2006), Jocob (2006), Chatterjee (2007), George (2007), Mohan (2007), Murty (2007), Parekh (2007), Radhakrishna (2007), Raju and Chand (2007), Vermani (2007), Chandrasekharan (2008), Kakar (2008), Khandelwal (2008), Verma (2008), Bharadwaj (2009), Chakraborty and Anita (2009), Chandrasekaran (2009), Chaudhary (2009), Easwaran (2009), Gopalakrishna (2009), Goyal (2009), James (2009), Kapoor (2009), Khandelwal (2009), Khandelwal (2009), Krishnamurthy (2009), Mishra (2009), Parasnis (2009), Parekh (2009), Prashad (2009), Priyadarshi (2009), Ramachandran (2009), Ramakrishnan (2009), Rao (2009), Rittershaus (2009), Singh (2009), Sridhar (2009), Sud (2009), The Hindu (2009), The Hindu (2009), Jaswal (2010), The Hindu (2010), Chaudhary and Kiran (2011), Gulati and Jain (2011), Malik (2011), Charumathi (2012), Gour and Gupta (2012), Bawa and Chatha (2013), Kumari (2013), Gupta and Aggarwal (2014), Hedge (2015), Venkatesan (2015), Kumar (2015)	It has raised new issues by promoting competition, breaking barriers, fair price to consumer, improvement in quality of services and led to entry of foreign players. In insurance sector it has helped in capital generation and also led the players to the untapped areas which were economically not so profitable but socially essential. Thus enhanced social security amongst masses. It has led to the protection of interests of policy holders and has enhanced risk taking capacity of the masses. These studies suggest that customer retention in life insurance is poor, still self employed and informal sector remain untapped, for health insurance there are instances of Third Party Administrators (TPAs) starting health care facility or some corporate hospitals themselves starting TPAs which is unethical. Often lack of medical history of individuals/groups causes repudiation of claim.

1.7 Inferences Drawn From the Review of Literature

Review of literature has brought about the importance of regulatory institutions including IRDAI in regulating insurance market equitably and also throws light on various inadequacies, which must be checked through strong regulatory process. The major inferences are as under:

(i) Inferences about Regulation:

Regulation must be enforced for the compliance of legal principles such as equal application of law and social concept of fairness and risk elimination. Regulation reduces fear, anxiety and risk factor amongst masses and promotes safety. Need for regulation arises in circumstances where market fails such as areas of criminal and civil justice. Regulation is often criticized for being expensive, dampening economic performance, causing delay and red-tapism.

(ii) Inferences about De-regulation:

De-regulation enhances competition and accountability, which enhances domain of public's choice. It is antithetic to the capture model in which regulator and regulated dominates over public interest.

(iii) Inferences on Regulation in Deregulated Environment

In order to check the accumulation of wealth in few hands the state regulations are necessary. Regulations promote competition and they should be fair and equitable to all enterprises.

Literature suggests an 'umbrella regulator' for whole financial sector instead of single regulator for each single financial market,

With IRDAI coming into being, insurance sector has witnessed a rapid growth with various players coming into the sector.

With various firms entering in the insurance market and product differentiation, policyholder is not able to cope up with the developments, due to lack of knowledge. Customer knowledge has not kept pace with the sophistication of technology.

Rural sector is still a potential and untapped area, insurers only cover this sector to the extent of percentage guidelines given by the regulator. The paid up capital for insurers such as some NGOs, or self help groups working in rural sector should be reduced.

Customer retention in life insurance is poor, often lapsation of policy is due to high premiums, negligence, and lack of incentive to agent for retention which results in loss of approximately Rs. 12,000 crore from the life insurance sector.

Percentage of overall population covered by insurance is very small. Also, percent of population covered under health insurance is approximately 2% and it is also from formal sector. Thus, self employed and informal sector still remain untapped.

IRDAI places stringent conditions on Third Party Administrators (TPAs) licensing. It has been observed that TPAs have started health care facility. Some corporate hospitals themselves have started TPAs which is unethical according to the IRDAI guidelines.

There are no standardized guidelines or accreditation system for health care facilities in India. A separate body within the regulator must be established to efficiently control health insurance sector.

Lack of medical history of individuals/groups cause repudiation of claim. Rigidity of policy terms and conditions and lack of professional control over the service providers in health care sector leads to inefficiency.

1.8 Inadequacies of Earlier Studies

Earlier studies could not depict the holistic picture of insurance sector vis-à-vis functioning of regulatory bodies like IRDAI. Studies were descriptive and lacked sound theoretical and empirical groundings. These studies focused much of their attention on urban population and have ignored the penetration of insurance in the rural sector. The studies have not tried to analyze, the role of IRDAI in promoting growth of insurance business by using rigorous methodology for policy impact analysis.

1.9 Rationale for the Present Study

Present study has comprehensively explored the functioning of IRDAI from multiple dimensions. It has studied economic aspect as well as social implications of insurance in India from the perspective of all the stakeholders. It has documented the theoretical foundations of regulations, deregulation and re-regulation and analysed the functioning of IRDAI by adopting a multi-dimensional approach. It has not only highlighted the achievements and inadequacies of IRDAI but also suggested policy measures to improve its role.

1.10 Scope of the Study

Insurance sector include life insurance, non-life insurance and re-insurance. Subject matter being complex and dynamic, was difficult to study all the facets of insurance. Thus the present study has confined to the analysis of life insurance sector.

1.11 Period of Study

IRDAI was set up in December 1999 and more than a decade and half has passed since it came into being. With market fluctuations and emerging challenges the role of IRDAI has undergone a sea change. It has cautiously reviewed and amended the policies so as to foster accountability and equity. Major slump in market and revival also falls under the study time. Therefore the study period covers a decadal and half of IRDAI functioning i.e. from 1999 to 2014.

1.12 Objectives of Study

Insurance is an instrument of risk diversification and a way of investment. Thus, it has economic and social repercussions. It generates a sense of security among people against unforeseen calamities.

The objectives of the study are thus, classified into four categories:

A. Promotional and efficiency role of IRDAI

B. Protection of interests of policyholders and dispute adjudication

C. Regulatory role of IRDAI for funds investment of insurance companies

D. Evaluation of IRDAI in consonance with features of best regulator

A. Promotional and efficiency role of IRDAI

For studying promotional and efficiency role the major objectives are to:

1. Examine the role of IRDAI in promoting the growth of life insurance business in India.
2. Evaluate the role of IRDAI in promoting efficiency in conduct of insurance business.
3. Study the role of IRDAI in spreading the life insurance business in rural areas.

B. Protection of interests of policyholders and dispute adjudication

For evaluating the role of IRDAI in protecting interests of policyholders the major objectives are to:

4. Analyse the effectiveness of IRDAI in protection of interests of policy holders.
5. Study the role of IRDAI in redressing grievances of Policyholders.

C. Regulatory role of IRDAI for funds investment of insurance companies:

In this regard the major objective is to:

6. Evaluate the effectiveness of IRDAI in regulating investment of funds by insurance companies.

D. Evaluation of IRDAI as the best regulator:

The major objectives examining IRDAI as best regulator are to:

7. Study the effectiveness of IRDAI for incorporating features of best regulator.
8. Suggest measures to improve the efficiency of IRDAI in regulating insurance sector.

1.13 Hypotheses of the Study

1. IRDAI has been an instrument in promoting the growth of life insurance business in India by promoting growth in number of agents, polices, single premium underwritten, total premium underwritten in comparison to pre-IRDAI period.
2. IRDAI has promoted efficiency in conduct of insurance business by making insurance firms to minimize inputs.
3. IRDAI has been effective in spreading life insurance in rural sector by fixing quota for rural sector.
4. IRDAI has been effective in regulating investment of funds by insurance companies by stipulating the percentages of investments in Government Securities, Infrastructure and Approved Investments and Other Investments.
5. IRDAI has been effective in protecting the interests of policy holders by making agents of insurers to dispense full information regarding policy proposal to prospective buyer.
6. IRDAI has effective machinery in the form of Grievance Redressal cell and Insurance Ombudsman for redressing grievances of policyholders.
7. IRDAI has been independent; competent; able to enforce powers and authority; and accountable and transparent in regulating insurance business.

1.14 Research Methodology

The study is based on both primary and secondary data. The primary data was collected from 314 policy holders of three life insurance firms namely, Life Insurance Corporation of India, ICICI Prudential and Exide Life through a questionnaire for analyzing the role of IRDAI in protecting interests of policyholders intrepidity; namely, Chandigarh, Mohali and Panchkula. These three firms are chosen as LIC is a sole government undertaking in insurance business. Exide Life is an Indian private firm without any foreign collaboration in life insurance and ICICI prudential has been selected as it is a firm with foreign collaboration and maximum volume of business in India. Tricity has been chosen as the locale of the study because it has higher percentage of policy holders per 1000 persons. Literacy rate is also higher suggesting greater awareness about policies among the customers. Per capita income is higher in the tricity indicating higher buying and sustaining policy capacity of the people. Further all the firms have their offices located in the tricity. All the three cities have rural segments which proved to be of immense importance for collecting data about rural policy holders. Second questionnaire was administered to managerial functionaries of all the three firms. Along with this the third questionnaire was administered to the agents of the three firms, as agent is the linch-pin between policy holder and insurer. Interview of Insurance Ombudsman was conducted to have the holistic picture regarding efficacy of IRDAI in redressing grievances of policyholders. Finally an interview with an official of IRDAI was conducted to assess the independence, enforcement powers, competence and transparency and accountability of IRDAI (Table 1.1).

IRDAI's Role in Insurance Sector:

Various secondary sources such as - annual reports of IRDAI, consultation papers, research papers, newspapers, and internet were widely used to complement the findings of primary data. To analyse the role of IRDAI in promoting growth in life insurance business or to assess 'Regulatory Impact Analysis' regression analysis and counterfactual tests were employed using secondary data along with calculating compound rate of growth. Regression analysis is undertaken by employing dummy variable- an artificial numerical variable used to represent subgroups of the sample study and it is used to distinguish different treatment groups. Regression analysis provides choice to researcher to separate information on certain variables into discreet categories by assuming 'dummy' values as 0 or 1 for each category. In the present case it is used t examine the impact of IRDAI by assigning dummy variable 0 for pre-IRDAI period and 1 for post IRDAI period. Counterfactual approach is also called as the potential outcome approach" or "Roy-Rubin model" which aims to estimate a potential outcome, or the state of the affairs that would have happened in the absence of the cause. In this study, the model is used to work out contours of insurance sector in case IRDAI had not been set up. To analyse the role of IRDAI in promoting efficiency in conduct of insurance business, Data Envelopment Analysis was used on secondary data. The secondary data was used to analyse the role of IRDAI in promoting insurance business in rural sector and regulating investments of life insurers.

Table 1.1: Data Collection Tools and Break-up of the Respondents

Sources of Data	Tools for Data Collection	Number of Respondents
Primary Data	1. Questionnaire Administered to Policy holders of Life Insurance Corporation; ICICI Prudential and Exide Life	314
	2. Questionnaire Administered to agents of Life Insurance Corporation; ICICI Prudential and Exide Life	67
	3. Questionnaire Administered to Managerial functionaries of Life Insurance Corporation; ICICI Prudential and Exide Life	32
	4. Interview conducted of official of IRDAI	1
	5. Interview conducted of Insurance Ombudsman	1
Secondary Data	1. Annual Reports of IRDAI	
	2. Annual Reports of LIC	
	3. Discussion Papers	
	4. Regulations of IRDAI	
	5. Reports of IRDAI	
	6. IRDAI Act	
	7. Journals	
	8. Books	
	9. Newspaper	
	10. Research papers	
	11. Internet (websites of IRDAI, Bima Bemissal, Consumer education website)	

The collected data was processed by editing, coding, classifying and tabulation. The data analysis was done by using Statistical Package for the Social Sciences (SPSS) software and simple frequencies were drawn along with graphical depiction such as bar diagrams and pie charts wherever appropriate to analyse the impact of functions of Insurance Regulatory and Development Authority of India on various issues mentioned above. Chi-square test was used to find variations across education level, income levels, urban-rural and gender of the respondents. In Chi-square test level of significance was checked at one and five percent level. In counterfactual t-test was used to check whether the difference between projected values and actual values is statistically significant or not.

1.15 Chapter-Scheme

The following is the chapter-scheme for the study:

1. Introduction

This chapter deals with - (i) the relationship between market and state; (ii) significance of the area of the study; (iii) selection of the research problem; (iv) introduction of the IRDAI; (v) review of literature and (vi) inferences drawn from review of literature. The chapter also contains objectives of the study; (a) hypotheses; (b) research methodology and (c) chapter-scheme of the study.

2. Theoretical Foundations of Regulation and De-regulation and Re-regulation

This Chapter is divided into three parts. **Part I** deals with regulation; rationale of regulation, kinds of regulation, theories and models of regulation and pitfalls of regulatory administration. **Part II** covers deregulation, case for deregulation of economy, types of privatization, theoretical basis of privatization. In **Part III** need for regulation in deregulation era, regulatory commissions, characteristics of best regulatory body, functions of regulatory bodies procedures used by regulatory bodies, challenges being faced by regulatory bodies are discussed.

3. Insurance Sector De-regulation in India and select Countries

The chapter is divided into three parts - (i) **Part I** provides an overview of deregulation in India. (ii) **Part II** deals with concept and types of insurance, principles of insurance, insurance sector in pre-liberalization era, liberalization of insurance sector in India, need for insurance regulation, types of insurance regulation and setting up of Insurance Regulatory and Development Authority of India. (iii) **Part III** provides a brief about insurance sector regulation in countries, namely USA, Australia, Japan, New Zealand and Hong Kong and also best practices/ principles for insurance sector.

4. Organization and Working of Insurance Regulatory and Development Authority of India

The chapter is divided into two parts: **Part I** covers establishment of Insurance Regulatory and Development Authority of India (IRDAI), aims, objectives, mission, organizational structure of IRDAI, tenure and removal of members, duties powers and functions of the Authority. **Part II** provides insights on website of Right to Information Act of the Authority, consumer grievance redressal mechanism, regulation of insurance and re-insurance companies, intermediaries associated with insurance business, professional institutes connected with the authority.

5. Role of Insurance Regulatory and Development Authority of India: An Assessment- I

The chapter deals with assessment of IRDAI in the form of promoting growth of life insurance business and efficacy of IRDAI in promoting efficiency in conduct of insurance business. The chapter also covers the role of IRDAI in spreading life insurance in rural sector and effectiveness of IRDAI in regulating investment of funds of life insurance firms.

6. Features of Sample-Population

In this chapter the salient features such as number of respondents of three life insurance firms, percentage of respondents from tricity, education level of respondents, monthly income of respondents, gender of respondents, proportion of urban and rural respondents of sample population have been described.

7. Role of Insurance Regulatory Development Authority in India: An Assessment- II

This chapter covers the role of IRDAI in protecting the interests of policy holders and efficacy of Grievance Redressal Cell of IRDAI and Insurance Ombudsman in redressing Grievances of Policyholders. The chapter also provides insights regarding IRDAI having features of a strong regulator or not.

8. Conclusions and Policy Prescriptions:

In this chapter major findings along with policy prescriptions for improving the role of IRDAI have been discussed.

2

Theoretical Foundations of Regulation and De-Regulation and Re-Regulation

The role of state has witnessed drastic changes overtime. The state adopted Smithian doctrine of laissez-faire in 17th and 18th century, limiting the role of the state only to internal and external security and provision of basic public utilities. The empirical evidence of Great Depressions (1929-1934) rejected the laissez-faire doctrine. Famous economist J.M. Keynes in contrast to classical economists' prescriptions suggested state intervention to overcome the Great Depressions and pitfalls of market failure. The Keynesian model dominated till the late 1960s and early 1970s. The predominance of State in most of the social and economic activities resulted to State failure according to New Right School of Thought and public choice theorists. Most of the social scientists and economists belonging to Neo-liberal school of thought suggested the doctrine of deregulation as panacea for ills of over-governance or state failure. Thus the pendulum of the economic policies has swung from free market to regulatory to free market. It is in this backdrop the present chapter deals with concepts and theoretical models of regulation, deregulation and re-regulation. The Chapter is divided into three parts. Part I deals with regulation, while part II elaborates deregulation paradigm. Regulation in deregulation era is discussed in part III.

I
REGULATION

Regulations are persistent since the inception of the State. In ancient civilizations, regulations existed in the form of standardized weights and measures, law and order, norms, customs, etc. With the development of the economic activities of the State and change in the role of the State from police state to welfare state, regulations were necessary to provide services to the people such as water, electricity, communication, etc. These regulations were trust busting (i.e. destruction and banning of monopolies), to create laws protecting interest of consumers and to introduce progressive tax structure.

2.1 Regulation:

Regulation can be defined as-

The totality of government control on the social and economic activities of its citizens, the rule making process of those administrative agencies charged with the official interpretation of laws[1].

Regulatory Administration represents a very direct use of governmental power to penetrate spheres of life that were once left primarily to the workings of private, social and economic forces[2].

Organization for Economic Co-operation and Development (OECD) defines regulation as follows:

"The word regulation itself can mean many things. At its most basic level, regulation is treated as synonymous with law. Regulations are rules or norms adopted by government and backed up by some threat of consequences, usually negative ones in the form of penalties. Often directed at businesses, regulations can also aim at non-profit organizations, other governmental entities and even individuals. Regulations can also derive from any number of institutional sources – parliaments or legislatures, ministries or agencies or even voters themselves through various kinds of plebiscites. Given their variety, regulations can be described using many different labels: constitutions, statutes, legislation, standards, rules, and so forth".[3]

2.2 Rationale For Regulation

Growth of regulation is associated with the growing economic, technological and social complexity of life. In order to discharge these functions, there is increasing division of labour and greater specialization which necessitates dependence of one person on another in various economic and social activities. Thus, to assure predictability and reliability of each other's behaviour, regulation is necessary.

Regulation is necessary to prevent undesirable industrial processes such as unhygienic conditions in food processing and packaging industry. It also helps in imposing safety standards by assuring safety of products, services, processes and technologies. This process largely makes use of scientific and engineering skills and relies on inspections and testing for enforcement, e.g. mandatory drug testing prior to marketing.

Regulation assures the proper functioning of markets. Anti-trust and fair trade regulations are prominent examples. It checks that market do not become non-competitive through monopolization. In case of prevailing monopolies the regulator may set the prices of the products and debars the monopolistic entity from exploiting the existing position. Otherwise, the spiral rise in prices may be witnessed in the market as a consequence of this monopolistic situation.

1. Shafritz and Russell, *op.cit.*, p. 36.
2. Rosenbloom, *op.cit.*, 369-375.
3. Cary Coglianese (2012), "Measuring Regulatory Performance: Evaluating the Impact of Regulation and Regulatory Policy", *Expert Paper No. 1,* Organization for Economic Co-operation and Development, p.8.

Environment regulation increases public awareness about long-term dangers to environment. It makes use of 'environment impact statements' which analyses ecological effects of economic development, production, processes and product uses on the environment. Regulation is necessary to prevent undesirable employment practices such as child labour, as it may weaken the social fabric of society. It promotes healthy and hygienic work places and practices.[4]

Economic regulation is necessary so as to develop efficient economic infrastructure for supporting competition in economy. In turn, competitive markets are best way to provide efficient and quality services to consumers.

In certain sectors, natural monopolies develop due to economies of scale etc. Thus, regulation is necessary to protect consumers' interests through provision of good quality, reliability and sustainable services[5].

2.3 Fundamental Kinds of Regulation

1. **Economic Regulation**: It involves entry condition as well as price controls in the market theory of natural monopoly which is the basic reason for evolution of economic regulation[6]. Economic regulations are further classified into structural regulations and conduct regulations. Structural regulations primarily concern regulations of market structure in the form of restrictions on entry or exit and rules for firms to provide professional services. Conduct regulations on the other hand are used to regulate market behavior of producers and consumers in the form of price controls, labeling of products rules against advertising and maintaining minimum quality standards[7].
2. **Product Regulation**: It involves how various kinds of goods are to be produced and delivered. It may involve directives that prohibit the use of certain dangerous materials or the sale of products that are potentially harmful to the consumers.[8]
3. **Social Regulation**: Social regulation is regulation in areas of environment protection, occupational health and safety, consumer protection and equal opportunities to all. Social regulations generally deals with the discharge of environmentally harmful substances, safety regulations in factories and workplaces, the obligation to include information on the packaging of goods, prohibiting discrimination on the basis of race, skin color, religion, sex, or nationality in the recruitment of personnel. [9].

2.4 Theories of Regulation

Government intervention in the economy can be interpreted in three major categories i.e. public interest theory and private interest and interest group theories of regulation.

---

4. Rosenbloom, *op.cit.*, pp. 354-359.
5. Department for Business, Innovation and Skills (2011), *Principles for Economic Regulation*, Government of United Kingdom, p.1.
6. Lane, *op.cit.*, pp. 118-119.
7. Hertog, *op.cit.*, pp. 2-5.
8. Lane, *op.cit.*, pp. 118-119.
9. Hertog, *op.cit.*, pp.2-5.

1. **Public Interest Theory**: It postulates that regulators have full information regarding market[10] and benevolent state intervenes in the market to maximize public welfare[11,12]. This theory is based on Pigovian welfare economics[13]. The basic assumptions underlying the theory are that economic markets are extremely fragile and if these markets are not regulated they may operate very inefficiently (or inequitably) and another assumption is that the government regulation is virtually costless[14]. This theory has been subjected to criticism mainly from Chicago School of Law and Economics. The critics argue that markets are capable of tackling market failures without government regulation and also government regulators being incompetent, corrupt and captured may further aggravate the problem rather than correcting the market failure[15].
2. **Private Interest Theory**: While Private Interest Theory contends that the state intervention is not to promote public interest rather private interest. Regulator suffers on account of information asymmetry in aspects of cost, demand, quality and other dimensions of firm behavior consequent to which; the economic agents exploit the situation and tend to promote private interest at the cost of public interest. Regulator work in accordance with the regulated practice and it has the systematic information on the basis of which the regulator decides[16],[17]. Regulators supply regulatory services in exchange of regulatory rents such as political income or personal gains[18].
3. **Economic Theory of Interest Groups**: Following the tradition of Chicago School Gary Becker proposed theory of interest groups which explains the trend towards deregulation in 1980[19]. The theory propounds that taxpayers and subsidy recipients compete with each other for getting favors from the government. Taxpayers will lobby for decreasing their taxes while subsidy recipients try to influence government for increasing their subsidies. The equilibrium of political favours depends on a range of factors, but most prominent being impact of the deadweight costs of taxes and subsidies on the production of pressure. High deadweight costs in case of subsidies will lower the effectiveness of subsidized groups to influence and raise the political power

10. *Ibid.* pp. 2-5.
11. Richard A. Posner (1974), "Theories of Economic Regulation", *The Bell Journal of Economics and Management Science*, Volume 5, Number 2, pp.335-339.
12. Andrei Shleifer (2005), "Understanding Regulation", *European Financial Management*, Volume 11, Number 4, p.440.
13. *Ibid*, pp.440-441.
14. Posner, *op.cit.*, p. 336.
15. *Ibid.*, p. 337.
16. George J. Stigler (1971), "The Theory of Economic Regulation", *The Bell Journal of Economics and Management Science*, Volume 2, Number 1, pp. 3-21
17. Anthony D. Williams (2004), "An Economic Theory of Self-Regulation", *Working Paper prepared for The Political Economy Doctoral workshop*, Department of Government, London School of Economics and political Science, pp.2-4
18. Stigler, *op.cit.*, pp. 3-21.
19. Gary Becker (1983), "A Theory of Competition among Pressure Groups for Political Influence", *Quarterly Journal of Economics*, Volume 98, pp. 371-399.

for taxpayers to influence, as more gains associated with their demand. The influence of subsidy seekers will wean because an increase in level of subsidy will eventually raise the marginal social cost to a point where deadweight costs will also increase and marginal social benefits will tend to fall and at last subsidy recipients would be discouraged from exerting additional pressure[20]. Thus, at last, Becker claims that policies that increase efficiency or raise output such as public goods with high social benefits will win in the competition because they produce gains rather than deadweight costs and are therefore more politically popular[21].

On the basis of these interventions in the economy the models of public regulations are as follows:

Normative Regulation Model: When there is a situation of natural monopoly i.e. less output with more input cost involved in an economy. The state intervention in the economic activity will turn the natural monopoly into legal monopoly by determining both output and price of the products. This model of regulation tacitly assumes that regulator and regulated act sincerely in the interest of the public or the consumers at large. Public regulation in this regard is based upon the notion that the benevolent State intervenes in the market to maximize social welfare by means of exercising its authority.

Positive Regulation Model: In order to overcome monopoly situations in the market, regulatory theory proposes a number of measures for decreasing efficiency loss and increasing consumer welfare. Positive regulation model proposes that all these initiatives for overcoming monopoly will be automatically, implemented once they are known to various actors in the regulation sphere. It is highly policy relevant, because it is concerned with the real life possibilities of the regulator and regulated. It lays emphasis on the notion that the practicality of invisible state regulating both the private and the public sectors, largely depends on the extent to which institutions may be motivated to come together and implement the mechanism for curbing monopoly in regulatory sphere.

The Capture Model: It implies that the special interest of both the regulator and the regulated will dominate over public interest. Moreover, it also predicts that the special interest of these two groups will converge towards some stable solution not far removed from the monopoly solution. The regulators work in accordance with the wishes of regulated because those regulated have the systematic information on the basis of which the regulator decides. Thus, both agree on a regulation policy that would remain stable over time, with maximization of their joint interest in stable and predictable outcomes.

The Rent Seeking Model: Public Interest Theory proposes government regulation on the grounds for decreasing average cost which has risen due to monopoly. But rent seeking model proposes that private entrepreneurs try to solicit favors from government in respect of concessions to entry barriers in the

20. Gary Becker (1985), "Public Policies, Pressure Groups, and Deadweight Costs", *Journal of Public Economics*, Volume 28, pp. 330-347.
21. Williams, *op.cit.*, p.7.

market by paying rents. Thus, if an entrepreneur pays rent then the social cost will be higher than the dead-weight loss because entrepreneur has to spend money on getting concessions. Actually rent seeking model is generalized in a situation where government restricts or creates barriers to entry. In other words, it is the tendency of the government towards asymmetric distribution of cost and benefits. Thus, the model proposes that government favors special interest groups (entrepreneurs who paid rent) while forcing the broad majority of the people to pay the costs of these rents[22].

2.5 Pit-falls of Regulatory Administration

Regulation is an expensive process, It affects cost, productivity and innovation, thus, impacts consumers and service providers. Due to strict regulation, often wastages are witnessed. Regulation dampens economic performance. It hampers free competition and also protects the weak companies at the stake of better performing companies. Regulatory process is too slow and it may take long time for commodities to get into market after going through the whole regulatory process. Thus, red-tapism and extravagance are endemic to regulatory bodies. Regulatory administration suffers from incompetence as regulatory bodies, at top of the hierarchy, are staffed by unqualified and politically appointed personnel. Regulatory administration promotes corruption. Regulators develop cozy relationship with the regulated because of frequent contact with industry and also as members of regulatory bodies being drawn from the industry being regulated. Thus, it leads to favourtism and corruption. Comprehensive rules often become over-inclusive, as new regulations are added and no attention is given to check the absoluteness of old rules.

The regulatory process is out of control[23]. Some economists such as-Nobel prize-winning economist, Milton Friedman as well as those of the Austrian School, have sought to limit economic regulation. They argue that government should limit its involvement in economies to protecting negative individual rights (life, liberty, property) rather than diminishing individual autonomy and responsibility for the sake of remedying any sort of putative "market failure." They tend to regard the notion of market failure as a misguided contrivance wrongly used to justify coercive government action to further various political agendas, such as mercantilistic or egalitarian goals.

These economists believe that government intervention creates more problems than it is supposed to solve, meaning thereby, these interventions may be chiefly because government officers are incapable of accurate economic calculation, lacking any reliable ability (or true incentive) to gather, integrate, or honestly evaluate the vast amounts of information that guide the "Invisible Hand" of a free market[24].

Regulation led to over regulation and it had jeopardized the public interest. At this juncture, two new issues arise. The optimistic theory of public regulation of

22. Lane, *op.cit.*, pp.118-120
23. Rosenbloom, *op.cit.*, pp. 369-375.
24. Van den Bergh, R. and P. Camesasca (2001), *European Competition Law and Economics: a Comparative Perspective*, Oxford, Intersentia, pp. 33-54.

Harvard School argues that the state can undo the negative outcomes of monopolistic behaviour i.e. *too little output at too high a cost.* On the other hand, literature by Chicago School put forth counter argument to Harvard School viewpoint. The *Chicago School* propounded that transforming a natural monopoly into a legal monopoly is bound to result in policy failure[25].

Thus, deregulation was best sought to undo the negative outcomes of regulation. Deregulation implies a shrinking public sector, but the chief aim is to enhance competition in the economy.

II

DE-REGULATION

In the aftermath of 1930s and till the 1960s, economists rejected the notion that free markets always optimized social welfare and believed that government intervention is necessary to prevent market failures. By the 1970s, the leading economists propagated the theory of government failure, and suggested that even if markets sometimes failed, public intervention was not a remedy to these failures since government failure is also evitable. Finally, as a major policy intervention in 1981 Ronald Reagan-Former President of USA in his first inaugural address announced that "government is not the solution to our problem; government is the problem". His approach is entirely consistent with a new generation of scholarship on government failure[26].

2.6 Deregulation:

Deregulation gained momentum in the 1970s, influenced by research at the University of Chicago and the theories of Ludwig von Mises, Friedrich von Hayek, and Milton Friedman. "De-regulation meaning thereby that areas hitherto reserved for the public sector will be henceforth opened to the private sector. In other words, it indicates the emergence of new culture in the society in which marketisation, competition and efficiency have become guiding principles in economic decision making[27]".

The contestable market theory also supports deregulation by postulating that equilibrium in market will not depend upon number of firms in markets rather its contestability i.e. absence of obstacles to the entry for new competitors[28]. In a contestable market, regulation is inappropriate as it creates obstacles to efficient behaviour by restraining potential competition, imposing administered prices and limiting entry of new firms. Contestable market requires three things, namely, free entry of firms, free exit of the firms from market without any sunk costs i.e. costs which are specific to investment and cannot be recovered if a firm leaves the market

25. Lane, *op.cit.*, p. 129.
26. David Moss (2010), "Reversing the Null: Regulation, Deregulation, and the Power of Ideas", *Working Paper. 10-080,* Harvard Business School, pp.5-6.
27. Simrit Kaur (2003), *Privatization and Public Regulation: The Indian Experience*, Macmillian India Ltd., New Delhi, p. 3.
28. W.J. Baumol, (1982), "Contestable markets: an uprising in the theory of market structure", *American Economic Review*, Volume 72, Number 1, pp. 1-15.

and lastly, the incumbent firm must not prevent the entry of firm and also force the exit of new firms by temporarily cutting its price[29].

Deregulation was oriented towards two goals: improved outcomes and cost savings. Deregulation led to replacement of planning with evaluation; line item budgets with performance budgets; control with management by objectives; detailed rule systems with framework legislation; and supervision with discretion.

2.7 Case for Deregulation of Economy

Free markets can provide more benefits to the society than the regulated ones. Free market induces price-competition by reducing the prices of products as large numbers of players will function and frequency of services will increase which will lead to rise in demand for anti-trust regulations.

Liability of law can be used to assure safety in many aspects of life. Potential of suits can make manufacturers or service providers to design safe products. It will make private sector innovative and responsible.

There is great potential for private sector to engage in self- regulation. Many firms and unions do employ safety inspectors and take active interest in establishing and maintaining healthful and safe conditions in the workplace. Public law may require enterprises to engage themselves in self-regulation, e.g. in hazardous waste disposal, trucking intravenous solutions by pharmaceutical firms.

If business enterprises disclose information relevant to safety, healthfulness and security of products, services or other offerings, then public could act as its own inspectors[30].

2.8 Privatization: Definition and Types

Privatization is a word of recent origin, the term privatization was first used by Professor *Peter Drucker* in his book the Age of Discontinuity in 1969[31]. He stated that government has poor managerial capabilities because it is bureaucratic in functioning. Drucker proposed that "systematic policy of using the other, the non-governmental institutions of the society of organizations, for the actual 'doing,' i.e., for performance, operations, execution. Such a policy might be called 're-privatization"[32].

In particular, politicians tend to equate privatization with commercialization and de-regulation. The revelation of productivity difficulties has encouraged a search for other public sector reform, namely privatization which has been a key term in western Europe since macro reforms were launched in relation to the public sector in 1980's. Privatization may cover the sell-off public ownership to private hands (denationalization); the transfer of public property from one form to another, such as creation of a joint stock company owned by the state or local government; the long term lease of public infrastructure to private enterprises, including franchising

29. *Ibid.*, pp. 2-10
30. Roosenbloom, *op.cit.*, pp. 376-378.
31. Peter F. Drucker (1969), *The Age of Discontinuity*, Harper & Row, New York, p.229.
32. *Ibid., p.*234.

the employment of decision making process like contracting and bidding; the replacement of authority as coordination mechanisms with market mechanism; and the insertion of market incentives into the reward system for public officials. Finally, privatization may mean deregulation, or more specifically, regulatory reform in the legal frameworks that govern different markets[33]. However, in economic terms, privatisation remains the transfer of ownership of goods and services from the public to the private sector.

With the advent of privatization the ex-ante model of governance, which was based on Webarian model and has strong footing in planning theory, was transformed into ex-post model which was termed as 'Public Management'. The features of both these models have been shown in Table 2.1 below.

Table 2.1: Features of Ex Ante and Ex Post governance

Ex Ante Model	Ex Post Model
Planning	Evaluation
Control	Discretion
Minute Regulation	Framework Legislation
Line Item Budgets	Block Grants
Means Focus	Management by Objectives
Steering	Measurement of Outputs and Outcomes
Collective Incentives	Individual Incentives
Taxation	User Fees
Authorities	Exchange

Source: Jan Erik Lane (2000), *The Public Sector: Concepts, Models & Approaches*, Sage Publication Ltd., London.

For cost savings, cut back strategies were used. These strategies reduce the costs for the public sector by downsizing the government.[34]

Types of Privatization

Major types of privatization are:

a. General roll back of state power [mega privatization]: It implies reduced power for the State in all its dimensions.

b. Marketization [macro privatization]: This implies reduced role for State as regulator, facilitator, welfare provider and producer.

c. Divestiture [Micro privatization]: It relates to the issue of transfer of ownership of public assets, in particular, public enterprises to private sector and implies a clear rollback as a producer State.

d. Economic reforms of socialist societies [socialist privatization]: It implies

33. Laxmi Narain (2005), *Public Enterprises Management and Privatization*, S. Chand & Co. Ltd., New Delhi, p. 289.
34. Lane, *op.cit.*, pp. 146-150.

deregulation with a view to enhancing competition among the economic agents.[35]

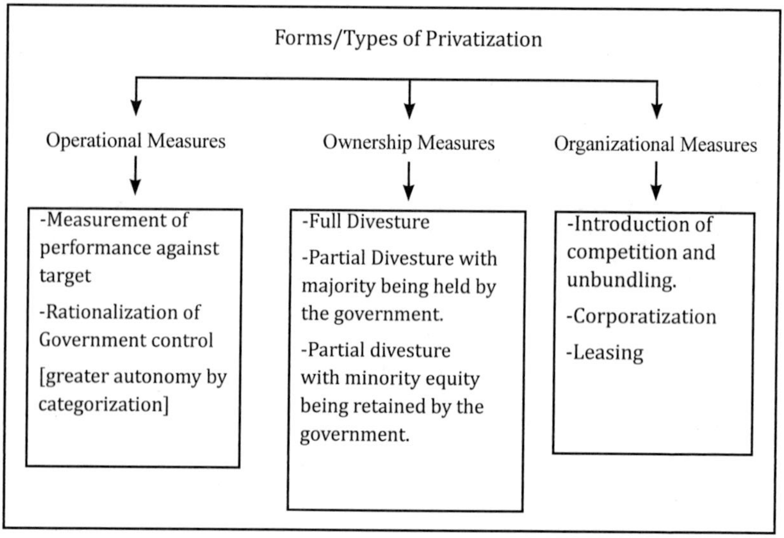

Figure 2.1: Forms/Types of Privatization

Source: Laxmi Narain (2005), *Public Enterprises Management & Privatisation*, New Delhi, S. Chand & Co. Ltd., pp. 299-300

2.9 Theoretical Bases of Privatization

The theoretical framework for privatization is provided by various strands of literature such as New Right Schools of Thought, Property Rights Literature, The Principal-Agent Relationship and Organization and Management Literature.

New Right Schools of Thought: There are four New Right Schools of Thought, i.e. - (i) the Chicago School led by Friedman; (ii) the Austrian School led by Hayek; (iii) Choice School led by Buchanan, Tullock and Niskanen and (iv) the supply side Economics School led by Laffer, Gilder and Wanniski.

Despite intellectual differences, New Right Schools commonly maintained that involvement of state leads to monopoly, increase in budgets, limits the choice for consumers, over production of unwanted services and enhance wastages and efficiencies. The New Right Schools propagated withdrawal of the state as regulator and producer. The schools emphatically propagated de-regulation and privatization. It also laid emphasis on reduction of inflation, lowering taxes and increasing role

35. Y.V. Reddy (1989), "State Market and Privatization: Statement in State Action in India", in T.L. Shankar and Y.Venugopal Reddy (Eds.), *Privatisation: Diversification of Ownership of Public Enterprises*, Institute of Public Enterprise Silver Jubilee Publication, Hyderabad, p. 23.

of market forces for delivery of services and goods[36]. The Public Choice approach premised on New Right School of thought propagating larger role for market was proposed by theorists such as Buchanan, Gordon Tullock and William Niskanen in 1970s. It is a theory of politics that explains and predicts political behavior on the assumptions that political actors are rational 'utility maximizers' seeking to promote their own self-interest. Thus, they propagated 'institutional pluralism which is anti-thetical to bureaucratic approach[37].

In nutshell the New Right Philosophy stands for a lesser role of the State in the society and economy and correspondingly, a larger role of the 'market' by way of replacement of the State's presence in selected spheres of activities.

Property Rights Literature: Property-rights literature deals with the efficient allocation of property rights over resources[38]. Property Rights Literature propounds that competitive markets can handle transactions at market prices because they rely heavily on formal and well defined property rights. On the other hand, lack of property rights limits amount of goods and services that can be exchanged in the market while well defined property rights is a significant factor for long term growth by increasing investment[39]. Variation in Property Rights arrangement also has impact on behavior of employees. Privatization proposes changes in property rights in favour of private ownership which ultimately leads to change in relationships between organization and management. In private organizations the profit rights are well defined which act as stimulant to perform better[40].

The Principal-Agent Relationship: Principal-agent theory focuses on the problems of superiors in monitoring the behavior of subordinates. It empathizes on creation of incentive structures for subordinates to align their behavior for achieving the organizational goals[41]. The Principal (owner) and Agent (management of the firm) follow different objectives. A Principal desires to control the behavior of agent and in order to achieve this, the principal thus, designs an incentive mechanism so that agents may be motive to pursue the goals of principal. In private sector, the principal is well informed and assigns the goal of profit maximization to the agent and the practice of sharing profits with agent motivates the agent to pursue the goal of principal. On the other hand in public sector these relations between principal and agent are complex and exist at various levels which render principal ineffective in

---

36. B.S. Ghuman, (1998), "Globalization, Liberalization, Privatization: Impact on Governance", Paper presented at *Third Annual Conference of New Public Administration Society of India*, held at Department of Public Administration, Dr. B.R. Ambedkar Open University, Hyderabad, p.2.
37. Mohit Bhatacharya (2007), "Rolling Back of The State: Public Administration in the Age of Market Supremacy", *Indian Journal of Public Administration*, Volume LII, Number 3, p. 255.
38. Gernod Gruening (2001), "Origin and theoretical basis of New Public Management", *International Public Management Journal*, Volume 4, p. 7.
39. Adnan Filipovic (2005), "Impact of Privatization on Economic Growth", *Issues in Political Economy*, Volume 14, p. 2.
40. Ghuman, *op.cit.*, p.2.
41. Gruening, *op.cit.*, p. 7.

controlling behavior of agent. Moreover the practice of sharing of profits (property rights) is not clearly defined in public sector leading to poor incentive mechanisms[42].

Organization and Management Literature

The Organization and Management literature criticized the Weberian model of bureaucracy. Two strands of literature emerged, one emphasizing the success of privatization and another emphasizing on adoption of private sector practices in the public sector[43]. The literature overall brought forward the inefficiencies induced by webarian style of functioning in public sector and suggested privatization and adoption of private sector practices in public sector. One of the offshoots of this literature is New Public Management.

2.10 Changes in Public Sector in Wake of Privatization

In 1980's and early 1990's remarkable changes took place in public sector management practices. The change was from rigid hierarchal bureaucratic form of public administration to a flexible market based form of management. This new model of public sector has been called as New Public Management, market based public administration, entrepreneurial government, etc. The thrust has been upon determined effort to implement the three E's of efficiency, economy and effectiveness[44]. The key idea of NPM is employment of private law contracts in order to provide public services. NPM is about contractualism or massive employment of short term contracts instead of using bureaucracy i.e. long term contracting.[45]

Thus, dia-grammatical representation of NPM model with its objectives and elements could be as follows:

42. Ghuman, *op.cit.*, 2.
43. *Ibid,* p. 3.
44. Mohit Bhatacharya (2007), *New Horizons of Public Administration*, Jawahar Publishers, New Delhi, p. 394.
45. Lane, *op.cit.*, p. 317.

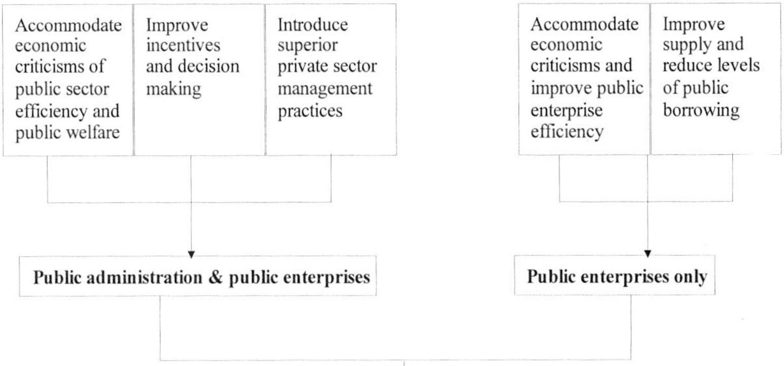

Elements of New Public Management Programmes			
Change traditional bureaucracy	Introduce private sector management practices	Increase competition in the public sector	Reduce the size of the public sector
De-politicise decision making and staffing Replace rigid hierarchy and specialised roles Terminate rigid career structure Decentralise decision making	Corporatisation Budget discipline Strategic planning Flexible organisational structure Output driven Total Quality Management	Competitive neutrality User pays and full cost recovery Internal contracting Eliminate Subsidies Deregulation of product market behaviour and controls Allow private sector to compete in the provision of public goods and services	Contracting out Outsourcing Joint public and private project Privatisation

Figure 2.2: General Model of New Public Management Reform Objectives

Source: Chris Aulich and Janine O' Flynn (2007), "From Public to Private: The Australian Experience of Privatisation", *The Asia Pacific Journal of Public Administration*, Hong Kong, Volume 29, Number 2, December, p. 66.

Deregulation, however does not automatically ensure operational efficiency. The risk, aversion on the part of the management and the profit maximization goals aggravate the problem to the disadvantage of the customers, thus leading to monopolies. Thus, in order to avoid deviation from the objectives of privatization regulation is necessary.

III
REGULATION IN DE-REGULATION

Although de-regulation enhances economic efficiency and promotes competition and institutional pluralism for service delivery but still government intervention is necessary for promoting fair competition amongst economic players by curbing predatory pricing and monopolistic nature and also protecting interests of consumers. The need for regulation in deregulation era is discussed in detail as under:

2.11 Need for Regulation in Deregulated Era

In the deregulated era, the context and style of regulation has a new form. Regulation shifts emphasis from supply side to demand side. Regulation under deregulated era is necessitated on the basis of the following:

1. Government has to provide legal framework and maintain law and order, including enforcement of contracts, property rights;
2. Government encourage competition by anti-monopoly and anti-restrictive practices legislations or by setting up competitive public enterprises, by trade liberalization and by taking over natural monopolies;
3. Government may regulate the processes of price formation, production of finance to make markets function better. Government can tax activities it wants to discourage (e.g. pollution) and can subsidize activities it wants to encourage e.g. public transport, education health etc.;
4. Government can intervene and minimize regional disparities;
5. Government has special role in promotion and development of human resources, by extension of services, retraining, research and publicity. Government can create new skills or improve existing skills; and
6. Government creates necessary infrastructure so that private activities may increase and diversify[46].

A successful regulation policy for public utilities requires strong, autonomous and technically proficient institutions whose existence diminishes the fear of the monopolies abusing their market power. Thus, prior to the commencement of the process of privatization, it is strongly recommended to constitute an autonomous regulatory authority for ensuring the customers' interests protection in terms of price and quality of service[47]. These agencies are in the form of Regulatory Commissions.

Countries across the globe adopted the U.S. style of regulation and restructured various sectors to allow privatization and also reorganized their public sectors so as to achieve greater competition, efficiency, quality of service and affordable pricing. Thus sectors such as telecommunication, water, insurance, infrastructure witnessed changes in consonance with these developments. Around 130 countries established 200 regulatory bodies, including independent agencies[48].

---

46. Bhatacharya, *op.cit.*, p. 255.
47. Narain, *op.cit.*, p. 168.
48. Lorenzo Bertolini (2004) "Regulating Utilities– Contracting out Regulatory Functions", *Public Policy for the Private Sector Note No. 269*, The World Bank Group, Washington DC, pp.1-4.

2.12 Regulatory Commissions

The proponents of deregulation also emphasized on creation of regulatory commissions for protecting interest of customers and regulating the industry in terms of licensing, rate setting, etc. The Regulatory Commissions are independent agencies created by a government to regulate some aspect of economic life[49].

A regulatory agency (also regulatory authority, Commission body or regulator) is a public authority or government agency responsible for exercising autonomous authority over some area of human activity in a regulatory or supervisory capacity. An independent regulatory agency is a regulatory agency that is independent from other branches or arms of the government.

Regulatory agencies deal in the area of administrative law—regulation or rulemaking (codifying and enforcing rules and regulations and imposing supervision or oversight for the benefit of the public at large). The existence of independent regulatory agencies is justified by the complexity of certain regulatory and supervisory tasks that require expertise, the need for rapid implementation of public authority in certain sectors, and the drawbacks of political interference. Some independent regulatory agencies perform investigations or audits, and some are authorized to fine the relevant parties and order certain measures.

Regulatory agencies are usually a part of the executive branch of the government or has statutory authority to perform its functions. Their actions are generally open to legal review. Regulatory authorities are commonly set-up to enforce standards and safety, to oversee use of public goods and regulate commerce. Examples of regulatory agencies are:- (i) the Interstate Commerce Commission and (ii) U.S. Food and Drug Administration in the United States, (iii) Telecom Regulatory Authority of India, (iv) Insurance Regulatory and Development Authority of India, etc.

The World Bank had encouraged privatization in the early 1990s as there was a consensus that private investment would not be possible unless it is regulated by a "de-politicized" independent regulator. The Bank wanted the policy makers to create regulatory entities whose decisions would be both transparent and independent of government/ political authorities[50].

2.13 Purpose of A Regulatory Authority

The economics literature emphasizes on regulation for curbing natural monopoly elements. To promote fair competition in an industry, economic efficiency is an essential pre-requisite which requires regulation of access rights and network use of system prices. Thus need is to enhance competition from natural monopoly. In US, the original objective of regulation was to protect interests of consumers from being exploited by the powerful. In countries of Asia, Latin America, Central and Eastern Europe and to some extent the regulation served the purpose of protecting investors from unacceptable risks. Also for foreign investors, an effective regulatory

49. Shafritz and Russell, *op.cit.*, p. 126.
50. World Bank (2003), "Regulation by Contract" *Working Paper No.14*, Washington DC, pp. 11-15.

agency with the appropriate powers provides credibility for the economic viability of their long-lived investments and low-cost monitoring and enforcement institutions. Thirdly, effective regulatory bodies are essential for enhancing transparency and accountability.

2.14 The Characteristics of Best Regulatory Body

In order to have an effective and efficient regulatory body in place following characteristics are desired so as to make it deliver as per the mandate (Figure 2.3)[51]:

Communication: Information should be made available to all stakeholders on a timely and accessible basis.

Consultation: Information exchange and education should be undertaken through participation of stakeholders in meetings.

Consistency: The logic, data sources, and legal basis for decisions should be consistent across market participants.

Predictability: In order to restore the confidence of investor and facilitate decisions by suppliers and customers these bodies should be predictable.

Flexibility: In order to cope with contingent market needs and balance, the regulatory discretion against the costs associated with uncertainty; these bodies should employ flexible instruments.

Independence: Freedom should be guaranteed from undue influence of various stakeholders so as to promote public confidence in the regulatory system.

Effectiveness and Efficiency: Cost effectiveness should be emphasized in data collection as also in the policies implemented by the regulator.

Accountability: Clear procedures should be laid down for various processes and decisions along with mechanisms of appeal so as to foster accountability.

Transparency: The openness of the decision making process to stakeholders promotes legitimacy.

51. Sanford Berg, Ali Nawaz Memon and Rama Skelton (2000), "Designing an Independent Regulatory Commission" *Public Utility Research Center eco. Research Papers*, Public Utility Research Center, University of Florida, p.6.

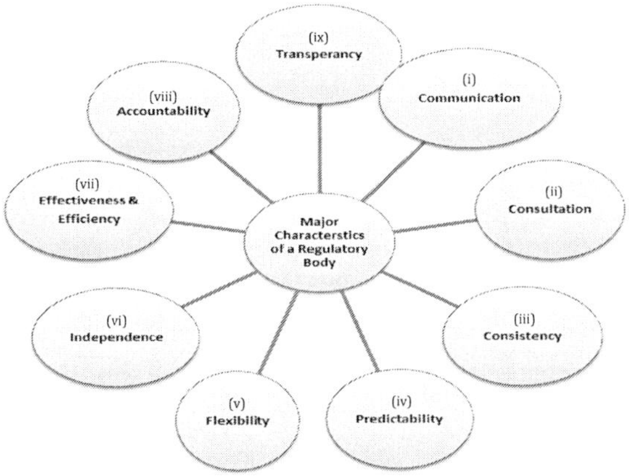

Figure 2.3: Major Characteristics of a Regulatory Body

Various international bodies and forums have also expressed their views regarding the best characteristics of the regulatory bodies (See - Table 2.2).

Table 2.2: Desired Characteristics/Best Practice Principles/Cultural Values of a Regulatory Body by Various Institutions

WFER 2003α	World Bank β	USAID Nexus study	CEER	PURC π	Utility Regulators Forum ∞	Stern (1997)
Indepen-dence	Indepen-dence	Indepen-dence	Indepen-dence	Legal Mandate, Values	Indepen-dence	Informal Indepen-dence
A minimum set of functions & public service obligations		Legal mandate & Financial resources	Enforce-ment Powers	Legal Mandate		
Impartiality, transpa-rency & simplicity	Legitimate / Accoun-tability	Trans-parency	Trans-parency & Accoun-tability	Values	Accoun-tability & Trans-parency	Accoun-tability & Trans-parency
Diligence and Ethics	Competency / Expertise	Expertise	Compe-tency	Resources	Effective-ness & Efficiency	Expertise
Appeals		Public Involve-ment μ	Inter-national activities		Communi-cation	
Dispute resolution in individual cases					Consul-tation	

Bench-marking					Consis-tency	
Predicta-bility					Predicta-bility	
Flexibility					Flexibility	

Source: Gürcan Gülen, Ruzanna Makaryan, Dmitry Volkov, Michelle Foss (?), "Improving Regulatory Agency Efficiency and Effectiveness: Best Practices, Processes and Organizational Structures", *Working Paper, Center for Energy Economics*, Bureau of Economic Geology, University of Texas at Austin, p. 7.

α- World Forum on Energy Regulation held in Rome in 2003.

β- Primarily from Bertolini (2004) and Estache (1997) but these factors are also discussed by Smith 1997a-c) as well as other World Bank publications.

μ- Public involvement is the central theme of the Nexus study (AEAI and PA Government Services, 2005). It can be seen as the necessary condition for transparency and accountability, but it is a necessary condition for success according to the study.

π- PURC list is mostly based on *Designing an Independent Regulatory Commission* by Berg et al.

∞- Office of Water Regulation (1999), Perth, WA, Australia.

2.15 Key Functions of Regulatory Bodies

Primarily, the regulatory bodies discharge following key functions:

1. **Issuing licenses related to regulatory functions:** Regulator has responsibility for issuing a license to a firm, when a capital investment has been completed stating the standards under which the facility is to be operated and standards that have impacts on cost and tariffs.

2. **Setting performance standards:** Performance standards for quality/ reliability having implications on cost/tariff, must be set as these involve resources. Standards for customer protection and investment of firms are also prescribed. In addition regulators also oversee infrastructure expansion overtime.

3. **Monitoring the performance of regulated firms:** Collecting and analyzing data on costs, revenues and performance is essential for tariff determination. Regulated firms prepare their account statements as prescribed by the regulator so as to have easy and fast review of the performance.

4. **Establishing the level and structure of tariffs:** Rate level is necessary for ensuring financial sustainability of the firms. These are essential to recover costs incurred, incentivize efficient use of scarce resources and promote fairness.

5. **Establishing a Uniform Accounting System:** Regulated firms are required to submit reports containing income statements, balance sheets, statements of cash flows, and operating statistics. All these are essential inputs in managerial

decision-making and regulatory review which are to be provided in the prescribed manner. The adherence to a uniform system of accounts allows the regulator and operator to compare the costs of operation over time and also across operators as well.

6. **Arbitrating disputes among stakeholders:** Often disputes may arise in a number of areas including tariffs and competitive access among various stakeholders. In order to deliver this role effectively and efficiently, it is desired from the regulator to establish a authority to look into such matters within its jurisdiction.
7. **Performing (usually via independent consultancy) management audits on regulated firms:** Regulators review companies' performance effectiveness to reach acceptable efficiency benchmarks. Thus, the commission needs to review the performance of firms through audit undertaken by independent external agency so as to see whether the goals are being met in a cost-effective manner.
8. **Developing human resources for the IRC:** Recruiting competent staff and training is essential part of regular managerial responsibilities, since the implementation of policies depends on the quality staff.
9. **Reporting sector activities to the appropriate government authority**: A regulator should submit regular reports regarding its working and activities to a higher authority which is essential in transmitting information regarding the regulator to concerned government departments. These reports help in establishing the public priorities for regulators, ensure transparency to stakeholders and accountability to political executive[52].

2.16 Procedures Used By Regulatory Agencies

Regulatory agencies regulate by making rules. Rules require a well designed advertising of statement of side-effects, contradictions and appropriate precautions and warnings. Rules not only prevent consumers from getting isled but also serve specific economic interests.

Regulatory agencies are engaged in "adjudication". They decide the cases of unfair labour practices, customer grievances, etc. Adjudicatory procedure is regulated by administrative law and constitutional concerns.

Regulatory agencies carry "testing" to implement their objectives. It is pronounced in the areas of health and safety and also some aspects of consumer affairs. Testing can be pre-market and post-market.[53]

Regulatory procedure must be predictably accountable and transparent. Regulatory bodies should[54]:-

52. Berg, *op.cit.*, p.7.
53. Rosenbloom, *op.cit.*, pp. 364-368.
54. Ioannis N. Kessides (2004), Reforming Infrastructure, Privatization, Regulation and Competition, *World Bank Policy Research Report,* World Bank and Oxford University Press, Washington DC, p. 18.

1. have competent, non-political and professional staff, who are expert in relevant economic, accounting, engineering and legal principles and familiar with good regulatory practice;
2. operate in a statutory framework that fosters competition and market like regulatory policies and practice; and -
3. be subject to substantive and procedural requirements that ensure integrity, independence, transparency and accountability.

2.17 Challenges Being Faced By Regulatory Bodies

The basic problem as reported seems to be a weak government. Following reasons have been identified[55]:

1. Most Commissions were never really independent.
2. Some Commissions were granted only limited legal independence.
3. Some Commissions faced with a legacy of tariffs, fell short of covering costs and were understandably reluctant to take politically explosive step of raising tariffs to cost covering level.
4. Operational autonomy is hampered owing to the staffing of regulatory authorities. Most of the legislations setting up the regulatory authorities include an enabling clause to have persons with administrative experience on the Board of Directors.
5. Often financial autonomy is not complete. The government must develop a market-oriented outlook. The regulatory authorities should be allowed to generate their own financial resources through licensing, administrative fee for regulations and charges for setting dispute.

2.18 Independence of A Regulatory Body

Amongst all the characteristics listed above independence of a regulatory body is the most important, which has been acknowledged almost by all the bodies. Independence connotes that regulator should not be influenced by the regulating and should also be free from undue government intervention.

The Council of European Energy Regulators (**CEER**), suggests that in order to be independent a regulator should have:

1. Independence from the interests of the regulated industry
2. Legal entity, separate from the ministries
3. Clear and sufficient competence
4. Financial independence from the state (revenues preferably from participant fees)
5. Board members:
    a. Meritocratic and impartial appointment process
    b. Fixed mandate, removal for cause only

55. World Bank, *op.cit.*, pp. 11-14.

c. No direct or indirect financial interests in the energy sector, no conflicts of interest, sufficient and highly qualified personnel and own management policy

6. Sufficient Infrastructure (budget, buildings, IT technology, etc.).

It is lamented to state that in the emerging economies regulators are not as independent as their counterparts in Anglo- Saxon type of regulators[56]. Having and independent regulatory agency in OECD countries is a rarity outside Anglo-Saxon economies. Norway has full retail competition and has an independent (but advisory) electricity regulator. In Norway there are no formal appeal rights against regulatory decision. Sweden also has same regulatory mechanisms as of Norway. An advisory regulator that makes fair and justifiable recommendations, uses fair and acceptable procedures and operates in a transparent and predictable way is better than a formally independent, decision-making regulator that does not act impartially. In emerging economies, where independent regulator is not possible due to political considerations following choices can be made:

First, establishing an advisory, non-decision making regulatory agency with limited formal legal independence, secondly, setting up a formally independent, decision-making regulator which the government ensures one way or another will not act against its wishes. In first case provided the agency can publish its recommendations and publicly present its case to appropriate bodies (eg committees of the legislature, the media etc), it is likely that in any substantive sense it is more genuinely "independent" than in second case. Thus, the government has to justify for non-compliance with the recommendations of the commission. In practice, effective regulation is intimately linked with reputation of the regulatory agency. Such regulatory reputation implies considerable informal as well as formal accountability to the regulated industry, to large and small consumers, to parliament, and to public opinion. The judgment of all of these is involved in creating and sustaining a reputation for fair and effective regulation.

Thus, notion of independent regulator may be discarded for emerging economies as government in the end is guarantor of regulatory reputation, however independent the law may specify the regulator to be. Governments may also try with certain sort of interim arrangements probably transitional for instance through openness and public debate as suggested above; or- alternatively; through contracts with investing companies, as has become common with independent gas suppliers, power generators and others. These arrangements will be most effective in having transparent, predictable and genuinely independent regulation machinery. It may give time to countries to work out their preferred methods of regulation compatible with their local economic, political and legal environment. These embryonic regulatory institutions may be able to build-up expertise, have reputation and credibility before having full fledged decision making responsibility. Finally, it is noteworthy to mention

56. Gülen, *op.cit.*, pp.9-12.

here that it is essential to have a regulatory agency, which has reputation of behaving fairly, than over-emphasize on having a formal independent regulator[57].

The regulatory bodies should also be open for periodic reviews of their performance. Regulatory oversight activities can be conducted by having cost benefit assessment of regulators, ex-post review of existing regulations, rejecting the regulations which are not supported by adequate analysis, etc[58]. In US regulatory oversight is undertaken by OMB Office of Information and Regulatory Affairs (OIRA) and US Congress[59]. Australian government has launched Regulator Performance Framework for improving the performance of the regulators. All the regulators subjected to the Framework are required for self-assessment once in a year and selected regulators are subjected for external review every three years[60].

2.19 Concluding Observations

It is evident from the above discussion that governance has witnessed changes from being regulatory to deregulatory with emerging challenges and fallacies. Regulations were persistent since ancient civilizations and with emerging complexities their nature had changed over time. Regulations helped in preventing undesirable industrial practices, enforcing safety standards, ensured proper functioning of markets by curbing monopolistic practices etc. On the other hand, regulatory administration suffers from lacunae such as being expensive, dampening economic performance, breeding corruption, etc leading to deregulation. Deregulation based on principles of marketisation, competition, efficiency and economy gained momentum in 1970s with the research at University of Chicago and theories of Ludwig von Mises, Friedrich von Hayek and Milton Friedman. With the advent of deregulation, it was also necessitated that sector specific regulatory commissions should be established before deregulating or in other words deregulation with re-regulation holds the key for successfully enhancing competition, facilitating entry of private and foreign players, promoting efficiency and protecting the interests of consumers. It was also emphasized that the regulatory commissions established during post de-regulation era must be politically, financially and functionally independent, transparent and accountable so as to deliver as per their mandate. Over the years, it was realized that these commissions were not independent in their functioning as their independence was compromised by executive interference. The personnel policies of these commissions, restricted their operational autonomy and these commissions had limited financial autonomy.

---

57. Jon Stern (1997), "What Makes an Independent Regulator Independent?", *Business Strategy Review*, Volume 8 Number 2, pp. 67-74.
58. W. Kip Viscusi (1996), "Regulating the Regulatory", *The University of Chicago Law Review*, Volume 63, Number 4, pp.1423-1431.
59. Dan Chenok (2015), "Regulatory Oversight: Lessons from the US and Others", presentation made at Bharti Institute of Public Policy at *Expert Group Meeting on Regulating the Regulators*, Mohali, pp.5-8.
60. Australian Government (2014), *Regulator Performance Framework*, Commonwealth of Australia, Canberra, pp. 1-9.

3

Insurance Sector De-Regulation in India and Select Countries

With advent of deregulation of economy, various sectors were unshackled from government monopoly by opening them to private sector accompanied by establishing sector specific regulatory bodies. The tide of deregulation also engulfed Indian economy. Government of India adopted liberalization, privatization and globalization policy in the early 1990s. Under the New Economic Policy, the sectors hitherto reserved for public sector - were opened to private players. In this backdrop, the present Chapter deals with insurance de-regulation in India. The Chapter is divided into three parts i.e. Part I deals with deregulation in India, Part II Insurance deregulation discusses and - Part III contains analysis of insurance deregulation of select countries of the world and also frames documents with best principles of insurance regulation.

I
DE-REGULATION IN INDIA

As stated earlier, during the 1970s, state failure paved way for deregulation of economy influenced by economists such as Ludwig Von Mises, Friedrich von Hayek and Milton Friedman. During this phase instead of minimal role of state –a complementarity between market and state was advocated which Joseph Stiglitz termed as 'third way'[1].

3.1 Deregulation in India

India was no exception to deregulation reforms taking place across the world. De-regulation was oriented towards two prominent goals, namely, improved outcomes and cost savings[2]. In Indian context, due to stagnation; high fiscal deficit (5.39% of GDP) adverse balance of payments and stagflation, New Economic Policy of 1991 was launched incorporating liberalization, privatization and globalization reforms[3].

1. Joseph Stilitz (2003), "Globalization and the economic role of the State in the new Millennium", *Industrial and Corporate Change,* Volume 12, Number 1, p.10.
2. Lane, *op.cit.,* pp. 118-119.
3. Mishra & Bhatt, *op.cit.,* p. 10.

The government adopted policy of de-licensing of industrial units. Initially compulsory license was required for all the industrial establishments. The process of obtaining license was cumbersome and overridden with bureaucratic red-tapism. In order to give fillip to investments in India, government followed the policy of de-licensing. Over the years, the list of compulsory licensing for establishing new industries was pruned down[4]. Currently-compulsory license is required for five types of industries namely, (i) alcoholic drinks, (ii) tobacco & cigar products, (iii) defense & electronics aerospace equipment, (iv) industrial explosives, including matchboxes and (v) hazardous chemicals industries.

In Public sector enterprises, policy of disinvestment was followed meaning thereby dilution of stake of government in public enterprises. The New Industrial Policy of 1991, also paved way for selling 20% of the shares of selected profit making public sector units to financial institutions, mutual funds etc. Further in 1993, Rangarajan Committee report emphasized on substantial disinvestment and it stated that disinvestment could go up to 49 percent in industries exclusively reserved for public sector and 74 percent in all other public sector undertakings. Subsequently, in 1999; government classified public sector units into strategic and non-strategic units for the purpose of disinvestment. Strategic areas would be such as defense production, atomic energy and railway transport where no disinvestment was to be done and in non-strategic areas disinvestment policy was to be followed in a phased manner. The receipts from disinvestment are submitted into National Investment Fund 2005.

The new economic policy unshackled government monopoly over most of the sectors and opened majority of the sectors for private players. As per Industrial Policy of 1956, seventeen industries were exclusively reserved for public sector whereas under Industrial Policy of 1991, only eight industries, namely, (i) defense production, (ii) atomic energy, coal and lignite, (iii) mineral oils, (iv) iron ore, (v) manganese, (vi) gold and diamond, (vii) atomic minerals and (viii) railways specifically for public sector operation were enlisted. Over the years, the number of industrial units reserved for public sector was brought down and currently, atomic energy, atomic minerals and rail transport are areas exclusively reserved for public sector.

This model is also termed as Rao-Manmohan model. The Public Enterprises reforms initiative included withdrawal of the state from non-core areas, reduction of government stake to bare minimum levels, greater autonomy by improving public enterprises-government interface through Memorandum of Understanding, recognition of flagship enterprises as ' Navratnas' and 'Miniratans'[5] and subsequently, a new category called 'Maharatnas' included in 2010.

Necessary changes were made in the financial system to adjust according to the new emerging global order. Thus sectors such as- telecom, infrastructure, power, insurance, etc. were liberalized and privatized with passage of necessary Acts.

---

4. R.K. Mishra (2014), "Role of State-Owned Enterprises In India's Economic Development", Background material for *Workshop on State-Owned Enterprises in the Development Process*, Held on 4 April, at OECD Conference Centre, Room 4, Paris, p.13.
5. Ibid .p.12.

Keeping in view, the need of regulation in the deregulated era, State and market has to be in synergic relationship with each other which could be termed as co-governance where State, market and civil sectors will coactively provide services to the citizens. Thus, in the emerging paradigm, the respective role of various organs is illustrated in Table 3.1. below:-

Table 3.1: A Tabular Presentation of Organs of State and their Respective Sphere of Activities

Domain or Sphere of Activities	Organs of State
Socio-economy policy formulation	Exclusive role of executive and legislature
Policy Regulations/enforcement of socio-economic policies	Respective role of statutory Independent Regulatory Authorities/ Commissions
Implementation of socio-economic policies	Gradually increasing role of NGOs & encouraging Public Private Partnership model.

Source: Minocha O. P. (2007), "Revamping The Role of Government As A Regulator", *Indian Journal of Public Administration*, VOL. LII, No. 3, July-September, p.400.

A successful regulation policy for public utilities requires strong, autonomous and technically proficient institutions whose existence diminishes the fear of the mono-polies abusing their market power. Thus, prior to the commencement of the process of privatization, it is strongly recommended to constitute an autonomous regulatory authority as such agency ensures that the interests of the customers in terms of price and quality of service are protected[6]. These agencies are in the form of regulatory commissions, namely, Telecom Regulatory Authority of India, Central Electricity Regulatory Commission, Securities and Exchange Board of India, Insurance Regulatory and Development Authority of India, Airport Authority of India, National Highway Authority of India, Petroleum and Natural Gas regulatory Board, etc. (*See - Table 3.2*). Keeping in tandem with this practice, insurance sector was de-regulated in 1999 with the passage of Insurance Regulatory and Development Authority Bill in December, 1999.

Table 3.2: Status of Sector-Specific Regulations in India

S. No.	Sector	Status of regulation
1	Power	Electricity Regulatory Commissions (ERC's) exist in almost all states and at the centre.
2	Energy	No Energy Regulator in India
3	Oil & Gas	The Petroleum & Natural Gas Regulatory Board (PNGRB) regulates refining, processing, storage, transportation, distribution and marketing of petroleum products.

6. Narain, *op.cit.*, p. 168.

4	Coal	The government owns the operators, the coal companies, and regulates.
5	Telecom	Telecom Regulatory Authority of India (TRAI). Facilitates competition through regulation and introducing pro-consumer elements relating to quality and access.
6	Ports	Tariff authority for Major Ports (TAMP), having limited authority in determining tariffs for major ports. There is no recourse, or performance standards, or consumer protection or competition.
7	Airports	The Airport Authority of India (AAI) is an operator and regulator of airports; and the Director General of Civil Aviation (DGCA) along with the Bureau of Civil Aviation Security is responsible for safety and technical aspects.
8	Roads	There is no regulatory authority as such and the National Highways Authority of India (NHAI) acts as one
9	Railways	The government owned Indian Railways is both operator and regulator
10	Water supply and sanitation	There is no regulatory authority. Central Ground Water Authority exists for control of ground water, pollution control and protect environment.
11	Social Sector	The social sector is lacking in any independent and transparent regulation. Higher education is regulated by the autonomous bodies like UGC, AICTE and self-regulatory bodies. Independent Regulatory Authority for Higher Education (IRAHE) is under consideration.
12	Forward Market	Forward Markets Commission for keeping forward markets under observation and to make recommendations for improving the organization and working of forward markets.
13	Medical	Medical Council of India for establishment of new medical college, new course of study etc. recognition of medical qualification granted by Universities or Medical Institutions in India, etc.
14.	Atomic Energy	Atomic Energy Regulatory Board
15.	Pollution Control	Central Pollution Control Board for prevention and control of water pollution and the maintaining of restoring of wholesomeness of water.

Source: Vijay Vir Singh and Siddhartha Mitra (2008), "Regulatory Management and Reform in India", *Background Paper for OECD,* CUTS International, Jaipur, India.

II
INSURANCE SECTOR DE-REGULATION IN INDIA

Keeping in view, the above mentioned sweeping reforms in India, the insurance sector was also de-regulated. Before moving to insurance deregulation, it is essential to understand the concept of insurance, types of insurance, principles of insurance, importance of insurance and scenario prevailing before deregulation of insurance.

3.2 Concept of Insurance

The practicality of insurance is based on three functions namely, (i) Risk Transfer, (ii)Risk Pooling and (iii) Risk Allocation. Risk transfer connotes transfer of risk from risk-averse individual to risk-neutral insurer. Risk pooling is based on the principle that by insuring numerous individuals, it is assumed that such risk would occur to some of the insured individuals[7]. It can be termed as the essence of "The Rule of Large Numbers", the fundamental principle underlying insurance[8]. In order to enable risk-pooling, the risks should be quite homogenous and independent. Finally, risk allocation signifies that the price each insured pays, reflects the risk that he contributes[9].

3.3 Types of Insurance

Broadly, insurance can be classified into life insurance, non-life insurance or general insurance and re-insurance. Life insurance is concerned with contracts of insurance on human life as it provides compensation/ sum assured to the dependent or insured in case of any peril covered under the policy such as death, permanent disability or maturity of policy. As per Insurance Act, 1938 Life insurance business means- "the business of effecting contracts of insurance upon human life, including any contract whereby the payment of money is assured on death (except death by accident only) or the happening of any". Various types of life insurance policies are (i) Endowment Policy, (ii) Whole Life Policy, (iii) Term Life Policy, (iv) Money-back Policy, (v) Joint Life Policy Group Insurance Policy, Loan Cover Term Assurance Policy, Pension Plan or Annuities and Unit Linked Insurance Plan.

3.4 Types of Insurance Policies

Life insurance can be classified generally as follows:

(i) **Term Insurance Policies:** These are the most basic form of life insurance policies which provide life cover without any profits component. In these policies, the premium is very less as compared to other insurance policies. In case the insured expires within the currency of the policy, he is paid fixed amount of money (sum assured) and if the policyholder survives, then no pay out is made.

(ii) **Endowment Plans:** Endowment plans are different from term plans on the aspect of maturity benefit. Endowment plans pay sum assured in both the cases of survival and indemnity. Under these plans higher premiums are charged to dispense the profits. The profits are outcome of premium being invested in asset markets such as equities and debt.

(iii) **Unit Linked Insurance Plans (ULIPs):** ULIPs are variants of the traditional endowment plan. They pay out, the sum assured (or the investment portfolio if it's higher) on death/maturity. ULIPs differ from traditional endowment

---

7. Doron Ziv-Av (2006), Competition versus Regulation In the Insurance Market: A law and Economic Analysis of Policy and Institutes, *Master Thesis: European Master Program in Law and Economics*, University of Hamburg, pp. 8-9.
8. Stephen M, Stigler (1986), *The History of Statistics: The Measurement of Uncertainty Before 1900*, Harvard University Press, pp 20-58.
9. Ziv-Av, *op.cit.* p.9.

plans in certain areas. Moreover, performance of ULIP is linked to markets. Individuals can choose the allocation for investments in stock/debt markets. The value of the investment portfolio is captured by the NAV (Net Asset Value). To that end, there are many similarities between ULIPs and mutual funds. ULIPs differ in one area, they are a combination of investment and insurance, while mutual funds are a pure investment avenue.

(iv) **Whole life policy:** It is a plan for whole life of policyholder having validity throughout the life instead of a specified duration. The policy expires only in case of an eventuality as there is no pre-defined policy tenure. The policyholder pays regular premiums until his death, upon which the corpus is paid out to the family.

(v) **Money back policy:** A money back policy is a variant of the endowment plan. It gives periodic payments over the policy term. To that end, a portion of the sum assured is paid out at regular intervals. If the policy holder survives the term, he gets the balance sum assured. In case of death over the policy term, the beneficiary gets the full sum assured.

3.5 General Insurance

Insurance other than Life Insurance falls under the category of General Insurance. Various types of general insurance are - (i) fire insurance, (ii) burglary insurance etc, (iii) personal insurance such as (a) accident and health insurance, (b) travel insurance and (c) liability insurance which cover legal liabilities. The non-life companies also offer policies covering machinery against breakdown such as policies covering the hull of ships and so on. A Marine Cargo policy covers goods in transit including by sea, air and road. There are also other covers available under general insurance such as Errors and Omissions insurance for professionals, credit insurance etc.

Re-insurance is an insurance of insured risk where the insurer retains a part and cedes the balance of a risk to the reinsurer. In other words, reinsurance is insurance that is purchased by an insurance company from an insurer (reinsurer) as a means of risk management thereby transferring risk from the insurer to the reinsurer. The reinsurer and the insurer enter into a reinsurance agreement which details the conditions upon which the reinsurer would pay the insurer's losses (in terms of excess of loss or proportional to loss). General Insurance Corporation is the re-insurance company in India.

3.6 Principles of Insurance

There are following seven principles of Insurance[10]:

1. Principle of *Uberrimae fidei* (Utmost Good Faith)
2. Principle of Insurable Interest
3. Principle of Indemnity
4. Principle of Contribution
5. Principle of Subrogation

10. [Online] Available from: www.mbcindia.com/Image/20%20insurance.pdf- The Meridian Business Consultants Pvt. Limited, [Accessed on 5 March 2015] pp.17-23.

6. Principle of Loss Minimization
7. Principle of *Causa Proxima* (Nearest Cause)

Principle of *Uberrimae fidei* (Utmost Good Faith): As per this principle, the insurance contract must be conceived by both the parties in good faith or trust. The prospective buyer of the policy must disclose all the relevant information concerned with the policy to the insurer. In case of concealing of the information, the liability of the insurer gets void or legally revoked. This principle is applicable to all the insurance contracts.

Principle of Insurable Interest: It means that the insured must have interest in the property or subject-matter of insurance. In other words, if the insured property or subject-matter is affected; it should also cause an adverse impact on insured. In general, insurance insurable interest is based on the ownership of the property, either absolute or partially. In life insurance, the close relationship such as of husband, wife, child etc. may give rise to insurable interest in each other's life.

Principle of Indemnity: As per the principle of indemnity, an insurance contract is signed only for getting protection against unforeseen losses. It is not for making profit but rather for giving compensation in case, the loss occurs. The compensation amount is paid in proportion to the incurred losses and it must not be more or less than the actual damage occurring in specified manner in prescribed time frame. However, the principle of indemnity do not apply in case of life insurance as insured life lost cannot be compensated with monetary means.

Principle of Contribution: Principle of contribution is a corollary of principle of indemnity. It applies only when the insured has taken more than one policy on the same subject matter. The insured can claim the compensation only to the extent of actual loss either from all insurers or from any one insurer. If one insurer pays full compensation then that insurer can claim proportionate claim from the other insurers.

For example: - If a house is insured with company X for Rs.5,000 and with company Y for Rs.10000 and the damage amounts to Rs.1200, company X will apparently be liable to contribute Rs.400 and company Y Rs.800. If he takes full compensation from both the insurance firms than he may be in a position of making profit and if this prevails then the insured may connive to cause loss to the property to make financial gains.

Essential Conditions for Contribution:

Thus, the essential conditions for contribution are **firstly** the insurance must relate to the same subject-matter, **secondly**, the policies concerned must cover the same interest of the same insured, **thirdly**, the policies concerned must cover the same peril which caused the loss and **fourthly**, the policies must have been in force and should be enforceable at the time of loss.

Principle of Subrogation: Subrogation means substituting one creditor for another. It is another corollary of principle of indemnity. It also applies to all contracts of indemnity and it is, generally, applicable to the contracts of fire insurance and marine insurance and does not apply to life and personal accidental policies. It means when the compensation is paid by the insured for the loss then the ownership right of the property shifts to the insurer[11].

3.7 Insurance Sector In Pre-Liberalization Era

Advent of modern day insurance in India could be traced back from 1818. Thus, during the past 196 years, insurance sector withstood radial transformations from being a private entity till 1956 to nationalization and finally, in 2000, unshackling of government's monopoly with incorporation of Insurance Regulatory and Development Authority of India or in other words, it could be termed as re-regulation in de-regulated insurance sector.

3.7.1 Life-Insurance

As stated earlier, history of modern insurance in India is traced back to British era with establishment of the Oriental Life Insurance Company in Calcutta (now Kolkata) in 1818, followed by Bombay Assurance Company in 1823 and the Madras Equitable Life Insurance Society in 1829. It is noteworthy to mention here that all these companies insured only European lives and did not extend their services to Indian lives. In 1870 Britishers enacted British Insurance Act. Subsequently, insurance firms namely, (i) Bombay Mutual, (ii) Oriental and (iii) Empire India started their operations from years 1871, 1874 and 1897 respectively in Bombay Presidency. During 19th century, there was no specific legislation to regulate the insurance industry. Insurers were subjected to the Indian Companies Act of 1866. Finally, in 1912 two legislations, namely, the Indian Life Assurance Companies Act and the Provident Insurance Societies Act were enacted to regulate life insurance industry in India.

In 1914, the Government of India started publishing returns of insurance companies in India. In 1928, the Indian Insurance Companies Act was enacted to enable the Government to collect statistical information about both life and non-life business transacted in India by Indian and foreign insurers including provident insurance societies.

In 1938, with a view to protect interests of the insurers, the earlier legislation was consolidated and amended by the Insurance Act, 1938 with comprehensive provisions for effective control over the activities of insurers. Subsequently, from 1935 to 1955 around 68 out of 215 insurance companies quitted the market or suffered heavy losses due to business mis-management and mal-practices, indulgence in speculative trading of life funds, large scale liquidation of insurance companies, inter-locking of funds etc. An Ordinance was issued on 19th January, 1956 nationalizing the Life Insurance sector. The Life Insurance Corporation (LIC) came into existence in the same year. The LIC absorbed total 245 insurers out of which 154 were Indian, 16 were foreign insurers and 75 were provident societies. LIC remained the sole life insurer in India till the de-regulation of insurance sector in 2000.

3.7.2 General Insurance:

Triton Insurance Company Ltd., was the first general insurance company established

11. Ibid, p. 23.

in the year 1850 in Calcutta (now Kolkata), which was owned and operated by the British. Indian Mercantile Insurance Company Limited was first indigenous general insurance company set up in 1907 at Bombay. Finally, New India Assurance Company Limited- a wholly Indian owned insurance company was set up in July, 1907[12].

During 19th century, there was no specific legislation to regulate the insurance industry. Insurers were subjected to the Indian Companies Act of 1866. A comprehensive legislation namely, Indian Insurance Act, 1938 was passed to regulate both life and general insurance industry as a whole[13]. General Insurance Council (GIC)- a wing of the Insurance Association of India, was formed in 1957. The GIC framed a code of conduct for ensuring fair conduct and sound business practices.

In 1968, the Insurance Act was amended to regulate investments and set minimum solvency margins and Tariff Advisory Committee was also set up.

In 1972, there were 107 general insurance companies in India out of which 50 percent were in poor financial health. The Government of India nationalized general insurance sector by passing General Insurance Business (Nationalization) Act. Consequent to this Act, General Insurance business was nationalized from 1st January, 1973 by amalgamating 107 general insurers and forming four subsidiaries namely: National Insurance Company Ltd., the New India Assurance Company Ltd., the Oriental Insurance Company Ltd and the United India Insurance Company Ltd. The General Insurance Corporation of India was incorporated as a company in 1971 and it commenced its operations from January 1st, 1973 onwards (see Table 3.3). Thus, it can be said that in pre-liberalization era, there was one life insurance firm, namely, Life Insurance Corporation and four non-life insurers such as National Insurance Company Ltd., the New India Assurance Company Ltd., the Oriental Insurance Company Ltd and the United India Insurance Company Ltd and General Insurance Corporation as re-insurer. The government had monopoly over the insurance sector before liberalization phase.

Table 3.3: Mile-stones of Insurance Regulations in the Twentieth Century

Year	Significant Regulatory Events
1912	First piece of insurance regulation promulgated—Indian Life Insurance Company Act, 1912.
1928	Promulgation of the Indian Insurance Companies Act.
1938	Insurance Act 1938 introduced, the first comprehensive legislation to regulate insurance business in India.
1956	Nationalization of life insurance business in India.
1972	Nationalization of general insurance business in India.

12. Tapen Sinha (2005), "An Analysis of the Evolution of Insurance in India", *Discussion Paper Series-III,* Centre for Risk and Insurance Studies, Instituto Tecnologico Autonomo de Mexico and University of Nottingham, pp 639-678, [Online] Available from: ww.nottingham.ac.uk/business/cris/papers 2005-3.pdf [Accessed on Aug.10, 2008].
13. Ibid. pp 639-642.

Year	Significant Regulatory Events
1993	Setting-up of the Malhotra Committee.
1994	Recommendations of Malhotra Committee released.
1996	Setting up of an (interim) Insurance Regulatory Authority (IRA).
1997	The government gives greater autonomy to LIC, General Insurance Corporation of India (GIC) and its subsidiaries with regard to the restructuring of boards and flexibility in investment norms aimed at channelling funds to the infrastructure sector.
1999	The Standing Committee headed by Murali Deora decides that foreign equity in private insurance should be limited to 26%. The IRA Act was renamed the insurance Regulatory and Development Authority (IRDA) Act.
1999	Cabinet clears IRDA Act.
2000	President gives assent to the IRDA Act.
2015	Government of India notification dated February 19, 2015 notified investment of up to 49% in the insurance sector.

Source: Anirban Dutta and Partha Pratim Sengupta (2011), "Efficiency Measurement of Indian Life Insurance Industry in Post-Reforms Era", *Global Business Review*, p. 417.

3.8 Liberalization of Insurance Sector In India

In early 1990s, due to sweeping tide of liberalization; globalization and privatization across the globe, Indian government also took effective steps in consonance with emerging global order for streamlining the economy. Thus, sectors such as telecom, infrastructure, power, insurance, etc. were liberalized and privatized with passage of necessary acts. To compliment, reforms initiated in financial sector to insurance industry; Government of India set up Malhotra Committee. The Committee submitted its report in 1994 and it recommended that the private players with a minimum paid-up capital of 1 Billion should be allowed in insurance sector and also foreign companies may also be permitted to enter in the insurance business as a joint venture with Indian firms. The other recommendations of the Committee include providing greater operational freedom to insurance companies, no company must be allowed to cater both life and general insurance as a single entity, mandatory reduction of investments of LIC Life Fund from 75 percent to 50 percent, upgradation of technology and computerization of operations by insurance companies, improving customer services and increasing coverage of insurance industry by promoting competition in insurance industry and finally, setting-up of an independent regulatory authority to provide greater autonomy to insurance companies in order to improve their performance and enable them to function independently. Thus, Malhotra Committee recommended the establishment of independent regulator for insurance sector in India.

3.9 Need For Insurance Regulation

Insurance regulation is essential because of industry protection and consumer protection. Industry protection provides an assurance for solvency of insurance firms, their stability and stability of insurance sector as a whole. Customer protection is must because customer's disadvantageous position due to lack of information may be exploited by insurer and he may be overcharged or may be duped[14].

3.10 Types of Regulations In Insurance Sector

Generally, three types of regulation are prevalent in insurance sector i.e. (i) solvency regulation, (ii) rate regulation and (iii) policy regulation each of amer regulation is discussed below:

1. **Solvency Regulation**: Solvency regulation is done through three methods. Firstly, application through technical reserve requirements and licensing conditions which includes licensing conditions such as - minimum capital required, limitations on corporate structure and ownership; prohibiting a firm to engage in other business except insurance[15]. It aims at assuring financial stability of potential insurance firms and it involves regulatory authorities in shaping the market structure. Secondly, regulatory safety and soundness supervision which involves guidelines such as insurers' assessment should be more than underwriting liabilities. It relies on processes such as examination of annual financial statements of insurers, supervision of companies investments, intensive investigation and solvency improvement requirements[16]. Thirdly, instrument of solvency regulation is the constitution of guaranty funds to protect policyholders in case of insolvency of insurance firms[17].
2. **Rate Regulation**: Rate regulation is grounded on three essentials, namely, disadvantageous bargaining position of consumers, information asymmetry which again puts consumer at weaker position and assuring that insurers' income is adequate to cover risks without being excessively expensive or discriminatory. Rate-setting is done by adopting few mechanisms such as administered prices; prior approval (the regulatory authority gives approval to the rates filed by insurers); file and use - (rates can be changed unilaterally by the insurers but the regulatory authority may reject them at a later stage) and flex rating (insurers are free to change the rates within a range prescribed by the regulator) and lastly, open competitions rate-setting (minimal government intervention and regulatory authority has power to reject the rates of insurers, if found unreasonable, unfair and excessive)[18]. Most widely used technique for rate setting is - *prior approval method* under which insurers file their rates to regulatory authority for prior approval and when such rates are approved the insurers launch such products or rates in market.
3. **Policy Regulation**: Policy regulation is aimed at protecting interests of

14. Ziv-Av, *op. cit.*, p.12.
15. H. Ellis (1990),"Government Regulation of Insurance Companies", in: Stephen Diacon, (ed) *A Guide to Insurance Management*, Palgrave Macmillan, Basingstoke, pp. 277-289.
16. Jonathan R. Macey and G. P. Miller, (1993) "The McCarran Ferguson Act of 1945: Re-conceiving the Federal Role in Insurance Regulation", *New York University Law Review* Volume 68, Number 14, pp.33-88.
17. Kenneth S. Abraham (2005), *Insurance Law and Regulation*, Foundation Press, pp. 531–536.
18. Macey and Miller, *op.cit.*, pp. 33-88.

customers[19]. It imbibes certain mandatory provisions such as prior approval of insurance contracts, information about premium and other charges to be paid, future benefits, etc. It essentially aims at tackling adverse selection and protects consumer from the effects of cognitive dissonances (over-optimism, influence of recent events, presentation style and underestimating future benefits such as pensions).

3.11 Setting Up of Insurance Regulator In India

After the submission of the Malhotra Committee Report, a new committee (called the Mukherjee Committee) was set up to make concrete plans for the requirements of the newly formed insurance companies. But the findings of the Mukherjee Committee were never made public. Thus, based on the recommendations of the Malhotra Committee, the Government constituted an interim authority (called the Insurance Regulatory Authority) - to look into the implementation aspects of the report. The Authority comprised a Government nominee and a member each from the life and general insurance industries. The Authority was assigned with two tasks of framing regulations on its functioning and acting as the insurance regulator. Subsequently, based on the recommendations of a standing committee, the Authority was vested with the responsibility of developing the insurance business in India and also train and develop professionals and intermediaries for the purpose. Subsequently, on 29th December, 1999, the Insurance Regulatory and Development Authority Bill received assent of the President of India which paved the way for establishment of an autonomous regulator for insurance sector in India.

III
INSURANCE REGULATION IN SELECTED COUNTRIES

With a view to improve the role of IRDAI, insurance regulation in couple of countries such as USA, Australia, Japan, New Zealand and Hong Kong has been briefly discussed as under:

3.12 Insurance Regulation in USA

In US, insurance is regulated by states and at federal level by National Association of Insurance Commissioners (NAIC). At state levels, in pursuant to the McCarran-Ferguson Act, insurance firms are principally regulated by respective Insurance Regulatory Department. The Insurance Regulatory Department includes an appointed or elected commissioner or director which oversees both the solvency and market-related aspects of the business of insurance. The state insurance regulators have jurisdictions over the laws enacted and regulations adopted in the state. All the states of US have the power to approve insurance rates; to periodically conduct financial examinations of insurers; to grant licenses to companies, agents, and brokers; and to monitor and regulate claims handling. At Federal level, the states use the National Association of Insurance Commissioners (NAIC) to coordinate and support their regulatory activities. NAIC is a voluntary association for standard-setting and regulatory support created and governed by the chief insurance regulators from the

19. Ziv-Av, *op. cit.*, p.13.

50 states, the District of Columbia and five U.S. territories. Through the NAIC, state insurance regulators establish standards and best practices, conduct peer review, and coordinate their regulatory oversight. NAIC members are the elected or appointed by state government officials who along with their departments and staff regulate the conduct of insurance companies and agents in their respective state or territory. NAIC envisages the mission of assisting state insurance regulators, individually and collectively, in serving the public interest and achieving the fundamental insurance regulatory goals of protecting public interest; promoting competitive markets; facilitating fair and equitable treatment of insurance consumers; promoting reliability, solvency and solidity of insurance institutions and finally, improving the state regulation of insurance. It aims at fostering a responsive, efficient and cost effective insurance market consistent with the wishes of its members.

It is relevant to mention here that the NAIC promulgates model laws and regulations, but states have discretion of enacting them. In areas such as risk based capital and solvency regulations, states have adopted models developed by NAIC with few modifications suitable to their local needs. In US, States philosophy towards insurance regulation is prescriptive in nature or rule based to regulate insurers' financial conditions and market practices. Regulators primarily focus on insurers' compliance with these prescriptions rather than their managements' competence and prudence. Regulators check insurers' compliance through their reported accounting values and financial statements. This approach permeats all aspects of solvency oversight, including capital requirements[20].

In US, there are 995 life insurance firms, 3438 non-life and 248 re-insurance companies. In the year 2013, total gross premium written is 2289921 Million US Dollar (USD). Market share of foreign companies in US is 20 percent for life and 10 percent for non-life. US had insurance penetration of 10.7 percent and total insurance density is 5690 USD[21].

3.13 Insurance Regulation in Australia

In Australia, the Australian Prudential Regulation Authority (APRA) is the chief insurance regulator for authorizing or registering a life, general or re-insurer. For protecting interest of policyholders Australian Securities and Investments Commission (ASIC) has been established. ASIC also issues licenses in the form of Australian Financial Services License (AFSL) to insurers and their intermediaries in the form of insurance brokers, agents and distributors. A reinsurer may operate from abroad without registering with APRA or holding an AFSL. In case of foreign investment of more than 15 percent in an Australian company by a foreigner through acquisition of shares or assets in the Australian company or any offshore parent of that company, the prior approval of Foreign Investment Review Board is mandatorily required.

---

20. Martin Eling, Robert W. Klein, and Joan T. Schmit (2009), Insurance Regulation in the United States and the European Union: A Comparison, *Independent Policy Report*, Independent Institute, Oakland, CA, pp.3-6.
21. OECD (2015), "International Comparison", in *OECD Insurance Statistics 2014*, OECD Publishing, Paris, pp.1-36.

The APRA has prescribed minimum capital to the tune of Australian Dollar 10 million for life insurers and Australian Dollar 5 million for General insurers. There are no minimum capital requirements for insurance brokers, agents and financial advisers[22].

Presently, there are 28 life insurers, 104 non-life insurers and 12 re-insurers operating in Australia. The total gross premium written by insurers is 87589 Million USD in 2014. Market share of foreign companies in Australian domestic market is 16.8 percent for life and 27.7 percent for non-life insurance. Australia has insurance penetration of 5.2 percent and insurance density of 3374 USD[23].

3.14 Insurance Regulation in Japan

In Japan, as per Insurance Business Act (IBA), the Prime Minister of Japan is the chief authority as insurance regulator. All the insurers and re-insurers are granted license by the Prime Minister of Japan. Except the powers of granting and cancelling the licenses the rest of the authority has been delegated to the Commissioner of the Financial Services Agency of the Japanese Government (FSA) and to the directors of the Local Finance Bureau and the Local Finance Branch Bureau of the Ministry of Finance (collectively LFB). Every insurance broker (Nakadachi-nin), agent and every officer for life insurance and employee of a corporate agent who individually acts as an agent must be registered. Entities carrying small amount and short term insurance business (SASTI) are separately registered. There are no FDI restrictions in Japan for a foreign investor. Minimum capital required for a Licensed Insurance Companies is Yen1 billion capital, for SASTI insurers Yen 10 million capital plus Yen 10 million (or more) deposit, for licensed Foreign Insurers Yen 200 million deposit and for Insurance brokers Yen 20 million (or more) deposited guarantee[24].

In Japan, there are 43 life insurers and more than 53 insurers for non-life sector. The insurance industry underwrites gross premium to the tune of 355931 Million USD. Market share of foreign companies in domestic market is 20.7 percent for life and more than 12.8 percent for non-life sector. In Japan, insurance penetration is 6.7 percent and insurance density is 2590 USD[25].

3.15 Insurance Regulation in New Zealand

In pursuant to Insurance (Prudential Supervision) Act 2010, the Reserve Bank of New Zealand (RBNZ) is the chief regulator of the insurance sector. RBNZ grants license and regulates all the insurers. All the insurance intermediaries and insurance brokers are regulated under the legislation although no authorization is required for operations. For foreign company to invest in insurance market of New Zealand requires consent of Minister of Crown if it acquires rights or interests of 25 percent or more or the equity is more than New Zealand Dollar 100 Million. Minimum capital for a life insurer is

22. Norton Rose Fullbirght (2015), "Insurance regulation in Asia Pacific: Ten things to know about 20 countries", [Online] Available from: http://www.nortonrosefulbright.com/files/insurance-regulation-in-asia-pacific-113885.pdf [Accessed on 30 July 2015].
23. OECD (2015) *op.cit.*, pp. 1-36.
24. Fullbirght, *op.cit.* pp. 17-18.
25. OECD, *op.cit.*, pp. 1-36.

Actual Solvency Capital (ASC) of NZD 5 million and for General insurer, it is ASC of NZD3 million ($1 million for captives).

There are 37 life insurers and 130 non-life insurers operating in New Zealand insurance market. The insurance market underwrote gross premium to the tune of 5139 million USD. Insurance penetration in New Zealand is 28 percent and insurance density is 1142 USD.

3.16 Insurance Regulation in Hong Kong

In Hong Kong, the insurance sector is regulated by Insurance Authority (IA), head of the Office of the Commissioner of Insurance (OCI). An insurer must have permission of IA to carry out the business. All insurance brokers must be members of - either the Hong Kong Confederation of Insurance Brokers (HKCIB) or - the Professional Insurance Brokers Association (PIBA). Insurance agents are registered by Insurance Agents Registration Board (IARB) established under the Hong Kong Federation of Insurers. Legislation is under consideration for establishment of Independent Insurance Authority by replacing OCI. Under the new regime compulsory licenses will be issued to insurance intermediaries replacing the existing system of self- regulatory regime. There are proposals to introduce a risk-based capital framework in line with core principles of the International Association of Insurance Supervisors (IAIS). Presently, there are no FDI limits on foreign investment in insurance sector. Minimum capital required for life and non-life insurers is to the tune of Hong Kong Dollar (HKD) 10 Million, for composite insurers and insurers writing statutory classes it is HKD 20 Million and for captive insurers it is HKD 2 million. Foreign branches have no capital deposit requirement but must maintain assets in Hong Kong equal to 80 per cent of net liabilities and applicable solvency margin.

There are 158 insurers operating in Hong Kong out of which 95 are general insurers, 44 pure long term insurers and 19 are composite insurers. The gross premium written by the insurance industry is to the tune of 299.5 billion HKD. The insurance penetration is 13.2 percent and insurance density is 5002 USD[26].

3.17 Select Best Practices/ Principles For Insurance Sector

Regulations are essential for proper functioning of markets and society. The challenge in front of governments is to design effective and efficient regulations. A regulation is effective, if it is capable of addressing an identified problem and efficient, if it maximizes the benefits to the community, taking account of the costs. Thus, in wake of changes in economic and social structure or obsoleteness of previous regulations; it is desirable that regulations should be amended and better way designed to meet the contingent needs.

OECD countries have identified various tools such as use of regulatory impact analysis (incorporating competition assessments), the systematic consideration of alternatives, wide public consultation, and improved accountability arrangements, in the review of existing regulations and development of new ones for improving the efficiency and effectiveness of regulation.

---

26. Office of Commissioner of Insurance (2013), *Annual Report 2013*, Hong Kong, pp. 5-7.

3.18 Australia

Though salient features of Australian regulation have been already discussed, Australian Model is also adjudged as one of the best model in the world.

For improving regulatory governance Australian Government has shown commitment towards improving consultation with stakeholders. Consultation is essential as it ensures both the regulator and regulated have good understanding of the problem, devise alternative options to address it, potential administrative and compliance mechanisms, and associated benefits, costs and risks. In face, lack of consultation may lead to designing and implementing regulation that is inappropriate to the circumstances, costly to comply and in certain cases, is not at all complied by those regulated. The Australian government established best practices principles for consultation while designing a regulation. The principles for consultation are as below:

1. **Continuity**: Consultation should be a continuous process which should start early in the policy development process.
2. **Targeting**: Consultation should be widely based so as to ensure that all the stakeholders being affected are captured. This includes state, territory and local governments, concerned Australian Government departments and agencies.
3. **Appropriate timeliness**: Consultation should start when policy objectives and options are being identified. Throughout the consultation process, stakeholders should be given sufficient time to provide considered responses.
4. **Accessibility**: Stakeholder groups should be informed of proposed consultation and be provided with information about proposals through a range of means appropriate to these groups.
5. **Transparency**: Policy agencies need to explain clearly the objectives of the consultation process and the regulation policy framework within which consultations will take place, and provide feedback on how they have taken consultation responses into consideration.
6. **Consistency and flexibility**: Consistent consultation procedures can make it easier for stakeholders to participate. However, this must be balanced with the need for consultation arrangements to be designed to suit the circumstances of the particular proposal under consideration.
7. **Evaluation and review**: Policy agencies should evaluate consultation processes and continue to examine ways of making them more effective.

Australian government adopt generally three mechanisms. These are - (i) Annual Regulatory Plans, (ii) a business consultation website, and (iii) the requirement for policy 'green papers' and exposure drafts for consultation.

Along with this, the other initiatives introduced to improve the policy development process include - use of rigorous cost-benefit analysis (qualitative and quantitative); the assessment of compliance costs and establishment of the Office of Best Practice Regulation (OBPR) to provide a one-stop-shop to assist departments and agencies in delivering the Government's best practice regulation requirements. The OBPR's main role include assisting and training departments and agencies to quantify compliance costs and prepare Regulatory Impact Statements (RISs); monitoring and reporting on compliance with the Government's regulation impact analysis requirements; promoting consultation; reporting on regulatory developments; and administering the Council of Australian Governments (COAG) guidelines for regulation making by national bodies. Every year OBPR publishes Best Practice Regulation Report incorporating compliance with the Government's regulation review and reform requirements. The Report covers all key aspects of the Government's requirements, including, assessment of compliance costs (using the BCC or an approved equivalent); preparation of RISs; post-implementation reviews and five-yearly reviews from 2012 onwards. The OBPR also reports more broadly on the regulatory environment in Australia, general trends in regulation, emerging pressures for its expansion and bottlenecks in its reduction[27].

3.19 Europe

European Insurance and Occupation Pension Authority (EIOPA) issued guidelines for insurance intermediaries in handling complaints of the customers. It has mandated that if customer is unaware about the appropriate authority to lodge complaint, it shall be duty of the intermediaries to guide the complainant to appropriate authority. The complaints management policy should include free of cost complaint lodging, fair treatment of complaints, providing adequate training to staff for complaints handling and process of internal reporting, follow up and monitoring. For handling complaints every insurance intermediary should appoint one or more senior manager, with overall regulatory responsibility for the complaints management process; ensure the necessary internal flows of information and reporting lines for complaints management; and control the effective and efficient treatment of complaints.

An insurance intermediary's register of complaints should contain necessary information on the complaints, such as subject of the complaint; data regarding the complainant; date of receiving and answering the complaint; and class of the insurance referred to. Documents relating to the complaint should be archived in a secure manner for a reasonable period of time as determined by the competent authority of the Member State based on the nature of the complaint and the insurance intermediary involved. Insurance intermediaries should share information with the complainants regarding their complaints, wherever sought by them. Collection of information on the cause of complaints should be done and in process, root cause of the complaint should be identified and done away with it[28].

---

27. Australian Government (2007), *Best Practice Regulation Handbook*, Government of Australia, Canberra, pp.1-58.
28. European Insurance and Occupation Pension Authority (2013), Report on Best Practices by Insurance Intermediaries in handling complaints, *EIOPA BoS 13/171*, pp.1-6, [Online] Available from: https://eiopa.europa.eu/Publications/Guidelines/EIOPA-BoS-13-164_Guidelines-on-complaints-handling-by-Insurance-Intermediaries.pdf [Accessed on 30 June 2015].

3.20 Concluding Observations

The forgone discussion highlighted that deregulation of Indian economy took place with the inception of New Industrial Policy of 1991. The new policy marked a paradigm shift by encouraging greater role for private sector players and lesser role for public sector. The sectors which were exclusively reserved for public sector such as telecom, insurance, electricity distribution, etc were opened for private players by establishing respective regulatory commissions. Insurance sector was deregulated in 1999 by constituting Insurance Regulatory and Development Authority now known as Insurance Regulatory and Development Authority of India on the recommendations of Malhotra Committee. Insurance sector regulation is mandated because of industry protection and consumer protection. Thus, the newly formulated IRDAI was entrusted with tasks of developing insurance business in India, training and developing professionals and intermediaries for the purpose and protecting interests of the consumers.

Further, insurance sector regulation of various countries also provided insights for insurance regulatory mechanisms adopted in federations and centralized nations ranging from two tier regulators and single regulators for the sector. The insurance sector regulation of other countries provides insights for the extent of maturity of insurance market in terms of foreign equity permissible, premium underwritten, number of insurers operating, insurance density and insurance penetration in those countries.

4

Organization and Working of Insurance Regulatory and Development Authority of India

Genesis: Back-Drops:

Insurance sector was deregulated in 1999 by establishing Insurance Regulatory and Development Authority of India (IRDAI) on the recommendations of Malhotra Committee. The Authority was established for protecting interest of consumers and regulating growth of insurance business and promoting competition. The aim of this Chapter is to examine the organization and working of Insurance Regulatory and Development Authority of India in discharging its functions as per the mandate.

This chapter covers various facets of Insurance Regulatory and Development Authority of India such as its setting up; mission; organizational structure; powers and functions. The Chapter is divided into two parts. Part I Deals with establishment of Insurance Regulatory and Development Authority of India, its mission, organization and statutory functions Part II covers policies, programmes, working and operations of Insurance Regulatory and Development Authority of India.

I
ESTABLISHMENT OF INSURANCE REGULATORY AND DEVELOPMENT AUTHORITY OF INDIA, ITS MISSION, ORGANIZATION AND STATUTORY FUNCTIONS

The recommendations of Malhotra Committee paved the way for establishment of an independent regulatory authority to regulate insurance industry. For implementing recommendations of the Malhotra Committee, Government of India in December 1996, introduced the Insurance Regulatory Authority (IRA) Bill in the Parliament. The Bill could not be passed and was withdrawn. This Bill was again introduced in the Lok Sabha in December 1998 but could not be taken up for consideration.

4.1 Establishment of Insurance Regulatory and Development Authority of India (IRDAI)

In 1998 IRA bill was renamed as Insurance Regulatory Development Authority bill and was introduced in Lok Sabha. On 2nd December, 1999 the IRDA bill was passed by

Lok sabha and subsequently on 7th December, 1999 Rajya Sabha passed the Bill. On 29th December, 1999, the Bill received assent of the President of India. Finally IRDA as an autonomous body was constituted on 19 April, 2000 vide Government of India notification number 277. IRDAI commenced its operations on 19 April, 2000 with N. Rangachary as its first Chairperson with 4 full-time and 2 part-time directors.

4.2 AIMS and Objectives

The key objectives of the IRDAI are to promote competition for enhancing customer satisfaction through increased consumer choice and lower premiums along with ensuring the financial security of the insurance market[1].

4.3 Mission of Insurance Regulatory and Development Authority of India (IRDAI)

The mission of IRDAI is to:

1. protect the interests of and secure fair treatment to policyholders;
2. bring about speedy and orderly growth of the insurance industry (including annuity and superannuation payments), for the benefit of the common man, and to provide long term funds for accelerating growth of the economy;
3. set, promote, monitor and enforce high standards of integrity, financial soundness, fair dealing and competence in those it regulates;
4. ensure speedy settlement of genuine claims, to prevent insurance frauds and other malpractices and put in place effective grievance redressal machinery;
5. promote fairness, transparency and orderly conduct in financial markets dealing with insurance and build a reliable management information system to enforce high standards of financial soundness amongst market players;
6. take action where such standards are inadequate or ineffectively enforced;
7. bring about optimum amount of self-regulation in day-to-day working of the industry consistent with the requirements of prudential regulation[2].

4.4 Organizational Structure of Insurance Regulatory and Development Authority of India

IRDAI comprises one Chairperson not more than five whole-time and four part-time members. The members of the Authority shall be appointed by the Central Government from amongst persons of ability, integrity and standing, who have knowledge or experience in life insurance, general insurance, actuarial science, finance, economics, law, accountancy, administration or any other disciplines which would, in the opinion of the Central Government - be useful to the Authority:

Provided that the Central Government shall, while appointing the Chairperson and the whole-time members, ensure that at least one person each is a person having knowledge or experience in life insurance, general insurance or actuarial science, respectively.

1. www.irda.gov.in, website of Insurance Regulatory Development Authority.
2. Insurance Regulatory Development Authority (2013), Annual Report 2012-13, October, Hyderabad.

Mr. T.S. Vijayan is the present Chairman of the IRDAI. His team includes 4 whole time members and 4 part time members (see Table 4.1) as shown below:

Table 4.1: Present Membership of IRDAI

Chairman Mr. T. S. Vijayan	
Members	Part Time Members
Shri Nilesh Sathe	Shri Anup Wadhawan
Mrs V. R. Iyer	Prof. V.K. Gupta
Ms. Pournima Gupte	Shri Subodh Kumar Agarwal
Shri D.D. Singh	Shri. S.B. Mathur

Source: IRDAI Website[3] as on 8 October, 2015

4.5 Tenure of the Members

The Chairperson office for a term of five years or till the age of 65 years whichever is earlier. Whole time members shall hold the office for 5 years or till they attain the age of 62 years whichever is earlier. Both chairperson and whole time members are eligible for reappointment. A part time member shall hold office for a term not exceeding five years[4].

4.6 Removal of the Members of the Authority

Central Government can remove a member from office if he is adjudged as an insolvent, physically or mentally incapable of acting as a member, has acquired financial or other interests which are likely to affect prejudicially his functions as a member has been convicted of an offence involving moral turpitude and has abused his position in such a manner that his continuation in office is detrimental to public interest[5].

4.7 Meetings of the Authority

The Authority shall meet at such time and places and shall observe such rules and procedures in regard to transaction of business at its meetings (including quorum at such meetings) as may be prescribed by the regulations. The Chairperson shall preside over the meetings and in his absence any other member chosen by the members present from amongst themselves at the meeting shall preside over the meeting. The decision shall be taken by the majority of votes by the members present and voting and in event of equality of votes the Chairperson or in his absence any other member presiding over shall have a casting vote[6].

---

3. www.irda.gov.in, website of Insurance Regulatory Development Authority.
4. The Insurance Regulatory and Development Authority Act, 1999, Universal Law Publishing Co. Pvt. Ltd., Delhi 2010, P. 7.
5. The Insurance Regulatory and Development Authority Act, 1999, *op.cit.*, p.7.
6. *Ibid.*, p.8.

4.8 Duties, Powers and Statutory Functions of Insurance Regulatory and Development Authority of India (IRDAI)

1. Subject to the provisions of this Act and any other law for the time being in force, the Authority shall have the duty to regulate, promote and ensure orderly growth of the insurance business and re-insurance business.
2. Without prejudice to the generality of the provisions contained in sub-section (1) the powers and functions of the Authority shall include,
   a. issue to the applicant, a certificate of registration, renew, modify, withdraw, suspend or cancel such registration;
   b. protection of the interests of the policy holders in matters concerning assigning of policy, nomination by policy holders, insurable interest, settlement of insurance claim, surrender value of policy and other terms and conditions of contracts of insurance;
   c. specifying requisite qualifications, code of conduct and practical training for intermediary or insurance intermediaries and agents;
   d. specifying the code of conduct for surveyors and loss assessors;
   e. promoting efficiency in the conduct of insurance business;
   f. promoting and regulating professional organisations connected with the insurance and re-insurance business;
   g. levying fees and other charges for carrying out the purposes of this Act;
   h. calling for information from, undertaking inspection of, conducting enquiries and investigations including audit of the insurers, intermediaries, insurance intermediaries and other organisations connected with the insurance business;
   i. control and regulation of the rates, advantages, terms and conditions that may be offered by insurers in respect of general insurance business not so controlled and regulated by the Tariff Advisory Committee under section 64U of the Insurance Act, 1938 (4 of 1938);
   j. specifying the form and manner in which books of account shall be maintained and statement of accounts shall be rendered by insurers and other insurance intermediaries;
   k. regulating investment of funds by insurance companies;
   l. regulating maintenance of margin of solvency;
   m. adjudication of disputes between insurers and intermediaries or insurance intermediaries;
   n. supervising the functioning of the Tariff Advisory Committee;

o. specifying the percentage of premium income of the insurer to finance schemes for promoting and regulating professional organisations referred to in clause (f);

p. specifying the percentage of life insurance business and general insurance business to be undertaken by the insurer in the rural or social sector; and

q. exercising such other powers as may be prescribed[7].

– Some of the Duties, Powers and Statutory Functions of the Insurance Regulatory and Development Authority of India are discussed in detail:

1. **Issuance of certificate of registration to an applicant:** Insurance Regulatory and Development Authority of India has been vested with power to issue certificate of registration, renewal, modification, withdrawal, suspension or cancelation of such certificate if need be. The opening up of the insurance market for private and global players has led to the entry of many firms in the business. For granting certificate the Authority follows two steps. First step involves preliminary satisfaction on the credibility and stability of the player followed by an in-depth assessment of the business plans submitted and upon satisfaction that the management is fit and proper. After exhaustive discussions between the promoters' representative and the officers of the Authority, the applications are accepted. The Authority seeks to satisfy itself that an insurer is committed for long term stay in the market and its entry would also bring innovation to the Indian insurance market as per the international standards[8]. In 2012-13 the Authority granted certificate of registration to CIGNA TTK Health insurance company. The Authority levied penalties on seven life insurers and twelve non-life insurers for not complying with its regulations, orders, directions, etc.

2. **Protection of the interests of the policy holders:** Insurance Regulatory and Development Authority of India is entrusted with the task of protection of interests of policy-holders in matters concerning assigning of policy, nomination by policyholders, insurable interest, settlement of insurance claim, surrender value of policy and other terms and conditions of contracts of insurance due to information asymmetry on the part of customer. It takes care of interests of policyholders through various guidelines, regulations designed from time to time[9]. Few steps that deserve special mention here include that the prospectus of insurance must clearly state warranties, exception, conditions of the insurance contract at the point of sale. Every prospective buyer must sign the policy himself, doing away with fine print on the policy prospectus, regular servicing of the policy holders, establishment of grievance redressal mechanism by an insurer[10].

7. *Ibid.,* p. 10.
8. Insurance Regulatory Development Authority (2001), Annual Report 2000-2001, October, Hyderabad, pp.35-36.
9. Insurance Regulatory Development Authority (2001), ibid, pp.35-38.
10. The Insurance Regulatory and Development Authority Act, 1999, *op.cit.,* p. 182.

Consumer activists are inducted into Insurance Advisory Committee and members are also drawn from industry, insurance agents, women organizations and interest groups in the Committee. The IRDAI has reconstituted Insurance Advisory Committee on 25 May, 2015 and its members are:

a. Chairman, Life Insurance Corporation of India
b. Chairman-cum-Managing Director, United India Insurance Co. Ltd.
c. Chairman-cum-Managing Director, General Insurance Corporation of India
d. MD and CEO, ICICI Prudential LIC Ltd.
e. MD and CEO, Bajaj Allianz GIC Ltd.
f. Chairman-cum-Managing Director, Star Health & Allied Insurance Co. Ltd.
g. Chairman-cum-Managing Director, Agricultural Insurance Co. Ltd.
h. Director, National Insurance Academy
i. Managing Director, Institute of Insurance and Risk Management
j. President, Institute of Actuaries of India
k. President, Insurance Brokers' Association of India
l. Chief Administrative Officer, United Healthcare Parekh TPA Pvt. Ltd.
m. Secretary General, Federation of Indian Chambers of Commerce and Industry (FICCI)
n. President, Indian Institute of Insurance Surveyors & Loss Assessors
o. Secretary General, National Federation of Insurance Field Workers of India
p. Chairman and Managing Director, Bank of Maharastra
q. Insurance Ombudsman, Guwahati
r. Secretary General, Insurance Institute of India
s. Smt. Rajyalakshmi Rao, Former Member, National Consumer Disputes Redressal Commission
t. Shri G.N. Agarwal, Actuary
u. Shri Asadulla Pasha, Hyderabad
v. Shri Sesha Bhattar Sreenivasa Chary, Hyderabad
w. Shri M. Kalyanasundaram, Chief Executive, International Network of Alternative Financial Institutions-India

The members of Insurance Advisory Committee are drawn from government and private life insurers, general insurers; insurance related institutes; Insurance Ombudsman; banks; consumer Disputes Redressal Commission and other such institutes.

Insurers have to get the approval for new products being launched in the market from the Authority. The authority closely examine details regarding the new products such as premium rating, policy conditions, proposal form, claim form, underwriting manual and the system in vogue to review the rates, terms and conditions in future. In the year 2013-14,

IRDAI received 780 products for approval out of which; it approved total 538 products and rejected 242 products.

3. **Promoting efficiency in the conduct of insurance business:** Insurance Regulatory and Development Authority of India in order to promote efficiency in conduct of insurance business is setting up norms for market conduct, ethical behavior of insurers and breach of regulations with the help of Insurance Association and Life Insurance and General Insurance Councils. The Insurance Association of India was established according to the provisions of the Insurance Act, 1938. It consists of all insurers conducting business in India. The IRDAI has established two councils of the Insurance Association of India, namely, the Life Insurance Council and the General Insurance Council. Members and chairmen to Executive Committee of both the councils are nominated by the IRDAI. The Executive Committees of the Councils are entrusted with the following functions such as advising and assisting insurers in setting up standards of conduct and sound practice and in the matter of rendering efficient service to policy holders; advising the Authority in the matter of controlling the expenses of insurers and informing the Authority of any insurer acting in a manner prejudicial to the interests of policy holders. IRDAI also helps in providing training and continuous professional development for all intermediaries. IRDAI has also mandated to set up call centres by all new players on 24/7 basis[11]. Recently the authority has launched Insurance Repository system. In this new system the policies are converted into electronic form and for submission of policy by agent, policy servicing are done electronically leading speedy process with reduced physical visits. Five companies, namely, NSDL Database Management Limited, Central Insurance Repository Limited, SHCIL Projects Limited, Karvy Insurance Repository Limited, and CAMS Repository Services Limited registered under Companies Act 1956 had been provided registration certificates for acting as Insurance Repositories. Thus, a policyholder can keep and buy all his policies under electronic Insurance Account (eIA)[12].

4. **Promoting and regulating professional organizations:** Insurance Regulatory and Development Authority of India also promotes and regulates professional organizations such as Actuarial Society of India and Insurance Institute of India which are connected with the insurance and re-insurance business. The Authority has also signed a MoU with the Indian Institute of Management, Bangalore to give impetus to insurance research and education. The Authority maintains good networking with the Institute of Chartered Accountants of India to enrich the acumen of its members in insurance accounting and audit. The authority had also established Indian Institute of Insurance Surveyors and Loss Assessors as a self regulatory body whose membership is mandatory for

---

11. Insurance Regulatory Development Authority (2001), *op.cit.* pp. 20-48.
12. Insurance Regulatory Development Authority (2013), "Insurance Repository a Step Towards e-world", [online] Available from: http://www.policyholder.gov.in/ uploads/ CEDocuments/ Insurance % 20 Repository%20System%20Handbook.pdf [Accessed on 18 August 2015].

granting surveyors license. The Authority in association with Government of Andhra Pradesh had established Institute of Insurance and Risk Management for providing training in professional courses related to insurance.

5. **Calling for information from, undertaking inspection of, conducting enquiries and investigations including audit of insurers, intermediaries and other organizations:** Insurance Regulatory and Development Authority of India is vested with powers to seek information from the insurers and the intermediaries. The Authority, also seeks time bound information from the insurer or intermediary when a complaint has been received against them. This information is also sought in order to address queries and questions of Parliament and Government. Thus to ensure that effective information is sought from the insurers the Authority meets the top management of the insurers twice a year and review the progress made in compliance with the Act and the regulations.

The authority is also vested with powers to undertake on-site and off-site inspections of insurers and insurance intermediaries through Inspection department. During 2013-14, nine life insurers and three non-life insurers were comprehensively investigated. Also eleven life insurers and three non-life insurers were investigated under focused investigations. The major areas under both types of investigations (focused and comprehensive) were grievance redressal mechanism of the insurers, payments to intermediaries and complaints received from the policyholders by the Authority, etc[13].

13. Insurance Regulatory Development Authority (2015), Annual Report 2014-15, October, Hyderabad, pp. 90-92.

Figure 4.1: Major Functions of Insurance Regulatory and Development Authority of India (IRDAI)

Source: Compiled and faried from IRDAI Act, 2010.

6. **Specifying the form and manner in which accounts shall be maintained:** Insurance Regulatory and Development Authority of India prescribes the insurers the manner in which their books of account and statement of accounts shall be maintained. In this regard the Authority has issued various guidelines and regulations, namely, Preparation of Financial Statements and Auditor's Report of Insurance Companies Regulations, 2000; Actuarial Report and Abstract Regulations, 2000; Assets, Liabilities and Solvency Margin of Insurers Regulations, 2000; Insurance Surveyors and Loss Assessors (Licensing, Professional Requirements and Code of Conduct) Regulations, 2000; Investment Regulations, 2000 and Investment (Amendment) Regulations, 2001.

   In year 2013-14 the Authority has consolidated all its circulars issued regarding maintain accounts into one master circular vide reference IRDA/F&A/cir/232/12/2013 issued on 11 December, 2013 for easy compliance by the life insurers. This document will serve as single point reference for all the life insurers with regard to accounting, financial reporting, corporate governance and public disclosures.

7. **Regulating investment of funds by insurance companies:** Insurance Regulatory and Development Authority of India (IRDAI) has specified manner in which funds of insurer shall be invested. The pattern of investment for life insurance, pension and general annuity and general and reinsurance is discussed in detail in Table 4.2 below.

Table 4.2: Pattern of Investments Specified by the Authority

Insurance	No	Type of Investment	Percentage
Life Insurance	i	Central Government Securities	Not less than 25%,
	ii	Government Securities or other approved securities (including above)	Not less than 50% including (i)
	iii iv	Approved investment as specified in Section 27 A of the Act and other investment as specified in Section 27 A (2) of the Act and Schedule I to these Regulations, (all taken together) subject to exposure/prudential norms as specified in Regulation 9 Other investment as specified under Section 27 A (2) of the Act, subject to exposure/prudential norms as specified in Regulation 9	Not exceeding 50% Not exceeding 15 %
	v	Investment in housing and Infrastructure	Not less than15 %
Pension and General Annuity	i	Government securities	not less than 20%
	ii	Government Securities or other approved securities inclusive of above, being not less than	not less than 40% including (i)
	iii	Balance to be invested in Approved Investments and to be governed by Exposure/ Prudential Norms	Not exceeding 60%
General Insurance and Reinsurance	i	Central Government Securities being not less than	not less than 20%
	ii	State Government securities and other Guaranteed securities including above being not less than	not less than 30% including (i)
	iii iv	Approved investment as specified in Section 27 B of the Act and other investment as specified in Section 27 B (3) of the Act and Schedule II to these Regulations, (all taken together) subject to exposure/ prudential norms as specified in Regulation 9 Other investment as specified under Section 27 B (3) of the Act, subject to exposure/prudential norms as specified in Regulation 9	Not exceeding 70% Not more than 25 percent
		Housing and Loans to State Government for Housing and Fire Fighting equipment, being not less than 5% Investment in Infrastructure	not less than 5% Not less than 10 percent

Source: Insurance Regulatory and Development Authority, Regulation (2013), vide REGD. No. D.L.33004.

For the year 2012-13, the pattern of investment specified for Life insurance is in government securities should not be less than 25 percent; approved securities including government securities including central government, state government securities not less than 50 percent; approved investments and other investments not exceeding 35 percent of the fund and investments in infrastructure should not be less than 15 percent of the fund.

8. **Adjudication of disputes between insurers and intermediaries or insurance intermediaries:** Insurance Regulatory and Development Authority of India has statutory obligation to adjudicate disputes between insurers and intermediaries. The Authority has adopted a consultative process for framing various regulations in this regard. Life Insurance Council and Non-Life Insurance Council provide a platform for consultation to all the insurers. Further, in case of grievance - the insurers and their intermediaries approach the Authority. The Authority after receiving the grievances, takes up the matter for discussion with respective insurance company and in extreme cases the Authority issues direction for resolution of disputes. In year 2010-11, the Authority received three complaints and adjudicated upon the complaints. The dispute adjudicated by the Authority pertains to PRMAN Reinsurance Brokers Pvt. Ltd Vs The Oriental Insurance Co. Ltd; Megatop Insurance Brooking Ltd Vs Agriculture Insurance Company of India Ltd and Key Insurance Brokers Pvt. Ltd Vs The Oriental Insurance Co. Ltd. From year 2011 to 2014 the Authority has received no application for dispute adjudication.

9. **Specifying the percentage of life insurance business and general insurance business to be undertaken by the insurer in the rural or social sector:** In order to increase coverage of insurance the Insurance Regulatory and Development Authority of India has made obligatory on the part of insurers to have certain percentage of insurance from rural and social sector. For Life insurer the percentage is 5% in the first financial year; 7% in the second financial year; 10% in the third financial year; 12% in the fourth financial year and 15% in the fifth year of total policies written direct in that year. In case of general insurance 2% in the first financial year; 3 % in the second financial year and 5% thereafter of total gross premium income written direct in that year. In case of social sector it is mandatory on the part of insurer to insure 5000 lives in the first financial year; 7500 lives in the second financial year; 10000 lives in the third financial year; 15000 lives in the fourth financial year and 20000 lives in the fifth year. It is noteworthy to mention here that over the years with maturity in insurance business IRDAI has increased percentage of Life insurance policies to be underwritten from rural sector along with increase in number of lives for general insurance. For Life insurance the rural sector latest obligations are 18 percent of the new policies in the seventh financial year; 19 percent of the new policies in eighth and ninth financial years; 20 percent of the new policies in the tenth financial year, of the total policies written direct in that year. The obligations for the tenth financial years i.e. 20 percent of the individual new policies shall be applicable in the future financial years. Along

with these for the existing insurers i.e. LIC the rural sector obligations 25 percent of the individual new policies written direct in that year. Further the amendment also elaborated that if an insurer commences operations in the second half of the financial year then rural sector obligations are not applicable to it for the said financial year and next financial year shall be counted as first financial year and specified regulations of the first financial year (7 percent of the individual new policies) shall be applicable. If insurer commences operations in the first half of the financial year then applicable obligation for the first financial year shall be 50 percent of the obligations specified in the regulation.

II
OTHER POLICIES AND FUNCTIONS OF INSURANCE REGULATORY AND DEVELOPMENT AUTHORITY OF INDIA (IRDAI)

Along with above mentioned statutory functions, IRDAI also performs other functions relating to regulation of insurance market. The other policies and functions of IRDAI are discussed as under:

4.9 Website For Right to Information Act

The Right to Information Act of Government of India is meant to give to the citizens of India access to information under control of public authorities to promote transparency and accountability in these organizations. The Insurance Regulatory and Development Authority of India being a public organization is obligated by the guidelines of RTI Act, 2005 to provide and furnish information to public.

IRDAI maintains its own website and furnish all the necessary information regarding acts/regulations; insurers and re-insurers, agents training institutes, appointed actuaries; surveyors, third party administrators, insurance brokers, corporate agents; insurance councils, insurance ombudsmen; Annual Report, IRDAI Journal and press releases. Website of IRDAI contains portal of RTI and it furnishes information how to seek grievance redressal by policy holders, how to make application under RTI Act, 2005, whom to send this application, etc. The website also contains name and designation, department and e-mail addresses of Central Public Information Officers as required to be published under Section 4(1)(b) of RTI Act 2005. IRDAI has designated appellate authority and also appointed Central Information Commissioner in consonance with terms of Chapter 3 of the Right to Information Act, 2005[14].

4.10 Consumer Grievances Redressal Mechanism

The Consumer Affairs Department of Insurance Regulatory and Development Authority of India handles policyholders grievances along with carrying out insurance awareness campaigns. In case of any grievances the Policy holder may register his compliant in the three stages, namely, Grievance redressal cell of insurer, Integrated

14. Insurance Regulatory Development Authority (2001), Annual Report 2000-2001, October, Hyderabad, pp.20-35.

Grievance Management System of Insurance Regulatory and Development Authority of India and Insurance Ombudsman.

a. Grievance redressal mechanism of Insurer

Grievance redressal mechanism of the insurer is the first point of interface during any complaint. A Policy holder has to first file his complaint with the insurer. If the insurer does not respond to the complaint within 15 days or if the complainant is not satisfied with the response of insurer he may register his complaint through Integrated Grievance Redressal Cell of IRDAI.

b. Integrated Grievance Management System

When a policy-holder is not satisfied with the response of insurer or insurer does not respond to complaint of policy holder within 15 days then a policy holder may lodge his complaint to Grievance Redressal Cell of IRDAI. Grievance Redressal Cell has Integrated Grievance Management System which receives complaints through Integrated Grievance Call centre which is a tool free number. IGMS is implemented by IRDAI which is helpful in providing information regarding status of complaints across the industry to the Authority on real time basis. IGMS is working as a repository of the industry's complaints including their status. In year 2012-13 Insurance Regulatory and Development Authority of India received 341012 grievances for life insurance segment and 78927 for general insurance (Table 4.3)

Table 4.3: Status of Grievances with Insurance Regulatory and Development Authority (IRDAI)

Insu-rance	Insurer	Outstanding as on 31stMarch 2012	Grievances Reported During 2012-13	Resolved During 2012-13	Outstanding as on 31 March 2013
Life	Public	165	73034	72655	544
	Private	1117	267978	268415	680
	Sub Total	1282	341012	341070	1224
Non-Life	Public	1548	18616	19057	1107
	Private	47	60311	60230	128
	Sub Total	1595	78927	79287	1235

Source: Insurance Regulatory and Development Authority (2013)[15], Annual Report (2012- 13), Hyderabad.

c. Insurance Ombudsman:

A policy holder with complaint relating to personal insurance, which claims for a value up to Rs.20 lakhs may directly approach Insurance Ombudsman in his area. IRDAI does not adjudicate on complaints. Thus complaints of adjudicatory nature are dealt by insurance ombudsman. If the complainant is looking for adjudication in respect of claims, he or she may approach the Insurance Ombudsman. The office of the Ombudsman was set up under the Redressal of Public Grievances Rules, 1998 framed by the Central Government. Any person who has a grievance against an insurer, may

15. Insurance Regulatory Development Authority (2013), *op.cit.*, pp.91-93.

himself or through his legal heirs make a complaint in writing to the Ombudsman within whose jurisdiction the branch or office of the insurer complained against is located. The Ombudsman may either make a recommendation through mediation or pass an award which he or she thinks is fair in the facts and circumstances of a claim.

4.11 Regulation of Insurance and Re-insurance Companies

For orderly growth of insurance business in India Insurance Regulatory and Development Authority of India has brought out many changes and issued the regulations such as IRDA (Appointed Actuary's) (First Amendment) Regulations, 2013; IRDA (Linked Insurance Products) Regulations 2013 and IRDA (Non-Linked Insurance Products) Regulations, 2013; IRDA (Life Insurance-Reinsurance) Regulations, 2013; IRDA (Investment) (Fifth Amendment) Regulations, 2013; IRDA (General Insurance-Reinsurance) Regulations, 2013; IRDA (Health Insurance) Regulations, 2013, etc.

Along with issuing these regulations IRDAI has made conducive for insurance firms to participate in repo/reverse repo transactions. IRDAI has also issued guidelines for servicing of orphan policies and know your customer.

a. **Participation in Repo/Reverse Repo Transactions in Corporate debt Securities:** Life insurers have been allowed to participate in reverse repo transactions in Government Securities and Corporate Debt Securities to the extent of 10 percent of their aggregate and respective fund size. Life insurers are not permitted to take part in repo transactions. Non-Life insurers are allowed to participate in both repo and reverse repo transactions to maximum limit 10 percent of their investment assets.

b. **Servicing to orphan policies:** As insurance agents are required to give proper service to policyholder regarding their policies. In case of death of agent or cancellation of license, etc the policyholder attached with the agent suffers in terms of post sales services. Under the new guidelines, the insurer is allowed to allot lapsed orphan policies to individual agent whose license is in place so that policy holder may get all the service benefits. The number of policies allotted to an agent should not exceed 20 percent of the total number of policies that were introduced by him/her and are in force as on date of allotment. If the allotted orphan policy is not revived within six months than insurance company has discretion to re-allot the policy to other agent.

c. **Know Your Customer (KYC):** Insurance company may consider the current passbook updated till last month or current statement of bank account with details of permanent address as official valid document for KYC. Above documents shall be sufficient towards Proof of Identity (PoI) and Proof of Address and written confirmation from the banks shall not be required hereafter. KYC is aimed at preventing money laundering and combating financing of terrorism via insurance especially non-life. IRDAI issued a circular in this regard and it has withdrawn exemptions from Anti Money laundering and Combating Financing of Terrorism (AML/CFT) requirements given standalone medical and health insurance policies. Insurers are advised to apply the AML/CFT requirements based on their risk assessment of each of the product's profile. Insurers are also required to identify and verify the beneficial owner to an insurance contract because of typical nature of insurance contracts driven by the principle of insurable interest and strict underwriting requirements.

d. **Insurance Fraud Monitoring Framework:** Insurance companies are required to have anti-fraud policy approved by board comprising procedures on fraud monitoring; identify potential areas of fraud; coordination with law enforcement agencies; framework for exchange of information; due diligence and regular communication channels. Also statistics regarding insurance should be submitted to the Authority in the prescribed format annually[16].

4.12 Intermediaries Associated With the Insurance Business

Insurance agents and other intermediaries such as corporate agents, surveyors and loss assessors acts as bridge between the insurer and the insured. IRDAI has not only assigned great importance to their training but also made compulsory eligibility test to acquire technical and product knowledge of the market. The authority also ensures that right type of persons undertake jobs so as to facilitate speedy service delivery to customers and helps insurer by providing report in stipulated time to enable them to settle a claim without delay.

In year 2013-14, the number of individual agents increased by 3.1 percent. The number increased from 21.22 lakh in 2013 to 21.88 lakh in 2014. In 2013-14, 7.25 lakh agents were appointed while 6.59 lakh agents were terminated. Private insurers appointed 3.83 lakh agents and terminated 3.40 lakh agents. In case of LIC, its appointed 3.41 lakh agents and 3.18 lakh agents were terminated. In 2014, there were 689 corporate agents while in 2013 the number stood at 739. This high attrition may adversely affect life insurance business, policy persistency and public perception of the agency channel as a stable career. This turnover of agents should be reduced and efforts should be to retain stable and growing workforce of agency.

Over the years there is perceptible shift away from the individual agency channel. The contribution of new business premium procured through individual agents increased to 78.40 percent during 2013-14 from 77.53 percent during 2012-13 (Table 4.4).

Table 4.4: Individual New Business Performance of Life Insurer

(Figures in percent of Premium)

Insurer	Individual Agents	Corporate Agents		Brokers	Direct selling	Total Individual New Business	Referrals
		Banks	Others				
Private	40.08	43.62	4	4.91	7.38	100	0.10
LIC	95.44	2.77	0.10	0.02	1.12	100	-
Industry Total	78.40	15.62	1.33	1.56	3.09	100	0.03

Source: Insurance Regulatory and Development Authority (2014),[17]

16. *Ibid.*, pp. 74-76.
17. Insurance Regulatory Development Authority (2014), *op.cit.*, p.63.

IRDAI is the authority which grants surveyor licenses and also regulates them. As per the notification of Insurance Surveyors and Loss Assessors (Licensing Professional Requirements and Code of Conduct) (Amendment) Regulations, 2013, Surveyors and Loss Assessors (SLAs) are persons who have membership of the Indian Institute of Insurance Surveyors and Loss Assessors (IIISLA). Thus all existing licensed SLAs would become members of IIISLA and are categorized as Licentiate, Associate and Fellow Member of the Institute. In order to increase the outreach of insurance in rural areas the Authority has incorporated to facilitate certain life and non-life insurance in India to market certain categories of Retail Insurance Policies and services through M/s Common Service centre e-Governance Services Limited – a special purpose vehicle to enable delivery of services through Common service centres. In year 2013-14 the Authority issued fresh licenses to 480 individual and 55 corporate SLAs. The Authority implemented web-based Integrated Licensing Management System for surveyors. This system facilitates online submission by individuals and corporate for grant of fresh/renewal/modified license.

The Authority allowed Insurance Brokers to operate in Indian market from 30 January, 2003 in pursuant to the provisions of the IRDA (Insurance Brokers) Regulations, 2002. In this regard a capital requirement of Rs. 50 Lakh for direct insurance brokers and Rs. 2 crore for reinsurance brokers and Rs. 2.5 crore for composite brokers is made obligatory. Foreign equity participation up to an extent of 26 percent is permissible in insurance broking. Insurance broking is becoming popular over the years as number of registrations has increased to 384 till 2014. Out of which 332 are direct brokers, 46 are composite brokers and 6 are reinsurance brokers[18].

4.13 Professional Institutes Connected With Insurance Education

Insurance Regulatory and Development Authority of India has accredited 495 training institutes to assist the training of agents across the country. IRDAI has made obligatory hundred hours pre-licensing training to agents. The accreditation process is transparent and a prospective institute is only accredited if it meets certain standards such as availability of a competent faculty, proper infrastructure facilities, etc. An assessment made on a "marks" system followed up by inspections, if necessary, by officers of the Authority before granting accreditation. The Authority normally recognises an institution for a period of three years at a time[19].

Indian Institute of Insurance Surveyors and Loss Assessors (IIISLA) is an institute promoted and established by Insurance Regulatory and Development Authority of India. The membership of the Institute is mandatory for getting license as surveyor and loss assessor. Insurance Institute of India is examining body for agents Pre-recruitment examinations. The institute also prepares course content for various examinations of surveyors and is also conducting the examination. The Authority also has statutory representation in the Council of the Institute of Actuaries of India- a statutory and professional body of Actuaries[20].

18. *Ibid.*, pp. 66.
19. Insurance Regulatory Development Authority (2001), Annual Report 2001-2002, October, Hyderabad, pp. 30-36.
20. Insurance Regulatory Development Authority (2013), *op.cit.*, pp.84-85.

4.14 International Cooperation in Insurance

In order to develop and maintain, fair, safe and stable insurance markets for the benefit and protection of policyholders; and to contribute to global financial stability the International Association of Insurance Supervisors (IAIS) was established at Basel, Switzerland in 1994 as a global standard setting body. The organization is run by funds raised by way of subscription from its members. The association has recently created a membership called the "observer status" to which insurance companies are admitted. Almost all the insurance regulators from different countries are members of the IAIS. IRDAI (India) is a member of the Association since 1996. Over the years the membership of insurance regulators and supervisors has grown to over 200 jurisdictions providing representation to 140 countries. The IAIS has over 130 organizations and individuals connected with it which represent professional associations, insurance and reinsurance companies, international financial institutions, consultants and other professionals as observers.

This mechanism of networking has helped in global knowledge sharing in insurance sector and helped in evolution of consistent supervisory standards and practices amongst various participants. IAIS undertakes its activities under the guidance of Executive Committee, which comprises members elected from different regions across the globe. Asian region is represented by five members and Chairman IRDAI is one member representing the region.

The aims and objectives of the IAIS are to usher in a regime of prudential regulations of the insurance industry, prescribe guidelines for the insurance supervisors to observe the industry within their jurisdiction, to promote international co-operation and understanding among the supervisors and to represent before world forums the cause of the insurance industry and the matter of its functioning and regulation. The Association has been entrusted gradually, by world financial organizations, with a role to play in the emerging financial architecture.

IAIS acts as a facilitator is establishing maintain, fair and efficient insurance markets by developing principles, standards and effective insurance supervisory regimes. IAIS also prepares 'Issue Papers' that provides background on specific areas of interest to insurance supervisors. In 2011, IAIS issued revised Insurance Core Principles (ICP). The 26 Core Principles also constitute the globally accepted framework used in evaluation of supervisory regimes under the Financial Sector Assessment Program (FSAP) conducted jointly by the World Bank and International Monetary Fund. Thus, in this regard; it is noteworthy to mention that India is also assessed under FSAP.

IAIS has developed an 'Initial Assessment Methodology' to assess the systematic importance of insurers. It is a three step process involving data collection, a methodical assessment of that data and a supervisory judgment and validation. The indicator based assessment approach is related to the approach developed by the Basel Committee for Global Systemically Important Banks or G-SIBs. This approach identifies five categories to measure relative systemic importance. These categories are non-traditional insurance and non-insurance (NTNI) activities; interconnectedness; substitutability; size and global activity. In July 2013, IAIS has released "Assessment Methodology and Policy Measures" for GSIIs which was endorsed by the Financial Stability Board (FSB). Based on this assessment methodology of IAIS and data of FSB, in consultation with IAIS and national authorities have identified nine Global Systemically Important Insurer (G-SIIs) to which the policy measures above should apply. These G-SIIs include Allianz SE, American International Group Inc., Assicurazioni Generali S.P.A., Aviva plc., Axa S.A., MetLife Inc., Ping An Insurance (Group) company of China Ltd., Prudential Financial Inc. and Prudential plc. Out of these insurers except one operating in China all other have joint ventures in India[21].

A good rapport exists between IRDAI and IAIS. IAIS has offered IRDAI its technical expertise in training its officers and members. Similarly, IRDAI has been receiving unstinted support from the National Association of Insurance Commissioners (NAIC), USA, the apex body of the American insurance regulators. NAIC has the distinction of bringing into effect prudential regulations and coordinating the activities of the state regulators of insurance to bring about a uniform approach to the regulation of the industry. NAIC periodically conducts training programmes and seminars to which the representatives of IRDAI have been invited.

IRDAI also has an ongoing relationship with the Canadian Institute of Actuaries in the professional meetings and seminars, actuaries of IRDAI are invited.

IRDAI participates in the exercise "Managing Regulatory Change in Life Insurance and Pensions" started by the Australian Agency for International Development (AusAID), the Asian Development Bank (ADB), the Commonwealth Bank of Australia, AXA Asia Pacific Holdings, and the Australian APEC Study Centre. The ADB has conducted a study of IRDAI's operation including the regulations formulated by it and have found them to be relevant and comparable to world standards. The USAID programme has allotted some grants for capacity building and technical training of the officers of the Authority[22].

IRDAI is a signatory to the Multilateral Memorandum of Understanding (MMoU) of IAIS as well, which provides an international platform for cooperation and information sharing[23].

The Authority, has thus established itself in the world stage and has participated in many international seminars and conferences where its Chairman has been invited to deliver theme or keynote addresses[24].

4.15 Insurance Ombudsman

The institution of Insurance Ombudsman was created by a Government of India Notification dated 11th November, 1998 with the purpose of quick disposal of the grievances of the insured customers and to mitigate their problems involved in redressal of those grievances. The institution of Insurance Ombudsman has great importance and relevance for the protection of interest of policyholders and also to

21. *Ibid.*, pp. 88-91.
22. Insurance Regulatory Development Authority (2001), *op.cit.* pp.20-46.
23. Insurance Regulatory Development Authority (2013), *op.cit.*p.91.
24. Insurance Regulatory Development Authority (2001), *op.cit.*, pp.25-28.

build up their confidence in the system. This institution has helped to generate and sustain the faith and confidence amongst the consumers in insurers.

a. Term of Office

The Person should not be more than 62 years of age. Ombudsman is appointed for a term of three years or till the incumbent attains the age of sixty five years, whichever is earlier.

b. Eligibility

He should have retired (or about to retire) as Chairman or Managing Director or Executive Director or General Manager of Public Sector Insurance Companies in India or have retired (or about to retire) from IAS or IRS. He should have held a post equivalent to or above the rank of Additional Secretary to the Government of India or any equivalent post under State Government or Persons who have retired (or about to retire) as High Court Judge or District & Sessions Court Judge. The person is selected by a Selection Committee comprising Chairman of IRDAI, Two Representatives of Insurance Council including each from Life Insurance and General Insurance and one Representative of Central Government. The selection will be made on the basis of the CVs of the applicants.

c. Removal from office:

An Ombudsman may be removed on the grounds of gross misconduct committed during his term of office. The governing body may appoint such person as it thinks fit to conduct enquiry in relation to misconduct of the Ombudsman. All enquiries on misconduct will be sent to Insurance Regulatory and Development Authority of India (IRDAI) which may take a decision on the proposed action to be taken against the Ombudsman. On recommendations of the IRDAI, the Governing Body may terminate his services, in case he is found guilty.

d. Offices of Insurance Ombudsman:

The Insurance Council which is the administrative body has appointed twelve ombudsmen across the country in cities of Ahmedabad, Bhopal, Bhubaneswar, Chandigarh, Chennai, Delhi, Guwahati, Hyderabad, Kochi, Kolkata, Lucknow and Mumbai. The Ombudsman has a secretarial staff provided to him by the insurance council to assist him in discharging his duties. The total expenses on Ombudsman and his staff are incurred by the insurance companies who are members of the insurance council in such proportion as may be decided by the governing body.

e. Power of Ombudsman

Insurance Ombudsman has two types of functions to perform, namely Conciliation and Award making. The insurance Ombudsman is empowered to receive and consider complaints from any person who has any grievance against an insurer. The complaint may relate to any grievance against the insurer such as

(a) any partial or total repudiation of claims by the insurance companies,

(b) dispute with regard to premium paid or payable in terms of the policy,

(c) dispute on the legal construction of the policy wordings in case such dispute relates to claims;

(d) delay in settlement of claims and

(e) non-issuance of any insurance document to customers after receipt of premium.

Insurance Ombudsman has power to deliver award on any complaint up to Rs. 20 lakhs. The insurance companies are required to honour the awards passed by an Insurance Ombudsman within three months.

f. Process of lodging complaint

A complainant can file complaint in writing addressed to the insurance Ombudsman of the jurisdiction under which the office of the insurer falls. The complaint can also be lodged through the legal heirs of the insured. Before lodging a complaint the complainant should have made a representation to his insurer and if the insurer has rejected the complaint or the complainant have not received any reply within a period of one month after the date of submission of the complaint or he is not satisfied with the reply of the insurer then he may approach Insurance Ombudsman. The complaint should be made within one year after the receipt of the reply of insurer. Also, the same complaint on the subject should not be pending with before any court, consumer forum or arbitrator.

g. Award

The ombudsman shall pass an award within a period of three months from the receipt of the complaint. The awards are binding upon the insurance companies. If the policy holder is not satisfied with the award of the Ombudsman he can make approach to other adjudicatory bodies like Consumer Forums and Courts of law for redressal of his grievances[25].

During year 2012-13, all the twelve Ombudsman received a total of 24, 782 complaints out of 64 percent were related to life insurance and remaining 37 percent were for general insurance (Table 4.5).

Table 4.5: Disposal of Complaints by Ombudsman during 2012-13

Insurer	Complaints as on 31.3.2012	Complaints received during 2012-13	Total	Complaints disposed during 2012-13	Complaints as on 31.03.2013
Life	2846	15711	18557	14673	3884
Non-Life	4330	9071	13401	8684	4717
Combined	7176	24782	31958	23357	8601

Source: Insurance Regulatory and Development Authority (2013), Annual Report (2012-13), Hyderabad.

25. www.irda.gov.in, website of Insurance Regulatory Development Authority.

In Year 2012-13, Insurance Ombudsman disposed of 23357 complaints. Out these total Ombudsman declared 16296 complaints (seventy percent) as non-acceptable/not-entertainable. It issued awards/recommendations for 2760 (twelve percent) of complaints. 2283 complaints (ten percent) were withdrawn while 2018 (nine percent) were dismissed[26].

4.16 Implementation of Official Language Policy

Insurance Regulatory and Development Authority of India has assigned task of promotion of official language to the Official Language Implementation department which explore creative ways for implementation of Official Language act and also implements Official language policy of government of India. In this regard employees are encouraged to respond to letters in Hindi which are received in Hindi language, conduct in-house meetings in Hindi and to sign documents in Hindi. The Consumer Affairs department of the Authority has launched website www.policyholder.gov. in which provides reference material for policy holders education in Hindi and English. All notifications which are related to public interest are published in Hindi on IRDAI website. IRDAI's monthly journal is bilingual and is published in Hindi and English. Along with this all important documents such as notifications, Circulars, Orders, Administrative and other reports, Annual Reports, Press Communiqués, Licenses, Contracts, Agreements and Official Papers are converted into Hindi. IRDAI also celebrated Hindi Fortnight from 14 September to 20 September 2012 and organized various competitions and activities for employees encouraging them to gain proficiency in Hindi[27].

4.17 Constitution of Funds:

As per Section 16 of the IRDA Act, there shall be Insurance Regulatory and Development Authority Fund. The fund would comprise Government grants, fees and charges received by the Authority; sums received by the Authority from such other source as may be decided time to time by the Central Government; the percentage of prescribed premium income received from the insurer/insurance intermediaries.

The Fund shall be applied for meeting the expenses of the Authority such as salaries, allowances and other remuneration of the members, officers and other employees of the Authority; the other expenses of the Authority related to the discharge of its functions and for the purposes of this Act.

4.18 Accounts and Audit:

As per Section 17 of the Act the Authority shall maintain proper accounts and other relevant records and prepare an annual statement of accounts in the manner prescribed by the Central Government in consultation with the Comptroller and Auditor-General of India (CGAI). The accounts of the Authority shall be audited by the Comptroller and Auditor-General of India as specified by him and any expenditure incurred in connection with such audit shall be payable by the Authority to the Comptroller and

26. Insurance Regulatory Development Authority (2013, op.cit., p.98.
27. *Ibid*, p.114.

Auditor-General. (CAGI) or any other person appointed by him in connection with the audit of the accounts of the Authority shall have the same rights, privileges and authority in connection with such audit as the Comptroller and Auditor-General. The accounts of the Authority as certified by the Comptroller and Auditor General of India (CGAI) with the audit-report thereon shall be forwarded annually to the Central Government and Government shall table that report before each House of Parliament.

4.19 Information and Technology in Insurance Regulatory and Development Authority of India

Information and technology has become enabler of speedy delivery of service in the organizations. Therefore, it has become necessary for all the organizations to transact business using IT. IRDAI in this regard has taken following initiatives in this regard:

a. **Business Analytics Solution:** The objective of Business Analytics Solution (BAS) is provision of necessary data and information for analyzing the insurance companies to facilitate decisions regarding regulations. The other objectives of BAS to make data capture simple and time bound; providing centralized facility to store and process captured data; reducing lag on data capturing and maintenance and focusing on analyzing the data; disseminating data within the Authority for regulatory purposes; providing Management Information System to various levels of Authority for administrative and regulatory purposes; automate the licensing processes of various departments like Brokers, Surveyors, Third Party Administrators and insurers. As per latest Annual Report 2013-14 of IRDAI 90 percent of the project development work has been completed. Finance and Accounts (life and non-life and corporate agent module) is operational, advertisement filling module for life department, hands-on training on help desk module are also operational.

b. **Integrated Grievances management System:** It is a repository of grievances of policyholders against insurers maintained by the Authority. The new features of this facility include new dashboards for operations and management, exclusive status report for senior citizens, enhanced ad-hoc and drill down facility in reporting; integration with internal application of the department, facility to update Branch codes. IGMS facility has been extended to applications being used through mobile phones. IGMS system is operational and policyholders can also track status of their complaints through mobile phones. When the complaint is lodged through IGMS the complaint flows to repository of the insurer and the Authority.

c. **Development and Implementation of an Application for Registration of Approved Persons of Insurance:** This application for registration of approved persons of Insurance repositories was developed in-house and the same has been implemented successfully. This software enables the insurance repositories to file the applications on-line.

d. **Setting up of Central Index Server for Insurance Repositories:** The central index server acts as the backbone for Insurance Repositories to issue unique e-account of the policyholders. The central index server for insurance repositories has been implemented and made operational.

IRDAI also maintains and upgrade its website through which it receives various feedbacks from various stakeholders. In year 2012-13, the a few new features in the website have been added such as advanced search facility and agent locator. IRDAI also use facility of video conferencing to facilitate speedy approval of products and to have regular interactions/reviews with insurer/ other regulated entities. For ensuring confidentiality, integrity and availability of information the authority has implemented Information Security Policy. The other activities in this regard also include implementation of Audio Conferencing facility, biometric Attendance System; enhancements to referral application; implementation of Data Loss Prevention software on all workstations and Centralized anti-virus management System, etc.

4.20 Future Agenda of Insurance Regulatory and Development Authority of India

As insurance regulation is at nascent-stage so much that it is desired to be done on regulatory perspective. Despite the guidelines of IRDAI regarding percentage of insurance from rural sector and the coverage of insurance in rural areas is less. With majority of population residing in rural areas it is necessary to cater to rural areas. In year 2012-13, life insurers out of total 441.57 lakh new policies underwrote 113.46 lakh policies i.e. 25.70 percent of the total policies in rural sector against the 68.3 percent total population. The Authority has prescribed that minimum of 25 percent of the policies should be from the rural sector for the year 2012-13. Health insurance is still underdeveloped in India but offers huge potential, as there will be increasing needs to purchase private health cover to supplement public programmes. Moreover coverage of health insurance will reduce out of pocket expenditure of the individual households and will usher in quality medical services.

AS opined by Law Commission that Insurance Act of 1938, is a colonial legislation and certain terms such as "provident societies" and "mutual insurance companies" have no relevance in modern context.

The IRDAI, while regulating the business activities of insurers, exercises quasi-judicial powers, in addition to its administrative powers, e.g. issue, renewal and cancellation of registration certificates to insurers, order with regard to investigation of the affairs of the insurers, making applications to the court for the winding-up of the insurance companies etc. It is felt necessary that there must be a provision of appeal against the decisions of the IRDAI to an independent body constituted under the Act itself. Recently in case of cancellation of registration the aggrieved party may appeal to Securities Appellate Tribunal of Security Exchange Board of India.

When consumers are dissatisfied with an insurance company, particularly in the area of claims settlement, they can go to the Ombudsman under the Redressal of Public Grievances Rules, 1998. They can also appeal under the Consumer Protection Act, 1986. Consumer courts are called upon to interpret the provisions of the Insurance Act 1938, which is a complex piece of legislation. If a special body of law develops, then a special tribunal is necessary to deal with insurance cases. This provision would parallel the Securities Appellate Tribunal functioning under the SEBI Act, 1992[28].

4.21 Concluding Observations

Insurance Regulatory and Development Authority of India was constituted in tune with deregulation of insurance sector in 1999. The Authority currently has one chairman and four part time and four full time members. The authority is entrusted with task of regulating insurance business and protecting interests of policyholders. The major powers and functions of the Authority are to regulate, promote and ensure orderly growth of the insurance business and re-insurance business; issuance to the applicant a certificate of registration, renew, modify, withdraw, suspend or cancel such registration; protection of the interests of the policy holders; specifying requisite qualifications, code of conduct and practical training for intermediary or insurance intermediaries and agents; specifying the code of conduct for surveyors and loss assessors; promoting efficiency in the conduct of insurance business; promoting and regulating professional organizations connected with the insurance and re-insurance business; specifying percentage of insurance business to be undertaken from rural and social sector, regulating investments of the insurers , etc.

The authority has been maintaining liaison with professional institutes connected with insurance business and also with international associations so as to develop and align Indian insurance market as per international standards. The Authority has been capable to keep itself abreast with information and technology development and has utilized the same for rendering services to stakeholders and policyholders. The insurance regulation in India is at nascent stage and IRDAI as a regulator may face lot of challenges in spreading insurance business in rural sector thereby increasing rural insurance density, establishing appellate mechanisms, making insurance firms to provide effective and efficient policy servicing.

28. Law Commission of India (2003), "Consultation Paper on Revision of the Insurance Act, 1938 and the Insurance Regulatory and Development Act, 1999", Government of India, New Delhi, pp. 1-18.

5

Role of Insurance Regulatory and Development Authority of India: An Assessment –I

Genesis/Backdrops:

Assessment of role of Insurance Regulatory and Development Authority of India is discussed in Chapter 5 and Chapter 7. Chapter 5 tends to assess the role of Insurance Regulatory and Development Authority of India (IRDAI) in terms of promoting the growth of life insurance in India; promoting efficiency in conduct of insurance business; spreading life insurance business in rural sector and regulating investment of funds of insurance companies on the basis of secondary data.

Organized into four parts. Part I of this chapter deals with assessment of IRDAI in promoting growth of life insurance in India. Similarly Part II covers assessment of IRDAI in promoting efficiency in conduct of insurance business. Part III contains assessment of IRDAI in terms of spreading life insurance business in rural grees and Regulation of investment of funds of insurance companies by IRDAI is assessed in Part IV.

Assessment of IRDAI in promoting growth of life insurance business in India is done by making comparison of growth rates of pre and post IRDAI phase data of various parameters such as number of offices of life insurers in India, premium underwritten, number of policies underwritten, etc. Further regulatory impact analysis is also done by using regression analysis and counterfactual analysis. Efficiency of life insurance business in India is measured by using Data Envelopment Analysis by taking commission expenses, operational expenses and benefits paid by life insurance companies as input variables and net premium earned by life insurers as output variable. Assessment of IRDAI in spreading life insurance business in rural sector is done by checking the percentage of policies underwritten in rural areas by life insurers against the standards set by IRDAI for life insurers for rural sector. Similarly, regulation of investment of funds of life insurance companies by IRDAI is done by comparing the investment patterns of life insurers against the norms laid down by IRDAI for various funds.

I
ASSESSMENT OF IRDAI IN PROMOTING GROWTH OF LIFE INSURANCE IN INDIA

It is essential to maintain growth in insurance sector as a well-developed insurance sector is needed for economic development. Insurance sector generates capital for long term funding and strengthen the risk taking ability. In India, insurance sector is growing at the rate of 15-20 percent annually and together with financing, real estate and business it contributes about 17.9 percent to national Income. Presently, there is 49 percent of foreign equity allowed in insurance sector and proposal is under consideration to enhance this up to 49 percent. The assessment of IRDAI in promoting growth of life insurance in India is undertaken on the basis of secondary data collected from IRDAI Annual Reports over the years. The assessment of IRDAI in promoting growth of life insurance was undertaken on the basis of the following parameters:

1. Growth in number of Insurers in life insurance
2. Growth in number of offices
3. Growth in number of individual agents
4. Number of policies issued
5. Growth in persistency of Policies
6. Number of products launched in the Market
7. Growth in first year (including single premium) life insurance premium
8. Growth in total premium underwritten in life sector
9. Growth in insurance penetration in life sector
10. Growth in insurance density in life sector

Compound Growth Rate

The compound growth rate has been calculated by using exponential relationship Y=ABt, where Y is variable for which compound rate of growth is calculated, t is time. Logarithm of variable was taken and linear regression equation was used by taking time as independent variable and log values of the variable as dependant variable to obtain beta coefficient. Anti logarithm of the beta coefficient was taken and the value was subtracted by one. The deducted value was multiplied by 100 and the value of the product was the compound rate of growth. The compound rate of growth was calculated for parameters such as growth in number of offices, individual agents, policies issued, products launched in the market, first year life insurance premium and total premium underwritten.

The hypothesis tested in this regard is, "IRDAI has been an instrument in promoting the growth of life insurance business in India by promoting growth in number of agents, polices, single premium underwritten, total premium underwritten in comparison to pre-IRDAI period".

5.1 Growth in Number of Life Insurance Companies in India

Prior to inception of IRDAI, insurance was the monopoly of government with six insurers, one catering to life insurance and four to non-life and one re-insurance Prior to deregulation, Life Insurance Corporation was the sole life insurance company in India without any foreign collaboration. After unshackling the government monopoly, in year 2000 the number of life insurers rose to 6 and further steadily rose. Presently there are 24 life insurers in India and 20 foreign insurers holding equity stakes (Table 5.1). IRDAI regulates registration, renewal, modifications and suspension of certificate of registration vide IRDAI (Registration of Indian Insurance Companies), Regulations, 2000 with amendments from time to time.

Table 5.1

Number of Insurance Companies in Life Sector

Sr. No.	INSURER	Foreign Partner	Date of Regis-tration	Year of Opera-tion	FDI in %
1.	AEGON Religare Life Insurance Company Limited	AEGONIndia Holdings BV, Netherlands	27.06.2008	2008-09	26
2.	Aviva Life Insurance Company India Limited	Aviva International Holdings LTD. UK.	14.05.2002	2002-03	26
3.	Bajaj Allianz Life Insurance Company Limited	Allianz, SE Germany	03.08.2001	2001-02	26
4.	Bharti Axa Life Insurance Company Limited	AXA India Holdings, France	14.07.2006	2006-07	22
5.	Birla Sunlife Life Insurance Company Limited	Sun Life Financial (India) Insurance Investment Inc, Canada	31.01.2001	2000-01	26
6.	Canara HSBC Oriental Bank of Commerce Life Insurance Company Limited	HSBC, Insurance (Asia Pacific) Ltd. UK	08.05.2008	2008-09	26
7*.	DLF Pramerica Life Insurance Company Limited	Prudential International Insurance Holdings Ltd. USA	27.06.2008	2008-09	26
8.	Edelweiss Tokio Life Insurance Company Limited	Tokio Marine & Nichido Fire Insurance Company Ltd. Japan	10.5.2011	2011-12	26

Sr. No.	INSURER	Foreign Partner	Date of Regis-tration	Year of Opera-tion	FDI in %
9.	Future Generali India Life Insurance Company	Participate Maatschapij Graafsschap Holland NV, Netherlands	04.09.2007	2007-08	25
10.	HDFC Standard Life Insurance Company Limited	Standard Life (Mauritius Holdings) 2006, Ltd. UK	23.10.2000	2000-01	26
11.	ICICI Prudential Life Insurance Company Limited	Prudential Corporation Holdings Ltd. UK	24.11.2000	2000-01	25
12**.	IDBI Federal Life Insurance Company Limited	Aegis Insurance International NV Netherlands	19.12.2007	2007-08	26
13.	India First Life Insurance Company Limited	Legal & General Middle East Ltd	5.11.2009	2009-10	26
14.***	Exide Life Insurance Company Limited	----	02.08.2001	2001-02	0
15.	Kotak Mahindra Old Mutual Life Insurance Ltd	Old Mutual Plc, UK	10.01.2001	2001-02	26
16****.	Max Life Insurance Company Limited	Mitsui Sumitomo Insurance Company Ltd. Japan	15.11.2000	2000-01	26
17*****.	PNB Metlife India Insurance Company Limited	Metlife International Holdings Inc, USA	06.08.2001	2001-02	26
18.	Reliance Life Insurance Company Limited	Nippon Life Insurance Company Ltd. Japan	03.01.2002	2001-02	26
19.	Sahara India Life Insurance Company Limited	-----	06.02.2004	2004-05	0
20.	SBI Life Insurance Company Limited	BNP Paribus Cardiff, France	29.03.2001	2001-02	26

Sr. No.	INSURER	Foreign Partner	Date of Regis-tration	Year of Opera-tion	FDI in %
21.	Shriram Life Life Insurance Company Limited	___	17.11.2005	2005-06	0
22.	Star Union Dai Chi Life Insurance Company Limited	Dai-ichi Life Insurance Company Ltd. Japan	26.12.2008	2009-10	26
23.	Tata Aia Life Insurance Company Limited	American International Assurance Company (Bermuda Ltd.)	12.02.2001	2000-01	26
24.	Life Insurance Corporation of India	----	01.09.1956	1956	0

*Now re-named as DHFL Pramerica Life Insurance Company Ltd with the signing of joint venture in July 2013 and was granted approval by the Insurance Regulator, IRDAI in December 2013.

** Now renamed as IDBI Federal Life Insurance Co Ltd- a joint-venture of IDBI Bank and Federal Bank, and Ageas, a multinational insurance giant.

*** Formerly known as ING Vysya Life Insurance Company Limited had a joint venture with ING Insurance International B.V., Netherlands.

**** Earlier had joint venture with New York Life.

***** Earlier named as Metlife India Insurance Company Limited.

5.2 Growth in Number of Offices of Life Insurance Companies

With growth in number of insurers there has been steady increase in number of offices of life insurers in India. In year 2000-01 there were 2199 offices and in 2012-13 this number stands at 10285 offices in pan India (Table 5.2). The number of offices helps in improving the outreach of insurance. As per the section 64 VC of Insurance Act 1938 it is mandatory for every insurer to get prior permission before opening new places of business in India. The place of Business includes a branch, a sub-branch, inspectorate, organization office and any other office. In pursuant to the above guidelines, IRDAI has issued guidelines vide circular No. 51/1/F&A/Misc/119/ Sept./ 2005-06 dated 26th September 2005advising insurers to have in place a Board approved annual branch expansion policy filed with the Authority. The insurers were also advised to keep in view the expansion of branches in semi-urban and rural areas. After the approval by the Authority it is mandatory for an insurer to open the office within one year from the date of approval.

In October, 2012 the authority has amended the Section 64 VC of Insurance Act of letting insurers open new branches with no prior approval of the Authority in semi urban and rural areas by notifying IRDAI (Places of Business) Regulations, 2013. As per the new regulations insurer having solvency ratio of 1.5 and expenses of management within the extant limits (Rule 17D/E of Insurance Rules, 1939) in the preceding financial year, are allowed to open new places of business, in Tier-2 and below centres, without prior approval; insurers should open new offices keeping in mind their long term presence in the area and avoid opening offices for shorter durations; all places of business other than those exempted with the Authority's prior approval are required to offer minimum policyholder services and in case of closure or relocation of office prior approval of the respective Boards of insurers shall be sought and policyholder should be notified two months in advance about the proposed closure or relocation. It is envisaged by the Authority that liberalization of branch opening in Tier –II and below centres would lead to expansions of branch networks of insurers and insurance penetration[1].

The number of offices increased from 2199 in 2000-01 to 12018 in 2009-10. After 2009-10 the growth in number of offices registered a decreasing trend. The number of offices decreased from 12018 in 2009-10 to 11546 in 2010-11 and further decreased to 11167 in 2011-12. Finally in 2012-13 the number of offices stands at 10285. The compound rate of growth for number of offices for the 20 years of pre IRDAI Phase (1980 to 2000) is 12.7 percent.

1. Insurance Regulatory Development Authority (2013), *op.cit.*, Hyderabad, p. 40.

Table 5.2: Number of Offices of Life Insurers in India

Insurer	2000-01	2001-02	2002-03	2003-04	2004-05	2005-06	2006-07	2007-08	2008-09	2009-10	2010-11	2011-12	2012-13
Aegon Religare	--	--	--	--	--	--	--	--	58	66	128	125	93
AVIVA	--	3	12	22	50	110	140	213	224	186	142	135	132
Bajaj Allianz	1	17	33	49	153	567	877	1007	1164	1151	1092	1044	992
Bharti AXA	--	--	--	--	--	1	16	77	200	202	181	128	127
Birla Sunlife	2	19	29	41	53	97	148	538	660	652	617	711	640
Canara HSBC	--	--	--	--	--	--	--	--	32	33	33	32	32
DLF Pramerica	--	--	--	--	--	--	--	--	15	32	41	40	56
Edelweiss Tokio	--	--	--	--	--	--	--	--	--	--	--	31	48
Future Generali	--	--	--	--	--	--	--	9	93	90	185	184	99
HDFC Standard	--	4	18	26	90	150	448	569	609	568	492	481	450
ICICI Prudential	6	14	29	69	109	175	583	1958	2102	1921	1402	990	557
IDBI Federal	--	--	--	--	--	--	--	2	33	37	60	62	62
India First	--	--	--	--	--	--	--	--	--	2	13	15	36
ING Life	--	4	16	26	38	68	183	265	265	254	247	216	207

Insurer	2000-01	2001-02	2002-03	2003-04	2004-05	2005-06	2006-07	2007-08	2008-09	2009-10	2010-11	2011-12	2012-13
Kotak Mahindra	--	9	28	39	43	46	75	151	198	215	203	205	200
Max Life	--	15	23	33	64	84	118	194	705	705	504	464	288
PNB Metlife	--	3	8	16	35	43	53	94	190	255	270	226	177
Reliance	--	17	35	48	80	157	159	745	1145	1247	1248	1230	1230
Sahara	--	--	--	2	18	18	33	33	49	49	135	143	142
SBILife	1	5	10	19	31	46	138	200	489	494	629	714	758
ShriramLife	--	--	--	--	--	11	12	53	98	162	162	208	195
Star Union Dai Chi	--	--	--	--	--	--	--	--	2	7	22	30	58
Tata AIA	3	6	13	26	40	72	89	283	454	439	363	298	180
LIC	2186	2190	2191	2196	2197	2220	2301	2522	3030	3250	3371	3455	3526
Grand Total	2199	2306	2445	2612	3001	3865	5373	8913	11815	12018	11546	11167	10285

Source: Annual Reports of Insurance Regulatory and Development Authority of India (2000-01 to 2012-13), Hyderabad.

The compound rate of growth of number of offices over the thirteen years is 18.8 percent, suggesting a higher rate of growth during post IRDAI phase (Table 5.3 and Figure 5.1).

Table 5.3: Annual Growth Rate of Offices of Life Insurers in India

Year	Total Offices	Simple Rate of Growth
2000-01	2199	
2001-02	2306	4.865848113
2002-03	2445	11.1869
2003-04	2612	18.78126
2004-05	3001	36.47112
2005-06	3865	75.76171
2006-07	5373	144.3383
2007-08	8913	305.3206
2008-09	11815	437.2897
2009-10	12018	446.5211
2010-11	11546	425.0568
2011-12	11167	407.8217
2012-13	10285	367.7126
Compound Rate of Growth		**18.8**

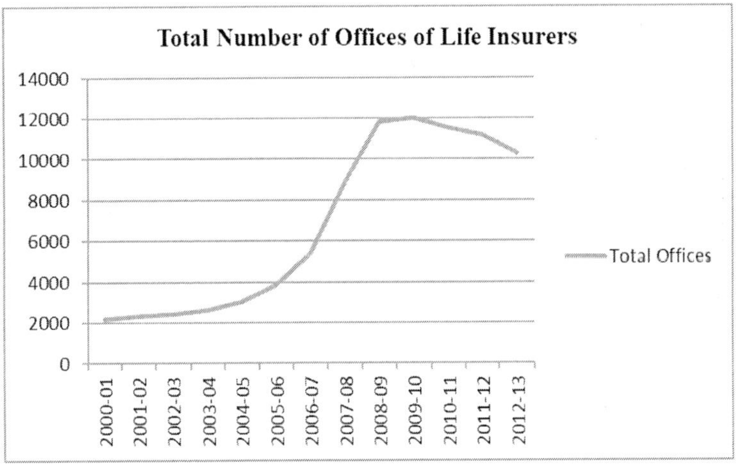

Figure 5.1

5.3 Growth in Number of Individual Agents of Life Insurance Companies

Growth in number of agents is essential for business growth, policy persistency and public perception of the agency channel as a stable career. IRDAI has issued (Licensing of Agents) Regulations, 2000 for licensing and code of conduct for agents. The Authority has prescribed the new course material for pre-recruitment qualification for life agents which helps an agent in gaining the knowledge and skills required to be licensed as a life insurance agent. An agent being a critical link between an insurer and insured should be capable of quality intermediation which requires the agents to follow code of conduct and have proper understanding of business and skills to sell the product. IRDAI has issued guidelines for agent's training institutes which include specific number of hours and duration of training, maintenance of attendance records of the trainees. Institutes are initially accredited for one year and it is mandatory for institutes to maintain database of candidates who have completed training with name of faculty and a record of test at the end of each chapter or at the end of training. In 2000-01, there were 115715 individual agents and in year 2012-13 the number of individual agents increased to 2122757 (Table 5.4). During pre IRDAI phase in last 20 years the compound growth rate of number of individual agents for LIC turns out to be 10.6 percent. It is noteworthy to mention here that recently IRDAI has exempted individual agents from its licensing process and now insurance companies can appoint agents of their own.

Table 5.4: Growth in Number of Individual Agents of Life Insurer

Insurer	2000-01	2001-02	2002-03	2003-04	2004-05	2005-06	2006-07	2007-08	2008-09	2009-10	2010-11	2011-12	2012-13
Aegon Religare	--	--	--	--	--	--	--	--	2309	7617	10861	7313	4488
Aviva	--		1868	5002	3806	10974	29052	35307	30838	32728	23219	19126	17470
Bajaj Allianz	--	4377	14157	36251	32565	109141	216191	250239	204941	167741	189667	173146	148000
Bharti AXA	--	--	--	--	--	0	1266	11749	28495	32661	15210	14842	13269
Birla Sunlife	211	2009	6179	12696	5288	17738	56490	109034	164363	168124	144573	131297	106823
Canara HSBC	--	--	--	--	--	--	--	--	--	0	0	0	0
DLF Pramerica	--	--	--	--	--	--	--	--	113	2115	5199	7122	5487
Edelweiss Tokio	--	---	--	--	--	--	--	--	--	--	0	825	3401
Future Generali	--	--	--	--	--	--	--	11	24437	42613	52666	41281	27437
HDFC Standard	185	3214	11237	19038	10305	34887	79109	144714	207626	198879	136009	106244	77503
ICICI Prudential	2114	10861	23825	46639	29890	72383	234460	306354	299879	241830	190407	13883	147547
IDBI Federal	--	--	--	--	--	--	--	279	6509	7737	7882	7400	8531
India First	--	--	--	--	--	--	--	--	--	0	296	1658	2959
ING Life	--	1135	3906	11671	7622	18683	33944	52760	76058	53273	34957	29396	28528
Kotak Mahindra	--	1348	3730	6511	2900	12523	24484	34723	42083	35897	38269	31297	33740

Insurer	2000-01	2001-02	2002-03	2003-04	2004-05	2005-06	2006-07	2007-08	2008-09	2009-10	2010-11	2011-12	2012-13
Max Life	227	2620	5773	10296	6997	15275	25044	36901	84651	72828	43542	35368	35384
PNB Metlife	--	417	1454	3155	3336	9985	20848	36798	60727	63300	28840	29418	24114
Reliance	--	484	1599	6381	5005	19956	95622	184194	149613	195565	189433	150590	124038
Sahara	--	--	--	--	0	78	9797	12839	13515	13856	14180	14578	11016
SBILife	--	719	2218	24690	2165	8128	25356	40643	68993	65332	79628	86989	94138
Shriram Life	--	--	--	--	--	5759	10384	17659	19759	21554	10139	6380	5351
Star Union Dai Chi	--	--	--	--	--	--	--	--	--	69	128	550	1189
TataAIA	--	7038	15451	32890	17737	35336	28105	52544	107670	151557	87223	46948	29361
Private Total	2737	34222	91380	215220	127616	370846	890152	1326748	1592579	1575476	1302-328	180651	949774
LIC	112-978	442-680	947-405	1341-597	353634	1052993	1103047	1193744	1344856	1402807	1337-064	1278-234	1172-983
Grand Total	115-715	476-902	1038-785	1556-817	481250	1423839	1993199	2520492	2937435	2978283	2639-392	2358-885	2122-757

Source: Annual Reports of Insurance Regulatory and Development Authority of India (2000-01 to 2012-13), Hyderabad

The number of individual agents increased from 2000-01 to 2003-04. In 2003-04, the number of individual agents stood at 15,56,817 while in 2004-05 it showed a steep fall to 4,81,250. In 2005-06 it started showing an increasing trend and stood at 29,78,283in 2009-10. After 2010-11, it started decreasing till 2012-13 and this number stood at 21,22,757. This trend shows high attrition rate of individual agents which may adversely affect life insurers' business. The high turnover of agents has financial implications for insurers who spend time and money on prospecting, appointing and training of these agents. High policies lapsation rate may also be attributed to this trend as after an agent quits the company the agencies procured by him are rendered orphan. The compound rate of growth of number of individual agents over the thirteen years of post IRDAI phase is 21.33 percent (Table 5.5 and Figure 5.2). The comparison of compound rate of growth in pre- and post IRDAI phase suggests that growth rate in post IRDAI phase is more than double that of pre-IRDAI period

Table 5.5: Annual Growth rate of Individual Agents of Life Insurers in India

Year	Total Number of Individual Agents	Annual Growth Rate
2000-01	1,15,715	
2001-02	4,76,902	312.135
2002-03	10,38,785	797.7099
2003-04	15,56,817	1245.389
2004-05	4,81,250	315.8925
2005-06	14,23,839	1130.471
2006-07	19,93,199	1622.507
2007-08	25,20,492	2078.19
2008-09	29,37,435	2438.508
2009-10	29,78,283	2473.809
2010-11	26,39,392	2180.942
2011-12	23,58,885	1938.53
2012-13	21,22,757	1734.47
The Compound Rate of Growth		21.33

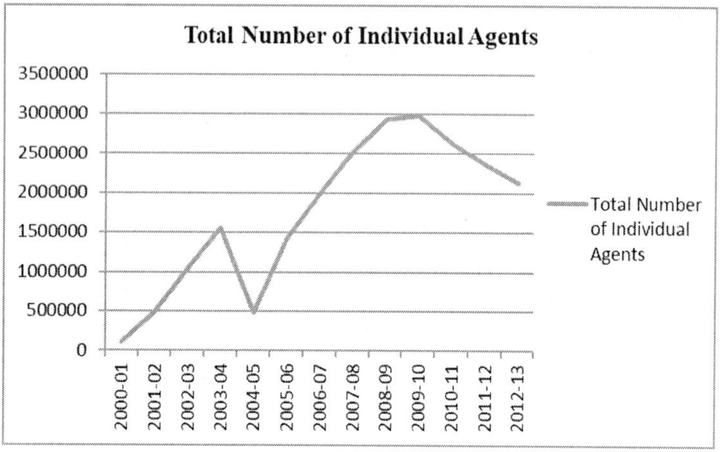

Figure 5.2

5.4 Growth in Number of Life Insurance Policies

Life Insurance provides an individual with protection against the risks enlisted in the policy along with providing an opportunity for investments. These investments are in the form of long-term for meeting various expenses in future. Policies can be said the primary tradable instrument between insurer and insured. It is the contract that binds both of them together. The growth in number of insurers in a country may lead to increased outreach of insurance to people and may ultimately result in increase in number of policies. In year 2004-05 there were 165358.196 thousand life insurance policies in force in India. The number of policies in force showed an increasing trend over the years and finally this number stood at 287857.32 thousand in 2012-13 (Table 5.6). The compound rate of growth life insurance policies for the 20 years of pre IRDAI Phase (1980 to 2000) is 8.8 percent.

Table 5.6: Number of Life Insurance Policies In Force (Policies in 2000)

Insurer	2004-05	2005-06	2006-07	2007-08	2008-09	2009-10	2010-11	2011-12	2012-13
Aegon Religare	--	--	--	--	5.51	14.83	54.18	95.51	121.27
Aviva	23.14	33.85	51	48	61.80	61.64	151.91	254.58	316.76
Bajaj Allianz	247.77	394.81	511	540	721.09	940.70	1820.32	2283.29	2507.15
Bharti AXA			1	10	38.83	44.79	1108.08	139.66	192.60
Birla Sunlife	102.18	159.32	234	325	675.92	993.18	851.98	942.46	769.19
Canara HSBC	--	--	--	--	0.17	0.81	15.31	30.23	54.17
DLF Pramerica					0.63	1.40	20.83	72.08	137.33
Edelweiss Tokio	--	--	--	--	--	--	5.90	5.59	22.43
Future Generali	--	--	0	1	56.39	178.47	366.51	344.34	353.27
HDFC Standard	410.44	589.97	752	996	1244.33	1497.30	1597.52	1762.67	1938.43
ICICI Prudential	373.79	473.21	744	1037	1311.84	971.50	1089.73	1293.45	1502.33
IDBI Federal	--	--	0	0	10.47	47.45	119.50	178.72	267.94
IndiaFirst	--	--	--	--	0	0	0.70	7.71	41.88
INGLife	152.24	193.33	253	289	362.65	432.07	572.25	657.38	743.44
Kotak Mahindra	96.54	108.28	123	149	156.83	162.71	265.20	384.45	473.07
MaxLife	353.45	561.90	713	896	1135.46	1342.27	1715.47	2026.73	2265.36
PNB Metlife	161.70	106.04	112	115	175.53	230.13	270.37	316.40	410.42
Reliance	47.72	76.78	189	220	234.10	600.21	1939.30	2154.94	2327.00
Sahara	10.00	22.17	42	76	101.10	116.27	149.80	196.76	228.70
SBILife	200.19	351.64	411	420	488.95	578.74	789.45	1204.99	1724.94
Shriram Life	0	20.79	53	39	38.36	39.80	72.41	167.80	247.05
Star Union Dai Chi	--	--.	--	--	0.62	12.23	36.99	86.89	153.95
Tata AIA	328.88	452.88	567	579	710.08	740.49	818.88	821.75	807.29
Private Total					7530.66	9006.99	1284-2.58	1542-8.38	1760-5.97
LIC	1629-50.92	1795-63.86	189-419	192-428	2101-54.04	2260-57.89	2403-81.21	2558-45.25	2702-51.35
GRAND TOTAL	1653-58.196	1831-08.83	194-164	198-168	21768-4.70	2350-64.88	2532-23.79	2712-73.62	2878-57.32

Source: Annual Reports of Insurance Regulatory and Development Authority of India (2004-05 to 2012-13), Hyderabad.

The number of life insurance policies in force grew at the compound rate of growth of 7.15 percent in post IRDAI phase which is marginally lower than the pre-IRDAI period. The annual rate of growth showed a continuous increasing trend from around 10 percent in 2005-06 in comparison to the base year of 2004-05. In subsequent years, it continuously grew and finally in 2012-13 - it pegged at 74 percent growth in comparison to the base year of 2004-05 (see - Table 5.7 and Figure 5.3 below)

Table 5.7: Annual Growth Rate of Life Insurance Policies In Force

Year	**Number of Insurance Policies in Force (Policies In 000)**	**Annual Growth Rate (%)**
2004-05	165358.196	
2005-06	183108.83	10.73466
2006-07	194164	17.42025
2007-08	198168	19.84166
2008-09	217684.70	31.64434
2009-10	235064.88	42.15496
2010-11	253223.79	53.13652
2011-12	271273.62	64.05212
2012-13	287857.32	74.08107
The Compound Rate of Growth		**7.15**

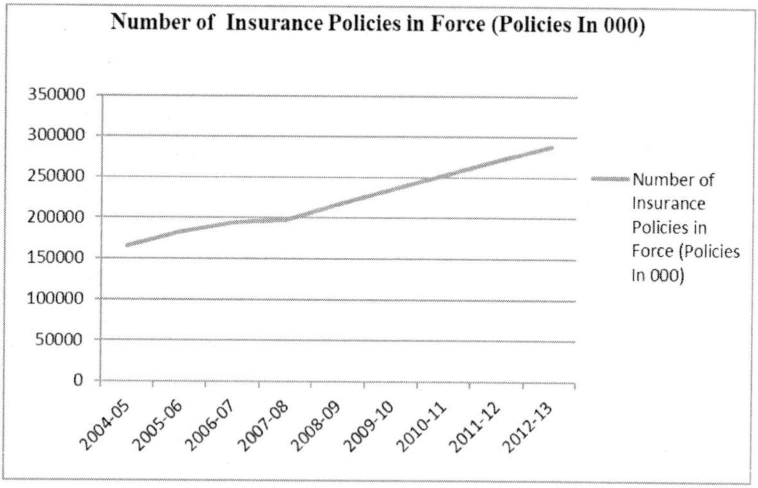

Figure 5.3

5.5 Growth in Persistency of Life Insurance Policies

Persistency of life insurance policies is in the interests of policy-holders, intermediaries and insurers. Persistency of policy depends on the factors such as suitability of the product; extraneous factors of policy holders such as changing socio-economic profile of policyholders and their ability to pay premiums regularly; and post sale-services delivered by agents. Among these factors, post-sale-services is most important factor in enhancing policy persistency. As life insurance policies are of long duration in nature, changing stages of life may warrant concomitant and simultaneous modifications in the policies. Thus, post-sale-services should be emphasized to maintain persistency levels. As stated earlier, due to high attrition rate of agents many policies are orphaned and thus, leads to policy lapsation. To ensure persistency of policies IRDAI has issued Circular (No IRDA/Life/GDL/GLD/ 217/09/2011) dated 20 September, 2011.As per these guidelines, minimum requirement for persistency has been kept 50 percent of the total number of policies. These requirements are applicable to both individual insurance agents as well as corporate agents[2].To evaluate persistency levels for the months mentioned, the four years data have been tested against the prescribed standards of IRDAI of 50 percent of the total number of policies. Although these guidelines were issued in 2011 September but for ease of evaluation of data for earlier years the same standards have been used.

Persistency requirements for 13 months in 2009-10 for majority of firms were at par with the IRDAI mandate. But various firms such as Aviva, Bharti Axa, DLF Praamerica, Future Genrali and TatAIA had persistency level below the prescribed limits of 50 percent. In year 2010-11, only one insurer, namely - Tata AIA did not have 13 month persistency at the prescribed levels. In 2009-10, 5 insurers did not recorded persistency for 25 months at par with prescribed standards while in 2010-11 this number increased to 6 insurers. Persistency levels for 37 months were not complied by 11 insurers in 2009-10 and 2010-11. In 2009 -10, persistency levels for 49 months were not met by 8 insurers while in 2010-11 this number stood at 10 insurers. Lastly persistency standards for 61 months was not met by 7 insurance firms in 2009-10 while in 2010-11, eight firms were unable to meet to the targets (Table 5.8).

Table 5.8: Persistency of Life Insurance Policies (Based on Number of policies)

Insurer	2009-10					2010-11				
	13	25	37	49	61	13	25	37	49	61
Aegon Religare	54	NA	NA	NA	NA	62	42	NA	NA	NA
Aviva	48	45	40	31	28	53	42	31	27	24
Bajaj Allianz	52	81	14	51	63	56.31	80.96	18.91	61.61	72.58
Bharti AXA	46.90	47	54	NA	NA	60	49	55	29	NA
Birla Sunlife	70.18	63.55	61.70	59.86	58.64	83	77	72	64	55
Canara HSBC	88.50	NA	NA	NA	NA	85	91	NA	NA	NA
DLF Pramerica	39	NA	NA	NA	NA	48.35	31.85	NA	NA	NA

2. Insurance Regulatory Development Authority (2012), Annual Report 2011-12, October, Hyderabad, pp. 26-27.

Edelweiss Tokio	NA	NA	NA	NA	NA	NA	NA	NA	NA	NA
Future Generali	35.33	NA	NA	NA	NA	55.46	50.19	NA	NA	NA
HDFC Standard	57.26	52.42	34.05	30	40.13	71.97	88.17	52.35	71.73	84.56
ICICI Prudential	72.74	87.19	37.29	55.46	72.37	75.80	88.70	30.10	46.30	65.20
IDBI Federal	66.74	NA	NA	NA	NA	71.65	88.57	NA	NA	NA
India First	NA	NA	NA	NA	NA	71.49	NA	NA	NA	NA
ING Life	57.31	50.75	34.91	51.58	42.86	67.70	51	26.60	23	16.10
Kotak Mahindra	69.11	61.86	33.70	33.45	36.15	70	60	49	40	39
Max Life	68	67	50	45	60	70	60	49	40	39
PNB Metlife	67.29	60.09	56.16	52.98	50.03	66.18	59.66	55.04	51.16	47.92
Reliance	51.23	52.29	23.21	39.72	46.57	52.70	81.50	34.40	74.50	85.80
Sahara	71.92	60.96	49.53	52.41	63.09	73.55	63.13	44.06	45.80	49.23
SBI Life	57.83	48.49	26.89	38.14	46.71	68.81	49.69	21.30	24.19	40.73
ShriramLife	54.26	45.48	25.52	25.77	NA	51.20	45.90	23.70	26	26.30
Star Union Dai Chi	NA	NA	NA	NA	NA	65	36	NA	NA	NA
Tata AIA	34.50	19.90	23.30	33.30	35.80	36.87	17	18.32	20.45	26.56
LIC	69	64	62	58	NA	64	58	47	53	49

Source: Annual Reports of Insurance Regulatory and Development Authority of India of India (2009-10 and 2010-11), Hyderabad.

In 2011-12, three insurers, namely - DLF Pramerica, Future Generali and Tata AIA were unable to meet the requirements of policy persistency for 13 months while in 2012-13, ten insurance firms were unable to meet the prescribed standards for 13 months. In 2011-12 four insurers were unable to meet the required standards of 50 percent policy persistency for the 25 months and in 2012-13, there were 10 insurers in list of non-compliance with standards. In 2011-12 fourteen insurers did not meet policy persistency standards of 37 months while in 2012-13 this number increased to eighteen insurers. Policy persistency standards for 49 months were not complied by 9 insurance firms in 2011-12 and in 2012-13, 18 insurance firms were unable to reach the targets. Finally, the 10 and 15 insurance firms were not able to meet the 61 months policy persistency standards in 2011-12 and 2012-13 respectively (Table 5.9).

Table 5.9: Persistency of Life Insurance Policies (Based on Number of policies)

Insurer	2011-12					2012-13				
	13	25	37	49	61	13	25	37	49	61
Aegon Religare	57	54	30	NA	NA	49	47	42	22	NA
Aviva	58	47	25	24	19	59	41	31	18	NA
Bajaj Allianz	54.57	85	19.03	51.85	43.50	48	43.44	13	7.47	4.02
Bharti AXA	58.20	51	46.80	52.20	39.60	45	42	50	36	32
Birla Sunlife	82	77	72	62	53	49	49	52	42	40
Canara HSBC	79.60	88	64.70	NA	NA	65	84	72	83	NA
DLF Pramerica	48.94	40.96	33.16	NA	NA	43	41.34	26	NA	NA
Edelweiss Tokio	NA	NA	NA	NA	NA	46	NA	NA	NA	NA
Future Generali	47.95	48.38	51.54	NA	NA	39	36	23.35	14.17	6.81
HDFC Standard	75.35	88.11	63.50	66.38	78.40	69	67	48	34	23

ICICI Prudential	77	86.70	31.80	50.60	65.30	67	63	28	14	10
IDBI Federal	66.38	85.91	83.55	NA	NA	70	61	43	20	NA
India First	72.43	71.56	NA	NA	NA	64	61	47	NA	NA
ING Life	65	55	38	36	38	56	50	38	30	24
Kotak Mahindra	70	61	50	40	40	64	61	38	28	33
Max Life	75	62	42	39	31	70	57	42	27	26
PNB Metlife	63.56	56.84	50.32	47.44	44.82	71	66	63	62.48	61.36
Reliance	55.90	78.10	29.10	70.30	76.70	61	53	21	17.87	21.09
Sahara	73.73	65.14	43.04	39.92	41.74	57	50	34	28	24
SBI Life	71.77	60.52	20.54	16.27	23.35	67	60	36	18	17.02
Shriram Life	51.40	82.30	39.10	80.30	84.70	30	27	9	5	4
Star Union Dai Chi	65	56	49	NA	NA	45	46	35	33	NA
Tata AIA	44.71	18.10	17.32	16.13	14.03	49	39	24	21	18
LIC	67	61	53	46	51	70	63	58	53	43

Source: Annual Reports of Insurance Regulatory and Development Authority of India (2011-12 and 2012-13)

5.6 Growth in Number of Life Insurance Products Launched in Market

IRDAI requires all the insurers to file their products with the Authority and after its approval the product can be launched in the market so as to ensure that the insurance products offered by the insurers are of value to the policyholder and that their pricing is appropriate and fair between the insurer and the insured. In this regard IRDAI has issued File & Use guidelines which makes it compulsory for every insurer to seek prior approval of IRDAI before selling any life/general insurance product in the Indian market. As per the File & Use guidelines, the insurer needs to justify the rates, terms and conditions of insurance policy to be offered while filing the product with IRDAI. The insurer is not permitted to offer any product for sale until IRDAI confirms in writing that it has no further queries in respect of that product. For Regulation of products of life insurers IRDAI issues guidelines and latest being IRDAI/Life/CIR/GDL/044/01/2014 in this regard. In year 2001-02, there were total 42 products approved by IRDAI of all life insurers. This number increased to 116 products in year 2002-03 and then started declining till 2005-06 and stood at 55. In year 2006-07 it had a quantum jump and stood at 208 products for the year. Subsequently the number of products fluctuated and finally in 2012-13, 118 products were approved by IRDAI of life insurers (Table 5.10). During twenty years of pre IRDAI phase the products of LIC grew at the compound growth rate of 0.92 percent.

Table 5.10: Number of Products Launched in Market by Life Insurers

Insurer	2001-02	2002-03	2003-04	2004-05	2005-06	2006-07	2007-08	2008-09	2009-10	2010-11	2011-12	2012-13
Aegon Religare	--	--	--	--	--	--	--	16	13	13	9	9
Aviva	--	--	10	4	2	24	19	14	16	18	1	6
Bajaj Allianz	9	8	12	10	6	20	14	15	26	13	8	8
Bharti AXA	--	--	--	--	--	10	5	5	19	13	9	5
Birla Sunlife	8	8	2	2	6	17	9	6	14	24	4	8
Canara HSBC	--	--	--	--	--	--	--	8	5	6	3	2
DLF Pramerica	--	--	--	--	--	--	--	11	14	9	1	4
Edelweiss Tokio	--	--	--	--	--	--	--	--	--		21	11
Future Generali	--	--	--	--	--	0	20	14	16	10	7	5
HDFC Standard	5	9	7	2	2	10	3	11	19	17	5	6
ICICI Prudential	8	15	13	13	9	30	11	11	17	14	13	4
IDBI Federal	--	--	--	--	--	0	6	8	6	9	5	1
India First	--	--	--	--	--	--	--		6	8	5	4
ING Life	6	5	4	4	5	9	7	3	10	11	7	2
Kotak Mahindra	9	13	5	6	1	16	6	8	26	11	3	5
Max Life	3	7	5		6	7	13	6	10	6	4	3
PNBMetlife	3	3	6	1	1	11	5	7	16	7	5	5
Reliance	5	4	8	3	0	9	8	13	35	7	5	7
Sahara				6	3	7	2	2	7	4	2	1
SBI Life	6	9	9	2	4	9	14	5	29	14	10	6
Shriram Life	--	--	--	--	3	11	8	2	14	7	4	2
Star Union Dai Chi	--	--	--	--	--.	--	--	11	13	6	3	4
Tata AIA	21	25	13	2	1	8	12	11	19	11	5	5
LIC	11	10		1	6	10	6	9	9	6	4	5
Grand Total	94	116	94	56	55	208	168	196	359	244	143	118

Source: Annual reports of Insurance Regulatory and Development Authority of India (2001-02 to 2012-13), Hyderabad.

Products launched by insurers grew at the compound rate of growth of 8.64 percent over 12 years, suggesting a massive growth in post IRDAI period. In year 2012-13, it showed an increase of around 23 percent from the base year 2001-02. In year 2004-05 and 2005-06 the trend was decelerating in terms of products. In subsequent years, it showed fluctuations and finally in year 2012-13, it registered the growth of around 25 percent in comparison to the base year (Table 5.11 and Figure 5.4).

Table 5.11: Annual Growth Rate of Number of Products Launched In Market by Life Insurers

Year	Total Products of Life Insurers	Annual Growth Rate (%)
2001-02	94	
2002-03	116	23.40426
2003-04	94	0
2004-05	56	-40.4255
2005-06	55	-41.4894
2006-07	208	121.2766
2007-08	168	78.7234
2008-09	196	108.5106
2009-10	359	281.9149
2010-11	244	159.5745
2011-12	143	52.12766
2012-13	118	25.53191
The Compound Rate of Growth		**8.64**

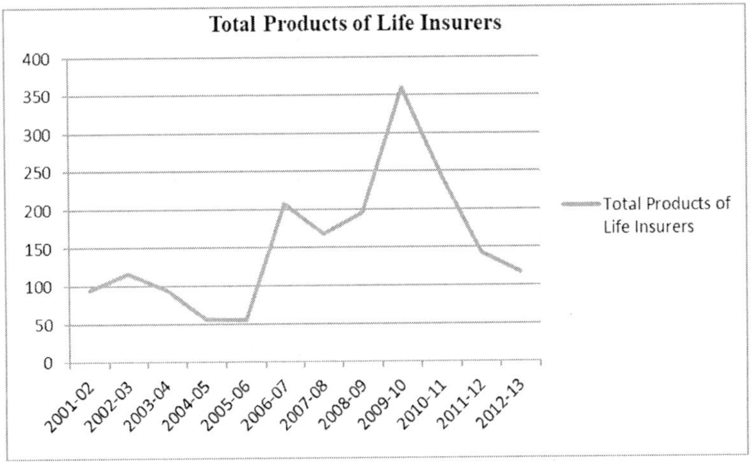

Figure 5.4

5.7 Growth in First Year (Including Single Premium) Life Insurance Premium

The first year premium recorded in 2000-01 was Rs. 9707.43 crore and it increased to Rs. 19857.28 crore in 2001-12. In year 2002-03, it fell down to Rs. 16942.4 crore. In subsequent years, it followed an upward trend till 2007-08 and stood at Rs. 93712.52 crore. In year 2008-09 it decreased to Rs. 87441.08 crore. In year 2009-10 and 2010-11 it showed a increasing trend but in year 2011-12 it decreased to Rs. 113966.03 crore and in 2012-13 it further decreased to Rs. 107361.08 crore (Table 5.12). In the twenty years of pre IRDAI phase the single premium grew at the 20.2 percent compound rate of growth.

Table 5.12: First Year (Including Single Premium) Life Insurance Premium

(Rupees Crore)

Insurer	2000-01	2001-02	2002-03	2003-04	2004-05	2005-06	2006-07	2007-08	2008-09	2009-10	2010-11	2011-12	2012-13
Aegon Religare	--	--	--	--	--	--	--	--	31.21	150.37	274.87	207.65	135.90
Aviva	--	--	13.47	76.96	192.29	407.12	721.35	1053.98	724.56	798.37	745.39	801.86	687.40
Bajaj Allianz	--	7.14	63.39	179.55	857.45	2716.77	4302.74	6674.48	4491.43	4451.10	3465.82	2717.31	2987.90
Bharti AXA	--	--	--	--	--	--	7.78	113.24	292.93	437.43	347.78	224.59	248.92
Birla Sunlife	0.32	28.11	129.57	449.86	621.31	678.12	882.72	1965.01	2820.85	2960.01	280.30	1926.17	1836.51
Canara HSBC	--	---	--	--	--	--	--	--	296.41	622.62	817.29	687.10	606.72
DLF Pramerica	--	--	--	--	--	--	--	--	3.37	37.38	74.15	103.16	140.01
Edelweiss Tokio	--	--	--	--	--	--	--	--	--	--	--	10.88	47.33
FutureGenerali	--	--	--	--	--	--	--	2.49	149.97	486.08	448.61	345.03	240.43
HDFC Standard	.002	32.78	129.31	209.33	486.15	1042.65	1648.85	2685.37	2651.11	3257.51	4059.33	3857.47	4436.07
ICICI Prudential	5.97	113.33	364.11	750.84	1584.34	2602.50	5162.13	8034.75	6811.83	6333.92	7862.14	4441.09	4808.62
IDBIFederal	--	--	--	--	--	--	--	11.90	316.78	400.56	444.95	311.01	345.14
IndiaFirst	--	--	--	--	--	--	--	--	--	201.59	704.77	982.31	1316.42
INGLife	--	4.19	17.66	72.10	282.42	283.98	467.66	704.44	688.95	642.43	660.49	638.14	638.20
KotakMahindra	--	7.58	35.21	125.51	373.99	396.06	614.94	1106.62	1343.03	1333.98	1253.14	1164.27	1188.10
MAXLife	0.16	38.80	67.31	137.28	233.63	471.36	912.11	1597.83	1842.91	1849.08	2061.39	1901.72	1899.34
PNBMetlife	--	0.48	7.70	23.41	57.52	143.53	340.44	825.35	1144.70	1061.85	706.22	1076.97	840.08
Reliance	--	0.28	6.32	27.21	91.33	153.56	232.11	2751.05	3513.98	3920.78	3034.94	1809.29	1376.57
Sahara	--	--	--	--	1.74	26.34	43.00	122.12	134.01	124.83	91.83	71.14	61.43
SBILife	--	14.69	71.88	207.05	484.85	827.82	2563.84	4792.82	5386.64	7040.72	7589.58	6531.32	5182.88
ShriramLife	--	--	--	--	--	10.33	181.17	309.99	314.47	419.50	571.99	390.99	420.65
Star Union Dai Chi	--	--	--	--	--	--	--	--	50.19	519.87	758.69	964.77	744.80
TataAIA	--	21.14	59.77	181.59	297.55	464.53	644.82	964.51	1142.67	1322.01	1332.21	939.55	560.16
LIC	9700.98	19588.77	15976.76	17347.62	20653.06	28515.87	56223.56	59996.57	53179.08	71521.90	87012.35	81862.25	76611.50
Grand Total	9707.43	19857.28	16942.45	19788.32	26217.64	38785.54	75649.21	93712.52	87331.08	109893.91	126398.18	113966.03	107361.08

Source: Annual Reports of Insurance Regulatory and Development Authority of India (2000-01 to 2012-13), Hyderabad.

The first year single premium registered the 27.05 percent compound rate of growth during post IRDAI phase higher by about 7 percent points from the pre-IRDAI phase. The annual growth rate showed fluctuation as it registered a growth of 104.55 percent in 2001- 02 from the preceding year. But in year 2002-03 it showed 74 percent growth rate in comparison to the base year 2000-01. After 2002-03, it followed a steady upward trend till 2007-08. In next year, it showed fluctuation with increasing trends in 2008-09 to 2010-11 and then a decreasing trend for the next two years (Table 5.13 and Figure 5.5)

Table 5.13: Annual Grow05th Rate of First Year (Including Single Premium) Life Insurance Premium

Year	Single Premium (in Rupees crore)	Annual Growth Rate
2000-01	9707.43	
2001-02	19857.28	104.5575
2002-03	16942.45	74.53075
2003-04	19788.32	103.8472
2004-05	26217.64	170.0781
2005-06	38785.54	299.5449
2006-07	75649.21	679.2918
2007-08	93712.52	865.369
2008-09	87331.08	799.6313
2009-10	109893.91	1032.06
2010-11	126398.18	1202.077
2011-12	113966.03	1074.008
2012-13	107361.08	1005.968
The Compound Rate of Growth		**27.05**

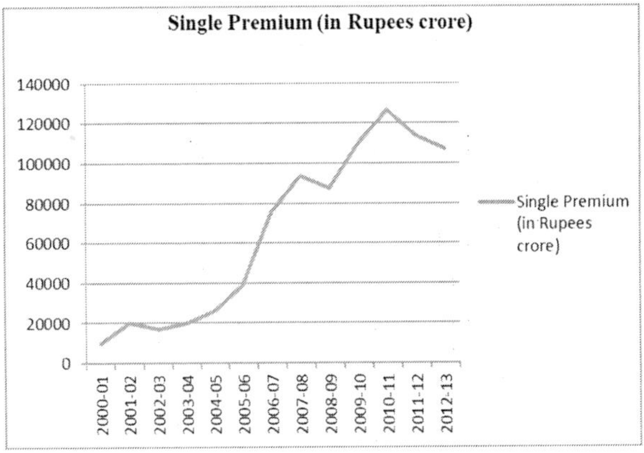

Figure 5.5

5.8 Growth in Total Premium Underwritten In Life Sector

The total premium underwritten in life segment in 2000-01 was Rs. 34,898.48 crore which increased to Rs. 2, 91,639 crore in 2010-11, but it showed a declining trend of 1.57 percent in 2011-12 and stood at 2,87,072 crore and which decreased to Rs.

2,87,202 crores in 2012-13 (Table 5.14). The total premium registered 20.5 percent compound rate of growth in last twenty years of pre IRDAI phase.

Table 5.14: Total Premium Underwritten By Life Insurer (Rupees Crore)

Insurer	2000-01	2001-02	2002-03	2003-04	2004-05	2005-06	2006-07	2007-08	2008-09	2009-10	2010-11	2011-12	2012-13
Aegon Religare	--	--	--	--	--	--	--	--	31.21	165.65	388.61	457.32	430.50
Aviva	--	--	13.47	81.50	253.442	600.27	1147.23	1891.88	1992.87	2378.01	2345.17	2415.8	2140.67
Bajaj Allianz	--	7.14	69.17	220.80	1001.68	3133.58	5345.24	9725.31	10624.52	11419.71	9609.95	7483.80	6892.70
Bharti AXA	--	--	--	--	--	--	7.78	118.41	360.41	669.73	792.02	774.16	744.52
Birla Sunlife	0.32	28.26	143.92	537.54	615.47	1259.68	1776.71	3272.19	4571.80	5505.66	5677.07	5885.36	5216.30
Canara HSBC	--	--	--	--	--	--	--	--	296.41	842.41	531.86	1861.08	1912.15
DLF Pramerica	--	--	--	--	--	--	--	--	3.37	38.44	95.04	167.01	236.79
Edelweiss Tokio	--	--	--	--	--	--	--	--	--	--	--	10.88	54.83
Future Generali	--	--	--	--	--	--	--	2.49	152.60	541.51	726.16	779.58	678.29
HDFC Standard	0.002	33.46	148.83	297.76	686.63	1569.91	2885.87	4858.56	5564.69	7005.10	9004.17	10202.40	11322.68
ICICI Prudential	5.97	116.38	417.62	989.28	2363.82	4251.05	7912.99	13561.06	15356.22	16528.75	17880.63	14021.58	13538.24
IDBIFederal	--	--	--	--	--	--	--	11.90	318.97	571.12	811.00	736.70	804.68
India First	--	--	--	--	--	--	--	--	--	201.60	798.43	1297.9	1690.08
ING Life	--	4.19	21.16	88.51	338.86	425.38	707.20	1158.87	1442.28	1642.65	1708.95	679.98	1742.36
Kotak Mahindra	--	7.58	40.32	150.72	466.16	621.85	971.51	1691.14	2343.19	2868.05	2975.51	2937.43	2777.78
Max Life	0.16	38.95	96.59	215.25	413.43	788.13	1500.28	2714.60	3857.26	4860.54	5812.63	6390.53	6638.70
PNBMetlife	--	0.48	7.91	28.73	81.53	205.99	492.71	1159.54	1996.64	2536.01	2508.17	2677.50	2429.52
Reliance	--	0.28	6.47	31.06	106.55	224.21	1004.66	3225.44	4932.54	6604.90	6571.15	5497.62	4045.39
Sahara	--	--	--	--	1.74	27.66	51.00	143.49	206.47	250.59	243.41	225.95	205.38
SBILife	--	14.69	72.39	225.67	601.18	1075.32	2928.49	5622.14	7212.10	10104.03	12945.29	13133.74	10450.03
ShriramLife	--	--	--	--	--	10.33	184.16	358.05	436.17	611.27	821.52	644.16	618.07
Star Union Dai Chi	--	--	--	--	--	--	--	--	50.19	530.37	933.31	1271.95	1068.80
TataAIA	--	21.14	81.21	253.53	497.04	880.19	1367.18	2046.35	2747.50	3493.78	3985.22	3630.30	2760.43
LIC	34892.02	49821.91	54628.49	63533.43	75127.29	90792.22	127822.84	149789.99	157288.04	186077.31	203473.40	202889.28	208803.58
Grand Total	34898.47	50094.46	55747.55	66653.75	82854.80	105875.76	156075.84	201351.41	221785.47	265447.25	291638.64	287072.11	287202.49

Source: Annual Reports of Insurance Regulatory and Development Authority of India (2000-01 to 2012-13), Hyderabad.

The total premium underwritten by life insurance industry registered compound growth rate to the tune of 23 percent from 2000-01 to 2012-13 suggesting an increase of 2.5 percent points in post IRDAI period. As per annual rate of growth it witnessed a increase of 43.5 percent in 20001-02 from the base year of 2000-01. The annual growth rate witnessed continuous increase till year 2010-11 by registering growth rate to the tune of 735.67 percent as compared to the base year. In 2011-12 it showed a decreasing trend and hovered around 722 percent (Table 5.15 and Figure 5.6).

Table 5.15: Annual Growth Rate of Total Premium Underwritten By Life Insurer

Year	Total Premium Underwritten (Rupees Crore)	Annual Growth Rate (%)
2000-01	34898.47	
2001-02	50094.46	43.54343
2002-03	55747.55	59.7421
2003-04	66653.75	90.99333
2004-05	82854.80	137.4167
2005-06	105875.76	203.3822
2006-07	156075.84	347.2283
2007-08	201351.41	476.9634
2008-09	221785.47	535.5163
2009-10	265447.25	660.6272
2010-11	291638.64	735.6774
2011-12	287072.11	722.5923
2012-13	287202.49	722.9658
The Compound Rate of Growth		**23.02**

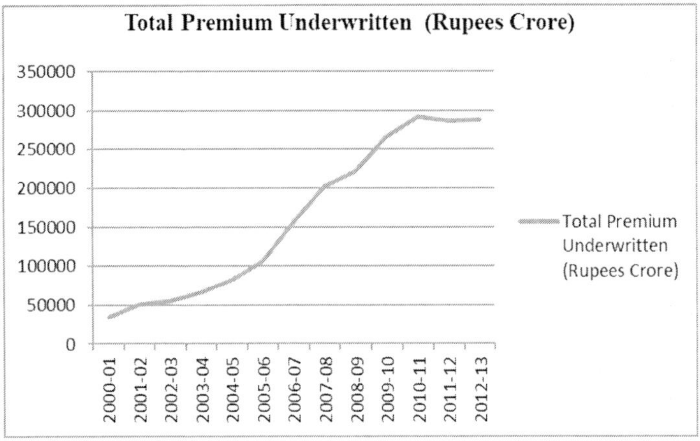

Figure 5.6

5.9 Growth in Life Insurance Penetration

Insurance penetration is the major determinant reflecting the development of insurance market in a country. Insurance penetration is percentage of insurance premium to Gross Domestic Product (GDP) of the country. Insurance penetration normally increases with increase in per-capita GDP[3-4]. India's growing consumer class, rising insurance awareness, increasing domestic savings and investments are among the most critical factors that have positively driven the market penetration of the insurance products among its consumer segments. However, there are many impediments such as lack of awareness and financial illiteracy which are hampering the growth of the insurance industry. Imparting financial literacy, incentivizing Indian households to transfer savings from physical assets to financial assets and taking the distribution network to rural areas will help bring more and more individuals within the insurance ambit. The sluggishness in Indian market due to international and domestic factors has led to deceleration in insurance sector. Insurance is largely viewed as a tax saving tool rather than protection against risk. Thus, there is need to reorient the consumer about the benefits of life insurance for both financial protections as well as for long-term wealth creation[5].

After insurance liberalization reforms, life insurance penetration consistently increased till 2006 and in subsequent years, it showed fluctuations. In year 2000, life insurance penetration was 1.77 percent whereas world life insurance penetration was 4.88 percent. In year 2009 and 2010, life insurance penetration was above the world average as Indian life insurance penetration in 2009 was 4.6 percent and in 2010 it was 4.4 percent whereas world life insurance penetration for these two years was 4 percent. In rest of the years Indian life insurance penetration was below the world levels. In year 2012, Indian life insurance penetration was 3.2 percent and world life insurance penetration was 3.7 percent. Barring two years 2009 and 2010, Indian life insurance penetration remained below the world average for other years (Table 5.16 and Figure 5.7).The comparison between Indian and World life insurance penetration was made by conducting t test. The results of t test highlights that the difference between Indian and World life insurance penetration was found to be statistically significant as $t=4.007$ and $p=.001$ at the level of significance $\alpha = 1$ percent.

3. DVS. Sastry (2011), "Life Insurance Penetration in India" *Journal of Social and Economic Policy*, Volume 8, Number 2, pp. 207-215.
4. RK Sinha, MM. Nizammudin and I. Alam (2012), "An Investigation of Insurance penetration and Density of India by Geography", *16th Conference of Asia-Pacific Risk and Insurance Association*, July, Seoul, South Korea, pp.4-11.
5. Priyanka Gupta and Vani Aggarwal (2014), "An Analysis of Insurance Sector: Penetration Perspective in India", *Working Paper No: 14*, Centre for WTO Studies (CWS), Indian Institute of Foreign Trade, New Delhi, pp. 6-23.

Table 5.16: Insurance Penetration in Life Sector (In %)

Year	Countries											
	India		World		China		South Korea		Japan		USA	
	Life	Total	Life	Total	Life	Total	Life	Total	Life	Total	Life	Total
2000	1.77	2.32	4.88	7.84	1.12	1.79	9.89	13.05	8.70	10.92	4.48	8.76
2001	2.15	2.71	4.68	7.83	1.34	2.20	8.69	12.07	8.85	11.07	4.40	8.97
2002	2.59	3.26	4.76	8.14	2.03	2.98	8.23	11.61	8.64	10.86	4.60	9.58
2003	2.26	2.88	4.59	8.06	2.30	3.33	6.77	9.63	8.61	10.81	4.38	9.61
2004	2.53	3.17	4.55	7.99	2.21	3.26	6.75	9.52	8.26	10.51	4.22	9.36
2005	2.53	3.14	4.34	7.52	1.78	2.70	7.27	10.25	8.32	10.54	4.14	9.15
2006	4.10	4.80	4.5	7.5	1.70	2.70	7.90	11.10	8.30	10.50	4	8.80
2007	4	4.70	4.40	7.50	1.80	2.90	8.20	11.80	7.50	9.60	4.20	8.90
2008	4	4.6	4.1	7.1	2.2	3.3	8	11.8	7.6	9.8	4.1	8.7
2009	4.6	5.2	4	7	2.3	3.4	6.5	10.4	7.8	9.9	3.5	8
2010	4.4	5.1	4	6.9	2.5	3.8	7	11.2	8	10.1	3.5	8
2011	3.4	4.1	3.8	6.6	1.8	3	7	11.6	8.8	11	3.6	8.1
2012	3.2	4.0	3.7	6.5	1.7	3.0	6.9	12.1	9.2	11.4	3.7	8.2

Source: Annual Reports of Insurance Regulatory and Development Authority of India (2000-01 to 2012-13), Hyderabad.

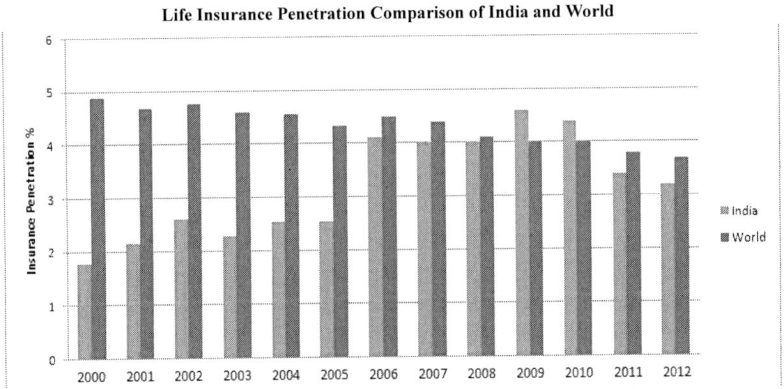

Figure 5.7

5.10 Growth in Insurance Density in Life Sector

Insurance density along with Insurance penetration is another major determinant reflecting the development of insurance market in a country. Insurance density is ratio of insurance total premium to the total population in the country. Thus, increase in insurance penetration may lead to reflect increasing insurance density but given the larger population base of India, insurance penetration could not make dent in comparison to world insurance density. After the inception of IRDAI, life insurance density steadily increased from (United States Dollar) USD 7.6 in 2001 to USD 55.7 in 2010 but in 2011 it decreased to USD 49 and further decreased to USD 42.70 in 2012. In 2000 Indian life insurance density was USD 7.6 whereas world average stood at USD 252.1. In terms of insurance density Indian insurance market is much below the world average and this may be attributed to the mass population base (Table 5.17 and Figure 5.8). The comparison between Indian and world life insurance density was made by conducting Mann-Whitney test because data is non-parametric (distribution free). In the Mann-Whitney test the difference between Indian life insurance density and world life insurance density was found to be statistically significant as the u=.0001 and p=.0001 at the level of significance $\alpha = 1$ percent.

Table 5.17: Insurance Density in Life Sector(in US $)

Year	Countries											
	India		World		China		South Korea		Japan		USA	
	Life	Total	Life	Total	Life	Total	Life	Total	Life	Total	Life	Total
2000	7.6	9.9	252.1	404.9	9.5	15.2	935.6	1234.1	3165.1	3973.3	1611.4	3152.1
2001	9.1	11.5	235	393.3	12.2	20	763.4	1160.1	2806.4	3507.5	1602	3266
2002	11.7	14.7	247.3	422.9	19.5	28.7	821.9	1159.8	2783.9	3498.6	1662.6	3461.6
2003	12.9	16.4	267.1	469.6	25.1	36.3	873.6	1243	3002.9	3770.9	1657.5	3673.7
2004	15.7	19.7	291.5	511.5	27.3	40.2	1006.8	1419.3	3044	3874.8	1692.5	3755.1
2005	18.3	22.7	229.5	518.5	30.5	46.3	1210.6	1706.1	2956.3	3746.7	1753.2	3875.2
2006	33.2	38.4	330.6	554.8	34.1	53.5	1480	2071.3	2829.3	3589.6	1789.5	3923.7
2007	40.4	46.6	358.1	607.7	44.2	69.9	1656.6	2384	2583.9	3319.9	1922	4086.5
2008	41.2	47.4	369.7	633.9	71.7	105.4	1347.7	1978.7	2869.5	3698.6	1900.6	4078
2009	44.7	54.3	341.2	595.1	81.1	121.2	1180.6	1890.3	3138.7	3979	1602.6	3710
2010	55.7	64.4	364.3	627.3	105.5	158.4	1454.3	2339.4	3472.8	4390.2	16318	3758.9
2011	49	59	378	661	99	163	1615	2661	4138	5169	1716	3846
2012	42.70	53.20	372.60	655.70	102.9	178.9	1578.1	2785.4	4142.5	5167.5	1808.1	4047.3

Source: Annual Reports of Insurance Regulatory and Development Authority of India (2000-01 to 2012-13), Hyderabad.

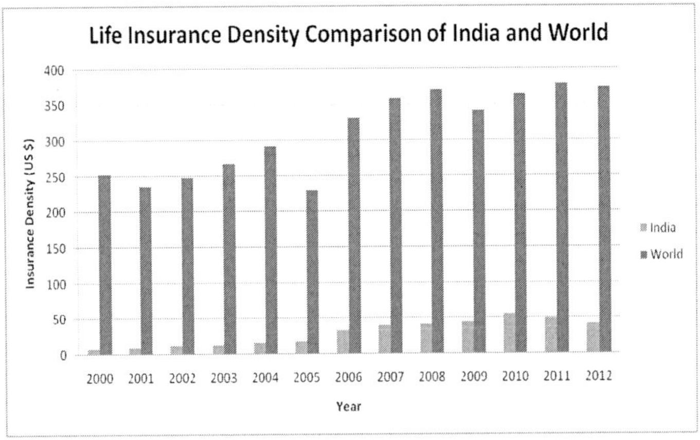

Figure 5.8

5.11 Regulatory Impact Analysis: Regression Analysis and Counter Factual Analysis

Efficacy of a policy intervention is judged from the analysis of its impact on the target group. For analyzing policy impact analysis a number of approaches are employed. Among these approaches two approaches, namely - regression analysis and counterfactual analysis are most suitable, thus, they are employed to study the efficacy of IRDAI in promoting growth in life insurance sector in India.

5.11 (a) Regression Analysis:

Regression analysis is used by employing dummy variable as an artificial numerical variable to represent subgroups of the sample study. It is used to distinguish different treatment groups or policies. Dummy variables provide choice to researcher to separate information on certain variables into discreet categories by assuming 'dummy' values as 0 or 1 for each category. Usage of dummy variables helps in indentifying the categories in data. Usage of dummy variables in regression also helps evaluating the 'treatment effect' of a policy intervention. As there are two categories of data one affected by policy and other neutral to the policy. In linear regression equation, $y = a + bx$, x denotes dummy variable and its value is zero for the category which is neutral to the effect of policy and unity for the category which is influenced by the policy intervention[6,7,8]. In a regression model, a dummy variable with a value of 0 causes its coefficient to disappear from the equation. Conversely, the

6. Meghnad Desai (1979), *Applied Econometrics*, Tata McGraw-Hill Publishing Company Ltd, New Delhi, pp.162-167
7. Potluri Rao and Roger LeRoy Miller (1972), *Applied Econometrics*, Prentice-Hall of India Private Limited, New Delhi, pp.88-93.
8. A. Koutsoyiannis (2003), Theory *of Econometrics: An Introductory Exposition of Econometric Methods*, Replika Press Pvt. Ltd., Kundli, pp.281-285.

value of 1 causes the coefficient to function as a supplemental intercept, because of the identity property of multiplication by 1.

5.11 (b) Counterfactual Analysis

In statistics and econometrics counterfactuals are used in policy evaluations. Counterfactual approach is also called as the potential outcome approach" or "Roy-Rubin Model" which aims to estimate a potential outcome, or the state of the affairs that would have happened in the absence of the cause[9].The counterfactual analysis of event causation proposes that c caused e, where c and e are individual events. Meaning thereby that e depended counterfactually on c and had c not occurred, e would not have also occurred[10]. It tends to describe the condition that would have occurred if a policy instrument had not been adopted. The counterfactual condition is used to assess the impact of an intervention by comparing outcomes for groups that have participated in the program with similar outcomes for groups that have not participated. Comparative analysis applying the counterfactual state is a central pre-condition for making valid assessments of impacts of public policy interventions ex-post[11]. In other words, counterfactual compares annex post realized outcome with a counterfactual outcome that could have obtained under certain assumptions regarding the policy variable.[12]

5.12 Results

5.12 (a) Regression Analysis Results

The data from 1980 to 2012-12 was analyzed by using regression analysis to assess the impact of IRDAI in promoting growth of the indicators, namely, growth in number of offices, agents, first year premium, total premium, products launched and policies in force (Table 5.18).

---

9. Massimo Loi and Margarida Rodrigues (2012), A note on the impact evaluation of public policies: the counterfactual analysis, Joint *Research Centre, Institute for the Protection and Security of the Citizen*, European Commission, Italy, p.9.
10. Jonathan Bennett (1987), "Event Causation: The Counterfactual Analysis", *Philosophical Perspectives*, Metaphysics, Volume 1, p.368.
11. Inge Ramberg and Mark Knell (2012), Challenges measuring effects of research and innovation policy interventions in ex-post impact evaluations. A synthesis report, retrieved online from www.forskningsradet.no/servlet/Satellite?...id..., last accessed on 5 April, 2015.
12. M. Hashem Pesaran and Ron P. Smith (2012), "Counterfactual Analysis in Macro-econometrics: An Empirical Investigation into the Effects of Quantitative Easing", Discussion Paper No. 6618, The Institute for the Study of Labor (IZA), Bonn, p. 2.

Table 5.18: Life Insurance Indicators from 1980 to 2013

Year	Offices	Agents	First Year premium (Rs. Crore)	Total Premium (Rs. Crore)	Prod-ucts Laun-ched	Policies in Force (Policies in 000)
1980-81	874	121257	177.8254	964.882	4	22772.88
1981-82	938	124589	193.1929	1092.906	1	23618.56
1982-83	1007	134742	242.6852	1217.962	--	24392.38
1983-84	1072	146473	262.2948	1355.098	--	25285.29
1984-85	1156	162478	324.8066	1559.327	--	26491.08
1985-86	1246	189496	405.0433	1782.98	5	28002.77
1986-87	1344	216606	532.2964	2097.208	3	29815.42
1987-88	1419	257959	803.1571	2671.879	2	32421.67
1988-89	1497	316927	1049.366	3432.718	1	36320.15
1989-90	1603	377929	1429.716	4489.394	2	40746.43
1990-91	1729	440830	1412.807	5600.799	3	46072.12
1991-92	1862	489660	1626.163	6959.919	2	51559.13
1992-93	2007	520809	1764.027	7987.239	4	57117.82
1993-94	2116	549454	2050.585	9735.318	1	61264.99
1994-95	2129	544892	2207.336	11527.8	3	65912.82
1995-96	2132	537117	2518.568	14181.77	2	71335.9
1996-97	2131	560636	3020.461	16239.79	5	78288.24
1997-98	2154	591198	3660.041	19252.07	2	85585.38
1998-99	2156	628301	4532.082	22805.8	2	92393.89
1999-2000	2156	714615	5735.934	27461.71	4	102258
2000-01	2199	115715	9707.43	34898.47	--	--
2001-02	2306	476902	19857.28	50094.46	94	---
2002-03	2445	1038785	16942.45	55747.55	116	---
2003-04	2612	1556817	19788.32	66653.75	94	---
2004-05	3001	481250	26217.64	82854.80	56	165358.196
2005-06	3865	1423839	38785.54	105875.76	55	183108.83
2006-07	5373	1993199	75649.21	156075.84	208	194164
2007-08	8913	2520492	93712.52	201351.41	168	198168
2008-09	11815	2937435	87331.08	221785.47	196	217684.70
2009-10	12018	2978283	109893.91	265447.25	359	235064.88
2010-11	11546	2639392	126398.18	291638.64	244	253223.79
2011-12	11167	2358885	113966.03	287072.11	143	271273.62
2012-13	10285	2122757	107361.08	287202.49	118	287857.32

Source: Right to information application on Life Insurance Corporation and Annual Reports of Insurance Regulatory and Development Authority of India.

To assess the impact of IRDAI on the indicators such as offices, agents, first year premium, total premium, products launched and policies in force linear regression equation $y = a + bx$ was used by taking these indicators as dependent variables and dummy variable (i.e. time) as independent variable.

In the above data the value of dummy variable has been taken as 0 for the pre IRDAI phase (1980-2000) time and for the post IRDAI phase (2000-01 to 2012-13) time the value of dummy variable is 1. SPSS software was used for regression analysis (Table 5.19).

The results of linear regression equation for the offices gives t value for α Intercept as 2.761 and t value for slope coefficient (β) as 5.399 which has been found to statistically significant at 1 percent level. In other words, set up of IRDAI has been helpful in growth of number of offices of insurance firms in India (Table 5.19).

Similarly, in case of growth of number of agents, t value for α Intercept was 3.295 and for slope coefficient t value was 3.748, which are statistically, significant at 1 percent level. In other words, IRDAI has positive impact on growth of number of agents in India (Table 5.19).

For first year (including single premium) the t value for α Intercept works out to be 0.395 and t value for slope coefficient was 3.379. The t value for α Intercept is statistically non-significant and t value for slope coefficient was found to be statistically significant at 1 percent level. The results reveal that IRDAI has been helpful in growth of first year (including single premium) (Table 5.19).

In case of total premium underwritten over the years the t value for α Intercept works out to be 0.548 and t value for slope coefficient was 4.207. The t value for α Intercept was statistically non-significant while for slope coefficient the t value was statistically significant at 1 percent level. The total premium underwritten witnessed more growth in post IRDAI phase vis-à-vis the phase under Life Insurance Corporation monopoly (Table 5.19).

Table 5.19: Regression Analysis Results

Indicators	α Intercept	β Slope Co-efficient	R Square
Offices	1636.400 (2.761)*	5097.831 (5.399)*	.485
Agents	248245.500 (3.295)*	391484.577 (3.748)*	.379
First Year premium (Rs. Crore)	704.946 (.395)	8372.143 (3.379)*	.332
Total Premium (Rs. Crore)	2768.756 (.548)	29495.900 (4.207)*	.435
Products Launched	2.556 (.225)	29.361 (1.951)	.167
Policies in Force (Policies in 000)	32291.490 (4.949)*	54321.314 (5.450)*	.610

Figures in parenthesis are t values

* Significant at 1 Percent level

In case of products launched, the t value was 0.225 for α Intercept and 1.951 for slope co-efficient. The t values of both the variables are statistically non-significant at 1 percent level but the slope coefficient was found to be statistically significant at 5 percent level. The results imply that IRDAI has positive impact in promoting growth in number of products launched by insurance firms. But in this case, the value of R square is very low that reflects poor specification of the model (Table 5.19 above).

On the other hand, in case of policies in force, the t value for α Intercept was found to be 4.49 and for slope co-efficient, it was 5.450. Both the values are statistically significant at 1 percent level. Thus, it implies that IRDAI has positively impacted the growth of the number of policies in force of insurance firms (Table 5.19).

5.12 (b) Counterfactual Analysis

For analyzing the role of IRDAI for growth of various indicators, the data from pre IRDAI phase (1980-2000) was plotted and equations best suitable to the data were obtained. By using the equation the projected values were obtained to make comparison with actual values (Table Annexure 1). The t test is used to evaluate difference between the actual values and projected values of post IRDAI phase (2000-01 to 2012-13).

Linear Equation $y = 0.051x + 6.811$ with $R^2 = 0.935$ and $r = 0.9669$ fits well with the actual data of pre-IRDAI (1980-2000) phase for number of offices in India. On the basis of the equation the projected values from 1980 to 2012-13 were obtained. Finally the comparison between the actual values and projected values from post IRDAI phase (2000-01 to 2012-13) was made by using t-test. In t-test, the difference between actual values and projected values was found to be statistically significant at 5 percent level as t value= 2.587 and p value= 0.023 (Table 5.20). Meaning thereby that inception of IRDAI has contributed in growth of number of insurance offices in India.

Linear equation $y = 0.101x + 11.62$ with $R^2 = 0.937$ and $r = 0.9679$ is most suitable for number of agents for obtaining projected values. The projected values and actual values of post IRDAI phase were compared using t test. The results of t-test revealed that difference between actual and projected values of post IRDAI phase were statistically non- Significant at 5 percent level with t value=2.51 and p= 0.804 (Table 5.20). It implies that IRDAI has not been helpful in growth of number of individual agents.

Table 5.20: Results of Counterfactual

Indicators	**Linear Equation**	**R Square**	**T Test Results**		
			t value	**p value**	**Significance/ non-significance level**
Offices	y = 0.051x + 6.811	0.935	2.587	0.023	Statistically significant at 5 percent level
Agents	y = 0.101x + 11.62	0.937	2.51	0.804	Statistically non- Significant at 5 percent level
First Year premium (Rs. Crore)	y = 0.183x + 5.021	0.977	2.929	0.01	Statistically Significant at 1 percent level

Total Premium (Rs. Crore)	y = 0.186x + 6.511	0.993	0.897	0.379	Statistically non-Significant at 5 percent level
Products Launched	y = 0.033x + 0.391	0.114	5.92	0.0001	Statistically significant at more that 1 percent level
Policies in Force (Policies in 000)	y = 0.084x + 16.71	0.985	0.537	0.599	Statistically non-Significant at 5 percent level

Linear regression equation y = 0.183x + 5.021 with R^2 = 0.977 and r = 0.9884 was found to be a good fit - for the actual values in pre IRDAI (1980 to 2000) phase data for first year (including single year) premium. The comparison through t test brought forward that difference between actual and projected values was found to be statistically significant at 1 percent level with p=2.929 and t=0.01 (Table 5.20). In nutshell IRDAI has influenced the growth of first year (including single year) premium.

For total premium underwritten, the linear equation y = 0.186x + 6.511 was found most suitable with R^2= 0.993 and r =0.9964 for pre IRDAI phase data. The t test reveals that the difference between actual and projected values was statistically non-significant at 5 percent level with value of t = 0.897 and p = 0.379 (Table 5.20). It implies that IRDAI did not have significant effect in growth of total premium underwritten.

On the basis of linear regression y = 0.033x + 0.391 with R^2=0.114 and r = 0.337 the projected values for products launched were obtained. The comparison of actual and projected values through t test revealed that difference between both the values was statistically significant at 1 percent level with t=5.92 and p=0.0001 (Table 5.20). The statistical analysis reveals that IRDAI has been helpful in growth of products launched by insurance firms.

Linear equation y = 0.084x + 16.71 with R^2=0.985 and r= =0.9924 fitted well with number of policies in force in pre-IRDAI phase (1980-2000) and thus, projected values were obtained. The results of t-test revealed that difference between actual and projected values was found to be statistically non-significant at 5 percent level with t=0.537 and p=0.599(Table 5.20). IRDAI has not been significant in growth of number of policies in force over the years of insurance firms.

5.13 Summing up of the Results of All the Three Statistical Tools

The results of regression analysis test and counterfactual analysis test reveals variation in certain indicators. On account of growth in number of individual agents, the dummy variable reveals statistically, significant difference in pre and post IRDAI phase whereas counterfactual test brings forth statistically non-significant difference between both the phases. Similar findings have been reported in case of total premium underwritten and policies in force by life insurance industry in India (see Table 5.21 below).

Table 5.21: Results of Compound Growth Rates, Regression Analysis and Counterfactual Analysis

Indicators	Compound Growth Rate	Regression Analysis	Counterfactual Analysis
Offices	High in post IRDAI Phase	Statistically significant at 1 percent level	Statistically significant at 5 percent level
Agents	High in pre-IRDAI Phase	Statistically significant at 1 percent level	Statistically non- Significant at 5 percent level
First Year premium (Rs. Crore)	High in post IRDAI Phase	Statistically significant at 1 percent level	Statistically Significant at 1 percent level
Total Premium (Rs. Crore)	High in post IRDAI Phase	Statistically significant at 1 percent level	Statistically non-Significant at 5 percent level
Products Launched	High in post IRDAI Phase	Statistically significant at 5 percent level	Statistically significant at more that 1 percent level
Policies in Force (Policies in 000)	High in post IRDAI Phase	Statistically significant at 1 percent level	Statistically non-Significant at 5 percent level

On the other hand, the results of indicators, namely, growth in number of offices, first year (including single year) premium and products launched was found to be statistically significant by dummy variable test and counter-factual analysis (Table 5.21 above).

5.14 Matrix Summing Up The Testing of Hypothesis 1

Matrix 5.1: Testing of Hypothesis 1- "IRDAI has been an instrument in promoting the growth of life insurance business in India by promoting growth in number of agents, polices, single premium underwritten, total premium underwritten in comparison to pre-IRDAI period"

Hypothesis	Sources of Data	Analysis	Status of Hypothesis Accepted
IRDAI has been an instrument in promoting the growth of life insurance business in India by promoting growth in number of agents, polices, single premium underwritten, total premium underwritten in comparison to pre-IRDAI period	Secondary data	The number of insurers had increased from one to 24 in post IRDAI phase. Growth in number of offices is higher in post IRDAI phase as the compound rate of growth was more than in pre IRDAI phase. Regression analysis and counterfactual analysis also proves that growth in number of offices was higher in post IRDAI phase. Growth in terms of agent is higher in pre IRDAI phase as compound rate of growth was more in pre IRDAI phase as compared to post-IRDAI phase. But regression analysis and counterfactual test reveals that it is more in post IRDAI phase. First year premium and total premium witnessed higher growth in post IRDAI phase as per counterfactual analysis, regression analysis and comparison of compound rate of growth. Products launched by insurance companies also witnessed higher rate of growth in post IRDAI phase as per comparisons of compound rate of growth, regression analysis and counterfactual analysis. Policies in force were more in post IRDAI phase as compared to pre-IRDAI phase as per comparison of compound rate of growth and regression analysis. But counterfactual analysis revealed that growth in policies was more in post IRDAI phase. Life insurance penetration in India had been less as compared to world average. Life insurance density in India had been consistently lower than the world average.	Yes

Thus, on the basis of analysis conducted on above data, the **Hypothesis 1:** "IRDAI has been an instrument in promoting the growth of life insurance business in India by promoting growth in number of agents, polices, single premium underwritten, total premium underwritten in comparison to pre-IRDAI period" **stands Validated.**

II
ROLE OF IRDAI IN PROMOTING EFFICIENCY IN CONDUCT OF LIFE INSURANCE BUSINESS

One of the functions of IRDAI is to enhance efficiency in conduct of insurance business. Efficiency consists of two types namely - technical efficiency and allocative efficiency. Technical efficiency refers to ability of a firm to obtain maximum output from given inputs or the use of minimum inputs to obtain fixed level of outputs. Allocative efficiency reflects the ability of a firm to use the inputs in optimal proportions, given their respective prices. The combination of technical and allocative efficiency provides economic efficiency[13].When a company is already established then optimal utilization of existing resources is first step for analyzing the efficiency rather than restricting or inducing changes to gain from reduced costs. Thus here only technical efficiency of insurers shall be examined[14].

5.15 Importance of Efficiency Measurement For Insurance Sector

Efficiency measurement is important in insurance sector from policy perspectives. In India due to deregulation of insurance sector public sector monopoly has been abolished. In the post deregulation era public sector firms has to reorient themselves so as to provide better services to customers and become competitive with private insurers. Efficiency studies also identify efficient and inefficient firms which are essential for improving competition and reposing trust of policyholders in insurance sector. Studying efficiency levels of insurance firms helps in identifying the causes of inefficiencies and thus by rectifying such causes efficiency of insurers can improve. Finally, efficiency is essential for market expansion and encourages wider participation to maximize social benefits of insurance to public.

5.16 Techniques For Measuring Efficiency

Two techniques, namely - parametric method like Stochastic Frontier Analysis (SFA); and non-parametric method like Data Envelopment Analysis (DEA) - are used to measure efficiency of firms or individuals especially banks' performance[15].Over the past years, the application of these techniques has increased in insurance industry for measuring technical efficiency[16], relationship between efficiency scale economies and

13. M.J. Farrell (1957), "The measurement of productive efficiency", *Journal of the Royal Statistical Society*, Series A, Volume 120, Number 3, pp. 253–281.
14. B.L. Rawson (2001), "Data envelopment analysis of technical efficiency in the UK insurance industry", *Ph.D. Thesis series,* Nottingham University, pp-20-90.
15. A.N. Berger and D.B. Humphrey (1992), "Measurement and efficiency issues in commercial banking", In Zvi Griliches (Eds.), *Output measurement in the services sector,* University of Chicago Press, Chicago, pp. 245–279.
16. F. Fecher, D. Kessler, S. Perelman, and P. Pestieau (1993), "Productive performance of the French insurance industry", *Journal of Productivity Analysis,* Volume 4, Number 1–2,pp. 77–93.

mergers and acquisitions[17].

Parametric approach marks a production, cost, revenue, or profit function with a specific shape and makes assumptions about the distribution of the inefficiency and error terms. This approach is principally of three types, namely, Stochastic Frontier Approach (SFA), Distribution-Free Approach (DFA) and Thick Frontier Approach (TFA). The SFA assumes a composed error model where inefficiencies follow an asymmetric distribution and the error term usually follows a normal distribution. On the other hand, DFA makes fewer specific assumptions and also requires several years of data. Efficiency of each company is assumed to be stable over time and the random noise averages out to zero. Lastly, the (TFA) assumes that inefficiencies differ between the highest and lowest quartile firms without making distributional assumptions for the random error and inefficiency terms,[18].

Non parametric approaches are of two types, namely - free-disposal hull (FDH) and Data Envelopment Analysis (DEA). The (FDH) approach is a special configuration of DEA. Under this approach, the points on the lines connecting the DEA vertices are excluded from the frontier and the convexity assumption on the efficient frontier is relaxed[19]. DEA was introduced by A. Charnes, W. W. Cooper and E. Rhodes in 1978[20] and it is the most widespread mathematical approach which uses linear programming to measure the relationship of outputs to assigned inputs.

DEA models can be categorized as constant returns to scale (CRS) and variable returns to scale (VRS) and can be used to further bifurcate cost efficiency into its various single components such as technical, pure technical, allocative, and scale efficiency. Based on constant returns to scale and variable returns to scale assumptions, two distinctive models were developed, that is, CCR model of Charnes et al., 1978 and BCC model of Banker et al., 1984[21]. The CCR model is built on the assumption of constant returns to scale. That is, if an activity (x, y) is feasible, the activity $(\lambda x, \lambda y)$ is also feasible. While the BCC model is built upon assumptions of variable returns to scale. Both CCR and BCC models can have two orientations, namely, Input oriented and output oriented versions. The input-oriented model aims to minimize inputs while satisfying at least the given output levels. The output-oriented model

17. J.D. Cummins, S. Tennyson, and M.A. Weiss, (1999), "Consolidation and efficiency in the US life insurance industry", *Journal of Banking and Finance,* Volume 23, Number 2–3, pp.325–357.
18. Martin Eling and Michael Luhnen (2009), "Frontier efficiency methodologies to measure performance in the insurance industry: Overview, systematization, and recent, *JEL classification: D23; G22; L11,* pp. 3-5.
19. A. N. Berger, and D. B. Humphrey, (1997), "Efficiency of Financial Institutions: International Survey and Directions for Future Research", *European Journal of Operational Research,* Volume 98, Number 2, pp. 175–212.
20. A. Charnes, W. W. Cooper and E. Rhodes (1978) "Measuring the Efficiency of Decision Making Units", *European Journal of Operational Research,* Volume 2, Number 6, pp. 429–444.
21. R.D. Banker, A. Charnes, and W.W. Cooper (1984), "Some models for estimating technical and scale inefficiencies in data envelopment analysis", *Management Science,* Volume 30, Number 9, pp.1078–1092.

attempts to maximize outputs without requiring more observed inputs[22]. Various studies employing different techniques in measuring efficiency in insurance sector are depicted in Table 5.22.

22. Anirban Dutta and Partha Pratim Sengupta (2011), "Efficiency Measurement of Indian Life Insurance Industry in Post-Reforms Era", *Global Business Review*, Volume 12, Number 3, pp. 415-430.

Table 5.22: Cross Country Studies on Efficiency

Weiss (1991)	World	Five OECD countries: France, Germany, Japan, Switzerland,	Aggregate economic data	1975-1987	Property–liability	Index numbers	Total factor productivity	1. US and Germany with overall high productivity 2. Productivity increase for France, Germany, and Switzerland, no clear results for US; Japan worse than average
Delhausse et al., (1995)	EU	Belgium, France	191 (BE) 243 (FR)	1984–1988	Non-life	DEA, SFA	Technical, scale	1. Efficiency French > Belgium 2. Overall low efficiency levels 3. Nonprofit companies are more efficient than for-profit companies
Rai (1996)	World	Denmark, Finland, France, Germany, Italy, Japan, Netherlands, Sweden, Switzerland, UK, US	106	1988-1992	Life including health, non-life	SFA, Distribution Free Approach	Cost	1. Efficiency Finland and France > UK 2. No result with regard to eff. over time 3. Small firms (specialized firms) more efficient than large firms (combined firms)
Donni and Fecher (1997)	World	Belgium, Canada, Finland, France, Germany, Iceland, Italy, Japan, Netherlands, New Zealand, Portugal, Switzerland, Turkey, UK, and US	Aggregate economic data	1983-1991	Life, nonlife	DEA	Technical	1. US, UK, France, and Germany best, Portugal worst 2. Efficiency levels high and Dispersed; growth in productivity in all countries due to technical progress

Mahlberg (1999)	EU	Austria and Germany	36 (AT) 118 (DE)	1992-1996	Life, health, property–liability	DEA	Technical	1. Efficiency Austria > Germany 2. Inefficiencies in both markets
Diacon (2001)	EU	France, Germany, Italy, Netherland, Switzerland, and UK	431	1999	General insurance	DEA	Technical	1. Efficiency UK > Germany > Netherlands > France > Switzerland > Italy 2. No result with regard to eff. over time (only one year considered)
Kessner (2001)	EU	Germany and UK	78 (GE) 87 (UK)	1994-1999	Life	DEA	Technical	1. Efficiency UK > Germany 2. Increasing efficiency in both markets
Diacon et al., (2002)	EU	Austria, Belgium, Denmark, France, Germany, Greece, Ireland, Italy, Luxembourg, Netherlands, Portugal, Spain, Sweden, Switzerland, and UK	454	1996–1999	Life incl. pension, and health	DEA	Pure technical, scale, mix	1. Striking international differences 2. Decreasing levels of average technical efficiency
Boon-yasai, Grace, Skipper (2002)	Asia	Korea, Philippines, Taiwan, and Thailand	33 (KR) 33 (PH) 31 (TW) 13 (TH)	1978–1997	Life	DEA	Technical, pure technical, scale	1. Productivity Korea and Philippines > Taiwan and Thailand 2. Efficiency increases 3. Welfare gains only minimal if deregulation does not closely follow liberalization

Hussels and Ward (2006)	EU	Germany and UK	31 (GE) 47 (UK)	1991–2002	Life	DEA, Distribution Free Approach	Cost, technical, allocative, scale	1. Efficiency UK > Germany 2. Limited evidence of improvement in post deregulation efficiency 3. Limited influence of deregulation on efficiency
Klumpes (2007)	EU	France, Germany, Italy, Netherlands, Spain, Switzerland, and UK	1183	1997–2001	Life, general insurance	DEA	Cost, technical, Allocative pure technical, scale, revenue	1. No country ranking in this study 2. No result with regard to eff. over time 3. Acquiring firms achieve greater efficiency gains than target firms or firms not involved in mergers
Fenn et al., (2008)	EU	Austria, Belgium, Denmark, Finland, France, Germany, Ireland, Italy, Luxembourg, Netherlands, Portugal, Sweden, Switzerland, and UK	Not specified	1995–2001	Life, nonlife, composite	SFA	Cost	1. Life: Portugal and Austria best, Netherlands and UK worst; Non-life: UK best, Luxembourg worst 2. No improvement in cost efficiency 3. Increasing returns to scale for most EU insurers operating; larger firms with high market shares less cost efficient

Vencappa, Fenn, and Diacon (2008)	EU	Austria, Belgium, Denmark, Finland, France, Germany, Ireland, Italy, Luxembourg, Netherlands, Portugal, Sweden, Switzerland, and UK	Not specified	1995–2001	Life, nonlife	SFA	Technical	1. Life: Italy best, UK among the worst; Non-life: Convergence of efficiency scores for France, Germany, Italy, and Spain 10 points above UK (worst) 2. Non-life: no improvement (except Spain); Life: no improvement (except for Germany), decrease for Spain 3. Total factor productivity growth decomposition indicates some growth from scale economies (particularly life), and improvements in technical efficiency
Davutyan and Klumpes (2008)	EU	France, Germany, Italy, Netherlands, Spain, Switzerland, and UK	472	1996–2002	Life, nonlife	DEA	Technical, pure technical, scale	1. Life: France best, Netherlands worst; Non-life: Switzerland best, Spain worst 2. Very low efficiency scores 3. In life insurance, after mergers, business inputs replace labor for both targets and acquirers; mergers do not significantly impact acquirer behavior

Source: Martin Eling and Michael Luhnen (2010), "Efficiency in the international insurance industry: A cross-country comparison", Journal of Banking & Finance, Volume 34, pp.1497-1509.

For checking efficiency of insurance firms in India, BCC and CCR input- oriented models were employed through usage of software Max DEA to calculate efficiency scores of insurance firms. Firms having efficiency score of one had been fully efficient in the time period under consideration. Thus efficiency score of one is the standard for making comparisons among insurance firms. For calculating efficiency scores operating expenses related to insurance business; commission paid to agents and net benefits paid to policyholders were taken as inputs while net premium revenues were taken as outputs of all the insurance firms (*See Annexure 2*). The data regarding these indicators was taken from annual reports of Insurance Regulatory and Development Authority of India. The data was run with the help of Max DEA software and efficiency scores of insurance firms were obtained. The average and standard deviation were calculated of the obtained efficiency scores to make intra-firm comparisons in terms of efficiency. Further to analyze the efficiency disparity over the years the coefficient of variation was also calculated of the efficiency scores.

The main hypothesis tested in this regard is "IRDAI has promoted efficiency in conduct of insurance business by making insurance firms to minimize inputs".

5.17 CCR Input Oriented Model At Constant Returns To Scale: Analysis

In year 2001-02, HDFC Standard, SBI Life and LIC with score one were fully efficient as per CCR input oriented model. The average score for the year 2001-02 was 0.6. Around 7 firms namely - HDFC Standard, SBI Life, LIC, Bajaj Alliance, Birla Sunlife, ICICI prudential, PNB Metlife, had efficiency score above the average. On the other hand firms such as ING Life, Kotak Mahindra, Max Life, Reliance, Tata AIA had efficiency score below the average. In year 2002-03, insurance firms such as Aviva Life, HDFC Standard, ICICI Prudential, SBI Life and LIC were fully efficient as per CCR input oriented model at constant returns to the scale. Six firms, namely, ING Life, Kotak Mahindra, Max Life, PNB Metlife, Reliance, Tata AIA had below average efficiency score in the same year.

In year 2003-04, Birla Sunlife, HDFC Standard, ICICI Prudential, Reliance, SBI Life, LIC were hundred percent efficient with efficiency score 1. While insurance firms such as Bajaj Allianz, ING Life, PNB Metlife and Tata AIA had below average efficiency score. In year 2004-05, three insurers, namely - Sahara, SBI Life and LIC with efficiency score of 1 had been fully efficient. On the other hand, insurers such as AVIVA, Bajaj Allianz, HDFC Standard, ING Life, Kotak Mahindra, Max Life, PNB Metlife and Tata AIA performed below average in terms of efficiency. In year 2005-06, six insurance companies namely - HDFC Standard, ICICI Prudential, Reliance, Sahara, Shriram Life and LIC were fully efficient while insurance firms such as AVIVA, Bajaj Allianz, Birla Sunlife, ING Life, Kotak Mahindra, Max Life, PNB Metlife and Tata AIA could not get average efficiency score of 0.79. For year 2006-07, insurance firms such as Bharti AXA, Sahara, SBI Life, Shriram Life and LIC were fully efficient. On the other hand, firms such as AVIVA, Bajaj Allianz, Birla Sunlife, ICICI Prudential, ING Life, Max Life, PNB Metlife, Reliance and Tata AIA performed below average in terms of efficiency. In year 2007-08, three life insurance firms namely - (i) Future Generali, (ii) IDBI Federal and (iii) Max Life were fully efficient. Around 12 insurers namely -

AVIVA, Bajaj Allianz, Birla Sunlife, HDFC Standard, ICICI Prudential, ING Life, Kotak Mahindra, PNB Metlife, Reliance, Sahara, SBI Life and Tata AIA performance in terms of efficiency was not up to the mark.

In year 2008-09, eight insurance firms such as Canara HSBC, DLF Pramerica, Edelweiss Tokio, IDBI Federal, India First, SBI Life, Star Union Dai Chi and LIC with efficiency score of one were fully efficient. On the other hand 14 life insurers namely - Aegon Religare, AVIVA, Bajaj Allianz, Bharti AXA, Birla Sunlife, Future Generali, HDFC Standard, ICICI Prudential, ING Life, Kotak Mahindra, Max Life, PNB Metlife, Reliance and Tata AIA could not obtain average 0.68 efficiency score. In year 2009-10, DLF Pramerica, ICICI Prudential, IDBI Federal, India First, SBI Life, Star Union Dai Chi and LIC were fully efficient. While insurers such as Aegon Religare, AVIVA, Bharti AXA, Birla Sunlife, Canara HSBC, Future Generali, Kotak Mahindra, Max Life, PNB Metlife, Reliance and Shriram Life performed below average in terms of efficiency. In year 2010-11, five life insurers namely - Canara HSBC, ICICI Prudential, India First, SBI Life and Star Union Dai Chi had score of one thus, exhibiting fully efficient behavior. Insurers such as Aegon Religare, AVIVA, Bajaj Allianz, Bharti AXA, Birla Sunlife, Future Generali, HDFC Standard, IDBI Federal, ING Life, Kotak Mahindra, Max Life, Reliance, Sahara, Shriram Life and Tata AIA had efficiency score below the average norms of the year. In year 2011-12 five life insurers, namely - (i) Edelweiss Tokio, (ii) India First, (iii) SBI Life, (iv) Star Union Dai Chi and (v) LIC were fully efficient. Insurers such as (i) Aegon Religare, (ii) AVIVA, (iii) Bajaj Allianz, (iv) Bharti AXA, (v) Birla Sunlife, (vi) DLF Pramerica, (vii) Future Generali, (viii) IDBI Federal, (ix) ING Life, (x) Max Life, (xi) PNB Metlife, (xii) Reliance, (xiii) Sahara, (xiv) Shriram Life, and (xv) Tata AIA had efficiency score of below average. In 2012-13, only three life insurers namely - (i) Edelweiss Tokio, (ii) India First and (iii) LIC got efficiency score of one thus, depicted being fully efficient. Insurers, namely - Aegon Religare, AVIVA, Bajaj Allianz, Bharti AXA, Birla Sunlife, Future Generali, IDBI Federal, ING Life, Kotak Mahindra, Max Life, PNB Metlife, Reliance Sahara and Shriram Life had efficiency score below the average.

Eight life insurers namely - Bajaj Allianz, Canara HSBC, DLF Pramerica, Edelweiss Tokio, India First, SBI Life, Star Union Dai Chi and LIC had been good performers in terms of efficiency over the years as the standard deviation of their efficiency scores hovered from 0 to 20. Similarly, in years 2003-04, 2005-06, 2009-10 and 2010-11 standard deviation of efficiency scores was below 20 meaning thereby - the firms in these years were efficient in relation to other years.

Co-efficient of variation was 65 percent in 2001-02 while in 2012-13, it decreased to 32.30 percent meaning thereby that disparity in efficiency amongst insurance firms has reduced over the years. Co-efficient of variation has shown a sharp declining trend from year 2001-02 to 2003-04, but in subsequent years, it fluctuated and further increased to 84 percent and then gain declined and stood at 32.30 percent in 2012-13. Thus, the behavior of co-efficient of variation is found to be erratic during the time period under review.

Table 5.23: Efficiency Scores of CCR Input Oriented model at Constant Returns to Scale

Insurer	2001 -02	2002 -03	2003 -04	2004 -05	2005 -06	2006 -07	2007 -08	2008 -09	2009 -10	2010 -11	2011 -12	2012 -13	Average	Standard Deviation
Aegon Religare								0.14	0.53	0.87	0.44	0.47318	0.49	0.26
AVIVA		1	0.89	0.38	0.76	0.62	0.12	0.59	0.80	0.74	0.52	0.56	0.64	0.24
Bajaj Allianz	0.93	0.74	0.65	0.61	0.62	0.51	0.15	0.58	0.82	0.71	0.54	0.61	0.62	0.19
Bharti AXA						1	0.47	0.23	0.59	0.70	0.58	0.45	0.58	0.24
Birla Sunlife	0.91	0.76	1	0.72	0.73	0.68	0.17	0.60	0.75	0.60	0.50	0.57	0.67	0.21
Canara HSBC								1	0.81	1	0.96	0.98	0.96	0.08
DLF Pramerica								1	1	0.90	0.60	0.69	0.84	0.18
Edelweiss Tokio											1	1	1	00
Future Generali							1	0.57	0.40	0.35	0.32	0.35	0.50	0.26
HDFC Standard	1	1	1	0.52	1	0.87	0.20	0.49	0.92	0.74	0.72	0.77	0.77	0.25
ICICI Prudential	0.73	1	1	0.77	1	0.10	0.27	0.61	1	1	0.69	0.78	0.75	0.29
IDBI Federal							1	1	1	0.64	0.52	0.50	0.78	0.24
India First									1	1	1	1	1	00
ING Life	0.13	0.64	0.73	0.52	0.49	0.66	0.17	0.59	0.90	0.50	0.40	0.44	0.52	0.21
Kotak Mahindra	0.15	0.37	0.96	0.62	0.71	0.79	0.16	0.54	0.81	0.72	0.66	0.62	0.59	0.25
Max Life	0.25	0.29	0.89	0.39	0.49	0.61	1	0.53	0.68	0.45	0.52	0.540	0.55	0.22
PNB Metlife	0.78	0.18	0.45	0.45	0.61	0.56	0.14	0.55	0.66	0.94	0.51	0.53	0.53	0.22
Reliance	0.05	0.14	1	0.88	1	0.72	0.16	0.62	0.74	0.53	0.38	0.43	0.56	0.33
Sahara				1	1	1	0.20	0.94	0.94	0.65	0.48	0.47	0.74	0.30
SBI Life	1	1	1	1	0.85	1	0.36	1	1	1	1	0.96	0.93	0.18
Shriram Life					1	1	0.40	0.93	0.66	0.73	0.40	0.40	0.69	0.26
Star Union Dai Chi								1	1	1	1	0.77	0.95	0.09
Tata AIA	0.27	0.53	0.74	0.36	0.56	0.69	0.14	0.55	0.94	0.62	0.57	0.70	0.56	0.21
LIC	1	1	1	1	1	1	0.70	1	1	0.97	1	1	0.97	0.08
Mean	0.6	0.66	0.87	0.66	0.79	0.74	0.38	0.68	0.82	0.75	0.64	0.65		
Standard Deviation	0.39	0.33	0.17	0.23	0.20	0.24	0.32	0.25	0.17	0.19	0.22	0.21		
Coefficient of Variation	65	50	19.54	34.84	25.31	32.43	84.21	36.76	20.73	25.33	34.37	32.30		

For making a comparison of the performance of the insurance firms on the basis of efficiency scores the firms were classified into highly efficient, moderate efficient and less efficient. The classification was done for the three years 2001-02 (beginning of de-regulation) 2007-08 (middle of the time period of analysis) and 2012-13 (the terminal year of analysis) by comparing their scores against the averages of the respective years.

In 2001-02, the mean of efficiency score was 0.6 thus, the highly efficient firms were those having efficiency score above 0.70. Similarly, moderate efficient firms with score ranging between 0.5 and 0.69, and firms having efficiency score less than 0.5 were classified as less efficient. In same year, there were 12 insurance firms operating in India and out of total 7 firms were found to be highly efficient. However, no firm was having moderate efficiency and 5 insurance firms were termed as less efficient (see Table 5.24 on next page).

In 2007-08, the average efficiency score was 0.38 thus firms scoring more than 0.48 were termed as highly efficient, firms with scores ranging between 0.28 and 0.47 were classified as moderate efficient firms and insurance firms with less than 0.28 efficiency score were referred as less efficient. In this year, our of 18 insurance firms operating in India 4 were termed as highly efficient, another three were moderately efficient and remaining eleven insurance firms were marked as less efficient (see Table 5.24 on next page).

In terminal year 2012-13, the average of efficiency score stood at 0.65. Thus, firms having score above 0.65 were termed as highly efficient, firms with scores ranging between 0.55 to 0.64 were moderately efficient on the other hand firms with efficiency score below 0.55 were termed as less efficient in the year under consideration. In the year, there were 24 insurance firms operating in India, out of which 8 insurance firms were highly efficient, six insurance firms had moderate efficiency scores while 10 firms were found to be less efficient (Table 5.24).

LIC was the only insurance firm remained highly efficient in three years under review. ING Life and reliance remained throughout - in less efficient category. Max Life showed wide variation in terms of efficiency because in 2001-02, it was less efficient but in 2007-08, it was in highly efficient category and in 2012-13, its efficiency witnessed a nose dive and fell into less efficient category (see Table 5.24 on next page).

The fluctuation of other insurance firms is also noticeable. Some of them are - Bajaj Allianz, Birla Sunlife, HDFC Standard, ICICI Prudential and PNB Metlife were highly efficient in 2001-02 but in 2007-08, these all firms are found to be less efficient. In year 2012-13, HDFC and ICICI Prudential improved their efficiency scores and were termed as highly efficient while Bajaj Allianz and Birla Sunlife remained in moderately efficient category. On the other hand, PNB Metlife remained in less efficient category in 2012-13 (see Table 5.24 below).

Table 5.24: Classification of Insurance firms on Account of their CCR Efficiency Scores in 2001-02, 2007-08 and 2012-13

Nature of Efficiency	2001-02	2007-08	2012-13
Highly Efficient	Bajaj Allianz Birla Sunlife HDFC Standard ICICI Prudential PNB Metlife SBI Life LIC	Future Generali IDBI Federal Max Life LIC	Canara HSBC Edelweiss Tokio HDFC Standard ICICI Prudential India First SBI Life Star Union Dai Chi LIC
Moderate Efficient	--	Bharti AXA SBI Life Shriram Life	AVIVA Bajaj Allianz Birla Sunlife DLF Pramerica Kotak Mahindra Tata AIA
Less Efficient	ING Life Kotak Mahindra Max Life Reliance Tata AIA	AVIVA Bajaj Allianz Birla Sunlife HDFC Standard ICICI Prudential ING Life Kotak Mahindra PNB Metlife Reliance Sahara Tata AIA	Aegon Religare Bharti AXA Future Generali IDBI Federal ING Life Max Life PNB Metlife Reliance Sahara Shriram Life

5.18 BCC Input Oriented Model At Variable Returns To Scale: Analysis

In year 2001-02, eight insurers, namely - Bajaj Allianz, Birla Sunlife, HDFC Standard, ICICI Prudential, PNB Metlife, Reliance, SBI Life and LIC had efficiency score of one meaning thereby that these firms were fully efficient as per BCC input-oriented model. While other four firms i.e. (i) ING Life, (ii) Kotak Mahindra, (iii) Max Life and (iv) Tata AIA performed below average in terms of efficiency. In year 2002-03, firms such as AVIVA, HDFC Standard, ICICI Prudential, PNB Metlife, Reliance, SBI Life and LIC were fully efficient while Bajaj Allianz, Birla Sunlife, ING Life, Kotak Mahindra, Max Life and Tata AIA performed below average mark in terms of efficiency. In year

2003-04, AVIVA, Birla Sunlife, HDFC Standard, ICICI Prudential, Kotak Mahindra, Max Life, PNB Metlife, Reliance, SBI Life and LIC had efficiency score of one exhibiting being fully efficient. Insurers such as Bajaj Allianz, ING Life and Tata AIA could not meet the average efficiency score of 0.94 in the year under review. For the year 2004-05, insurers, namely - Birla Sunlife, HDFC Standard, ICICI Prudential, ING Life, Kotak Mahindra, Reliance, Sahara, SBI Life and LIC were fully efficient while remaining insurers such as AVIVA, Bajaj Allianz, Max Life, PNB Metlife and Tata AIA were unable to meet the average efficiency score of the year. For the year 2005-06, AVIVA, HDFC Standard, ICICI Prudential, Reliance, Sahara, Shriram Life and LIC were fully efficient. On the other hand Bajaj Allianz, Birla Sunlife, ING Life, Kotak Mahindra, Max Life and Tata AIA performed below average in terms of efficiency scores. In year 2006-07, insurance firms such as Bajaj Allianz, Bharti AXA, Sahara, SBI Life, Shriram Life and LIC were fully efficient as they had efficiency score of one. AVIVA, Birla Sunlife, ICICI Prudential, ING Life, Kotak Mahindra, Max Life, Reliance and Tata AIA performed below average in terms of efficiency as they were not able to meet the average target of 0.84 in the year under consideration. In year 2007-08 five insurance firms, namely, Bharti AXA Future Generali IDBI Federal Max Life and LIC were fully efficient. Majority of the insurers such as AVIVA, Bajaj Allianz, Birla Sunlife, HDFC Standard, ICICI Prudential, ING Life, Kotak Mahindra, PNB Metlife, Reliance, SBI Life, Shriram Life and Tata AIA performed below average in terms of efficiency.

In year 2008-09, insurers such as Bajaj Allianz, Canara HSBC, DLF Pramerica, IDBI Federal, Reliance, Sahara, SBI Life, Star Union Dai Chi, Tata AIA and LIC were fully efficient as they had efficiency score of one. On the other hand, Aegon Religare Bharti AXA Birla Sunlife Future Generali HDFC Standard ING Life Kotak Mahindra PNB Metlife had below the average efficiency score in the year under review. In 2009-10 Canara HSBC, DLF Pramerica, ICICI Prudential, IDBI Federal, India First, Sahara, SBI Life, Star Union Dai Chi, Tata AIA and LIC were fully efficient by having efficiency score of one. While Aegon Religare, AVIVA, Bharti AXA, Birla Sunlife, Future Generali, Kotak Mahindra, Max Life, PNB Metlife, Reliance and Shriram Life were the average efficiency score of the year under review. In year 2010-11, Canara HSBC DLF Pramerica ICICI Prudential India First PNB Metlife Sahara SBI Life Star Union Dai Chi and LIC were fully efficient. In year 2011-12, eight insurers, namely - (i) Canara HSBC, (ii) Edelweiss Tokio, (iii) HDFC Standard, (iv) India First, (v) Sahara, (vi) SBI Life, (vii) Star Union Dai Chi and (viii) LIC while in 2012-13 nine insurers namely - (i) Bajaj Allianz, (ii) Canara HSBC, (iii) Edelweiss Tokio, (iv) HDFC Standard, (v) India First, (vi) Sahara, (vii) SBI Life, (viii) Tata AIA and (ix) LIC were fully efficient in terms of variable returns to the scale.

Four life insurers namely - (i) Canara HSBC, (ii) Edelweiss Tokio, (iii) India First and (iv) LIC had been fully efficient in terms of BCC input- oriented model throughout the review period. While four insurers namely - DLF Pramerica, Sahara, SBI Life and Star Union Dai Chi were also good performers as standard deviation of their efficiency scores hovered between 0.06 to 0.20. Similarly, in years 2002-03, 2003-04, 2004-05, 2005-06, 2009-10, 2010-11 and 2012-13; the standard deviation of efficiency scores of all the firms - had been below 20 meaning thereby that in these years, the firms were more efficient as compared with other years.

The co-efficient of variation of efficiency scores has overall shown a downward trend from initial year to terminal year. In year 2001-02 the co-efficient of variation of efficiency scores was 48 while it decreased to 25.31 in year 2012-13 meaning thereby that disparity in efficiency amongst insurance firms had reduced over the years (see Table 5.25 on next page).

Table 5.25: Efficiency Scores of BCC Input Oriented model at Variable Returns to Scale (Technical Efficiency)

Insurer	2001-02	2002-03	2003-04	2004-05	2005-06	2006-07	2007-08	2008-09	2009-10	2010-11	2011-12	2012-13	Average	Standard Deviation
Aegon Religare								0.24	0.59	0.90	0.48	0.72	0.59	0.24
AVIVA		1	1	0.61	1	0.79	0.12	0.97	0.82	0.74	0.71	0.61	0.76	0.25
Bajaj Allianz	1	0.81	0.67	0.79	0.62	1	0.15	1	0.92	0.74	0.67	1	0.78	0.24
Bharti AXA						1	1	0.27	0.77	0.70	0.58	0.52	0.69	0.26
Birla Sunlife	1	0.79	1	1	0.75	0.71	0.18	0.72	0.77	0.69	0.63	0.80	0.75	0.21
Canara HSBC								1	1	1	1	1	1	00
DLF Pramerica								1	1	1	0.79	0.83	0.92	0.10
Edelweiss Tokio											1	1	1	00
Future Generali							1	0.67	0.55	0.44	0.35	0.50	0.59	0.22
HDFC Standard	1	1	1	1	1	0.93	0.20	0.75	0.95	0.88	1	1	0.89	0.23
ICICI Prudential	1	1	1	1	1	0.10	0.27	0.88	1	1	0.88	0.97	0.84	0.31
IDBI Federal							1	1	1	0.64	0.58	0.60	0.80	0.21
India First									1	1	1	1	1	00
ING Life	0.28	0.79	0.88	1	0.49	0.74	0.17	0.79	0.94	0.54	0.41	0.45	0.62	0.27
Kotak Mahindra	0.18	0.66	1	1	0.74	0.82	0.16	0.63	0.84	0.80	0.84	0.77	0.70	0.27
Max Life	0.26	0.38	1	0.61	0.49	0.83	1	0.94	0.72	0.82	0.95	0.81	0.73	0.24
PNB Metlife	1	1	1	0.65	0.97	0.87	0.14	0.73	0.86	1	0.57	0.591	0.78	0.26
Reliance	1	1	1	1	1	0.81	0.16	1	0.77	0.69	0.47	0.53	0.78	0.27
Sahara				1	1	1	0.59	1	1	1	1	1	0.95	0.13
SBI Life	1	1	1	1	0.87	1	0.37	1	1	1	1	1	0.93	0.18
Shriram Life					1	1	0.40	0.95	0.68	0.83	0.59	0.521	0.74	0.23
Star Union Dai Chi								1	1	1	1	0.85	0.97	0.06
Tata AIA	0.31	0.57	0.75	0.55	0.56	0.82	0.14	1	1	0.99	0.83	1	0.71	0.28
LIC	1	1	1	1	1	1	1	1	1	1	1	1	1	00
Mean	0.75	0.84	0.94	0.87	0.83	0.84	0.45	0.84	0.88	0.84	0.76	0.79		
Std. Deviation	0.36	0.20	0.11	0.18	0.20	0.22	0.36	0.22	0.14	0.16	0.21	0.20		
Coefficient of Variation	48	23.80	11.70	20.68	24.09	26.19	80	26.19	15.90	19.04	27.63	25.31		

For making a comparison of the performance of the insurance firms on the basis of BCC efficiency scores at the variable returns to scale, the firms were classified into highly efficient, moderate efficient and less efficient. The classification wass done for the three years 2001-02 (beginning of de-regulation) 2007-08 (middle of the time period of analysis) and 2012-13 (the terminal year of analysis) by comparing their scores against the averages of the respective years.

In 2001-02, the mean of BCC efficiency score was 0.75 thus, the highly efficient firms were those having efficiency score 0.85 and above, moderate efficient firms with score ranging between 0.65 and 0.84, whereas firms having efficiency score less than 0.65 were classified as less efficient. In same year there were 12 insurance firms operating in India and out of total, 8 insurance firms were classified as highly efficient and 4 were termed as less efficient (see Table 5.25 on preceding page 175).

In 2007-08, the average BCC efficiency score was 0.45. Thus firms scoring more than 0.55 and above, were termed as highly efficient, firms with scores ranging between 0.35 and 0.54 were classified as moderately efficient firms and insurance firms with less than 0.35 efficiency score were termed as less efficient. In very year, there were 18 insurance firms operating in India, 6 insurance firms were categorized as highly efficient, 2 were noted as moderately efficient and 10 insurance firms fell into less efficient category (see Table 5.25 on preceding page 175).

In terminal year 2012-13 the average of efficiency score stood at 0.79. Thus firms having score above 0.89 and above were termed as highly efficient, firms with scores ranging between 0.69 to 0.88 were moderately efficient. On the other hand, firms with efficiency score below 0.69 were less efficient in the year under consideration. In very year, there were 24 insurance firms operating in India, 10 insurance firms were classified as highly efficient, 6 as moderately efficient and 8 as less efficient (see Table 5.25 on preceding page 175).

LIC is the only insurance firm which remained in highly efficient category throughout the period under review. On the other hand ING Life had been less efficient category throughout the analysis of three years. TATA AIA was less efficient for 2001-02 and 2007-08 while in 2012-13, it improved its efficiency and entered into highly efficient category. Other insurance firms such as - Bajaj Allianz, Birla Sunlife, HDFC Standard, ICICI Prudential, PNB Metlife and Reliance were in highly efficient category in 2001-02 but in 2007-08 they fell into less efficient category. In 2012-13, Bajaj Allianz, HDFC Standard and ICICI Prudential improved their efficiency scores and were termed as highly efficient while Birla Sunlife jumped up into moderately efficient category. On the other hand, Reliance and PNB Metlife also remained in less efficient category in the year 2012-13 (Table 5.26 below).

Table 5.26: Classification of Insurance firms on Account of their BCC Efficiency Scores in 2001-02, 2007-08 and 2012-13

Nature of Efficiency	2001-02	2007-08	2012-13
Highly Efficient	Bajaj Allianz Birla Sunlife HDFC Standard ICICI Prudential PNB Metlife Reliance SBI Life LIC	Bharti AXA Future Generali IDBI Federal Max Life Sahara LIC	Bajaj Allianz Canara HSBC Edelweiss Tokio HDFC Standard ICICI Prudential India First Sahara SBI Life Tata AIA LIC
Moderate Efficient	--	SBI Life Shriram Life	Aegon Religare Birla Sunlife DLF Pramerica Kotak Mahindra Max Life Star Union Dai Chi
Less Efficient	ING Life Kotak Mahindra Max Life Tata AIA	AVIVA Bajaj Allianz Birla Sunlife HDFC Standard ICICI Prudential ING Life Kotak Mahindra PNB Metlife Reliance Tata AIA	AVIVA Bharti AXA Future Generali IDBI Federal ING Life PNB Metlife Reliance Shriram Life

The analysis also reveals that in year 2001-02 firms such as LIC, SBI Life and HDFC Standard were found to efficient by both the models i.e. BCC and CCR. Firms had shown fluctuations in terms of being 100 percent efficient over the years. In nutshell, LIC had been efficient over the years (see Table 5.27 on next page). Similar findings have been confirmed by Dutta and Sengupta[23].

23. Dutta and Sengupta, *op.cit.,* p 423.

Table 5.27: Fully Efficient Insurance Firms as per BCC and CCR Models

Years	BCC Efficient insurance Firms	CCR Efficient insurance firms
2001-02	Bajaj Allianz, Birla Sunlife, HDFC Standard, ICICI Prudential, PNB Metlife, Reliance, SBI Life and LIC	HDFC Standard, SBI Life and LIC
2002-03	AVIVA, HDFC Standard, ICICI Prudential, PNB Metlife, Reliance, SBI Life and LIC	Aviva Life, HDFC Standard, ICICI Prudential, SBI Life and LIC
2003-04	AVIVA, Birla Sunlife, HDFC Standard, ICICI Prudential, Kotak Mahindra, Max Life, PNB Metlife, Reliance, SBI Life and LIC	Birla Sunlife, HDFC Standard, ICICI Prudential, Reliance, SBI Life and LIC
2004-05	Birla Sunlife, HDFC Standard, ICICI Prudential, ING Life, Kotak Mahindra, Reliance, Sahara, SBI Life and LIC	Sahara, SBI Life and LIC
2005-06	AVIVA, HDFC Standard, ICICI Prudential, Reliance, Sahara, Shriram Life and LIC	HDFC Standard ICICI Prudential Reliance Sahara Shriram Life LIC
2006-07	Bajaj Allianz, Bharti AXA, Sahara, SBI Life, Shriram Life and LIC	Bharti AXA, Sahara, SBI Life, Shriram Life and LIC
2007-08	Bharti AXA Future Generali IDBI Federal Max Life and LIC	Future Generali, IDBI Federal and Max Life
2008-09	Bajaj Allianz, Canara HSBC, DLF Pramerica, IDBI Federal, Reliance, Sahara, SBI Life, Star Union Dai Chi, Tata AIA and LIC	Canara HSBC, DLF Pramerica, Edelweiss Tokio, IDBI Federal, India First, SBI Life, Star Union Dai Chi and LIC
2009-10	Canara HSBC, DLF Pramerica, ICICI Prudential, IDBI Federal, India First, Sahara, SBI Life, Star Union Dai Chi, Tata AIA and LIC	DLF Pramerica,ICICI Prudential,IDBI Federal,India First,SBI Life,Star Union Dai Chi and LIC
2010-11	Canara HSBC DLF Pramerica ICICI Prudential India First PNB Metlife Sahara SBI Life Star Union Dai Chi and LIC	Canara HSBC, ICICI Prudential, India First, SBI Life and Star Union Dai Chi
2011-12	Canara HSBC, Edelweiss Tokio, HDFC Standard, India First, Sahara, SBI Life, Star Union Dai Chi and LIC	Edelweiss Tokio, India First, SBI Life, Star Union Dai Chi and LIC
2012-13	Bajaj Allianz, Canara HSBC, Edelweiss Tokio, HDFC Standard, India First, Sahara, SBI Life, Tata AIA and LIC	Edelweiss Tokio, India First and LIC

An analysis of the insurance firms was done to identify the firms which had been inefficient by BCC and CCR models. It was found that in year 2001-02, ING Life, Kotak Mahindra, max Life and TATA AIA were found to inefficient by both the models.

Although there are various firms proved to be inefficient on yearly basis, but no firm had been consistently inefficient throughout the study (see Table 5.28 below).

Table 5.28: Inefficient Insurance Firms as per BCC and CCR Models

Years	BCC Inefficient insurance Firms	CCR Inefficient insurance firms
2001-02	ING Life, Kotak Mahindra, Max Life, Tata AIA	ING Life, Kotak Mahindra, Max Life, PNB Metlife, Reliance, Tata AIA
2002-03	Kotak Mahindra, Max Life, Tata AIA	Kotak Mahindra, Max Life, PNB Metlife, Reliance, Tata AIA
2003-04	Bajaj Allianz, Tata AIA	Bajaj Allianz, ING Life, PNB Metlife, Tata AIA
2004-05	AVIVA, Max Life, PNB Metlife, Tata AIA	AVIVA, HDFC Standard, ING Life, Max Life, PNB Metlife, Tata AIA
2005-06	Bajaj Allianz, ING Life,Max Life,Tata AIA	Bajaj Allianz, ING Life, Max Life, PNB Metlife, Tata AIA
2006-07	Birla Sunlife, ICICI Prudential	AVIVA, Bajaj Allianz, ICICI Prudential, Max Life, PNB Metlife
2007-08	AVIVA, Bajaj Allianz, Birla Sunlife, HDFC Standard, ICICI Prudential, ING Life, Kotak Mahindra, PNB Metlife,Reliance, Tata AIA	AVIVA, Bajaj Allianz, Birla Sunlife, HDFC Standard, ICICI Prudential, ING Life, Kotak Mahindra, PNB Metlife, Reliance, Sahara, Tata AIA
2008-09	Aegon Religare, Bharti AXA, Birla Sunlife, Future Generali, Kotak Mahindra, PNB Metlife	Aegon Religare, Bharti AXA, Future Generali, HDFC Standard, Kotak Mahindra, Max Life, PNB Metlife, Tata AIA
2009-10	Aegon Religare, Bharti AXA, Birla Sunlife, Future Generali, Max Life, Reliance, Shriram Life	Aegon Religare, Bharti AXA, Future Generali, Max Life, PNB Metlife, Shriram Life
2010-11	AVIVA, Bajaj Allianz, Bharti AXA, Birla Sunlife, Future Generali, IDBI Federal, ING Life, Reliance	Birla Sunlife, Future Generali, IDBI Federal, ING Life, Max Life, Reliance, Sahara, Tata AIA
2011-12	Aegon Religare, Bharti AXA, Birla Sunlife, Future Generali, IDBI Federal, ING Life, PNB Metlife, Reliance, Shriram Life	Aegon Religare, AVIVA, Birla Sunlife Future Generali, IDBI Federal, ING Life, Max Life, PNB Metlife, Reliance, Sahara, Shriram Life
2012-13	AVIVA, Bharti AXA, Future Generali, IDBI Federal, ING Life, PNB Metlife, Reliance, Shriram Life	Aegon Religare, Bharti AXA, Future Generali, IDBI Federal, ING Life, Max Life, PNB Metlife, Reliance, Sahara, Shriram Life

5.19 Matrix Summing Up The Testing of The Hypothesis 2

Matrix 5.2: Testing of Hypothesis 2- "IRDAI has promoted efficiency in conduct of insurance business by making insurance firms to minimize inputs"

Hypothesis	Sources of Data	Analysis	Status of Hypothesis Accepted
IRDAI has promoted efficiency in conduct of insurance business by making insurance firms to minimize inputs	Secondary data	Analysis of results revealed that in year 2001-02, out of 13 insurance firms 8 were found to efficient by BCC model and 3 by CCR Model. In year 2012-13, out of 24 insurance firms, 9 were found efficient by BCC model and 3 by CR model. Only one life insurance firm, namely - LIC has been proved to be efficient by both the models. Also during all these years, insurance firms had been found to be inefficient by both the models.	NO

Thus, on the basis of analysis of the **Hypothesis 2**: "IRDAI has promoted efficiency in conduct of insurance business by making insurance firms to minimize inputs" **stands rejected**.

III
Assessment of IRDAI in Spreading Life Insurance In Rural Sector

Life insurance is skewed in rural areas vis-à-vis urban areas and general insurance is bought because of compulsions by authorities and laws such as traffic laws for vehicle insurance etc. But growth of life insurance in rural sector is low and rural market is still untapped[24].

Post liberalization of insurance sector, spread of insurance in rural sector is governed by regulation, namely, Insurance Regulatory and Development Authority (Obligations of Insurers to Rural and Social sectors) Regulations, 2000. The Regulation aims at increasing the outreach of insurance in rural sector. Over the years with maturity of insurance market it has issued various notifications in consequent to above mentioned regulation for increasing the percentage of policies to be underwritten in rural sector.

The hypothesis tested in this regard is, "IRDAI has been effective in spreading life insurance in rural sector by fixing quota for rural sector".

In 2000, IRDAI issued notification dated 14 July, vide F.No. IRDA/Reg/7/2000 which defines rural sector as a place having population less than 5000 and population

24. Aditya Kumar Gupta (2014), "Life Insurance Market: The Rural India Connect" *Management Insight*, Volume. X, Number 1, PP. 81-85.

density of less than 400 persons per square kilometer and lastly at least 75 percent of the male working population should be engaged in agricultural activities. Through this notification, IRDAI also made obligatory on the part of insurers to have certain percentage of insurance from rural sector. For Life insurer the percentage is 5 % in the first financial year, 7% in the second financial year; 10% in the third financial year; 12% in the fourth financial year; 15% in the fifth financial year of total policies written direct in that year.

For the existing insurers IRDAI stipulated that the percentage of policies issued in the rural sector for the year shall not fall below the quantum of insurance business done in the counting year ended 31 March 2000. It is also enlisted that in case the first financial year of an insurer is less than 12 months then the proportionate percentage of policies shall be underwritten in rural sector.

Since data is not available for the year 2000-01, verification of the above cannot be done. It is noteworthy to mention here that the data pertaining to rural policies was obtained through Right to Information Act.

For the year 2001-02 to 2005-06, the data of different insurers regarding individual new business in terms of number of policies underwritten and rural policies was not provided through Right to Information Act. Thus data for these years is only in the form of total number individual new policies of whole life insurance sector vis-à-vis data for whole private players and Life Insurance Corporation (Public sector entity). The comparison has been made on the basis of available data and also the Annual Reports of IRDAI have been relied upon. But the data for the subsequent years from 2006-07 to 2012-13, regarding rural policies had been provided by IRDAI through RTI. Data for total individual new business of various insurers has been retrieved from Annual Reports of IRDAI. Thus for these years comparison will be done on the basis of available data and Annual Reports of IRDAI.

5.20 Analysis of Rural Sector Spread of Insurance Firms

As per IRDAI Annual Report for the 2001-02 out of 11 insurers 10 were able to meet the rural sector obligations of 5% percent. One private insurance firm had marginal deficiency in meeting the stipulated target. In case of LIC, it was unable to meet the target of existing insurers i.e. percentage of policies issued in the rural sector for the year should not fall below the quantum of insurance business done in the accounting year ending on 31 March 2002[25].

In 2002, IRDAI issued regulation vide notification dated 16 October, 2002, vide F.No.IRDA/Reg/10/2002 explaining worker in agricultural pursuits as working as cultivators, laborers, and working in livestock, forestry, fishery, hunting and plantations, orchards and allied activities. The obligations specified for life insurers for rural sector were 7% in the first financial year, 9% in the second financial year; 12% in the third financial year; 14% in the fourth financial year; 16% in the fifth financial year of total policies written direct in that year. It was also enlisted that in case the first financial year of an insurer is less than 12 months then the proportionate

25. Insurance Regulatory Development Authority (2002), Annual Report 2001-02, October, Hyderabad, p.81.

percentage of policies shall be underwritten in rural sector. This amendment came into effect from the year from the financial year 2002-03.

In year 2002-03, total 253.71 lakh individual new policies were issued and out of which 4654338 (18.04 percent) were underwritten in rural sector. LIC issued total 245.46 lakh individual new policies and 4546148 (18.52 percent) were underwritten in rural sector. On the other hand, private sector as a whole issued 8.25 lakh individual new policies out of which 108190 (13.11 percent) were specifically issued for rural sector (Table 5.29). As per IRDAI Annual report 2002-03, barring one private insurer all the life insurers who had entered the market in last three years complied with the specified norms of 12 percent. This private insurer had a shortfall in meeting the rural sector obligation on a proportionate basis as it commenced its operations in 2002, October[26].

In year 2003-04, around 286.27 lakh individual new policies were underwritten out of which 6393638 (16.25 percent) were in rural sector. LIC underwrote 269.68 lakh new policies and 4546148 (16.85 percent) specifically for rural sector (Table 5.29). While private insurers together underwrote 16.59 lakh individual new policies out of which 108190 (6.52 percent) were undertaken in rural sector. As per IRDAI Annual Report 2003-04 all the life insurers complied with the rural sector norms[27].

In year 2004-05, 262.11 lakh individual new policies were underwritten out of which 5908301 policies (22.54 percent) were in rural sector. LIC underwrote 239.78 lakh individual new policies and 5484514policies (22.87 percent) specifically for rural sector. Private insurers underwrote 22.33 lakh policies out of which 423787 policies (18.97 percent) pertain to rural sector (Table 5.29). As per IRDAI Annual report 2004-05 all the life insurers who had commenced operations in the last five years were able to meet the rural sector obligations[28].

In year 2005-06, 354.62 lakh total individual new life insurance policies were underwritten out of which 8309902 policies (23.43 percent) were from rural sector. LIC underwrote 315.91 lakh individual new policies and 7471202 policies (23.64 percent) were from rural sector. All the private players underwrote 38.71 lakh individual new policies out of 838700 policies (21.62 percent) were from rural sector (Table 5.29). As per IRDAI Annual Report 2005-06 all the life insurers complied with rural sector obligations[29].

Table 5.29: Number of Total Rural Policies of Life Insurers

	Rural Policies				
Insurer	2001-02	2002-03	2003-04	2004-05	2005-06
Aviva	--	96	13302	16763	33819

26. Insurance Regulatory Development Authority (2003), Annual Report 2002-03, October, Hyderabad, p.217.
27. Insurance Regulatory Development Authority (2004), Annual Report 2003-04, October, Hyderabad, p.40.
28. Insurance Regulatory Development Authority (2005), Annual Report 2004-05, October, Hyderabad, p.43.
29. Insurance Regulatory Development Authority (2006), Annual Report 2005-06, October, Hyderabad, p.82.

Bajaj Allianz	3874	19368	23994	48019	133031
Birla Sunlife	2005	10422	25893	48128	63934
HDFC Standard	1365	15352	39075	57773	86481
ICICI Prudential	6940	29376	64763	101267	156433
ING Life	658	3883	12071	16940	21449
Kotak Mahindra	770	5170	7129	9978	29047
MAX Life	5551	8211	24110	40627	151730
PNB Metlife	84	2916	6826	7314	17294
Reliance	72	1510	6086	5698	13235
Sahara	--	--	--	2793	6540
SBILife	148	2749	19195	27684	55555
ShriramLife	--	--	--	--	8990
TataAIA	3894	9137	23034	40803	61162
Private Sector Total	25361	108190	265478	423787	838700
LIC	4305835	4546148	6128160	5484514	7471202
Grand Total	4331196	4654338	6393638	5908301	8309902

Source: Information Retrieved through Right to Information Act from Insurance Regulatory and Development Authority of India.

In 2005, IRDAI issued regulation vide notification dated 26 December 2005, vide F.No.IRDA/Reg/4/2005/37. This regulations added regulation 3A i.e. the obligation for life insurer in the sixth financial year shall be 18 % of the total policies written directly in that year. The other regulations specifying the obligations for life insurers for rural sector were unaltered. Thus, the previous regulations were7% in the first financial year, 9% in the second financial year; 12% in the third financial year; 14% in the fourth financial year; 16% in the fifth financial year of total policies written direct in that year. It is also enlisted that in case the first financial year of a insurer is less than 12 months then the proportionate percentage of policies shall be underwritten in rural sector.

In year 2006-07 total 26127798 individual new policies were underwritten out of which 10524111 (22.81 percent) were from rural sector. All the sixteen life insurance firms complied with the norms specified by the IRDAI for the year[30]. Shriram Life in second financial year of its operation underwrote maximum 40.87 percent policies from rural areas followed by Sahara Life and others. The insurers such as Bajaj Allianz Life, LIC, Birla Sun Life, Exide Life, HDFC Standard Life ICICI Prudential, SBI Life and ING underwrote more than 20 percent of their new individual policies from rural areas. Bharti Axa commenced operations around 8 months earlier and was able to meet the target of proportionate policies from the total policies from rural sector (Table 5.30).

IRDAI further amended the obligations of life insurers for rural sector on 3 January 2008 vide F.No.IRDA/Reg./1/42/2008. It prescribed the obligations of life insurers for seventh financial year and thereafter. On 25 January, 2008, it introduced minor amendments to the above notification vide F.No. IRDA/Reg./2/43/2008.

30. Insurance Regulatory Development Authority (2007), Annual Report 2006-07, October, Hyderabad, p.38.

Thus, the new obligations for rural sector for life insurers are 18 percent of the new policies in the seventh financial year; 19 percent of the new policies in eighth and ninth financial years; 20 percent of the new policies in the tenth financial year, of the total policies written direct in that year. The obligations for the tenth financial years i.e. 20 percent of the individual new policies shall be applicable in the future financial years. Along with these for the existing insurers i.e. LIC, the rural sector obligations for 2007-08 are 24 percent of the individual new policies and 25 percent of the individual new policies for 2008-09 and 2009-10 written direct in that year. Further the amendment also elaborated that if an insurer commences operations in the second half of the financial year then rural sector obligations were not applicable to it for the said financial year and next financial year shall be counted as first financial year and specified regulations of the first financial year (7 percent of the individual new policies) shall be applicable. If insurer commences operations in the first half of the financial year then applicable obligation for the first financial year shall be 50 percent of the obligations specified in the regulation.

For the year 2007-08, all the eighteen life insurers fulfilled their rural sector obligations[31]. Shriram Life in third financial year of its commencement registered maximum rural policies followed by Sahara life. LIC underwrote 24.05 percent rural policies against the target of 24 percent. Other insurers, namely, Tata AIG Life, SBI Life, Kotak Mahindra, Bajaj Allianz, HDFC Standard, ICICI Prudential, Birla Sunlife and Max Life underwrote more than 20 percent policies from the rural sector. Bharti Axa being in second financial year of its commencement registered 9.29 percent policies from the rural sector against the target of 9 percent individual new policies. Future Generali and IDBI Life commenced operations in second half of the financial years they may be exempted from the rural sector obligations for the said financial year (Table 5.30).

In the year 2008-09, total 50904871 individual new policies were underwritten out of which 16631429 (32.67 percent) policies were from rural sector. All the 22 life insurers except HDFC Standard Life and LIC complied with rural sector norms[32]. HDFC Standard issued 11.6 percent individual new policies against the mandate of 19 percent policies in ninth financial year. LIC underwrote 24.29 percent policies against the mandate of 25 percent policies for the said financial year. All the insurers in ninth year of their commencement underwrote more than 19 percent of the policies. Future Generali Life in second year of its commencement underwrote 10.34 percent rural policies against the mandate of 9 percent. Canara HSBC commenced operations in the first half of the financial year underwrote 8.62 percent rural policies against the prescribed norm of 3.5 percent (50 percent of the first year obligations i.e. 7 percent). Similarly IDBI Federal, DLF PRAMERICA and Ageon Religare commenced operations in first half of the financial year and underwrote 8.42 percent, 5.43 percent and 3.83 percent rural policies respectively against the specification of 3.5 percent of the total individual new policies (Table 5.30).

31. Insurance Regulatory Development Authority (2008), Annual Report 2007-08, October, Hyderabad, p.49.
32. Insurance Regulatory Development Authority (2009), Annual Report 2008-09, October, Hyderabad, pp. 35-36.

Table 5.30: Number of Total Policies, Rural Policies and Percent of Rural Policies

Insurer	2006-07			2007-08			2008-09		
	Total Policies	Rural Policies	% of Rural Policies	Total Policies	Rural Policies	% of Rural Policies	Total Policies	Rural Policies	% of Rural Policies
Aegon Religare	--	--	--	--	--	--	23585	904	3.83
Aviva	297095	57107	19.22	388342	77638	19.99	374188	78459	20.96
Bajaj Allianz	2078933	431765	20.76	3744346	961196	25.67	2589943	808387	31.21
Bharti AXA	5700	480	8.421	74074	6884	9.29	211575	25719	12.15
Birla Sunlife	426584	87695	20.55	688311	149290	21.68	1383469	4428795	20.12
Canara HSBC	--	--	--	--	--	--	35729	3080	8.62
DLF Pramerica	--	--	--	--	--	--	2777	151	5.43
Future Generali	--	--	--	800	23	2.87	103660	10721	10.34
HDFC Standard	522982	124337	23.77	948612	217583	22.93	1074015	124629	11.60
ICICI Prudential	1959575	434005	22.14	2913110	637867	21.89	2637675	774725	29.37
IDBI Federal	--	0	--	3158	0	0	84001	7077	8.42
ING Life	229189	46879	20.45	360069	71287	19.79	358208	74058	20.67
Kotak Mahindra	165002	30677	18.59	313490	81085	25.86	494876	103323	20.87
MAX Life	552505	104026	18.82	873331	189088	21.65	1206716	301774	25.01
PNB Metlife	119406	23133	19.37	235152	44076	18.74	328134	63412	19.32
Reliance	450683	83579	18.54	1073715	206619	19.24	2219273	487647	21.97
Sahara	41396	14136	34.14	109084	44088	40.41	110547	34471	31.18
SBI Life	565389	118262	20.91	925529	258936	27.97	937493	254787	27.17
Shriram Life	96077	39276	40.87	109129	50704	46.46	126612	68490	54.09
Star Union Dai Chi	--	--	---	--	--	--	13245	0	0
Tata AIA	408707	78368	19.17	496949	1790909	36.03	697818	266158	38.14
LIC	38208575	8850386	23.16	37589995	9043413	24.05	35891332	8714662	24.28
GRAND TOTAL	46127798	10524111	22.81	50847196	13830686	27.20	50904871	16631429	32.67

Source: Information retrieved through Right to Information Act from IRDAI and Annual Reports of IRDAI (2006-07 to 2008-09), Hyderabad.

In year 2009-10 total 5,31,95,191 individual new policies were issued out of which 1,44,25,404 policies (27.11 percent) were from rural sector. All the 23 life insurance firms complied with the rural sector norms specified by the IRDAI[33]. Shri Ram Life underwrote maximum (56.34 percent) policies in the rural sector. All the insurers in their 10th financial year commencement complied with the laid down norm of 20 percent policies from the rural sector. LIC underwrote 26.39 percent policies in the rural sector against the mandate of 25 percent. Bharti Axa life in fourth year of its commencement registered 18.13 percent rural policies against the mandate of 14 percent. Canara HSBC life, IDBI Federal and Aegon Religare in second year of their commencement underwrote 16.7 percent, 12.49 percent and 9.31 percent rural policies respectively against the specified norm of nine percent (see Table 5.31 on next page).

In year 2010-11, 4,81,06,668 individual new policies were underwritten by life insurers out of which 1,49,82,638 policies (31.14) percent pertained to rural sector. All the twenty three life insurers barring Bharti AXA complied with rural sector norms[34]. Bharti AXA in fifth year of its commencement underwrote 15.97 percent policies in the rural sector against the mandate of 16 percent. LIC underwrote 32.75 percent policies against the mandate of 25 percent for the said financial year. Insurers such as IDBI Federal, India first and Aegon Religare in third year of their commencement underwrote 15.97 percent, 13.85 percent and 13.44 percent rural policies respectively against the mandate of 12 percent. It is surprising to see that DLF PRAMERICA in third year of its commencement underwrote maximum (46.15 percent) policies in rural sector (Table 5.31).

In year 2011-12, total 4,41,60,341 individual new policies were underwritten by all the life insurers out of 1,39,83,265 (31.66 percent) policies were underwritten specifically from rural sector. All the twenty four life insurance firms complied with the rural sector norms[35]. DLF PRAMERICA underwrote maximum (53.4 percent) policies in the rural sector. All the insurers with more than 10th financial year of their commencement registered at least 20 percent policies from the rural sector (see Table 5.31 on next page).

33. Insurance Regulatory Development Authority (2010), Annual Report 2009-10, October, Hyderabad, p.35.
34. Insurance Regulatory Development Authority (2011), Annual Report 2010-11, October, Hyderabad, p.50.
35. Insurance Regulatory Development Authority (2012), *op.cit.*, pp. 64-65.

Table 5.31: Number of Total Policies, Rural Policies and Percent of Rural Policies

Insurer	2009-10	2010-11	2011-12						
	Total Policies	Rural Policies	% of Rural Policies	Total Policies	Rural Policies	% of Rural Policies	Total Policies	Rural Policies	% of Rural Policies
Aegon Religare	49848	4643	9.31	93183	12121	13.01	79393	11242	14.15
Aviva	239543	53809	22.46	191003	45663	23.90	180014	44758	24.86
Bajaj Allianz	2229489	683450	30.65	1542005	330963	21.46	1052336	263505	25.04
Bharti AXA	178750	32408	18.13	168307	26890	15.97	98284	20955	21.32
Birla Sunlife	1770721	704456	39.78	1004093	316954	31.56	847278	256226	30.24
Canara HSBC	99856	16677	16.70	111298	25701	23.09	71633	19330	26.98
DLF Pramerica	19484	7699	39.51	36890	17025	46.15	69925	37341	53.40
Edelweiss Tokio	--	-	--	--	--	---	6588	390	5.91
Future Generali	335693	81271	24.20	313954	81339	25.90	167761	44309	26.41
HDFC Standard	950260	245642	25.84	830532	167271	20.14	814726	178055	21.85
ICICI Prudential	1761227	423670	24.05	1350494	352899	26.13	1028826	331133	32.18
IDBI Federal	96764	12093	12.49	108390	15014	13.85	84714	14918	17.60
India First	--	--	--	111850	15042	13.44	114881	12745	11.09
ING Life	290755	59824	20.57	274401	57353	20.90	233800	49516	21.17
Kotak Mahindra	320173	64339	20.09	258783	52927	20.45	207525	46053	22.19
MAX Life	951840	274486	28.83	816259	229302	28.09	571485	131055	22.93
PNB Metlife	291737	71460	24.49	199211	44552	22.36	202755	45744	22.56
Reliance	2325631	706918	30.39	1902685	608981	32.01	1093624	384347	35.14
Sahara	84033	30118	35.84	69532	25169	36.19	70887	32847	46.33
SBI Life	1353231	378162	27.94	939978	212031	22.55	881550	190719	21.63
Shriram Life	139359	78525	56.34	120610	46569	38.61	130250	56144	43.10
Star Union Dai Chi	108192	26690	24.66	97730	21839	22.34	150932	31198	20.67
Tata AIA	689196	219421	31.83	553203	152154	27.50	276425	62966	22.77
LIC	38838653	10249643	26.39	37012277	12124879	32.75	35724749	11717769	32.80
Grand Total	53195191	14425404	27.11	48106668	14982638	31.14	44160341	13983265	31.66

Source: Information retrieved through Right to Information Act from IRDAI and Annual Reports of IRDAI (2009-10 to 2011-12), Hyderabad.

LIC underwrote 32.8 percent policies from the rural sector against the mandate of 25 percent. IDBI Federal and Aegon Religare in their fourth year of commencement underwrote 17.6 percent and 14.15 percent rural policies respectively against the mandate of 14 percent in the said financial year. India First in its second year of commencement registered 11.09 percent rural policies against the mandate of 9 percent. EDELWEISS TOKIO commenced its operations in the first half of the financial year was able to underwrite 5.91 percent policies from the rural sector against the mandate of fifty percent (3.5 percent) policies from rural sector (Table 5.32).

Table 5.32: Number of Total Policies, Rural Policies and Percent of Rural Policies

Insurer	2012-13		
	Total Policies	Rural Policies	% of Rural Policies
Aegon Religare	64,303	11,445	17.79
Aviva	1,40,073	36,641	26.15
Bajaj Allianz	7,30,554	2,07,353	28.38
Bharti AXA	99,622	19,857	19.93
Birla Sunlife	5,58,602	1,23,147	22.04
Canara HSBC	73,343	21,523	29.34
DLF Pramerica	1,02,384	69,111	67.50
Edelweiss Tokio	22,955	2,499	10.88
Future Generali	1,13,182	35,479	31.34
HDFC Standard	10,25,739	2,28,889	22.31
ICICI Prudential	9,59,958	3,05,909	31.86
IDBI Federal	1,21,950	23,497	19.26
India First	1,23,846	22,784	18.39
ING Life	2,04,602	43,326	21.17
Kotak Mahindra	1,69,479	36,091	21.29
MAX Life	5,04,250	1,05,583	20.93
PNB Metlife	2,11,856	50,050	23.62
Reliance	7,62,532	2,66,994	35.01
Sahara	64,848	27,028	41.67
SBI Life	8,88,670	2,07,051	23.29
ShriramLife	1,53,215	76,555	49.96
Star Union Dai Chi	1,52,527	31,385	20.57
Tata AIA	1,50,683	35,849	23.79
LIC	3,67,55,451	93,48,789	25.43
GRAND TOTAL	4,41,54,624	1,13,36,835	25.67

Source: Information retrieved through Right to Information Act from IRDAI and Annual Report of IRDAI (2012-13), Hyderabad.

In year 2012-13, total 4,41,54,624 individual new policies were underwritten by life insurers out of which 1,13,36,835 (25.67 percent) were from rural sector. All the twenty four life insurance firms complied with the norms specified by the IRDAI for the rural sector[36]. LIC underwrote 25.43 percent rural policies against the mandate of 25 percent. All the insurers with more than eleven years in the industry complied

36. Insurance Regulatory Development Authority (2013), *op.cit.*,pp. 60-61.

with the norm of 20 percent individual policies from the rural sector. Bharti AXA in seventh year of its commencement registered 19.93 percent rural policies against the mandate of 19 percent. IDBI Federal and Aegon Religare in fifth year of their commencement underwrote 19.26 percent and 17.79 percent rural policies against the mandate of 16 percent. India First in third year of its commencement underwrote 18.39 percent rural policies against the mandate of 12 percent. While EDELWEISS TOKIO in second year of its operation undertook 10.88 percent rural policies against the specified norm of 9 percent (Table 5.32).

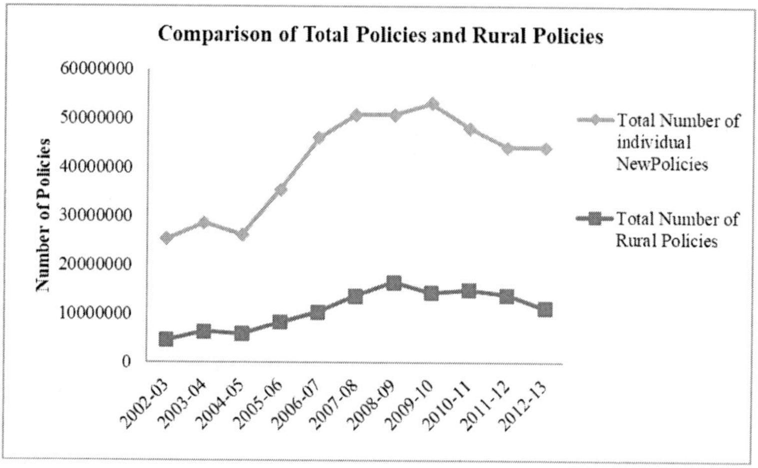

Figure 5.9

Table 5.33: Yearly Status of Life Insurance Defaulters for Rural Sector Obligations of the IRDAI

Year	Name of the Insurer
2001-02	One Private Insurer defaulted (name unknown) and Life Insurance Corporation
2002-03	One Private Insurer defaulted (name unknown)
2003-04	No Insurer Defaulted
2004-05	No Insurer Defaulted
2005-06	No Insurer Defaulted
2006-07	No Insurer Defaulted
2007-08	No Insurer Defaulted
2008-09	HDFC Standard Life and Life Insurance Corporation Defaulted
2009-10	No Insurer Defaulted
2010-11	Bharti AXA Defaulted

2011-12	No Insurer Defaulted
2012-13	No Insurer Defaulted

From the above table, it is all evident that barring few exception such as in years 2001-02 by one private insurer and LIC, in 2002-03 one private player, in 2008-09 HDFC Standard Life and LIC; and finally in 2010-11 Bharti AXA all other insurers complied with rural sector obligations of IRDAI (see Table 5.33 above).

5.21 Perception of Managerial Functionaries of the Insurance Companies and Irdai Official

Majority of the functionaries of the insurance firms were of the view that IRDAI should play more active role on spreading life insurance business in rural sector. The functionaries pointed out that due to lower education levels of the people in rural areas it is difficult to sell insurance policies in rural sector. Products such as ULIPs sometimes are difficult for rural people to comprehend and after selling the policy they feel cheated. Moreover rural people assume insurance as an instrument of investment rather than for risk coverage. IRDAI should proactively organize insurance awareness campaigns in rural areas thereby increasing financial literacy of the masses.

For first five years IRDAI granted gestation period for insurers so that they may settle down in business atmosphere and exempted firms from penalties. But after this period insurers continued violating minimum prescribed norms and IRDAI has only punished nine insurers in this regard. In case of violations of rural and social sector obligations, IRDAI can impose financial penalty from Rs 5 to 25 lakh, imprisonment and cancellation of registration. But IRDAI has only slapped a fine of Rs 5 lakh, irrespective of the fact whether it is the social or the rural target that insurers have not realized and no criminal proceedings have been initiated against the defaulters[37]. The IRDAI officials during telephonic interview stated that IRDAI has penalized the insurance firms for not complying with rural sector norms.

37. Neha Shukla (2012), "IRDA Soft on Insurance Companies Flouting Norms" *TNN*, 12 June.

5.22 Matrix Summing Up The Testing Of Hypothesis 3

Matrix 5.3: Testing of Hypothesis 3- "IRDAI has been effective in spreading life insurance in rural sector by fixing quota for rural sector."

Hypothesis	Sources of Data	Analysis	Status Hypothesis Accepted
IRDAI has been effective in spreading life insurance in rural sector by fixing quota for rural sector	Secondary data and primary data	Barring for the years 2001-02, 2002-03, 2008-09 and 2010-11 all the insurers obliged with the rural sector norms specified by the IRDAI. Managerial functionaries of the insurance firms revealed that due to lack of financial literacy in rural areas it is difficult to cater insurance products in rural markets. Rural people think insurance an instrument of investment rather than risk diversification. IRDAI officials stated that the Authority has penalized insurance firms for not complying with rural sector norms.	Yes

Thus, on the basis of above analysis, the **Hypothesis 3**: "IRDAI has been effective in spreading life insurance in rural sector by fixing quota for rural sector", **stands validated.**

IV
EVALUATION OF IRDAI IN REGULATING INVESTMENT OF FUNDS OF LIFE INSURERS

Investment income is a key determinant in the calculation of premium rates for any insurance company under the various insurance policies/schemes and for declaration of bonuses by life insurers. Therefore, insurance companies essentially invest these funds judiciously with the combined objectives of liquidity, maximization of yield and safety. An investment policy has to be submitted to the Authority by an insurer before the start of an accounting year. Since the insurance companies keep the policy-holders money in their fiduciary capacity, they are also required to maintain a minimum level of solvency to meet the reasonable expectations of the policy-holders.

Generally, there are two regulatory models, namely, Prescriptive Model and Prudent- Man Model governing investments of insurance companies. In Prescriptive Model the asset allocation decisions of these institutional investors are dictated by a mandated investment pattern. This model is followed in countries like India, Canada, Italy, Japan and South Korea. As per Prudent-Man Model there is no mandated investment pattern, but "eligible assets" and" admissibility limits" must back the prescribed minimum solvency related to eligible assets. Countries such as US, UK, France and Spain follows this model.

Moreover, Rakesh Mohan committee also highlighted that in order to meet the fund deficit for infrastructure building within the country, funds of insurance sector should be tapped. IRDAI has also instructed all the insurers to build in-house capacities for investment of funds and discontinue outsourcing of funds by 31st December, 2004. Insurers shall form Investment Committee consisting of two non executive directors, appointed actuary, chief investment officer, etc. of the insurer to frame Investment Policy on an annual basis and review it periodically. IRDAI has also initiated steps towards investment audit on periodic basis with a view to monitor the investment decisions of the insurers, compliance with the regulations, prudent investment of the funds and adequate provisioning on regular basis. The inspection team for the purpose includes chartered accountant maintained by the Authority and an officer of the Authority.

The hypothesis tested in this regard is, "IRDAI has been effective in regulating investment of funds by insurance companies by stipulating the percentages of investments in Government Securities, infrastructure and Approved Investments and Other Investments".

5.23 Analysis of Investment Pattern of Insurance Firms

For regulating the funds of insurance firms, IRDAI has specified the pattern of investment to be followed by insurance companies. For the year 2000-01 IRDAI mandated that investments in government securities should be 25 percent and approved securities including government securities not less than 50 percent. Approved investments as specified in Schedule I includes

(a) infrastructure and social sector not less than 15 percent,

(b) Others to be governed by exposure/prudential norms (specified in Regulation 5) not exceeding 20 percent; and

other than in approved investments to be governed by exposure/prudential norms specified in Regulation 5 Not exceeding 15 percent out of the total investment fund.

In year 2000-01, total life fund stood at Rs. 1,94,00,959.55 lakhs and almost all the insurers complied with investment pattern specified for Government securities. Three insurers, namely, Birla Sunlife, ICICI, Max life, and LIC did not comply with the standards of IRDAI set up for infrastructure and social sector investments. Kotak Mahindra, Tata AIA and LIC did not complied with specifications of not exceeding 20 percent for approved investments and all insurers complied with specifications of other than approved investments (Table 5.34).

Table 5.34: Pattern of Investments of Life Insurers (2000-01)
(Rupees in Lakhs)

Insurer	Government Securities	Government and other approved Securities	Infra-structure Investments/ Social Sector	Approved investments)	Other than approved investments	Total
Birla Sunlife	3660.91 (35.08)	3804.45 (36.45)	1522.09 (14.58)	991.66 (9.50)	455.62 (4.36)	10434.73
HDFC Standard	10236.13 (65.48)	0 (0)	2641.97 (16.90)	2753.42 (17.61)	0 (0)	15631.52
ICICI Prudential	8801.28 (70.59)	959.02 (7.69)	1866.34 (14.97)	840.39 (6.74)	0 (0)	12467.03
Kotak Mahindra	9237.11 (60.66)	0 (0)	2466.29 (16.19)	3288.74 (21.60)	233.17 (1.53)	15225.31
MAX Life	1806.81 (24.99)	3920.45 (54.24)	1000 (13.83)	500 (6.91)	0 (0)	7227.26
Tata AIA	5820.51 (49.85)	0 (0)	0 (0)	5854.19 (50.14)	0 (0)	11674.70
LIC	4711705.00 (24.37)	5243711.00 (27.12)	2479189.00 (12.82)	5036000.00 (26.05)	1857694.00 (9.61)	19328299.00
Total	4751267.75 (24.48)	5252394.92 (27.07)	2488685.69 (12.82)	5050228.40 (26.03)	1858382.79 (9.57)	19400959.55

Source: Insurance Regulatory and Development Authority of India (2001), Annual Report 2000-01, Hyderabad

Note: Figures in the parenthesis are percentages

For the year 2001-02, IRDAI mandated that investments in government securities should be 25 percent; approved securities including government securities not less than 50 percent; approved investments as specified in Schedule I includes

(a) infrastructure and social sector not less than 15 percent, (b) others to be governed by exposure/prudential norms (specified in Regulation 5) not exceeding 20 percent; and other than in approved investments to be governed by exposure/ prudential norms specified in Regulation 5 Not exceeding 15 percent out of the total investment fund.

In year 2001-02, total life insurance fund stood at Rs. 2,46,868.56 crore whereas in previous year it was Rs. 1,94,009.59 crore, thus registering an increase of 27.24 percent from the preceding year. All the insurers adhered to the patterns set up for government securities for the year under review. Three insurers, namely, Birla Sunlife, PNB Metlife and LIC were not able to meet the norms set up for investments in infrastructure and social sector whereas seven insurance companies did not comply with norms set up for approved investments of not exceeding 20 percent. All insurers met the norm established for other than approved investments (Table 5.35).

Table 5.35: Pattern of Investments of Life Insurers (2001-02)
(Rupees in Crore)

Insurer	Central Government Securities	State Government Securities and other Guaranteed securities	Infra-structure Investments/	Approved investments)	Other than approved investments	Total
Bajaj Allianz	73.45 (53.74)	73.45 (53.74)	24.44 (17.88)	38.51 (28.17)	0.26 (0.19)	136.66
Birla Sunlife	42.48 (37.02)	61.57 (53.66)	15.18 (13.23)	32.72 (28.52)	5.26 (4.58)	114.72
HDFC Standard	86.43 (60.77)	86.43 (60.77)	32.12 (22.58)	23.67 (16.64)	9.18 (6.45)	142.22
ICICI Prudential	117.94 (58.87)	117.94 (58.87)	32.55 (16.24)	35.72 (17.83)	14.10 (7.03)	200.31
ING Life	42.98 (90.75)	47.98 (59.66)	14.99 (18.64)	17.44 (21.68)	--	80.41
Kotak Mahindra	59.82 (41.80)	73.71 (51.50)	23.57 (16.46)	45.83 (32.02)	12.64 (8.83)	143.11
MAX Life	42.19 (25)	106.93 (63.36)	27.17 (16.09)	27.67 (16.39)	7 (4.14)	168.76
PNB Metlife	57.59 (55.38)	57.59 (55.38)	15.23 (14.64)	15.66 (15.06)	15.50 (14.90)	103.98
Reliance	--	--	--	119.75 (100)	--	119.75
SBI Life	76.32 (58.11)	76.32 (58.11)	26.93 (20.50)	12.38 (9.426)	15.70 (11.95)	131.33
Tata AIA	74.86 (53.62)	74.86 (53.62)	29.98 (21.47)	34.76 (24.90)	--	139.59
LIC	128139.04 (52.21)	131400.71 (53.54)	20498.72 (8.35)	77046.29 (31.39)	16442.00 (6.70)	245387.72
Total	128813.10 (52.17)	132177.48 (53.54)	20740.87 (8.401)	77450.38 (31.37)	16521.65 (6.69)	246868.56

Source: Insurance Regulatory and Development Authority of India (2002), Annual Report 2001-02, Hyderabad

Note: Figures in the parenthesis are percentages

For the year 2002-03, IRDAI mandated that investments in government securities should be 25 percent; approved securities including government securities not less than 50 percent; approved investments as specified in Schedule I includes

(a) infrastructure and social sector not less than 15 percent,

(b) others to be governed by exposure/ prudential norms (specified in Regulation 5) not exceeding 35 percent;

(investments other than approved investments not exceeding 15 percent out of the total investment fund).

In year 2002-03, life insurance fund decreased to Rs. 2,29,648.54 crore from Rs. 2,46,868.56 crore in 2001-02, showing a decrease of 7.49 percent from the preceding year. All the insurers adhered to the norms set up for government securities. Two insurers, namely LIC and ICICI did not meet the terms for infrastructure and social sector investments. All life insurers were able to meet the requirements for investments subject to exposure norms and investment for other than approved investments specified by IRDAI (Table 5.36).

Table 5.36: Pattern of Investments of Life Insurers (2002-03)
(Rupees in Crore)

Insurer	Central Government Securities	State Government Securities (Including Central Govt. securities)	Infrastructure Investments/ Social Sector	Investments subject to exposure norms (including other than approved investments)	Other than approved investments	Total
Aviva	66.39 (57.06)	66.39 (57.06)	23.08 (19.83)	26.88 (23.10)	3.49 (2.99)	116.35
Bajaj Allianz	100.14 (52.36)	105.14 (54.98)	47.68 (24.93)	48.41 (25.31)	-0.38 (-0.198)	191.23
Birla Sunlife	31 (39.76)	50.05 (64.20)	15.14 (19.42)	12.76 (16.36)	2.98 (3.82)	77.95
HDFC Standard	133.89 (61.92)	133.89 (61.92)	39.20 (18.12)	43.12 (19.94)	9.11 (4.21)	216.22
ICICI Prudential	229.58 (54.11)	229.58 (54.11)	63.56 (14.98)	131.08 (30.89)	35.84 (8.44)	424.21
ING Life	53.80 (54.86)	58.80 (59.96)	15.25 (15.55)	24 (24.47)	0 (0)	98.05
Kotak Mahindra	78.91 (55.51)	78.91 (55.51)	26.49 (18.63)	36.73 (25.84)	18.25 (12.84)	142.13
MAX Life	38.01 (24.99)	104.10 (68.46)	27.12 (17.83)	20.83 (13.69)	5 (3.28)	152.05
PNB Metlife	57.17 (63.23)	57.17 (63.23)	15.18 (16.79)	18.06 (19.97)	7.54 (8.33)	90.41
Reliance	65.56 (69.53)	65.56 (69.53)	18.80 (19.94)	9.92 (10.52)	0 (0)	94.28
SBILife	122.18 (60.84)	122.18 (60.84)	31.29 (15.58)	47.34 (23.57)	17.96 (8.94)	200.81
TataAIA	99.33 (68.86)	99.33 (68.86)	24.93 (17.28)	19.98 (13.85)	4.39 (3.04)	144.24
LIC	122629.02 (53.85)	145914.39 (64.08)	32624.91 (14.32)	49161.30 (21.59)	6792.85 (2.98)	227700.60
Total	123468.97 (53.76)	147085.49 (64.04)	32962.63 (14.35)	39600.40 (17.24)	6897.04 (3.00)	229648.54

Source: Insurance Regulatory and Development Authority of India (2003), Annual Report 2002-03, Hyderabad.

Note: Figures in the parenthesis are percentages

For the year 2003-04, IRDAI mandated that investments in government securities should be 25 percent; approved securities including government securities not less than 50 percent; approved investments as specified in Schedule I includes (a) infrastructure and social sector not less than 15 percent, (b) others to be governed by exposure/ prudential norms (specified in Regulation 5) not exceeding 35 percent; (investments other than approved investments not exceeding 15 percent out of the total investment fund).

In 2003-04, Life insurance funds available with the industry stood at Rs. 3,07,308.91 crore as against Rs. 2,29,648.54 crore in the previous year, therefore witnessing an increase of 33.81 percent. All the insurers complied with the norms relating to central and state government securities. Except LIC and Sahara all other followed norms relating to investments in infrastructure and social sector. All life insurers were able to comply with the norms laid down for investments subject to exposure norms and other than approved investments by the IRDAI (Table 5.37).

Table 5.37: Pattern of Investments of Life Insurers (2003-04)
(Rupees in Crore)

Insurer	Central Government Securities	State Government Securities (Including Central Govt. securities)	Infra-structure Invest-ments/ Social Sector	Investments subject to exposure norms (including other than approved investments)	Other than approved invest-ments	Total
Aviva	78.99 (54.60)	78.99 (54.60)	29.65 (20.49)	36.01 (24.89)	0.19 (0.13)	144.65
Bajaj Allianz	141.37 (63.70)	141.37 (63.70)	46.27 (20.85)	34.27 (15.44)	0 (0)	221.91
Birla Sunlife	70.55 (50.25)	77.03 (54.87)	28.43 (20.25)	34.92 (24.87)	2.18 (1.55)	140.38
HDFC Standard	181.86 (59.54)	189.69 (62.10)	57.84 (18.93)	57.91 (18.96)	18.06 (5.91)	305.43
ICICI Prudential	382.25 (58.05)	382.25 (58.05)	104.58 (15.88)	171.61 (26.06)	55.00 (8.35295)	658.45
ING Life	37.68 (50.05)	37.68 (50.05)	15.68 (20.82)	21.92 (29.11)	6.44 (8.55)	75.28
Kotak Mahindra	66.78 (50.04)	66.78 (50.04)	27.69 (20.75)	38.96 (29.19)	0	133.43
MAX Life	2.17 (0.897)	168.94 (69.85)	41.36 (17.10)	31.55 (13.04)	12.27 (5.07)	241.86
PNB Metlife	69.06 (57.46)	69.06 (57.46)	25.82 (21.48)	25.31 (21.06)	11.79 (9.81)	120.18
Reliance	58.23 (59.00)	58.88 (59.66)	15.96 (16.17)	23.85 (24.16)	12.07 (12.23)	98.69
Sahara	60.19 (42.00)	115.09 (80.31)	5.73 (3.99)	22.47 (15.68)	3.60 (2.51)	143.29

SBILife	211.34 (57.45)	211.34 (57.45)	62.09 (16.87)	94.42 (25.66)	30.50 (8.29)	367.84
Tata AIA	178.78 (81.02)	178.78 (81.02)	34.80 (15.77)	7.07 (3.20)	0	220.65
LIC	143126.27 (47.01)	172917.76 (56.79)	38140.94 (12.52)	93378.18 (30.67)	16693.50 (5.48)	304436.88
Total	14465.52 (4.707)	174693.64 (56.84)	38636.84 (12.57)	93978.43 (30.58)	16845.63 (5.48)	307308.91

Source: Insurance Regulatory and Development Authority of India (2003), Annual Report 2003-04, Hyderabad.

Note: Figures in the parenthesis are percentages

For the year 2004-05, IRDAI mandated that investments in government securities should be 25 percent; approved securities including government securities not less than 50 percent; approved investments as specified in Schedule I includes

(a) infrastructure and social sector not less than 15 percent,

(b) others to be governed by exposure/ prudential norms (specified in Regulation 5) not exceeding 35 percent;

(investments other than approved investments not exceeding 15 percent out of the total investment fund).

In 2004-05, life insurance fund increased to Rs. 3,66,219.85 crore from Rs. 3,07,308.91 crore registering growth of around 19 percent from the preceding year. The pattern of investments for central and state government securities were in consonance with the specifications of IRDAI. Except for LIC all other insurers adhered to the norms specified by IRDAI for infrastructure and social sector investments. All life insurers complied with the norms laid down for investments subject to exposure norms and other than approved investments (see Table 5.38 below).

Table 5.38: Pattern of Investments of Life Insurers (2004-05)
(Rupees in Crore)

Insurer	Central Government Securities	State Government Securities (Including Central Govt. securities)	Infrastructure Investments/ Social Sector	Investments subject to exposure norms (including other than approved investments)	Other than approved investments	Total
Aviva	79.70 (54.98)	79.70 (54.98)	30.21 (20.84)	35.04 (24.17)	0	144.95
Bajaj Allianz	235.67 (61.64)	235.67 (61.64)	74.02 (19.36)	72.59 (18.98)	20.89 (5.46)	382.28
Birla Sunlife	84.73 (49.82)	110.75 (65.12)	31.74 (18.66)	27.58 (16.21)	9.56 (5.62)	170.06
HDFC Standard	286.2 (59.54)	286.29 (59.54)	85.80 (17.84)	108.67 (22.60)	19.68 (4.09)	480.77

ICICI Prudential	552.82 (56.95)	552.82 (56.95)	159.04 (16.38)	258.77 (26.66)	75.82 (7.81)	970.63
ING Life	79.70 (54.98)	79.70 (54.98)	30.21 (20.84)	35.04 (24.17)	0	144.95
Kotak Mahindra	108.11 (53.87)	133.10 (66.32)	46.92 (23.38)	40.64 (20.25)	0.73 (0.36)	200.67
MAXLife	109.09 (24.99)	315.67 (72.33)	89.08 (20.41)	31.62 (7.24)	15.06 (3.45)	436.37
PNB Metlife	101.51 (64.58)	101.51 (64.58)	30.05 (19.11)	25.63 (16.30)	13.34 (8.48)	157.18
Reliance	63.54 (57.39)	65.30 (58.98)	22.94 (20.72)	22.47 (20.29)	6.58 (5.94)	110.71
Sahara	60.47 (42.44)	102.90 (72.22)	24.27 (17.03)	15.32 (10.75)	0.01 (0.0070)	142.48
SBILife	587.78 (61.17)	592.78 (61.69)	155.26 (16.15)	212.86 (22.15)	88.46 (9.20)	960.89
Tata AIA	311.91 (79.41)	311.91 (79.41)	64.66 (16.46)	16.19 (4.12)	1.33 (0.33)	392.76
LIC	167718.86 (46.40)	206906.87 (57.24)	44660.40 (12.35)	109861.60 (30.39)	26111.98 (7.22)	361428.87
Total	170433.39 (46.53)	209908.18 (57.31)	45521.01 (12.42)	110790.66 (30.25)	26373.73 (7.20)	366219.85

Source: Insurance Regulatory and Development Authority of India (2005), Annual Report 2004-05, Hyderabad

Note: Figures in the parenthesis are percentages

For 2005-06, IRDAI mandated that investments in government securities should be 25 percent; approved securities including government securities including central government, state government securities not less than 50 percent; approved investments as specified in Schedule I includes

(a) infrastructure and social sector not less than 15 percent,

(b) others to be governed by exposure norms (specified in Regulation 5) not exceeding 35 percent.

Out of this 35 percent, not more than 15 percent shall be invested in other than approved investments.

In years 2005-06, life insurance investments rose to Rs. 3,97,188.65 crore from Rs. 3,66,219.85 crore in the preceding year thus, registering the growth of 8.4 percent. ING Life insurance company was not able to meet the investment patterns specified for state and central government securities - as it invested around 25 percent against the mandate of 50 percent. LIC and ING Life did not meet the 15 requirement for investment in social and infrastructure investments. ING Life and LIC were able to invest 9.83 and 12.37 percent respectively in infrastructure and social sector investment category. All the life insurance firms complied with the norms laid down for investments subject to exposure norms and other than approved investments (Table 5.39).

Table 5.39: Pattern of Investments of Life Insurers (2005-06)
(Rupees in Crore)

Insurer	Central Govern-ment Securities	State Govern-ment Securities (Including Central Govt. securities)	Infra-structure Invest-ments/ Social Sector	Invest-ments subject to exposure norms (including other than approved invest-ments)	Other than approved invest-ments	Total
Aviva	128.91 (59.05)	128.91 (59.05)	38.15 (17.47)	51.24 (23.47)	4.93 (2.25)	218.29
Bajaj Allianz	403.04 (55.73)	403.04 (55.73)	141.91 (19.62)	178.15 (24.63)	30.94 (4.27)	723.10
Birla Sunlife	141.95 (56.18)	141.95 (56.18)	41.97 (16.61)	68.72 (27.20)	7.25 (2.86)	252.64
HDFC Standard	463.82 (50.93)	463.82 (50.93)	213.28 (23.42)	233.43 (25.63)	14.82 (1.62)	910.53
ICICI Prude-ntial	683.64 (217 .6574)	683.64 (217.6574)	226.11 (71.98 892)	404.34 (128.7338)	67.37 (21.44 927)	314.09
ING Life	196.16 (25.41)	196.16 (25.42)	75.93 (9.83)	99.64 (12.91)	49.01 (6.35)	771.73
Kotak Mahindra	128.97 (38.09)	180.53 (53.32)	59.99 (17.72)	98.02 (28.95)	1.98 (0.58)	338.54
MAX Life	505.97 (72.91)	505.97 (72.91)	130.90 (18.86)	57.03 (8.21)	29.80 (4.29)	693.90
PNB Metlife	127.20 (60.95)	127.20 (60.95)	43.87 (21.02)	37.60 (18.01)	17.69 (8.47)	208.67
Reliance	95.80 (58.42)	95.80 (58.42)	34.34 (20.94)	33.84 (20.63)	6 (3.65)	163.98
Sahara	48.42 (33.23)	90.92 (62.40)	28.37 (19.47)	26.80 (18.39)	2.71 (1.86)	145.69
SBI Life	758.38 (49.05)	780.18 (50.46)	264.96 (17.13)	500.76 (32.39)	167.70 (10.84)	1545.91
Shriram Life	65.25 (50.28)	65.25 (50.28)	34.95 (26.93)	29.55 (22.77)	7.59 (5.84)	129.75
Tata AIA	511.43 (70.61)	511.43 (70.61)	121.50 (16.77)	91.37 (12.61)	4.69 (0.64)	724.30
LIC	197419.39 (50.69)	241103.52 (61.90)	48182.22 (12.37)	161.78 (0.04)	26286.06 (6.74)	389447.52
Total	201678.32 (50.77)	2245477.93 (56.53)	49638.45 (12.49)	102072.27 (25.69)	26706.15 (6.72)	397188.65

Source: Insurance Regulatory and Development Authority of India (2006), Annual Report 2005-06, Hyderabad.

Note: Figures in the parenthesis are percentages

For 2006-07, IRDAI mandated that investments in government securities should be 25 percent; approved securities including government securities including central government, state government securities not less than 50 percent; approved investments as specified in Schedule I includes

(a) infrastructure and social sector not less than 15 percent,

(b) others to be governed by exposure norms (specified in Regulation 5) not exceeding 35percent.

Out of this 35 percent, not more than 15 percent shall be invested in other than approved investments.

In year 2006-07 the investments of life insurers rose to Rs. 4,65,555.30 crore from Rs. 3,97,188.65 crore in 2005-06. The fund witnessed an increase of 17.2 percent from the preceding year. All the life insurers complied with the specified patterns of investment for central government and state government securities. SBI Life and LIC by making investments to the tune of 0.28 and 14.91 percent respectively were not able to meet the mandate of minimum 15 percent investment for infrastructure and social sector investments. Bajaj Allianz and ING Life did not complied with the investment norm for Investments subject to exposure norms and other than approved investments as their investments exceeded mandate of not more than 35 percent of total investments in these categories (Table 5.40).

Table 5.40: Pattern of Investments of Life Insurers (2006-07)
(Rupees in Crore)

Insurer	Central Govern-ment Securities	State Govern-ment Securities (Including Central Govt. securities)	Infra-structure Invest-ments/ Social Sector	Invest-ments subject to exposure norms (including other than approved invest-ments)	Other than approved invest-ments	Total
Aviva	222.71 (56.75)	222.71 (56.75)	80.09 (20.40)	89.62 (22.83)	0 (0)	392.42
Bajaj Allianz	616.95 (40.91)	755.25 (50.08)	245.35 (16.27)	507.22 (33.63)	72.45 (4.80)	1507.82
Bharti AXA	37.66 (32.39)	62.06 (53.38)	24.51 (21.08)	29.66 (25.51)	2.0 (1.72)	116.24
Birla Sunlife	193.40 (51.76)	193.40 (51.76)	74.40 (19.91)	105.73 (28.29)	20.86 (5.58)	373.63
HDFC Standard	464.002 (33.53)	725.61 (52.43)	250.86 (18.12)	407.27 (29.43)	25.01 (1.80)	1383.73
ICICI Prude-ntial	973.67 (53.12)	973.67 (53.12)	308.39 (16.82)	550.47 (30.03)	108.00 (5.89)	1832.63

ING Life	287.39 (48.28)	303.16 (50.93)	99.45 (16.70)	192.59 (32.35)	53.29 (8.95)	595.20
Kotak Mahindra	200.29 (44.90)	255.03 (57.18)	77.87 (17.45)	113.12 (25.36)	8.97 (2.01)	446.0
MAX Life	695.95 (59.88)	708.82 (60.99)	238.93 (20.55)	214.40 (18.44)	62.01 (5.33)	1162.1
PNB Metlife	256.68 (56.80)	256.68 (56.80)	104.65 (23.15)	90.56 (20.04)	32.91 (7.28)	451.89
Reliance	123.05 (139.79)	148.63 (168.85)	48.30 (54.87)	91.09 (103.48)	24.88 (28.26)	88.02
Sahara	47.11 (29.67)	81.17 (51.12)	29.99 (18.88)	47.61 (29.98)	9.63 (6.06)	158.77
SBI Life	931.78 (44.21)	1107.23 (52.53)	4.19 (0.19)	6.07 (0.28)	168.15 (7.97)	2107.48
Shriram Life	73.63 (50.59)	73.63 (50.59)	34.96 (24.02)	36.94 (25.38)	13.86 (9.52)	145.53
Tata AIA	863.21 (74.80)	863.21 (74.80)	202.70 (17.56)	88.00 (7.62)	3.41 (0.29)	1153.91
LIC	227676.79 (50.21)	272578.68 (60.11)	67616.17 (14.91)	113245.21 (24.97)	29443.19 (6.49)	453440.06
Total	233664.31 (50.19)	279308.95 (59.99)	69836.78 (15.00)	116409.57 (25.004)	30048.61 (6.45)	465555.30

Source: Insurance Regulatory and Development Authority of India (2007), Annual Report 2006-07, Hyderabad

Note: Figures in the parenthesis are percentages

For 2007-08, IRDAI mandated that investments in government securities should be 25 percent; approved securities including government securities including central government, state government securities not less than 50 percent; approved investments as specified in Schedule I includes

(a) infrastructure and social sector not less than 15 percent,

(b) others to be governed by exposure norms (specified in Regulation 5) not exceeding 35percent.

Out of this 35 percent, not more than 15 percent, shall be invested in other than approved investments.

In year 2007-08, the life insurance fund stood at Rs. 5,41,629.99 crore whereas in 2006-07 it pegged at Rs. 4,65,555.30 crore meaning thereby that the fund has shown an increase of 16.3 percent All life insurers complied with the investment norms for central government and state government securities. Except LIC all life insurance complied with infrastructure and social sector norms by investing at least 15 percent in this category. All life insurance firms fulfilled the mandate of approved investments subject to exposure norms and other than approved investments (Table 5.41).

Table 5.41: Pattern of Investments of Life Insurers (2007-08) (Rupees in Crore)

Insurer	Central Government Securities	State Government Securities	Infrastructure Investments	Approved Investments	Other Investments	Total
Aviva	228.72 (54.72)	0 (0)	95.14 (22.76)	94.07 (22.50)	0 (0)	417.93
Bajaj Allianz	646.95 (25.44)	697.11 (27.41)	404.53 (15.91)	712.62 (28.02)	81.31 (3.19)	2542.53
Bharti AXA	78.79 (44.30)	19.68 (11.06)	29.81 (16.76)	41.98 (23.60)	7.37 (4.14)	177.83
Birla Sunlife	233.82 (39.64)	64.35 (10.91)	137.54 (23.32)	97.23 (16.48)	56.80 (9.63)	589.75
Future Generali	103.96 (73.96)	0 (0)	25.10 (17.85)	10.44 (7.42)	1.08 (0.76)	140.56
HDFC Standard	1095.10 (49.32)	84.22 (3.79)	364.77 (16.42)	625.79 (28.18)	50.28 (2.26)	2220.16
ICICI Prude-ntial	1352.92 (49.45)	69.10 (2.52)	452.08 (16.52)	509.40 (18.62)	352.00 (12.86)	2735.49
IDBI Federal	44.95 (29.96)	63.25 (42.16)	32.43 (21.62)	9.36 (6.24)	0 (0)	149.99
ING Life	254.68 (35.79)	124.78 (17.53)	153.97 (21.63)	130.80 (18.38)	47.32 (6.65)	711.55
Kotak Mahindra	329.60 (51.39)	25.03 (3.90)	122.29 (19.07)	144.78 (22.57)	19.55 (3.04)	641.25
MAX Life	897.17 (50.13)	116.62 (6.51)	429.41 (23.99)	186.46 (10.41)	159.83 (8.93)	1789.48
PNB Metlife	275.26 (45.29)	77.21 (12.70)	176.61 (29.06)	48.88 (8.04)	29.76 (4.89)	607.72
Reliance	235.75 (49.19)	28.81 (6.01)	78.59 (16.40)	120.44 (25.13)	15.59 (3.25)	479.18
Sahara	83.50 (30.89)	63.67 (23.55)	56.09 (20.75)	53.00 (19.61)	14 (5.18)	270.26
SBI Life	1503.42 (44.55)	363.77 (10.78)	652.02 (19.32)	658.92 (19.52)	196.12 (5.81)	3374.25
Shriram Life	77.71 (45.80)	10.14 (5.97)	26.49 (15.61)	46.51 (27.41)	8.82 (5.19)	169.66
Tata AIA	1091.51 (67.05)	0 (0)	309.82 (19.03)	202.12 (12.41)	24.39 (1.49)	1627.84
LIC	242259.49 (46.32)	65237.68 (12.47)	59715.45 (11.41)	114645.90 (21.92)	41126.24 (7.86)	52298 4.76
Total	250791.31 (46.30)	67045.41 (12.37)	63262.13 (11.67)	11838.70 (2.18)	42190.44 (7.78)	54162 9.99

Source: Insurance Regulatory and Development Authority of India (2008), Annual Report 2007-08, Hyderabad

Note: Figures in the parenthesis are percentages

For 2008-09, IRDAI mandated that investments in government securities should not be less than25 percent; approved securities including government securities including central government, state government securities not less than 50 percent; approved investments and other investments not exceeding 35 percent of the fund and investments in infrastructure should not be less than 15 percent of the fund.

In 2008-09, the life insurance investment fund increased to Rs. 629650.40 crore from Rs. 541629.99 crore in 2007-08. The fund registered a growth of 16.2 percent from the preceding year. DLF PR AMERICA and Reliance did not meet the specified investment patterns for central government and state government securities. LIC and IDBI Federal did not meet the minimum requirement of 15 percent investment in infrastructure. Reliance and IDBI Federal did not complied with norms for approved and other investments as they exceeded the mandatory requirement of 35 percent for these two investments. Barring these two insurers all other complied with the norms specified for approved and other investments (Table 5.42).

Table 5.42: Pattern of Investments of Life Insurers (2008-09) (Rupees in Crore)

Insurer	Central Government Securities	State Government Securities	Infrastructure Investments	Approved Investments	Other Investments	Total
Aegon Religare	20.49 (34.78)	9.37 (15.90)	14.41 (24.46)	10.03 (17.02)	4.59 (7.79)	58.90
Aviva	298.72 (54.19)	0 (0)	116.99 (21.22)	135.50 (24.58)	0 (0)	551.21
Bajaj Allianz	928.58 (31.52)	725.74 (24.63)	510.40 (17.32)	775.97 (26.34)	5 (0.16)	2945.69
Bharti AXA	45.46 (39.48)	14.86 (12.90)	24.04 (20.87)	23.19 (20.14)	7.59 (6.59)	115.14
Birla Sunlife	443.02 (51.59)	9.83 (1.14)	211.37 (24.61)	188.39 (21.94)	16.00 (1.86)	858.61
Canara HSBC	159.36 (51.38)	115.50 (37.24)	72.71 (23.44)	62.57 (20.17)	0 (0)	310.14
DLF Pramerica	5.43 (6.86)	0 (0)	17.36 (21.94)	5.29 (6.68)	3.04 (3.84)	79.12
Future Generali	111.33 (63.58)	0 (0)	40.81 (23.30)	17.94 (10.24)	5.02 (2.86)	175.10
HDFC Standard	1248.42 (49.21)	75.54 (2.97)	496.61 (19.57)	681.34 (26.86)	34.70 (1.36)	2536.60
ICICI Prudential	1187.06 (38.17)	491.20 (15.79)	526.27 (16.92)	761.85 (24.49)	143.35 (4.60)	3109.73

IDBI Federal	151.16 (47.74)	35.17 (11.10)	47.38 (14.96)	170.91 (53.98)	12 (3.79)	316.61
ING Life	322.94 (39.69)	128.87 (15.84)	171.97 (21.13)	128.72 (15.82)	61.08 (7.50)	813.57
Kotak Mahindra	471.54 (53.40)	69.99 (7.92)	230.57 (26.11)	109.44 (12.39)	1.41 (0.15)	882.95
MAX Life	1451.75 (58.51)	121.44 (4.89)	504.84 (20.34)	368.68 (14.86)	34.16 (1.37)	2480.87
PNB Metlife	314.46 (39.56)	121.25 (15.25)	207.90 (26.16)	103.38 (13.01)	47.73 (6.01)	794.72
Reliance	197.22 (26.15)	95.26 (12.63)	138.43 (18.35)	311.2 (41.26)	12.05 (1.59)	754.08
Sahara	95.14 (33.85)	63.64 (22.64)	71.04 (25.28)	45.72 (16.27)	5.44 (1.93)	280.99
SBI Life	1484.59 (40.73)	439.48 (12.05)	663.98 (18.21)	963.57 (26.43)	92.80 (2.54)	3644.45
Shriram Life	84.61 (43.18)	16.68 (8.51)	40.02 (20.42)	44.57 (22.74)	10.05 (5.12)	195.92
Star Union Dai Chi	66.48 (53.15)	0 (0)	27.59 (22.05)	27.21 (21.75)	3.80 (3.03)	125.07
Tata AIA	1058.64 (49.84)	325.62 (15.33)	473.20 (22.27)	241.60 (11.37)	24.88 (1.17)	2123.94
LIC	25899 6.79 (42.70)	85955.62 (14.17)	62065.43 (10.23)	148693.48 (24.51)	50735.69 (8.36)	60648 7.01
Total	26909 1.17 (42.73)	88755.04 (14.09)	66673.33 (10.58)	153870.47 (24.43)	51260.39 (8.14)	62965 0.40

Source: Insurance Regulatory and Development Authority of India (2009), Annual Report 2008-09, Hyderabad

Note: Figures in the parenthesis are percentages

For 2009-10, IRDAI mandated that investments in government securities should not be less than25 percent; approved securities including government securities including central government, state government securities not less than 50 percent; approved investments and other investments not exceeding 35 percent of the fund and investments in infrastructure should not be less than 15 percent of the fund.

In 2009-10 life insurance investment fund increased to Rs. 731290.86 crore from Rs. 629650.40 crore in year 2008-09, thus, registering a growth of 16.1 percent. Four life insurance firms, namely, HDFC Standard, IDBI Federal, Indian First and Reliance Life Insurance did not meet the minimum investment requirements for government securities. India First and Life Insurance Corporation of India did not meet the minimum requirement of 15 percent of the total investment for infrastructure sector. Barring India First and LIC all other life insurers met the specified requirement for approved investments and other investment (Table 5.43).

Table 5.43: Pattern of Investments of Life Insurers (2009-10)
(Rupees in Crore)

Insurer	Central Govern-ment Securi-ties	State Govern-ment Securi-ties	Infra-structure Invest-ments	Approved Invest-ments	Other Invest-ments	Total
Aegon Religare	66.52 (56.57)	9.34 (7.94)	23.67 (20.13)	7.83 (6.65)	10.21 (8.68)	117.58
Aviva	277.50 (55.86)	6.58 (1.32)	99.62 (20.05)	113.01 (22.75)	0 (0)	496.71
Bajaj Allianz	1278.47 (27.89)	1193.44 (26.04)	1045.11 (22.80)	1062.53 (23.18)	2.79 (0.06)	4582.34
Bharti AXA	67.72 (49.27)	10.11 (7.35)	29.06 (21.14)	27.88 (20.28)	2.66 (1.93)	137.43
Birla Sunlife	758.78 (52.22)	0 (0)	414.21 (28.51)	268.53 (18.48)	11.25 (0.77)	1452.77
Canara HSBC	128.78 (55.03)	15.47 (6.61)	37.78 (16.14)	47.68 (20.37)	4.30 (1.83)	234.01
DLF Pramerica	51.18 (60.02)	0 (0)	28.14 (33.01)	5.87 (6.88)	0.08 (0.09)	85.26
Future Generali	99.05 (35.46)	61.59 (22.05)	59.74 (21.38)	58.20 (20.83)	0.72 (0.25)	279.30
HDFC Standard	2042.86 (45.89)	139.86 (3.14)	843.82 (18.95)	1326.27 (29.79)	98.28 (2.20)	4451.08
ICICI Prudential	1797.86 (41.55)	598.96 (13.84)	688.31 (15.90)	1126.00 (26.02)	115.16 (2.66)	4326.29
IDBI Federal	90.67 (31.42)	43.18 (14.96)	73.69 (25.53)	76.56 (26.53)	4.44 (1.53)	288.55
India First	150.85 (45.85)	0 (0)	38.69 (11.76)	101.41 (30.82)	38.03 (11.56)	328.98
ING Life	411.99 (36.90)	149.09 (13.35)	262.98 (23.55)	174.99 (15.67)	117.31 (10.50)	1116.36
Kotak Mahindra	574.08 (47.19)	145.13 (11.93)	284.07 (23.35)	211.52 (17.39)	1.52 (0.12)	1216.32
MAX Life	1683.17 (48.25)	462.58 (13.26)	765.19 (21.93)	575.69 (16.50)	1.30 (0.03)	3487.93
PNBMetlife	462.72 (44.90)	119.96 (11.64)	316.58 (30.72)	119.98 (11.64)	11.27 (1.09)	1030.52
Reliance	287.69 (32.43)	139.91 (15.77)	169.44 (19.10)	281.46 (31.73)	9.13 (1.02)	886.92

Sahara	127.17 (33.43)	73.11 (19.21)	98.47 (25.88)	68.92 (18.11)	12.72 (3.34)	380.40
SBILife	2040.46 (42.50)	429.36 (8.94)	775.20 (16.14)	1542.24 (32.12)	13.37 (0.27)	4800.63
ShriramLife	90.43 (38.08)	29.89 (12.58)	70.16 (29.54)	41.18 (17.34)	5.78 (2.43)	237.43
Star Union Dai Chi	172.38 (46.82)	151.50 (41.15)	70.46 (19.14)	69.52 (18.88)	4.25 (1.15)	368.11
Tata AIA	1533.89 (54.15)	337.10 (11.90)	489.14 (17.26)	448.66 (15.83)	23.68 (0.83)	2832.47
LIC	292901.34 (41.95)	109629.03 (15.70)	78991.01 (11.31)	182643.05 (26.16)	33989.06 (4.86)	698153.49
Total	307095.57 (41.99)	113644.46 (15.54)	85674.54 (11.71)	190398.99 (26.03)	34477.30 (4.71)	731290.86

Source: Insurance Regulatory and Development Authority of India (2010), Annual Report 2009-10, Hyderabad

Note: Figures in the parenthesis are percentages

For 2010-11, IRDAI mandated that investments in government securities should not be less than25 percent; approved securities including government securities including central government, state government securities not less than 50 percent; approved investments and other investments not exceeding 35 percent of the fund and investments in infrastructure should not be less than 15 percent of the fund.

In year 2010-11, the volume of life insurers' investment fund decreased to Rs. 4,41,074.55 crore from Rs. 7,31,290.86 crore. Three life insurance firms, namely, ICICI Prudential, IDBI Federal, and reliance life insurance could not meet the minimum requirement of at least 50 percent of the total investments for government securities. ICICI Prudential and Life Insurance Corporation were not able to meet the minimum 15 percent investment requirement for infrastructure investments. All life insurers followed the mandatory requirements for investments for approved investments and other investments (see Table 5.44 ahead below).

Table 5.44: Pattern of Investments of Life Insurers (2010-11) (Rupees in Crore)

Insurer	Central Government Securities	State Government Securities	Infrastructure Investments	Approved Investments	Other Investments	Total
Aegon Religare	113.61 (49.06)	17.85 (7.70)	40.43 (17.46)	59.64 (25.75)	0 (0)	231.53
Aviva	338.81 (40.65)	137.66 (16.52)	178.79 (21.45)	178.01 (21.36)	0 (0)	833.28
Bajaj Allianz	2125.63 (37.23)	890.25 (15.59)	1081.98 (18.95)	1553.22 (27.20)	57.68 (1.01)	5708.76

Bharti AXA	90.84 (45.12)	10.06 (4.99)	31.99 (15.89)	66.52 (33.04)	1.91 (0.94)	201.32
Birla Sunlife	1138.02 (52.25)	0 (0)	535.32 (24.57)	501.89 (23.04)	2.66 (0.12)	2177.89
Canara HSBC	134.25 (48.18)	24.76 (8.88)	75.23 (27.01)	44.36 (15.92)	0 (0)	278.60
DLF Prame-rica	80.59 (56.34)	0 (0)	34.37 (24.03)	26.12 (18.26)	1.95 (1.36)	143.02
Future Generali	185.11 (41.14)	60.56 (13.47)	130.53 (29.01)	73.06 (16.23)	0.65 (0.14)	449.90
HDFC Standard	2276.66 (42.47)	456.77 (8.52)	1301.75 (24.28)	1274.23 (23.77)	50.72 (0.94)	5360.12
ICICI Prude-ntial	2619.75 (30.52)	813.75 (9.48)	1080.84 (12.59)	1934.78 (22.54)	113.26 (1.31)	8582.38
IDBI Federal	150.32 (26.92)	54.84 (9.82)	83.86 (15.01)	261.27 (46.79)	8.08 (1.44)	558.38
India First	190.66 (54.55)	12.21 (3.49)	59.08 (16.90)	87.56 (25.05)	0 (0)	349.50
ING Life	575.01 (40.37)	152.28 (10.69)	335.53 (23.56)	315.42 (22.14)	45.82 (3.21)	1424.06
Kotak Mahindra	682.46 (44.05)	163.03 (10.52)	370.86 (23.93)	331.08 (21.36)	1.85 (0.11)	1549.28
MAX Life	2517.25 (51.58)	521.02 (10.67)	1131.22 (23.17)	709.36 (14.53)	1.33 (0.02)	4880.19
PNB Metlife	784.60 (57.08)	120.21 (8.74)	57.06 (4.151)	112.49 (8.18)	0 (0)	1374.36
Reliance	476.80 (36.40)	171.28 (13.07)	253.20 (19.33)	403.82 (30.83)	4.67 (0.35)	1309.77
Sahara	191.93 (41.47)	63.03 (13.62)	123.94 (26.78)	80.86 (17.47)	3.01 (0.65)	462.77
SBI Life	2161.51 (45.85)	319.30 (6.77)	746.50 (15.83)	1377.42 (29.21)	109.39 (2.32)	4714.12
Shriram Life	107.09 (41.20)	25.46 (9.79)	63.27 (24.34)	62.81 (24.16)	1.29 (0.49)	259.92
Star Union Dai Chi	195.42 (48.32)	53.71 (13.28)	70.00 (17.31)	77.84 (19.25)	7.38 (1.82)	404.35

Tata AIA	2146.83 (60.47)	360.08 (10.14)	603.50 (17)	418.74 (11.79)	20.85 (0.58)	3550.00
LIC	334092.91 (41.85)	136929.55 (17.15)	80491.49 (10.08)	205050.46 (25.68)	4172 6.63 (5.22)	7982 91.03
Total	353376.05 (80.11)	141357.66 (32.04)	89180.75 (20.21)	215000.98 (48.74)	4215 9.12 (9.55)	4410 74.55

Source: Insurance Regulatory and Development Authority of India (2011), Annual Report 2010-11, Hyderabad.

Note: Figures in the parenthesis are percentages

For 2011-12, IRDAI mandated that investments in government securities should not be less than25 percent; approved securities including government securities including central government, state government securities not less than 50 percent; approved investments and other investments not exceeding 35 percent of the fund and investments in infrastructure should not be less than 15 percent of the fund.

In year 2011-12, the life insurance investment fund increased to Rs. 9,74,620.33 crore from Rs. 4,41,074.55 crore in 2010-11. It shows that the fund had a quantum jump from with 120 percent increase from the preceding year. Four life insurance firms, namely, Edelweiss Tokio, HDFC Standard, ICICI Prudential and Reliance life did not meet the minimum investment requirement for government securities. Barring LIC all other life insurer met the investment requirement for infrastructure. Edelweiss Tokio and Reliance life were not able to meet investment requirements for approved investments and other investments (Table 5.45).

Table 5.45: Pattern of Investments of Life Insurers (2011-12) (Rupees in Crore)

Insurer	Central Government Securities	State Government Securities	Infrastructure Investments	Approved Investments	Other Investments	Total
Aegon Religare	87.35 (35.75)	37.64 (15.40)	62.33 (25.51)	46.68 (19.10)	10.31 (4.22)	244.31
Aviva	483.02 (40.60)	157.86 (13.27)	267.97 (22.52)	280.59 (23.58)	--	1189.45
Bajaj Allianz	3431.95 (42.08)	838.26 (10.28)	1614.18 (19.79)	2148.58 (26.34)	121.19 (1.48)	8154.16
Bharti AXA	149.59 (50.03)	--	50.11 (16.76)	80.12 (26.80)	19.13 (6.39)	298.95
Birla Sunlife	1454.23 (54.59)	--	810.11 (30.41)	367.35 (13.79)	32.15 (1.20)	2663.85
Canara HSBC	167.26 (42.05)	32.87 (8.26)	142.88 (35.92)	54.69 (13.751)	--	397.69

DLF Paramerica	91.58 (58.26)	--	49.11 (31.24)	13.38 (8.51)	3.12 (1.98)	157.19
Edelweiss Tokio	61.11 (12.41)	--	119.54 (24.28)	261.25 (53.07)	50.35 (10.22)	492.25
Future Generali	237.10 (34.37)	125.31 (18.14)	181.50 (26.28)	145.86 (21.12)	0.74 (0.10)	690.50
HDFC Standard	3119.66 (41.79)	594.53 (7.96)	1636.71 (21.92)	1952.72 (26.16)	160.30 (2.14)	7463.93
ICICI Prudential	2638.53 (29.46)	1134.31 (12.66)	1686.00 (18.82)	3333.99 (37.23)	161.37 (1.80)	8954.20
IDBI Federal	341.80 (45.89)	59.86 (8.03)	137.44 (18.45)	202.89 (27.24)	2.79 (0.37)	744.79
India First	241.45 (52.90)	12.13 (2.65)	93.03 (20.38)	108.55 (23.78)	1.25 (0.27)	456.41
ING Life	824.20 (42.68)	157.40 (8.15)	482.99 (25.01)	367.92 (19.05)	98.48 (5.09)	1931.00
Kotak Mahindra	835.84 (39.79)	285.47 (13.59)	541.48 (25.78)	436.63 (20.78)	0.83 (0.03)	2100.25
MAX Life	3368.10 (46.58)	765.13 (10.58)	1779.46 (24.61)	1287.86 (17.81)	29.59 (0.40)	7230.14
PNB Metlife	1282.39 (62.83)	120.45 (5.90)	472.37 (23.14)	165.62 (8.11)	--	2040.83
Reliance	833.72 (30.95)	213.28 (7.91)	417.17 (15.48)	1122.60 (41.67)	106.98 (3.97)	2693.74
Sahara	228.42 (42.26)	59.54 (11.01)	159.30 (29.47)	81.05 (14.99)	12.09 (2.23)	540.40
SBI Life	2872.26 (46.86)	412.48 (6.72)	1104.88 (18.02)	1593.48 (25.99)	145.96 (2.38)	6129.05
Shriram Life	139.37 (43.06)	29.87 (9.23)	73.78 (22.80)	74.75 (23.10)	5.82 (1.79)	323.59
Star Union Dai Chi	247.33 (50.78)	61.88 (12.70)	99.72 (20.47)	75.21 (15.44)	2.91 (0.59)	487.05
Tata AIA	2955.03 (63.92)	325.58 (7.043)	805.41 (17.42)	515.73 (11.15)	20.78 (0.44)	4622.53
LIC	368688.82 (40.31)	172509.45 (18.86)	84532.45 (9.24)	243607.2 (26.63)	45276.07 (4.95)	914614.07
Total	394780.11 (40.50)	177933.28 (18.25)	97319.92 (9.98)	258324.79 (26.50)	46262.23 (4.74)	974620.33

Source: Insurance Regulatory and Development Authority of India (2012), Annual Report 2011-12, Hyderabad

Note: Figures in the parenthesis are percentages

For 2012-13, IRDAI mandated that investments in government securities should not be less than25 percent; approved securities including government securities including central government, state government securities not less than 50 percent; approved investments and other investments not exceeding 35 percent of the fund and investments in infrastructure should not be less than 15 percent of the fund.

For the year 2012-13, the life insurance fund pegged at Rs. 11,20,000 crore from

Rs. 9,74,620.33 crore in 2011-12 which shows an increase of 14.9 percent from the preceding year. Edelweiss Tokio, ICICI Prudential and Reliance Life were not become able to meet the standards laid down for government securities. Two life insurance firms, namely - Reliance Life and LIC did not meet the statutory requirement for infrastructure investments. Two life insurance firms, namely - Edelweiss Tokio and Reliance Life did not meet the mandatory investment pattern for approved investment and other than approved investments (see Table 5.46 on next page).

Table 5.46: Pattern of Investments of Life Insurers (2012-13)
(Rupees in Crore)

Insurer	Central Government Securities	State Government Securities	Infrastructure Investments	Approved Investments	Other Investments	Total
Aegon Religare	132.86 (58.90)	22.11 (9.80)	42.16 (18.69)	20.06 (8.89)	8.37 (3.71)	225.56
Aviva	870.70 (49.64)	188.19 (10.72)	416.61 (23.75)	278.40 (15.87)	0.01 (0.01)	1753.91
Bajaj Allianz	4666.84 (42.57)	1253.27 (11.43)	2024.46 (18.46)	2880.23 (26.27)	196.52 (1.79)	10961.22
Bharti AXA	171.89 (52.23)	--	66.77 (20.29)	85.26 (25.91)	5.18 (1.57)	329.04
Birla Sunlife	1512.62 (53.06)	58.89 (2.06)	815.73 (28.61)	417.79 (14.65)	45.55 (1.59)	2850.58
Canara HSBC	402.25 (53.09)	31.03 (4.09)	160.41 (21.17)	146.22 (19.29)	17.75 (2.34)	757.66
DLF Pramerica	104.34 (48.72)	15.24 (7.11)	61.94 (28.92)	29.53 (13.79)	3.07 (1.43)	214.12
Edelweiss Tokio	88.73 (20.98)	--	60.25 (14.25)	270.79 (64.04)	3.03 (0.71)	422.80
Future Generali	358.48 (35.79)	159.59 (15.93)	302.78 (30.23)	180.19 (17.99)	0.43 (0.04)	1001.47
HDFC Standard	4423.02 (42.58)	742.66 (7.15)	2038.39 (19.62)	2848.54 (27.42)	333.19 (3.20)	10385.80
ICICI Prudential	4602.07 (37.24)	1320.11 (10.68)	2418.10 (19.57)	3768.77 (30.50)	245.67 (1.98)	12354.71
IDBI Federal	433.90 (39.85)	125.60 (11.53)	427.45 (39.25)	101.54 (9.32)	0.34 (0.03)	1088.83
India First	220.07 (48.56)	40.27 (8.88)	91.06 (20.09)	100.53 (22.18)	1.25 (0.27)	453.18
ING Life	1252.55 (45.65)	162.58 (5.92)	711.41 (25.93)	574.68 (20.94)	42.09 (1.53)	2743.30
Kotak Mahindra	1060.51 (38.19)	514.37 (18.52)	708.46 (25.51)	488.36 (17.58)	5.00 (0.18)	2776.70
MAX Life	4853.89 (49.14)	1003.67 (10.16)	2152.29 (21.79)	1801.79 (18.24)	65.02 (0.65)	9876.67

PNB Metlife	2006.95 (66.39)	102.17 (3.380)	682.04 (22.56)	224.09 (7.41)	7.39 (0.24)	3022.64
Reliance	947.16 (18.51)	757.34 (14.80)	648.93 (12.68)	2604.57 (50.91)	57.76 (1.12)	5115.74
Sahara	262.35 (39.90)	95.71 (14.55)	173.91 (26.45)	105.31 (16.01)	20.21 (3.07)	657.49
SBI Life	4232.47 (50.68)	598.54 (7.16)	1398.19 (16.74)	1937.09 (23.19)	183.60 (2.19)	8349.89
Shriram Life	209.14 (40.91)	47.82 (9.35)	123.75 (24.20)	123.49 (24.15)	6.98 (1.36)	511.20
Star Union Dai Chi	368.10 (52.99)	83.57 (12.03)	131.98 (19.01)	106.36 (15.31)	4.60 (0.66)	694.61
Tata AIA	3746.89 (64.64)	326.11 (5.62)	1120.45 (19.33)	582.87 (10.05)	20.14 (0.34)	5796.36
LIC	404122.92 (38.94)	206808.07 (19.93)	102000.90 (9.82)	276914.03 (26.68)	47810.55 (4.60)	1037656.47
Total	440990.60 (36.99)	214456.88 (17.99)	118878.37 (9.97)	296590.39 (24.88)	49083.72 (4.11)	1120000

Source: Insurance Regulatory and Development Authority of India (2010), Annual Report 2009-10, Hyderabad

Note: Figures in the parenthesis are percentages

Table 5.47: Names of Life insurers Defaulted on Investment Pattern as Mandated by the IRDAI

Year	Government Securities	Infrastructure Investments	Approved Investments and Other Investments
2000-01	----	Birla Sunlife, ICICI, Max life, and LIC	Kotak Mahindra, Tata AIA and LIC
2001-02	----	Birla Sunlife, PNB Metlife and LIC	Bajaj Allianz, Birla Sunlife, ING Life, Kotak Mahindra, Reliance, Tata AIA, LIC
2002-03	----	LIC and ICICI Prudential	---
2003-04	----	LIC and Sahara	---
2004-05	----	LIC	----
2005-06	ING Life	LIC and ING Life	----
2006-07	----	SBI Life and LIC	Bajaj Allianz and ING Life
2007-08	----	LIC	---
2008-09	DLF PRAMERICA and Reliance	LIC and IDBI Federal	Reliance and IDBI Federal
2009-10	HDFC Standard, IDBI Federal, Indian First and Reliance Life	India First and LIC	India First and LIC

2010-11	ICICI Prudential, IDBI Federal, and Reliance life	ICICI Prudential and LIC	---
2011-12	Edelweiss Tokio, HDFC Standard, ICICI Prudential and Reliance life	LIC	Edelweiss Tokio and Reliance life
2012-13	Edelweiss Tokio, ICICI Prudential and Reliance Life	Reliance Life and LIC	Edelweiss Tokio and Reliance Life

5.24 Perception of Managerial Functionaries of the Insurance Companies and IRDAI Official

Along with comparing the stipulated guidelines issued by IRDAI regarding the investment of funds of insurance companies, the perceptions of the functionaries were also solicited in regarding to regulation of funds of insurance companies. Majority (81.2 percent) of the functionaries of the insurance firms expressed satisfaction with the IRDAI regarding regulation of investment of funds of insurance firms.

The IRDAI Official expressed that IRDAI has imposed fines on insurance firms for not following investment patterns specified by the Authority.

5.25 Matrix Summing Up The Testing of Hypothesis 4

Matrix 5.4: Testing of Hypothesis 4- "IRDAI has been effective in regulating investment of funds by insurance companies by stipulating the percentages of investments in Government Securities, infrastructure and Approved Investments and Other Investments"

Hypothesis	Sources of Data	Analysis	Status of Hypothesis Accepted
IRDAI has been effective in regulating investment of funds by insurance companies by stipulating the percentages of investments in Government Securities, infrastructure and Approved Investments and Other Investments	Secondary data and primary data	During all the years one or another insurance firm has defaulted with the norms specified for the investment of funds by IRDAI. Moreover majority of the firms had followed the investment specifications issued by IRDAI. Around 81.2 percent of the total Management functionaries of the life insurance firms expressed their satisfaction with the IRDAI for regulating investments funds of insurance firms IRDAI officials also opined that IRDAI has imposed fines on insurance firms for not adhering to investment norms specified by the authority.	Yes

Thus, on the basis of above analysis; the **Hypothesis 4-** "IRDAI has been effective in regulating investment of funds by insurance companies by stipulating the percentages of investments in Government Securities, infrastructure and Approved Investments and Other Investments" **stands validated.**

5.26 Concluding Observations:

The assessment of IRDAI is undertaken in terms of promoting growth in life insurance business, promoting efficiency in conduct of insurance business, spreading life insurance business in rural sector and regulating investment of funds of insurance companies. In this regard the study tested four hypotheses, namely, (i) IRDAI has been an instrument in promoting the growth of life insurance business in India by promoting growth in number of agents, polices, single premium underwritten, total premium underwritten in comparison to pre-IRDAI period; (ii) IRDAI has promoted efficiency in conduct of insurance business by making insurance firms to minimize inputs; (iii) IRDAI has been effective in spreading life insurance in rural sector by fixing quota for rural sector and (iv) IRDAI has been effective in regulating investment of funds by insurance companies by stipulating the percentages of investments in Government Securities, infrastructure and Approved Investments and Other Investments.

For testing the hypothesis related to role of IRDAI in promoting growth in life insurance business the study relied on various parameters such as growth in number of insurers, policies in force, total premium underwritten etc. Regression analysis test and counterfactual analysis were used to make a comparative analysis in pre and post IRDAI phase. The study finds that IRDAI has remained effective in promoting growth in life insurance business in India and the hypothesis, namely - IRDAI has become an instrument in promoting the growth of life insurance business in India by promoting growth in number of agents, polices, single premium underwritten, total premium underwritten in comparison to pre-IRDAI period - stands validated.

For testing the efficacy of IRDAI in enthusing efficiency in conduct of insurance business in India, Data Envelopment Analysis was applied through BCC and CCR input-oriented models. It was found that barring few exceptions majority of insurance firms were inefficient by both the models during period under review. There had not been a single year where no firm was found to be inefficient. The hypothesis, namely, IRDAI has promoted efficiency in conduct of insurance business by making insurance firms to minimize inputs stands rejected. In terms of testing the hypothesis regarding role of IRDAI in spread of insurance business in rural sector, the mandatory requirements laid by IRDAI for rural sector were checked against the actual business undertaken in rural sector. It was found that barring few exceptions such as LIC and Bharti Axa for few years the insurance firms adhered to the norms of rural sector laid by IRDAI. The hypothesis, namely, IRDAI has been effective in spreading life insurance in rural sector by fixing quota for rural sector is validated.

In analysis of regulation of investment of funds of life insurers by IRDAI it was found that majority of the life insurers have followed norms laid down by IRDAI. For all the years there had been one or more defaulters who did not adhere to norms of investments stipulated by IRDAI. But majority of the managerial functionaries of three life insurance firms have expressed their satisfaction with the way IRDAI regulates investment funds. The hypothesis, namely - IRDAI has become effective in regulating investment of funds by insurance companies by virtue of stipulating the percentages of investments in Government Securities, infrastructure and Approved Investments and Other Investments - stands validated.

6

Role of Insurance Regulatory and Development Authority of India: An Assessment –II

Role of IRDAI Thoroughly discussed Background

Chapter 6 aims to assess the role of Insurance Regulatory and Development Authority of India (IRDAI) in protecting interests of policyholders and efficacy of IRDAI in redressing grievances of policyholders. The chapter also examines the IRDAI as a best regulator on the basis of primary and secondary data.

The Chapter is organized into three parts. Part I contains assessment of IRDAI in protecting interests of policyholders. Efficacy of IRDAI in redressing grievances of policyholders is discussed in Part II. While assessment of IRDAI in terms of having features of a good regulator is dealt in part III.

Basis of Interest Protecting of policy-holders:

Assessment of IRDAI in protecting interest of policyholders is undertaken on the basis of indicators such as efficacy of IRDAI in making policy proposal form policyholder-centric, adherence to the norm of mandatory information disclosure by agents of insurance firms to prospective buyer at the point of sale of policy, satisfaction of respondents with the information imparted and product sold by the agent. Finally, efficacy of grievance redressal mechanism of insurer is done on the perceptions of the policyholders. Efficacy of IRDAI in redressing grievances of policyholders is done on the basis of number of cases of grievances pending with Grievance Redressal Cell of IRDAI and Insurance Ombudsman along with perceptions of policyholders regarding grievance redressal cell of IRDAI and Insurance Ombudsman. Also decisions of Insurance Ombudsman are also analyzed as case studies to judge nature of complaint filed and decision of Insurance Ombudsman keeping in mind the principles of insurance also justice delivery to the aggrieved party. Examination of IRDAI as a best regulator was done on the basis of independence of IRDAI, enforcement powers of IRDAI, transparency and accountability mechanisms in the working of IRDAI and competency of IRDAI.

I

ASSESSMENT OF IRDAI IN PROTECTING INTERESTS OF POLICY HOLDERS

Consumer Affairs Department of Insurance Regulatory and Development Authority of India Development (IRDAI) entrusted with the task of protection of interests of policyholders in matters concerning assigning of policy, nomination by policyholders, insurable interest, settlement of insurance claim, surrender value of policy and other terms and conditions of contracts of insurance. As stated earlier that there are three types of insurance regulations namely - (i) solvency regulation, (ii) rate regulation and (iii) policy regulation prevalent in insurance market. It is noteworthy to mention here that policy regulation specifically focuses on policyholder's interest protection because of information asymmetry on the part of customers. In this regard, IRDAI has issued various guidelines and regulations and also has a dedicated website namely, *Bima Bemissal*, for spreading awareness regarding insurance among people. In order to curb fraudulent practices by insurers IRDAI has mandated that the prospectus of insurance must clearly state warranties, exceptions, conditions of the insurance contract at the point of sale. Every prospective buyer must sign the policy himself, making policy proposal form legible without fine printing, regular servicing of the policy holders. Regulation 5 of the IRDA (Protection of Policyholders' Interest) Regulations 2002 stipulates that every insurer shall have in place proper procedures and effective mechanism to address complaints and grievances of policyholders efficiently and within stipulated time period of 15 days. Every insurer will spread information regarding Insurance Ombudsman to policyholders.

The hypothesis tested in this regard is "IRDAI has been effective in protecting the interests of policy holders by making agents of insurers to dispense full information regarding policy proposal to prospective buyer".

The main hypothesis was split into following sub-hypotheses:

1. IRDAI has been effective in making policy proposal form policyholder-centric.
2. IRDAI has been effective in stimulating agents to share all the necessary information regarding policy with the prospective buyer at point of sale of policy proposal.
3. Policyholders are satisfied with the information provided by the agent at the point of sale of policy proposal.
4. Policyholders are satisfied with the final policy of the insurance firm.
5. Insurers have effective grievance redressal mechanism for redressing grievances of policyholders.

The hypotheses testing satisfaction of the policyholders were split to check variations across education, monthly Income, urban rural and gender of the respondents.

6.1 Making Policy Proposal Form - Policyholder-Centric

The first interface of the buyer with the insurance firm occurs at the point of sale of policy by an agent of insurer. IRDAI mandates that prospective buyer should fill the proposal form himself/herself or he should provide his consent to the concerned person to fill the proposal on his/her behalf if he is not in a position to fill the form. The prospective buyer should clearly read the instructions of the policy document. If prospective buyer is not in a position to fill the form himself an agent should share full information with him/her.

Sub-Hypothesis tested regarding policy proposal form is that 'IRDAI has been effective in making policy proposal form policyholder-centric'.

6.2 Policyholders and Form Filling Process

The field survey results revealed that around one third respondents had filled policy proposal themselves. For example out of total 314 respondents only 114 (36.3 %) have filled policy proposal themselves. Variations have a been noticed across insurance companies as 32.7 percent respondents of LIC, 43.5 percent respondents of ICICI Prudential and 31.8 percent respondents of Exide life stated that they have filled policy proposal of their own (Table 6.1).

Table 6.1: Policy Proposal Form Filling and Variations across Insurers

Policyholders filled policy proposal Form themselves	LIC	ICICI Prudential	Exide Life	Total
Yes	53 (32.7)	47 (43.5)	14 (31.8)	114 (36.3)
No	109 (67.3)	61 (56.5)	30 (68.2)	200 (63.7)
Total	162 (100)	108 (100)	44 (100)	314 (100)

Note: Figures in the parenthesis are percentages.

However variations have been observed in terms of education level. For example 23.5 percent respondents with below matric education and 40 percent respondents with education of matric and plus two have filled policy proposal form themselves. In case of graduates and above, around 41 percent of respondents have filled policy proposal of their own (Table 6.2). The findings of Chi-square test reveals that these variations are statistically significant at 5 percent level as χ^2= 7.84(2, N= 314), p= .020.

Table 6.2: Policy Proposal Form Filling and Variations across Education level

Policyholders filled policy proposal Form themselves	Below Matric	Matric and Plus 2	Graduation and above	Total
Yes	19 (23.5)	24 (40)	71 (41)	114 (36.3)
No	62 (76.5)	36 (60)	102 (59)	200 (63.7)
Total	81 (100)	60 (100)	173 (100)	314 (100)

Note: Figures in the parenthesis are percentages.

Variations were also noticed across income groups as 36.1 percent respondents with monthly income below Rs. 10,000 filled policy proposal form by themselves. On the other hand 30.1 percent respondents having monthly income ranging from Rs. 10,000 to 30,000 and 45.3 percent respondents having monthly income above Rs. 30,000 stated that they have filled policy proposal of their own (see Table 6.3). The variations across income groups are found to be statistically insignificant at 5 percent level by Chi-square test as value of χ^2 is 5.528(2, n=314), p =0.063.

Table 6.3: Policy Proposal Form Filling and Variations across Income Levels

Policyholders filled policy proposal Form themselves	Below Rs. 10,000	Rs. 10,000-30,000	Above Rs. 30,000	Total
Yes	30 (36.1)	41 (30.1)	43 (45.3)	114 (36.3)
No	53 (63.9)	95 (69.9)	52 (54.7)	200 (63.7)
Total	83 (100)	136 (100)	95 (100)	314 (100)

Note: Figures in the parenthesis are percentages

Variations have also been observed in case of urban and rural respondents. As37.4 percent urban respondents and 33.3 percent rural respondents have filled policy proposal form of their own (see Table 6.4 below). The findings of Chi-square test reveal that rural-urban variations are insignificant at 5 percent level as χ^2= 0.460 (1, n= 314), p =0.498.

Table 6.4: Policy Proposal Form Filling and Variations across Urban and Rural Areas

Policyholders filled policy proposal Form themselves	Urban	Rural	Total
Yes	85 (37.4)	29 (33.3)	114 (36.3)
No	142 (62.6)	58 (66.7)	200 (63.7)
Total	227 (100)	87 (100)	314 (100)

Note: Figures in the parenthesis are percentages.

An attempt was also made to check variations across gender. The field survey reveals that, 38.2 percent males and 31.4 percent females have filled policy proposal form themselves (Table 6.5). The Chi-square test reveals that these variations are statistically insignificant as value of χ^2= 1.235 (1, n= 314), p=0.266.

Table 6.5: Policy Proposal Form Filling and Variations across Gender

Policyholders filled policy proposal Form themselves	Male	Female	Total
Yes	87 (38.2)	27 (31.4)	114 (36.3)
No	141 (61.8)	59 (68.6)	200 (63.7)
Total	228 (100)	86 (100)	314 (100)

Note: Figures in the parenthesis are percentages.

6.3 Language of the Policy Proposal

The language of the policy proposal form should be simple which acts as an incentive for filling proposal form by the policyholders. Policy proposal form with technical language overridden with clauses and terms, often gets beyond comprehension of the prospective buyer and agent may exploit the situation by misleading him or her. It is relevant to mention here that the target-centric approach of the insurance firms is also one of the major factors for mis-selling policies by agents. In the process when customer feels cheated by not having the desired product sold to him, the policies may lapse.

The survey results show that majority (65.6 percent) of respondents expressed that the language of the policy document was technical in nature and beyond comprehension. This was because only 34.4 percent of the respondents found the language of the policy document warts understanding. Variations have been noticed across insurance firms as 38.3 percent respondents of LIC, 29.6 percent respondents of ICICI Prudential and 31.8 percent respondents of Exide Life, expressed that they found the language of the policy proposal easy to comprehend (see Table 6.6).

Table 6.6: Language of the Policy Proposal and Variations across Insurance Firms

Language of the Policy Proposal	LIC	ICICI Prudential	Exide Life	Total
Easy to Understand	62 (38.3)	32 (29.6)	14 (31.8)	108 (34.4)
Technical	100 (61.7)	76 (70.4)	30 (78.2)	218 (65.6)
Total	162 (100)	108 (100)	44 (100)	314 (100)

Note: Figures in the parenthesis are percentages.

Variations were also noticed across education level of the respondents. Around 72.8 percent respondents with below matric education level, 63.3 percent respondents with matric and plus two education level and 64 percent respondents having education level of graduation and above stated that they found language of the policy proposal technical in nature (Table 6.7). But the variations across education level are found to be statistically insignificant at 5 percent level as per Chi-square test [χ^2 =2.534 (2, n = 314), p =0.282].

Table 6.7: Language of the Policy Proposal and Variations across Education Levels

Language of the Policy Proposal	Below Matric	Matric and Plus 2	Graduation and above	Total
Easy to Understand	22 (27.2)	22 (36.7)	64 (37)	108 (34.4)
Technical	59 (72.8)	38 (63.3)	109 (63)	206 (65.6)
Total	81 (100)	60 (100)	173 (100)	314 (100)

Note: Figures in the parenthesis are percentages.

Variations were also seen in terms of monthly income level. For example 72.6 percent respondents with monthly income less than Rs. 10,000 stated that the language of the policy document was technical. Around 64.7 percent respondents with monthly income ranging from Rs. 10,000 to Rs. 30,000 and 59 percent respondents having monthly income above Rs. 30,000 have revealed that they found the language of policy document technical in nature (see Table 6.8). As per Chi- square test, the variations across income are found to be statistically insignificant as χ^2= 3.715 (2, n=314), p =0.156.

Table 6.8: Language of the Policy Proposal and Variation across Income Levels

Language of the Policy Proposal	Below Rs. 10,000	Rs. 10,000-30,000	Above Rs. 30,000	Total
Easy to Understand	26 (27.4)	48 (35.3)	34 (41)	108 (34.4)
Technical	69 (72.6)	88 (64.7)	49 (59)	206 (65.6)
Total	95 (100)	136 (100)	83 (100)	314 (100)

Note: Figures in the parenthesis are percentages.

Variations are also noticed across urban and rural areas. Around 64.8 percent urban and 67.8 percent rural respondents are of the opinion that language of the policy proposal was technical and was difficult to understand (see Table 6.9). But rural-urban variation turns out to be statistically insignificant as per the Chi-square test [χ^2= 0.261 (1, n = 314), p =0.610].

Table 6.9: Language of the Policy Proposal Variations across Urban and Rural Areas

Language of the Policy Proposal	Urban	Rural	Total
Easy to Understand	80 (35.2)	28 (32.2)	108 (34.4)
Technical	147 (64.8)	59 (67.8)	206 (65.6)
Total	227 (100)	87 (100)	314 (100)

Note: Figures in the parenthesis are percentages.

Variations across gender were also witnessed because 67.1 percent male and 61.6 percent female respondents were of the view that policy document had technical language (see Table 6.10). But the variations across gender are found to be statistically insignificant as per Ch-square test as value of χ^2= 0.830 (1, n=314), p =0.362.

Table 6.10: Language of the Policy Proposal and Variation across Gender

Language of the Policy Proposal	Male	Female	Total
Easy to Understand	75 (32.9)	33 (38.4)	108 (34.4)
Technical	153 (67.1)	53 (61.6)	206 (65.6)
Total	228 (100)	86 (100)	314 (100)

Note: Figures in the parenthesis are percentages.

6.4 Font Size of the Policy Proposal

The terms and conditions of the policy proposal should be bold and clear so that a potential buyer may get the product in consonance with his needs. If policy proposal form is fine printed (i.e. very small font size), then a customer may not be well aware about its terms and conditions and thus, he may be denied benefits of the policy in long run by insurer. Out of total respondents, only 26.4 percent stated that they found the policy proposal legible. Variations were also observed across insurance companies. For example, 22.2 percent respondents of LIC, 29.6 percent respondents of ICICI Prudential and 34.1 percent respondents of Exide Life opined that policy proposal was easily readable (see Table 6.11).

Table 6.11: Legibility of Policy Proposal and Variations across Insurance Firms

Was Policy Proposal legible?	LIC	ICICI Prudential	Exide Life	Total
Yes	36 (22.2)	32 (29.6)	15 (34.1)	83 (26.4)
No	126 (77.8)	76 (70.4)	29 (65.9)	231 (73.6)
Total	162 (100)	108 (100)	44 (100)	314 (100)

Note: Figures in the parenthesis are percentages.

Education level of respondents also showed variation. For example, 23.5 percent respondents with below matric education level; 18.3 percent respondents having education level of matric and plus two and 30.6 percent respondents with graduation and above educational qualifications expressed that the policy proposal form was legible (see Table 6.12). The variations in terms of education level are found to be statistically insignificant as χ^2=3.965 (2, n=314), p=.0138.

Table 6.12: Legibility of Policy Proposal and Variations across Education Levels

Was Policy Proposal legible	Below Matric	Matric and Plus 2	Graduation and above	Total
Yes	19 (23.5)	11 (18.3)	53 (30.6)	83 (26.4)
No	62 (76.5)	49 (81.7)	120 (69.4)	231 (73.6)
Total	81 (100)	60 (100)	170 (100)	314 (100)

Note: Figures in the parenthesis are percentages.

Variations were also observed across income levels. For example, 32.5 percent respondents with monthly income less than Rs. 10,000 have expressed that the policy proposal was readable. On the other hand 924.3 percent respondents with monthly income ranging from Rs. 10,000 to Rs. 30,000 have stated that policy proposal was not fine printed (readable). Around 24 percent respondents with monthly income above Rs. 30,000 have opined that policy proposal was legible (see Table 6.13. The variations across income level, turn out to be statistically insignificant as per Chi-square test [χ^2= 2.157 (2, n=314), p= 0.340].

Table 6.13: Legibility of Policy Proposal and Variations across Income Levels

Was Policy Proposal legible	Below Rs. 10000	Rs. 10000-Rs. 30000	Above Rs. 30000	Total
Yes	27 (32.5)	33 (24.3)	23 (24.2)	83 (26.4)
No	56 (67.5)	103 (75.7)	72 (75.8)	231 (73.6)
Total	83 (100)	136 (100)	95 (100)	314 (100)

Note: Figures in the parenthesis are percentages.

Variations were also seen across urban and rural respondents as 27.3 percent urban respondents and 24.3 percent rural respondents were of the view that policy proposal was legible (Table 6.14). The rural-urban variations are found to be statistically insignificant as χ^2= 0.326 (1, n=314), p = 0.568.

Table 6.14: Legibility of Policy Proposal and Variations across Rural and Urban Areas

Was Policy Proposal legible	Urban	Rural	Total
Yes	62 (27.3)	21 (24.1)	83 (26.4)
No	165 (72.7)	66 (75.9)	231 (73.6)
Total	227 (100)	87 (100)	314 (100)

Note: Figures in the parenthesis are percentages.

Responses across gender also showed variation as 22.8 percent male respondents and 36 percent female respondents stated that the policy proposal was legible (Table 6.15).The variations across gender are found to be statistically significant at 5 percent level as χ^2=5.629(1, n =314), p=.018.

Table 6.15: Legibility of Policy Proposal and Variations across Gender

Was Policy Proposal legible	Male	Female	Total
Yes	52 (22.8)	31 (36)	83 (26.4)
No	176 (77.2)	55 (64)	231 (73.6)
Total	228 (100)	86 (100)	314 (100)

Note: Figures in the parenthesis are percentages.

6.5 Delivery of Policy Proposal

IRDAI has mandated that once policy proposal is accepted by the insurance companies, it must reach to the policyholder with in stipulated time period of fifteen working days from the date of acceptance of the policy proposal. In case of delay, a insurer must communicate with the prospective policyholder stating reasons for delay.

Majority (80.9 percent) of the respondents stated that they received finalized policy document with in stipulated time period. Variations were noticed across insurers as 74.1 percent respondents of LIC; 91.7 percent respondents of ICICI prudential and 79.5 percent respondents of Exide Life have stated that they received final policy proposal well in time (see Table 6.16).

Table 6.16: Delivery of Policy Proposal and Variations across Insurance Firms

Was Policy delivered on time	LIC	ICICI Prudential	Exide Life	Total
Yes	120 (74.1)	99 (91.7)	35 (79.5)	254 (80.9)
No	42 (25.9)	9 (8.3)	9 (20.5)	60 (19.1)
Total	162 (100)	108 (100)	44 (100)	314 (100)

Note: Figures in the parenthesis are percentages.

However variations were also observed across education levels. Around 70.4 percent respondents with education level less than matric; 61.7 percent respondents with educational level matric and plus 2 and 92.5 percent respondents with education level graduation and above, have expressed that - they received policy document within stipulated time (Table 6.17).

Table 6.17: Delivery of Policy Proposal and Variations across Education Levels

Was Policy delivered on time	Below Matric	Matric and Plus 2	Graduation and above	Total
Yes	57 (70.4)	37 (61.7)	160 (92.5)	254 (80.9)
No	24 (29.6)	23 (38.3)	13 (7.5)	60 (19.1)
Total	81 (100)	60 (100)	173 (100)	314 (100)

Note: Figures in the parenthesis are percentages.

Variations across income level suggest that 74.7 percent respondents with monthly income less than Rs, 10,000; and 74.3 percent respondents with monthly income ranging from Rs. 10,000 to Rs. 30,000 and 95.8 percent respondents with monthly income above Rs. 30,000 have stated that they had received policy document on time (see Table 6.18).

Table 6.18: Delivery of Policy Proposal and Variations across Income Levels

Was Policy delivered on time	Below Rs. 10000	Rs. 10000- Rs. 30000	Above Rs. 30000	Total
Yes	62 (74.7)	101 (74.3)	91 (95.8)	254 (80.9)
No	21 (25.3)	35 (25.7)	4 (4.2)	60 (19.1)
Total	83 (100)	136 (100)	95 (100)	314 (100)

Note: Figures in the parenthesis are percentages.

Variations were also noticed across urban and rural respondents. For example, 78.4 percent urban respondents and 87.4 percent rural respondents had expressed that they had received final policy document on time (see Table 6.19).

Table 6.19: Delivery of Policy Proposal and Variations across Rural and Urban Areas

Was Policy delivered on time	Urban	Rural	Total
Yes	178 (78.4)	76 (87.4)	254 (80.9)
No	49 (21.6)	11 (12.6)	60 (19.1)
Total	227 (100)	87 (100)	314 (100)

Note: Figures in the parenthesis are percentages.

Around 77.6 percent male respondents and 89.5 percent female respondents have expressed that they had received final policy document on time (see Table 6.20).

Table 6.20: Delivery of Policy Proposal and Variations across Gender

Was Policy delivered on time	Male	Female	Total
Yes	177 (77.6)	77 (89.5)	254 (80.9)
No	51 (22.4)	9 (10.5)	60 (19.1)
Total	228 (100)	86 (100)	314 (100)

Note: Figures in the parenthesis are percentages.

6.6 Information Disclosure By the Agent at the Point of Sale of Policy Proposal

IRDAI has mandated that at point of sale of policy the agent has to provide all the necessary information such as name of the plan governing the policy, whether policy includes profits, premium to be paid, its periodicity, date of commencement of risk, free look period, documents required for claim settlement, address and contact number of insurer, etc regarding policy to the prospective buyer which is essential ingredient of customer interest protection.

Sub Hypothesis tested in this regard is 'IRDAI has been effective in stimulating agents to share all the necessary information regarding policy with the prospective buyer at point of sale of policy proposal'.

6.7 Information Disclosure By The Agent About The Name Of The Plan Governing The Policy

Every agent should share information regarding name of the plan proposal governing the policy. In life insurance various names of the plans are term plan, endowment plan, Unit Linked Insurance Product, money back and whole life plan. Out of total respondents, majority (81.5) percent stated that the agent shared information regarding name of the plan governing the policy. Inter insurance companies variation were noticed. For example, 84.6 percent respondents of LIC; 76.9 percent respondents of ICICI Prudential and 81.8 percent respondents of Exide Life have stated that agent shared information regarding name of the plan governing the policy (see Table 6.21).

Table 6.21: Information Shared by an Agent Regarding Plan Governing the Policy and Variations across Insurance Firms

Did agent made aware about name of the plan governing the policy	LIC	ICICI Prudential	Exide Life	Total
Yes	137 (84.6)	83 (76.9)	36 (81.8)	256 (81.5)
No	25 (15.4)	25 (23.1)	8 (18.2)	58 (18.5)
Total	162 (100)	108 (100)	44 (100)	314 (100)

Note:- Figures in the parenthesis are percentages.

Variations were also noticed across education level of respondents. It was brought forward that 67.9 percent respondents with education level less than matric and 85 percent respondents having education between matric and plus two and 86.7 percent respondents with education level of graduation and above have stated that the agent shared information regarding name of the plan governing the policy (Table 6.22). But these variations are found to be statistically insignificant as per Chi-square test [^{2}= 0.212 (2, N = 314), p= 0.900].

Table 6.22: Information Shared by an Agent Regarding Plan Governing the Policy and Variations across Education Levels

Did agent made aware about name of the plan governing the policy	Below Matric	Matric and Plus 2	Graduation and above	Total
Yes	55 (67.9)	51 (85)	150 (86.7)	256 (81.5)
No	26 (32.1)	9 (15)	23 (13.3)	58 (18.5)
Total	81 (100)	60 (100)	173 (100)	314 (100)

Note: Figures in the parenthesis are percentages.

Variations were also observed across income levels. Around 75 percent respondents with monthly income less than Rs. 10,000 and 87.5 percent respondents with monthly income ranging from Rs. 10,000 and Rs. 30,000 have stated that agent shared information regarding name of the policy plan. Approximately, 79 percent respondents having monthly income above Rs. 30,000 have stated that agent shared information regarding name of plan (Table 6.23). As per Chi-square test these variations are found to be statistically insignificant as χ^2= 3.651 (2, N = 314), p = 0.161.

Table 6.23: Information Shared by an Agent Regarding Plan Governing the Policy and Variations across Income Levels

Did agent made aware about name of the plan governing the policy	Below Rs. 10000	Rs. 10000- Rs. 30000	Above Rs. 30000	Total
Yes	62 (74.7)	119 (87.5)	75 (78.9)	256 (81.5)
No	21 (25.3)	17 (12.5)	20 (21.1)	58 (18.5)
Total	83 (100)	136 (100)	95 (100)	314 (100)

Note: Figures in the parenthesis are percentages.

Variations have also been noticed in terms of urban and rural respondents. In terms of urban respondents, 82.4 percent and in terms of rural respondents 79.3

percent stated that the agent imparted information regarding the name of the plan governing the policy (Table 6.24). But these variations are found to be statistically insignificant as per Chi-square test as χ^2= 0.255 (1, N = 314), p= 0.614.

Table 6.24: Information Shared by an Agent Regarding Plan Governing the Policy and Variations across Rural and Urban Areas

Did agent made aware about name of the plan governing the policy	Urban	Rural	Total
Yes	187 (82.4)	69 (79.3)	256 (81.5)
No	40 (17.6)	18 (20.7)	58 (18.5)
Total	227 (100)	87 (100)	314 (100)

Note: Figures in the parenthesis are percentages.

Responses across gender showed variation as around 81 percent male respondents and 82.6 female respondents stated that agent imparted information regarding name of the plan governing the policy (Table 6.25).Variations in terms of gender turns out to be statistically insignificant as per Chi-square test [χ^2=0.310(2, N = 314), p = 0.578].

Table 6.25: Information Shared by an Agent Regarding Plan Governing the Policy and Variations across Gender

Did agent made aware about name of the plan governing the policy	Male	Female	Total
Yes	185 (81.1)	71 (82.6)	256 (81.5)
No	43 (18.9)	15 (17.4)	58 (18.5)
Total	228 (100)	86 (100)	314 (100)

Note: Figures in the parenthesis are percentages.

6.8 Information Disclosure By The Agent Regarding Inclusion of Profits/Bonus In The Policy

Here certain policies include sharing of the profits/bonuses with the policy-holders and they are termed as with-profit plans. The declaration of various bonuses/ profits varies from one insurance firm to another. In general, profits can be simple reversionary bonuses that are declared per thousand Sum Assured annually at the end of each financial year. Finally, (Additional) Bonus may be payable to the policyholder if a policy continues for a minimum time period.

It is also mandatory on the part of the agent to share information regarding inclusion of benefits/bonus in the policy proposal to the prospective buyer. Around 72 percent of the respondents stated that agent shared information regarding inclusion or exclusion of the benefits/profits in the policy. Variations were also noticed across insurance firms. For example, around 70 percent respondents of LIC; 75.9 percent respondents of ICICI Prudential and 72.7 percent respondents of Exide Life have reported that agent disclosed information regarding inclusion of benefits in the policy at point of sale of policy (Table 6.26).

Table 6.26: Information Shared by an Agent Regarding Inclusion of Profits in policy and Variations across Insurance Companies

Did agent tell whether policy includes profits/Bonus	LIC	ICICI Prudential	Exide Life	Total
Yes	113 (69.8)	82 (75.9)	32 (72.7)	227 (72.3)
No	49 (30.2)	26 (24.1)	12 (27.3)	87 (27.7)
Total	162 (100)	108 (100)	44 (100)	314 (100)

Note: Figures in the parenthesis are percentages.

Variations were also noticed across education levels. Around 61 percent respondents with education below matric level and 65 percent respondents with matric and plus2 education level have stated that agent shared information regarding inclusion of profits in the policy. In case of respondents with education level with graduation and above 80.3 percent stated that agent shared information regarding bonuses included in the policy (Table 6.27). The variations in terms of education level are found to be statistically insignificant as per Chi-square test [$\chi^2 = 3.975$ (2, N = 314), p = 0.137].

Table 6.27: Information Shared by an Agent Regarding Inclusion of Profits in Policy and Variations across Education Levels

Did agent tell whether policy includes profits/Bonus	Below Matric	Matric and Plus 2	Graduation and above	Total
Yes	49 (60.5)	39 (65.0)	139 (80.3)	227 (72.3)
No	32 (39.5)	21 (35.0)	34 (19.7)	87 (27.7)
Total	81 (100)	60 (100)	173 (100)	314 (100)

Note: Figures in the parenthesis are percentages.

Variations were also noticed across income levels as 66.3 percent respondents with monthly income less than Rs. 10,000 and 72.8 percent respondents with monthly income ranging from Rs. 10,000 and Rs. 30,000 have reported that agent disclosed that whether policy includes profits or not. Around 77 percent respondents having monthly income above Rs. 30,000 have stated that agent shared information regarding inclusion or exclusion of profits in the policy (Table 6.28). As per Chi-square test these variations are found to be statistically insignificant at 5 percent level as χ^2= 2.678 (2, N = 314), p = 0.262.

Table 6.28: Information Shared by an Agent Regarding Inclusion of Profits in Policy and Variations across Income Levels

Did agent tell whether policy includes profits/Bonus	Below Rs. 10000	Rs. 10000-Rs. 30000	Above Rs. 30000	Total
Yes	55 (66.3)	99 (72.8)	73 (76.8)	227 (72.3)
No	28 (33.7)	37 (27.2)	22 (23.2)	87 (27.7)
Total	83 (100)	136 (100)	95 (100)	314 (100)

Note: Figures in the parenthesis are percentages.

Similarly, variations were also observed in terms of urban and rural respondents. In terms of urban respondents, around 73.1 percent and 70.1 percent rural respondents expressed that agent shared information regarding inclusion of profits/ bonus in the policy at the point of sale of policy (Table 6.29).These variations are found to be statistically insignificant as per Chi-square test as χ^2= 0.160 (1, N = 314), p = 0.689.

Table 6.29: Information Shared by an Agent Regarding Inclusion of Profits in policy and variations across Rural and Urban Areas

Did agent tell whether policy includes profits/Bonus	Urban	Rural	Total
Yes	166 (73.1)	61 (70.1)	227 (72.3)
No	61 (26.9)	26 (29.9)	87 (27.7)
Total	227 (100)	87 (100)	314 (100)

Note: Figures in the parenthesis are percentages.

In terms of gender variations were also noticed as 71.5 percent male respondents and 74.4 percent female respondents reported that agent disclosed information regarding inclusion of profits in the policy (Table 6.30).These variations are found to be statistically insignificant as per Chi-square test as χ^2= .297 (1, N = 314), p = .440.

Table 6.30: Information Shared by an Agent Regarding Inclusion of Profits in Policy and Variations across Gender

Did agent tell whether policy includes profits/Bonus	Male	Female	Total
Yes	163 (71.5)	64 (74.4)	227 (72.3)
No	65 (28.5)	22 (25.6)	87 (27.7)
Total	228 (100)	86 (100)	314 (100)

Note:- Figures in the parenthesis are percentages.

6.9 Information Disclosure By The Agent Regarding Various Benefits Payable In The Policy

It is mandated by the IRDAI that an agent must disclose all the benefits being paid under the policy cover; as it provides an opportunity to the prospective buyer to buy the policy as per his/her needs. Out of total respondents, 73.6 percent stated that agent made them aware about various benefits covered in the policy. Variations were observed across insurers as 74.1 percent respondents of LIC; 75 percent respondents of ICICI prudential and 68.2 percent respondents of Exide Life stated that agent shared information regarding various benefits payable under the policy cover (Table 6.31).

Table 6.31: Information Shared by an Agent Regarding Benefits Payable in Policy and Variations across Insurance Firms

Did agent make aware about benefits payable in policy	LIC	ICICI Prudential	Exide Life	Total
Yes	120 (74.1)	81 (75)	30 (68.2)	231 (73.6)
No	42 (25.9)	27 (25)	14 (31.8)	83 (26.4)
Total	162 (100)	108 (100)	44 (100)	314 (100)

Note: Figures in the parenthesis are percentages.

Variations were also noticed in terms of education levels as 58 percent respondents having below matric education and 75 percent respondents with matric and plus two education level stated that agent disclosed information regarding various benefits covered under the policy. Around 80 percent respondents with education level of graduation and above expressed that agent disclosed information regarding benefits payable under the policy (Table 6.32). As per Chi-square test these variations are found to be statistically significant at one percent level [χ^2= 9.670(2, N = 314), p = .008].

Table 6.32: Information Shared by an Agent Regarding Benefits Payable in Policy and Variations across Education Levels

Did agent made aware about benefits payable	Below Matric	Matric and Plus 2	Graduation and above	Total
Yes	47 (58)	45 (75)	139 (80.3)	231 (73.6)
No	34 (42)	15 (25)	34 (19.7)	83 (26.4)
Total	81 (100)	60 (100)	173 (100)	314 (100)

Note: Figures in the parenthesis are percentages.

Across income levels variations were also noticed. For example 62.7 percent respondents with monthly income less than Rs. 10,000; 75.7 percent respondents with monthly income ranging between Rs. 10,000 and Rs. 30,000 and 80 percent respondents with monthly income above Rs. 30,000 expressed that agent shared information regarding various benefits payable under the policy cover (Table 6.33). These variations are found to be statistically insignificant as per Chi-square test as χ^2= .496 (2, N = 314), p= .781.

Table 6.33: Information Shared by an Agent Regarding Benefits Payable in Policy and Variations across Income Levels

Did agent made aware about benefits payable	Below Rs. 10000	Rs. 10000- Rs. 30000	Above Rs. 30000	Total
Yes	52 (62.7)	103 (75.7)	76 (80.0)	231 (73.6)
No	31 (37.3)	33 (24.3)	19 (20.0)	83 (26.4)
Total	83 (100)	136 (100)	95 (100)	314 (100)

Note: Figures in the parenthesis are percentages.

Perceptions of urban and rural respondents also varied as 76.2 percent urban respondents and 66.7 percent rural respondents were of the view that agent disclosed information regarding various benefits payable under the policy (Table 6.34). The variations across rural and urban areas are found to be statistically insignificant as per Chi-square test [χ^2= 2.412 (1, N = 314), p = 0.120].

Table 6.34: Information Shared by an Agent Regarding Benefits Payable in Policy and Variations across Urban and Rural Areas

Did agent made aware about benefits payable	Urban	Rural	Total
Yes	173 (76.2)	58 (66.7)	231 (73.6)
No	54 (23.8)	29 (33.3)	83 (26.4)
Total	227 (100)	87 (100)	314 (100)

Note: Figures in the parenthesis are percentages.

Variations were also noticed across gender. For example, 76.3 percent male respondents and 66.3 percent female respondents were of the opinion that agent disclosed information regarding various benefits payable under the policy (see Table 6.35).These variations are found to be statistically significant at 5 percent level as per Chi-square test as ^{2}= 5.054 (1, N = 314), p= .025.

Table 6.35: Information Shared by an Agent Regarding Benefits Payable in Policy and Variations across Gender

Did agent made aware about benefits payable	Male	Female	Total
Yes	174 (76.3)	57 (66.3)	231 (73.6)
No	54 (23.7)	29 (33.7)	83 (26.4)
Total	228 (100)	86 (100)	314 (100)

Note: Figures in the parenthesis are percentages.

6.10 Information Shared By An Agent Regarding Date Of Commencement Of Risk

When the buyer buys the policy, the policy is assessed by the insurer in terms of sum assured, income of the policyholder and premium payment etc. This process in insurance parlance is called underwriting. If insurer is satisfied then a policy bond is prepared, and it is from this point that a cover becomes active or commencement of the risk takes place. From this date onwards, one is entitled for the various risks such as death claim.

Out of total respondents, majority (71 percent) reported that agent made them aware about the date of commencement of risk. The findings across insurance companies show variance as 66.7 percent respondents of LIC; 76.9 percent respondents of ICICI Prudential and 72.7 percent respondents of Exide Life stated that agent made them aware about the date of beginning of risk coverage under the policy (Table 6.36).

Table 6.36: Information Shared by an Agent Regarding Commencement of Risk and Variations across Insurance Firms

Were you told about date of commencement of risk by agent	LIC	ICICI Prudential	Exide Life	Total
Yes	108 (66.7)	83 (76.9)	32 (72.7)	223 (71.0)
No	54 (33.3)	25 (23.1)	12 (27.3)	91 (29)
Total	162 (100)	108 (100)	44 (100)	314 (100)

Note: Figures in the parenthesis are percentages.

Variations in this regard were also observed across education levels of respondents. For example, 59.3 percent respondents with below matric education; 61.7 percent respondents having educational qualification between matric and plus two and 79.8 percent respondents with graduation and above education stated that agent made them aware about date of commencement of risk (Table 6.37). As per Chi-square test, these variations are found to be statistically insignificant at 5 percent level as $\chi^2 = 5.338$ (2, N = 314), p = .069.

Table 6.37: Information Shared by an Agent Regarding Commencement of Risk and Variations across Education Levels

Were you told about date of commencement of risk by agent	Below Matric	Matric and Plus 2	Graduation and above	Total
Yes	48 (59.3)	37 (61.7)	138 (79.8)	223 (71)
No	33 (40.7)	23 (38.3)	35 (20.2)	91 (29)
Total	81 (100)	60 (100)	173 (100)	314 (100)

Note: Figures in the parenthesis are percentages.

In terms of income levels, variations were also noticed as 71.1 percent respondents with monthly income less than Rs. 10,000 and 68.4 percent respondents having monthly income ranging between Rs. 10,000 and Rs. 30,000 reported that agent shared information regarding date of commencement of risk (Table 6.38).These variations are found to be statistically insignificant as per Chi-square test as χ^2= 2.943 (2, N = 314), p = .230.

Table 6.38: Information Shared by an Agent Regarding Commencement of Risk and Variations across Income Levels

Were you told about date of commencement of risk by agent	Below Rs. 10000	Rs. 10000- Rs. 30000	Above Rs. 30000	Total
Yes	59 (71.1)	93 (68.4)	71 (74.7)	223 (71)
No	24 (28.9)	43 (31.6)	24 (25.3)	91 (29)
Total	83 (100)	136 (100)	95 (100)	314 (100)

Note: Figures in the parenthesis are percentages.

Around 74 percent urban respondents and 64.4 percent rural respondents were of the opinion that agent shared information regarding date of commencement of risk at the point of sale of policy (Table 6.39).These variations are found to be statistically insignificant as per Chi-square test as χ^2= .110 (1, N = 314), p = .740.

Table 6.39: Information Shared by an Agent Regarding Commencement of Risk and Variations across Rural and Urban Areas

Were you told about date of commencement of risk by agent	Urban	Rural	Total
Yes	167 (73.6)	56 (64.4)	223 (71)
No	60 (26.4)	31 (35.6)	91 (29)
Total	227 (100)	87 (100)	314 (100)

Note: Figures in the parenthesis are percentages.

Variations were also noticed across gender as70.6 percent male respondents and 72.1 percent female respondents reported that agent shared the information regarding date of initiation of risk coverage of the policy (Table 6.40).These variations are found to be statistically insignificant as per Chi-square test [χ^2= .016 (1, N = 314), p = .899].

Table 6.40: Information Shared by an Agent Regarding Commencement of Risk and Variations across Gender

Were you told about date of commencement of risk by agent	Male	Female	Total
Yes	161 (70.6)	62 (72.1)	223 (71)
No	67 (29.4)	24 (27.9)	91 (29.0)
Total	228 (100)	86 (100)	314 (100)

Note: Figures in the parenthesis are percentages.

6.11 Information Disclosure By Agent Regarding Maturity of Policy

After the initiation of the policy, if no indemnity happens in between the policy matures after stipulated time period as per the insurance contract. Generally, on maturity of the policy the policyholder is paid sum assured and bonus of the policy. Thus the policyholder receives back lump sum amount of money that he had paid by small installments as premium over the years.

Out of total respondents 79.6 percent stated that agent told them about date of maturity of the policy. In case of LIC 76.5 percent respondents; 84.3 percent respondents of ICICI and 79.5 percent respondents of Exide life have reported that agent told them about date of maturity of the policy (Table 6.41).

Table 6.41: Information Shared by an Agent Regarding Maturity of Policy and Variations across Insurance Firms

Did agent tell about date of maturity	LIC	ICICI Prudential	Exide Life	Total
Yes	124 (76.5)	91 (84.3)	35 (79.5)	250 (79.6)
No	38 (23.5)	17 (15.7)	9 (20.5)	64 (20.4)
Total	162 (100)	108 (100)	44 (100)	314 (100)

Note: Figures in the parenthesis are percentages.

Variations were also noticed across education levels as 63 percent respondents with below matric education; 76.7 percent respondents having education from Matric to plus two and 88.4 percent respondents having graduation and above education expressed that agent made them aware about date of maturity of the policy (Table

6.42). These variations are found to be statistically insignificant as per Chi-square test as χ^2= 3.783 (2, N = 314), p = .151.

Table 6.42: Information Shared by an Agent Regarding Maturity of Policy and Variations across Education Levels

Did agent tell about date of maturity	Below Matric	Matric and Plus 2	Graduation and above	Total
Yes	51 (63)	46 (76.7)	153 (88.4)	250 (79.6)
No	30 (37)	14 (23.3)	20 (11.6)	64 (20.4)
Total	81 (100)	60 (100)	173 (100)	314 (100)

Note: Figures in the parenthesis are percentages.

Income levels of the respondents also showed variation. For example, 66.3 percent respondents having monthly income less than Rs. 10,000; whereas 79.4 percent respondents having monthly income ranging from Rs. 10,000 to Rs. 30,000 and 91.6 percent respondents with monthly income above Rs. 30,000 have stated that agent told them about date of maturity of the policy (Table 6.43). These variations are found to be statistically insignificant as per Chi-square test as χ^2= .673 (2, N = 314), p = .714.

Table 6.43: Information Shared by an Agent Regarding Maturity of Policy and Variations across Income levels

Did agent tell about date of maturity	Below Rs. 10000	Rs. 10000-Rs. 30000	Above Rs. 30000	Total
Yes	55 (66.3)	108 (79.4)	87 (91.6)	250 (79.6)
No	28 (33.7)	28 (20.6)	8 (8.4)	64 (20.4)
Total	83 (100)	136 (100)	95 (100)	314 (100)

Note: Figures in the parenthesis are percentages.

Perceptions of urban and rural respondents varied on this front as 85 percent urban respondents and 65.5 percent rural respondents were of the opinion that agent made them aware about date of maturity of the policy (Table 6.44). These variations are found to be statistically significant at one percent level as per Chi-square test [χ^2= 18.403 (1, N = 314), p = .001].

Table 6.44: Information Shared by an Agent Regarding Maturity of Policy and Variations across Urban and Rural areas

Did agent tell about date of maturity	Urban	Rural	Total
Yes	193 (85)	57 (65.5)	250 (79.6)
No	34 (15)	30 (34.5)	64 (20.4)
Total	227 (100)	87 (100)	314 (100)

Note: Figures in the parenthesis are percentages.

In terms of gender, around 83.3 percent male respondents and 69.8 percent female respondents reported that agent shared information regarding date of maturity of the policy at the point of sale of policy proposal (Table 6.45). These variations are found to be statistically significant at one percent level as per Chi-square test [χ^2= 16.362 (1, N = 314), p = .001].

Table 6.45: Information Shared by an Agent Regarding Maturity of Policy and Variations across Gender

Did agent tell about date of maturity	Male	Female	Total
Yes	190 (83.3)	60 (69.8)	250 (79.6)
No	38 (16.7)	26 (30.2)	64 (20.4)
Total	228 (100)	86 (100)	314 (100)

Note: Figures in the parenthesis are percentages.

6.12 Information Shared By An Agent Regarding Free Look Period

Among the protection of policyholders' interest issues, free look period deserves special mention as it is a customer friendly provision. Free look period provides option to policyholder to change policy plan or discontinue the policy within 15 days from receipt of finalized policy document and get money refund after deducting the charges for policy processing. It means on receiving final policy document the policyholder can evaluate all the terms and conditions of the document and can check whether the product sold to him/her is the same desired by him/her. If the policyholder is not satisfied with the policy/product he can change or return the policy within 15 days by paying nominal processing charges and getting money refund.

Out of total respondents, 27.1 percent stated that agent disclosed information regarding free look period. Inter insurer variations are also documented as only 16 percent respondents of LIC; 40.7 percent respondents of ICICI Prudential and 34.1 percent respondents of Exide Life expressed that agent made them aware about free look period at point of selling the policy (Table 6.46).

Table 6.46: Information Shared by an Agent Regarding Free Look Period and Variations across Insurance Firms

Agent imparted information regarding free look period	LIC	ICICI Prudential	Exide Life	Total
Yes	26 (16)	44 (40.7)	15 (34.1)	85 (27.1)
No	136 (84)	64 (59.3)	29 (65.9)	229 (72.9)
Total	162 (100)	108 (100)	44 (100)	314 (100)

Note: Figures in the parenthesis are percentages.

Sharing of information regarding free look period also varied across education level of respondents. Around 7.4 percent respondents with below matric education; 20 percent respondents with matric and plus two education level and 38.7 percent respondents having education of graduation and above stated that agent shared information regarding free look period (Table 6.47). These variations are found to be statistically significant at one percent level as per Chi-square test [χ^2= 29.292 (2, N = 314), p = .001].

Table 6.47: Information Shared by an Agent Regarding Free Look Period and Variations across Education Levels

Agent imparted information regarding free look period	Below Matric	Matric and Plus 2	Graduation and above	Total
Yes	6 (7.4)	12 (20)	67 (38.7)	85 (27.1)
No	75 (92.6)	48 (80)	106 (61.3)	229 (72.9)
Total	81 (100)	60 (100)	173 (100)	314 (100)

Note: Figures in the parenthesis are percentages.

Variations were also noticed across income levels of respondents as 12 percent respondents with monthly income below Rs. 10,000 and 30.9 percent respondents having monthly income ranging from Rs. 10,000 and Rs. 30,000 stated that agent shared information about free look period while 34.7 percent respondents having monthly income above Rs. 30,000 were made aware by agent on this account (Table 6.48). As per Chi-square test these variations are found to be statistically significant at one percent level as χ^2= 13.317 (2, N = 314), p = .001.

Table 6.48: Information Shared by an Agent Regarding Free Look Period and Variations across Income Levels

Agent imparted information regarding free look period	Below Rs. 10000	Rs. 10000-Rs. 30000	Above Rs. 30000	Total
Yes	10 (12)	42 (30.9)	33 (34.7)	85 (27.1)
No	73 (88)	94 (69.1)	62 (65.3)	229 (72.9)
Total	83 (100)	136 (100)	95 (100)	314 (100)

Note: Figures in the parenthesis are percentages.

Rural-Urban variations were also noticed and it was found that 30.4 percent urban respondents and 18.4 percent rural respondents were made aware about free look period by the agent (Table 6.49).These variations are found to be statistically significant at 5 percent level as per Chi-square test [χ^2= 4.592 (1, N = 314), p = .032].

Table 6.49: Information Shared by an Agent Regarding Free Look Period and Variations across Rural and Urban Areas

Agent imparted information regarding free look period	Urban	Rural	Total
Yes	69 (30.4)	16 (18.4)	85 (27.1)
No	158 (69.6)	71 (81.6)	229 (72.9)
Total	227 (100)	87 (100)	314 (100)

Note: Figures in the parenthesis are percentages.

Around 29 percent male respondents and 22.1 percent female respondents were made aware about free look period by the agent (Table 6.50).These variations are found to be statistically insignificant as per Chi-square test as χ^2= 1.486 (1, N = 314), p = .223.

Table 6.50: Information Shared by an Agent Regarding Free Look Period and Variations across Gender

Agent imparted information regarding free look period	Male	Female	Total
Yes	66 (28.9)	19 (22.1)	85 (27.1)
No	162 (71.1)	67 (77.9)	229 (72.9)
Total	228 (100)	86 (100)	314 (100)

Note: Figures in the parenthesis are percentages.

6.13 Information Discloser By Agent Regarding Premium To Be Paid And Its Periodicity, Grace Period For Premium Payment, Last Premium Installment

Agent should provide information regarding amount of premium to be paid its periodicity, grace period and last premium installment. If premium amount is not in consonance with the income of the prospective buyer the policy may lapse in future. As per latest guidelines of IRDAI this is termed as miss-selling on the part of agent. Information regarding periodicity of the premium also avoids lapsation of policy. Also, the policy contract provides for a grace period, which gives the policyholder an additional period of time after the due date for the payment of the premium. During this period, a policyholder can still pay premium and the life policy will continues to be in force. Thus grace period prevents lapsation of policy.

Out of total respondents, majority (81.5 percent) reported that agent shared information regarding premium to be paid and its periodicity, grace period for premium payment, last premium installment. Inter insurer variations were also observed. It was found that 80.9 percent respondents of LIC; 82.4 percent respondents of Exide Life and 81.8 percent respondents of Exide Life revealed that agent made them aware about premium to be paid and its periodicity, grace period for premium payment, last premium installment (Table 6.51).

Table 6.51: Information Shared by an Agent Regarding Premium, its Periodicity, Grace Period and Variations across Insurance Firms

Agent made aware about premium to be paid and its periodicity, grace period for premium payment, last premium installment	LIC	ICICI Prudential	Exide Life	Total
Yes	131 (80.9)	89 (82.4)	36 (81.8)	256 (81.5)
No	31 (19.1)	19 (17.6)	8 (18.2)	58 (18.5)
Total	162 (100)	108 (100)	44 (100)	314 (100)

Note: Figures in the parenthesis are percentages.

Education level of respondents also showed variation on this front. Around 77 percent respondents with below matric education; 81.7 percent respondents with matric and plus two education and 83.8 percent respondents having graduation and above education stated that agent shared information regarding premium to be paid, its periodicity, grace period and last installment of the premium (Table 6.52).These variations are found to be statistically insignificant as per Chi-square test as $\chi^2= 1.938$ (2, N = 314), p = .379.

Table 6.52: Information Shared by an Agent Regarding Premium, its Periodicity, Grace Period and Variations across Educational Levels

Agent made aware about premium to be paid and its periodicity, grace period for premium payment, last premium installment	Below Matric	Matric and Plus 2	Graduation and above	Total
Yes	62 (76.5)	49 (81.7)	145 (83.8)	256 (81.5)
No	19 (23.5)	11 (18.3)	28 (16.2)	58 (18.5)
Total	81 (100)	60 (100)	173 (100)	314 (100)

Note: Figures in the parenthesis are percentages.

Variations were also observed across income levels of the respondents. It was found that 81.9 percent respondents with monthly income below Rs. 10,000 and 77.9percent respondents with monthly income ranging from Rs. 10,000 to Rs. 30,000 and 86.3 percent respondents with monthly income above Rs. 30,000 expressed that agent made them aware about premium to be paid and its periodicity, grace period for premium payment, last premium installment (Table 6.53). These variations are found to be statistically insignificant at 5 percent level as per Chi-square test as χ^2= 2.617 (2, N = 314), p = .270.

Table 6.53: Information Shared by an Agent Regarding Premium, its Periodicity, Grace Period and Variations across Income Levels

Agent made aware about premium to be paid and its periodicity, grace period for premium payment, last premium installment	Below Rs. 10000	Rs. 10000- Rs. 30000	Above Rs. 30000	Total
Yes	68 (81.9)	106 (77.9)	82 (86.3)	256 (81.5)
No	15 (18.1)	30 (22.1)	13 (13.7)	58 (18.5)
Total	83 (100)	136 (100)	95 (100)	314 (100)

Note: Figures in the parenthesis are percentages.

Responses of urban and rural respondents also showed variation as 83.3 percent urban respondents and 77 percent rural respondents were of the view that agent made aware about premium to be paid and its periodicity, grace period for premium payment, last premium installment (Table 6.54). These variations are found to be statistically insignificant as per Chi-square test as χ^2= 1.631 (1, N = 314), p = .202.

Table 6.54: Information Shared by an Agent Regarding Premium, its Periodicity, Grace Period and Variations across Rural and Urban Areas

Agent made aware about premium to be paid and its periodicity, grace period for premium payment, last premium installment	Urban	Rural	Total
Yes	189 (83.3)	67 (77)	256 (81.5)
No	38 (16.7)	20 (23)	58 (18.5)
Total	227 (100)	87 (100)	314 (100)

Note: Figures in the parenthesis are percentages.

Variations across gender were also observed and it was found that 82.5 percent male respondents and 79.1 percent female respondents reported that agent made them aware about premium to be paid and its periodicity, grace period for premium payment, last premium installment (Table 6.55). As per Chi-square test these variations are found to be statistically insignificant [χ^2 =0.476 (1, N = 314), p = .490].

Table 6.55: Information Shared by an Agent Regarding Premium, its Periodicity, Grace Period and Variations across Gender

Agent made aware about premium to be paid and its periodicity, grace period for premium payment, last premium installment	Male	Female	Total
Yes	188 (82.5)	68 (79.1)	256 (81.5)
No	40 (17.5)	18 (20.9)	58 (18.5)
Total	228 (100)	86 (100)	314 (100)

Note: Figures in the parenthesis are percentages.

6.14 Information Disclosure By An Agent Regarding Contingencies Excluded From The Risk Cover

All policies cover different risks. Generally, life insurance policies do not include deaths in war, death in plane crash, death due to suicide, deaths due to various ailments, etc. Thus a prospective buyer should be fully acquainted with various risks cover so that he may buy product as per his needs. Masking of such information by agent may tend to deliver a product which is not in consonance with needs of the buyer.

Out of total respondents, 43.9 percent reported that they were made aware regarding various contingencies excluded from the scope of the risk cover. In terms of insurance companies variations were observed on this front. In case of LIC 42.6 percent respondents; 46.3 percent respondents of ICICI Prudential and 43.2 percent respondents of Exide Life revealed that agent shared information regarding various contingencies excluded from the scope of the risk at the point of sale of policy (Table 6.56).

Table 6.56: Information Shared by an Agent Regarding Contingencies Excluded from the Risk Cover and Variations across Insurance Companies

Agent imparted information regarding contingencies excluded from the scope of risk cover	LIC	ICICI Prudential	Exide Life	Total
Yes	69 (42.6)	50 (46.3)	19 (43.2)	138 (43.9)
No	93 (57.4)	58 (53.7)	25 (56.8)	176 (56.1)
Total	162 (100)	108 (100)	44 (100)	314 (100)

Note: Figures in the parenthesis are percentages.

Variations were also noticed in terms of education level of respondents as 34.6 percent respondents with below matric education level; 40 percent respondents having education level of matric and plus two and 49.7 percent respondents with graduation and above education level reported that agent shared information regarding exclusion of various contingencies from risk cover (Table 6.57). These variations are found to be statistically insignificant at 5 percent level as per Chi-square test [χ^2= 5.605 (2, N = 314), p = .061].

Table 6.57: Information Shared by an Agent Regarding Contingencies Excluded from the Risk Cover and Variations across Education Levels

Agent imparted information regarding contingencies excluded from the scope of risk cover	**Below Matric**	**Matric and Plus 2**	**Graduation and above**	**Total**
Yes	28 (34.6)	24 (40)	86 (49.7)	138 (43.9)
No	53 (65.4)	36 (60)	87 (50.3)	176 (56.1)
Total	81 (100)	60 (100)	173 (100)	314 (100)

Note: Figures in the parenthesis are percentages.

Similarly, variations in terms of income level of respondents were also documented. It was found that 43.4 percent respondents having monthly income below Rs. 10,000; around 44 percent respondents having monthly income ranging from Rs. 10,000 to Rs. 30,000 and 44.2 percent respondents having monthly income above Rs. 30,000 stated that agent imparted information regarding contingencies excluded from scope of risk cover (Table 6.58). These variations are found to be statistically insignificant as per Chi-square test as χ^2= 0.015 (2, N = 314), p = 0.992.

Table 6.58: Information Shared by an Agent Regarding Contingencies Excluded from the Risk Cover and Variations across Income Levels

Agent imparted information regarding contingencies excluded from the scope of risk cover	**Below Rs. 10000**	**Rs. 10000- Rs. 30000**	**Above Rs. 30000**	**Total**
Yes	36 (43.4)	60 (44.1)	42 (44.2)	138 (43.9)
No	47 (56.6)	76 (55.9)	53 (55.8)	176 (56.1)
Total	83 (100)	136 (100)	95 (100)	314 (100)

Note: Figures in the parenthesis are percentages.

Variations were also noticed in terms of urban and rural respondents. For example, 46.7 percent urban respondents and 36.8 percent rural respondents stated that agent imparted information regarding contingencies excluded from the scope of risk cover (Table 6.59). These variations are found to be statistically insignificant as per Chi-square test as χ^2= 2.510 (1, N = 314), p = .113.

Table 6.59: Information Shared by an Agent Regarding Contingencies Excluded from the Risk Cover and Variations across Rural and Urban Areas

Agent imparted information regarding contingencies excluded from the scope of risk cover	Urban	Rural	Total
Yes	106 (46.7)	32 (36.8)	138 (43.9)
No	121 (53.3)	55 (63.2)	176 (56.1)
Total	227 (100)	87 (100)	314 (100)

Note: Figures in the parenthesis are percentages.

Variations were also observed across gender and it was found that 37.7 percent male respondents and 60.5 female respondents revealed that agent imparted information regarding contingencies excluded from the scope of risk cover (Table 6.60). As per Chi-square test these variations are found to be statistically significant at one percent level as χ^2= 13.115 (1, N = 314), p = .001.

Table 6.60: Information Shared by an Agent Regarding Contingencies Excluded from the Risk Cover and Variations across Gender

Agent imparted information regarding contingencies excluded from the scope of risk cover	Male	Female	Total
Yes	86 (37.7)	52 (60.5)	138 (43.9)
No	142 (62.3)	34 (39.5)	176 (56.1)
Total	228 (100)	86 (100)	314 (100)

Note: Figures in the parenthesis are percentages.

6.15 Information Disclosure By Agent Regarding Contact Number And Address of Insurer

IRDAI mandated that agent should share information regarding address of the insurer to the prospective buyer of the policy. This is also helpful in availing various post sale services, also lodging grievances related to the policy.

Out of total respondents, 70.1 percent expressed that agent imparted details regarding contact and address of insurer at point of sale of policy. Inter insurer variations reveals that in terms of LIC 66.7 percent respondents; 73.1 percent respondents of ICICI Prudential and 75 percent respondents of Exide Life stated that agent shared information regarding contact and address of insurer (Table 6.61).

Table 6.61: Information Shared by an Agent Regarding Contact Number and Address of Insurer and Variations across Insurance Companies

Agent imparted details regarding contact number and address of the insurer for addressing your queries	LIC	ICICI Prudential	Exide Life	Total
Yes	108 (66.7)	79 (73.1)	33 (75)	220 (70.1)
No	54 (33.3)	29 (26.9)	11 (25)	94 (29.9)
Total	162 (100)	108 (100)	44 (100)	314 (100)

Note: Figures in the parenthesis are percentages.

Variations were also observed in terms of education level of respondents. For example, 61.7 percent respondents with below matric education and 70 percent respondents having matric and plus two education level expressed that agent imparted information regarding contact and address of the insurer. While this percentage stands at 74 percent in case of respondents having graduation and above education level (Table 6.62).These variations are found to be statistically insignificant as per Chi-square test [χ^2= 3.954 (2, N = 314), p = .139].

Table 6.62: Information Shared by an Agent Regarding Contact Number and Address of Insurer and Variations across Education Levels

Agent imparted details regarding contact number and address of the insurer for addressing your queries	Below Matric	Matric and Plus 2	Graduation and above	Total
Yes	50 (61.7)	42 (70)	128 (74)	220 (70.1)
No	31 (38.3)	18 (30)	45 (26)	94 (29.9)
Total	81 (100)	60 (100)	173 (100)	314 (100)

Note: Figures in the parenthesis are percentages.

Variations across income levels, reveals that - 69.9 percent respondents with monthly income less than Rs. 10,000 and 64 percent respondents with monthly income ranging between Rs. 10,000 and 30,000 stated that agent disclosed information regarding contact number and address of insurer. On the other hand 78.9 percent respondents having monthly income above Rs. 30,000 expressed that agent disclosed information regarding address and contact number of insurer (see Table 6.63).Chi-square test shows that these variations are found to be statistically significant at 5 percent level [χ^2= 5.983 (2, N = 314), p = .050].

Table 6.63: Information Shared by an Agent Regarding Contact Number and Address of Insurer and Variations across Income Levels

Agent imparted details regarding contact number and address of the insurer for addressing your queries	Below Rs. 10000	Rs. 10000- Rs. 30000	Above Rs. 30000	Total
Yes	58 (69.9)	87 (64)	75 (78.9)	220 (70.1)
No	25 (30.1)	49 (36)	20 (21.1)	94 (29.9)
Total	83 (100)	136 (100)	95 (100)	314 (100)

Note: Figures in the parenthesis are percentages.

Variations were also observed in terms of urban and rural respondents. For example, 72.2 percent urban respondents and 64.4 percent rural respondents were of the view that agent shared information regarding contact number and address of insurer (Table 6.64). These variations are found to be statistically insignificant as per Chi-square test as χ^2= 1.861 (1, N = 314), p = .172.

Table 6.64: Information Shared by an Agent Regarding Contact Number and Address of Insurer and Variations across Urban and Rural Areas

Agent imparted details regarding contact number and address of the insurer for addressing your queries	Urban	Rural	Total
Yes	164 (72.2)	56 (64.4)	220 (70.1)
No	63 (27.8)	31 (35.6)	94 (29.9)
Total	227 (100)	87 (100)	314 (100)

Note: Figures in the parenthesis are percentages.

Variations were also reported across gender as 73.2 percent male respondents and 61.6 percent female respondents stated that agent disclosed information regarding address and contact number of insurer at the point of sale of policy proposal

(Table 6.65). Chi-square test reveal that these variations are statistically, significant at 5 percent level [χ^2= 4.018 (1, N = 314), p = .045].

Table 6.65: Information Shared by an Agent Regarding Contact Number and Address of Insurer and Variations across Gender

Agent imparted details regarding contact number and address of the insurer for addressing your queries	Male	Female	Total
Yes	167 (73.2)	53 (61.6)	220 (70.1)
No	61 (26.8)	33 (38.4)	94 (29.9)
Total	228 (100)	86 (100)	314 (100)

Note: Figures in the parenthesis are percentages.

6.16 Information Shared By An Agent Regarding Documents Required During Claim Settlement

Agent should mandatorily impart information regarding various documents required during claim settlement. An informed policyholder may avail hassle free claim settlement within stipulated time period. Otherwise if application for claim settlement lacks various supporting documents claim settlement can be delayed till further submission of those documents.

Out of total respondents majority (53.8 percent) respondents stated that agent made them aware about various documents required during claim settlement. Inter insurer variations were also noticed and it was found that 48.1 percent respondents of LIC; 60.2 percent respondents of ICICI Prudential and 59.1 percent respondents of Exide Life expressed that agent shared information regarding various document required during claim settlement (Table 6.66).

Table 6.66: Information Shared by an Agent Regarding Documents Required during Claim and Variations across Insurance Companies

Agent told about documents required during claim settlement	LIC	ICICI Prudential	Exide Life	Total
Yes	78 (48.1)	65 (60.2)	26 (59.1)	169 (53.8)
No	84 (51.9)	43 (39.8)	18 (40.9)	145 (46.2)
Total	162 (100)	108 (100)	44 (100)	314 (100)

Note: Figures in the parenthesis are percentages.

Variations were also observed across education level of respondents. For example it was found that 39.5 percent respondents with below matric education; 58.3 percent respondents having education between matric and plus two and 59 percent respondents having education level of graduation and above stated that agent shared information regarding documents required during claim settlement (Table 6.67). These variations are found to be statistically significant at 5 percent level as per Chi-square test [χ^2= 9.008 (2, N = 314), p = .011].

Table 6.67: Information Shared by an Agent Regarding Documents Required during Claim and Variations across Education Levels

Agent told about documents required during claim settlement	Below Matric	Matric and Plus 2	Graduation and above	Total
Yes	32 (39.5)	35 (58.3)	102 (59)	169 (53.8)
No	49 (60.5)	25 (41.7)	71 (41)	145 (46.2)
Total	81 (100)	60 (100)	173 (100)	314 (100)

Note: Figures in the parenthesis are percentages.

Income level of respondents also showed variation on this account. For example, 42.2 percent respondents with monthly income less than Rs. 10,000; around 56 percent respondents with monthly income ranging from Rs. 10,000 to Rs. 30,000 and 61.1 percent respondents with monthly income above Rs. 30,000 expressed that agent told them regarding various documents required during claim settlement (Table 6.68. As per Chi-square test these variations are found to be statistically significant at 5 percent level [χ^2= 6.766 (2, N = 314), p = .034].

Table 6.68: Information Shared by an Agent Regarding Documents Required during Claim and Variations across Income Levels

Agent told about documents required during claim settlement	Below Rs. 10000	Rs. 10000-Rs. 30000	Above Rs. 30000	Total
Yes	35 (42.2)	76 (55.9)	58 (61.1)	169 (53.8)
No	48 (57.8)	60 (44.1)	37 (38.9)	145 (46.2)
Total	83 (100)	136 (100)	95 (100)	314 (100)

Note: Figures in the parenthesis are percentages.

Perceptions of urban and rural respondents also varied as 54.6 percent urban respondents and 51.7 percent rural respondents revealed that agent imparted information regarding various documents required during claim settlement (Table 6.69).These variations are found to be statistically insignificant as per Chi-square test as χ^2= .213 (1, N = 314), p = .644.

Table 6.69: Information Shared by an Agent Regarding Documents Required during Claim and Variations across Rural and Urban Areas

Agent told about documents required during claim settlement	Urban	Rural	Total
Yes	124 (54.6)	45 (51.7)	169 (53.8)
No	103 (45.4)	42 (48.3)	145 (46.2)
Total	227 (100)	87 (100)	314 (100)

Note: Figures in the parenthesis are percentages.

Variations were also noticed across gender of respondents. For example, 51.3 percent male respondents and 60.5 female respondents opined that agent shared information regarding various documents required during claim settlement (see Table 6.70). Chi-square test shows that these variations are found to be statistically insignificant at 5 percent level [χ^2= 2.103 (1, N = 314), p = .147].

Table 6.70: Information Shared by an Agent Regarding Documents Required during Claim and Variations across Gender

Agent told about documents required during claim settlement	Male	Female	Total
Yes	117 (51.3)	52 (60.5)	169 (53.8)
No	111 (48.7)	34 (39.5)	145 (46.2)
Total	228 (100)	86 (100)	314 (100)

Note: Figures in the parenthesis are percentages.

6.17 Information Discloser By An Agent Regarding Grievance Redressal Mechanisms

While selling the policy as per the *Bima Bemissal website* an insurer along with spreading awareness regarding in-house grievance procedure should also spread awareness regarding insurance ombudsman. Informing a prospective buyer about existence of grievance redressal mechanisms of IRDAI along with terms and conditions of policy, may help in reposing his trust in insurer and he may pursue policy without much apprehension.

Out of total respondents, only 8.3 percent reported that agent made them aware about existence of grievance redressal cell of IRDAI and Insurance Ombudsman at point of sale of policy proposal. In terms of insurers, 7.4 percent respondents of LIC; 11.1 percent respondents of ICICI Prudential and 4.5 percent respondents of Exide Life stated that agent made them aware about existence of various grievance redressal mechanisms (Table 6.71).

Table 6.71: Information Shared by an Agent Regarding Grievance Redressal Mechanisms and Variations across Insurance Companies

Agent made aware about grievance redressal cell of IRDAI and Insurance ombudsman	LIC	ICICI Prudential	Exide Life	Total
Yes	12 (7.4)	12 (11.1)	2 (4.5)	26 (8.3)
No	150 (92.6)	96 (88.9)	42 (95.5)	288 (91.7)
Total	162 (100)	108 (100)	44 (100)	314 (100)

Note: Figures in the parenthesis are percentages.

Variations were also noticed across education levels of respondents and it was found that 4.9 percent respondents with below matric education level; 8.3 percent respondents having education between matric and plus two and 9.8 percent respondents having education level of graduation and above were made aware by agent regarding existence of various grievance redressal mechanisms (Table 6.72). These variations are found to be statistically insignificant as per Chi-square test as χ^2= 1.736 (2, N = 314), p = .420.

Table 6.72: Information Shared by an Agent Regarding Grievance Redressal Mechanisms and Variations across Education Levels

Agent made aware about grievance redressal cell of IRDAI and Insurance ombudsman	Below Matric	Matric and Plus 2	Graduation and above	Total
Yes	4 (4.9)	5 (8.3)	17 (9.8)	26 (8.3)
No	77 (95.1)	55 (91.7)	156 (90.2)	288 (91.7)
Total	81 (100)	60 (100)	173 (100)	314 (100)

Note: Figures in the parenthesis are percentages.

In terms of income level of respondents variations were also noticed. For example 6.6 percent respondents with monthly income less than Rs. 10,000 and 7.4 percent respondents with monthly income ranging from Rs. 10,000 to Rs. 30,000 and 12 percent respondents with monthly income above Rs. 30,000 reported that agent made them aware about grievance redressal cell of IRDAI and Insurance Ombudsman (Table 6.73). As per Chi-square test these variations are found to be statistically insignificant [χ^2= 2.151 (2, N = 314), p = .341].

Table 6.73: Information Shared by an Agent Regarding Grievance Redressal Mechanisms and Variations across Income Levels

Agent made aware about grievance redressal cell of IRDAI and Insurance ombudsman	Below Rs. 10000	Rs. 10000- Rs. 30000	Above Rs. 30000	Total
Yes	9 (6.6)	7 (7.4)	10 (12)	26 (8.3)
No	127 (93.4)	88 (92.6)	73 ()88	288 (91.7)
Total	136 (100)	95 (100)	83 (100)	314 (100)

Note: Figures in the parenthesis are percentages.

Variation Shown by Participants:

Perceptions of urban and rural respondents also showed variation. For example, 10.3 percent urban respondents and 7.5 percent rural respondents stated that agent made them aware about existence of various grievance redressal mechanisms (Table 6.74). These variations are found to be statistically insignificant as per Chi-square test as ^{2}= .675 (1, N = 314), p = .411.

Table 6.74: Information Shared by an Agent Regarding Grievance Redressal Mechanisms and Variations across Rural and Urban Areas

Agent made aware about grievance redressal cell of IRDAI and Insurance ombudsman	Urban	Rural	Total
Yes	9 (10.3)	17 (7.5)	26 (8.3)
No	78 (89.7)	210 (92.5)	288 (91.7)
Total	87 (100)	227 (100)	314 (100)

Note: Figures in the parenthesis are percentages.

Variations were also observed across gender as 6.6 percent male respondents and 12.8percent female respondents were of the opinion that agent made them aware about grievance redressal cell of IRDAI and Insurance Ombudsman at point of sale of policy (Table 6.75).These variations are found to be statistically insignificant at 5 percent level as per Chi-square test [χ^2= 3.173 (1, N = 314), p = .075].

Table 6.75: Information Shared by an Agent Regarding Grievance Redressal Mechanisms and Variations across Gender

Agent made aware about grievance redressal cell of IRDAI and Insurance ombudsman	Male	Female	Total
Yes	15 (6.6)	11 (12.8)	26 (8.3)
No	213 (93.4)	75 (87.2)	288 (91.7)
Total	228 (100)	86 (100)	314 (100)

Note: Figures in the parenthesis are percentages.

6.18 Satisfaction Of The Policyholders With Information Shared By Agent

The overall assessment of information sharing by agent was done on the basis of policyholders' satisfaction with the information provided by an agent of the insurance firm at point of sale of policy.

The sub-hypothesis tested in this regard is 'Policyholders are satisfied with the information provided by the agent at the point of sale of policy proposal'.

Out of total respondents majority (61.1 percent) expressed satisfaction with the information shared by agent of the insurer at point of sale of policy proposal. In terms of insurers 65.4 percent respondents of LIC; 55.6 percent respondents of ICICI Prudential and 59.1 percent respondents of Exide Life stated that they were satisfied with the information shared by agent (Table 6.76).

Table 6.76: Satisfaction of the Policyholders with Information Shared by an Agent and Variations across Insurance Companies

Satisfied with the information provided by agent of the insurer	LIC	ICICI Prudential	Exide Life	Total
Satisfied	106 (65.4)	60 (55.6)	26 (59.1)	192 (61.1)
Neutral	32 (19.8)	21 (19.4)	14 (31.8)	67 (21.3)
Dissatisfied	24 (14.8)	27 (25)	4 (9.1)	55 (17.5)
Total	162 (100)	108 (100)	44 (100)	314 (100)

Note: Figures in the parenthesis are percentages.

Whether education level of respondents make a difference or not in overall satisfaction with the information provided by the agent of the insurer was checked by testing sub-hypothesis namely, 'Education level of respondents has bearing on satisfaction of respondents with the information shared by the agent'

Around 56 percent respondents with below matric education; 61.7 percent respondents with matric and plus two education level and 63.6 percent respondents having education level of graduation and above expressed satisfaction with the information provided by agent of insurer (Table 6.77). The Chi-square test reveals that education level of respondents and satisfaction with the information provided by the agent are related. The above sub-hypothesis is validated as the variations across education level are found to be statistically significant at one percent level as per Chi-square test as χ^2= 29. 858 (4, N = 314), p = .001.

Table 6.77: Satisfaction of the Policyholders with Information Shared by an Agent and Variations across Education Levels

Satisfied with the information provided by agent of the insurer	Below Matric	Matric and Plus 2	Graduation and above	Total
Satisfied	45 (55.6)	37 (61.7)	110 (63.6)	192 (61.1)
Neutral	8 (9.9)	20 (33.3)	39 (22.5)	67 (21.3)
Dissatisfied	28 (34.6)	3 (5)	24 (13.9)	55 (17.5)
Total	81 (100)	60 (100)	173 (100)	314 (100)

Note: Figures in the parenthesis are percentages.

The relation between satisfaction of respondents with the information provided by the agent of the insurer and income was tested through sub-hypothesis namely, 'Income of respondents and satisfaction of respondents with the information shared by the agent are related'.

Field survey results reveals that, 65.1 percent respondents having monthly income less than Rs. 10,000 and 58.8 percent respondents with monthly income ranging from Rs. 10,000 to Rs. 30,000 stated that they were satisfied with the information shared by agent. On the other hand 61.1 percent respondents with monthly income above Rs. 30,000 expressed satisfaction with the information shared by agent (Table 6.78). Monthly income of respondents and satisfaction are related to each other. Thus the above sub-hypothesis stands validated as Chi-square test shows that variations across income levels of respondents are found to be statistically significant at one percent [χ^2= 15.170 (4, N = 314), .004].

Table 6.78: Satisfaction of the Policyholders with Information Shared by an Agent and Variations across Income Levels

Satisfied with the information provided by agent of the insurer	Below Rs. 10000	Rs. 10000-Rs. 30000	Above Rs. 30000	Total
Satisfied	54 (65.1)	80 (58.8)	58 (61.1)	192 (61.1)
Neutral	12 (14.5)	41 (30.1)	14 (14.7)	67 (21.3)
Dissatisfied	17 (20.5)	15 (11)	23 (24.2)	55 (17.5)
Total	83 (100)	136 (100)	95 (100)	314 (100)

Note: Figures in the parenthesis are percentages.

The difference between area of residence (rural or urban) of respondents and overall satisfaction with the information provided by the agent of the insurer was tested through sub-hypothesis namely, 'perceptions of urban and rural respondents and satisfaction with the information shared by the agent are related'.

Satisfaction level of urban and rural respondents showed variation. Around 61 percent urban respondents and 60.9 percent rural respondents revealed that they were satisfied with the information shared by agent (Table 6.79).The Chi-square test reveals that the urban rural variations are statistically insignificant at 5 percent level as $\chi^2 = .294$ (2, N = 314), p = .863 hence, the sub- hypothesis is not validated.

Table 6.79: Satisfaction of the Policyholders with Information Shared by an Agent and Variations across Urban and Rural Areas

Satisfied with the information provided by agent of the insurer	Urban	Rural	Total
Satisfied	139 (61.2)	53 (60.9)	192 (61.1)
Neutral	47 (20.7)	20 (23)	67 (21.3)
Dissatisfied	41 (18.1)	14 (16.1)	55 (17.5)
Total	227 (100)	87 (100)	314 (100)

Note: Figures in the parenthesis are percentages.

Whether gender of the respondents make a difference or not in overall satisfaction with the information provided by the agent of the insurer was tested through sub-hypothesis namely, 'Gender of respondents and satisfaction of respondents with the information shared by the agent are related'.

Field survey results reveals that 59.6 percent male respondents and 65.1 percent female respondents expressed overall satisfaction with the information provided by agent of insurer during selling of the policy proposal (Table 6.80).The variations across gender are found to be statistically insignificant at 5 percent level as per Chi-square test [χ^2= 1.173 (2, N = 314), p= .556]. Thus, Gender of the respondents and information shared by the agent are not related and above sub-hypothesis is rejected.

Table 6.80: Satisfaction of the Policyholders with Information Shared by an Agent and Variations across Gender

Satisfied with the information provided by agent of the insurer	Male	Female	Total
Satisfied	136 (59.6)	56 (65.1)	192 (61.1)
Neutral	49 (21.5)	18 (20.9)	67 (21.3)
Dissatisfied	43 (18.9)	12 (14)	55 (17.5)
Total	228 (100)	86 (100)	314 (100)

Note: Figures in the parenthesis are percentages.

6.19 Satisfaction Of The Policyholders With Product Of The Insurer

The overall assessment of information sharing by agent was also done on the basis of policyholders' satisfaction with the final product they received from insurer.

The sub-hypothesis tested in this regard is 'Policyholders are satisfied with the final policy of the insurance firm'.

Out of total respondents 70.1expressed overall satisfaction with product received from the insurer. Variations were noticed in terms of insurance companies. For example, 73.5 percent respondents of LIC; 64.8 percent respondents of ICICI Prudential and 70.5 percent respondents of Exide life opined that they were satisfied with the final product received from insurer (See Table 6.81).

Table 6.81: Satisfaction of the Policyholders with Product of the Insurer and Variations across Insurance Companies

Satisfied with the policy/ product given to you by your insurer	LIC	ICICI Prudential	Exide Life	Total
Satisfied	119 (73.5)	70 (64.8)	31 (70.5)	220 (70.1)
Neutral	19 (11.7)	12 (11.1)	6 (13.6)	37 (11.8)
Dissatisfied	24 (14.8)	26 (24.1)	7 (15.9)	57 (18.2)
Total	162 (100)	108 (100)	44 (100)	314 (100)

Note: Figures in the parenthesis are percentages.

The relationship between education of the respondents and overall satisfaction with the product/policy of the insurer was analyzed through sub-hypothesis, namely, 'Education of respondents and satisfaction of respondents with the product of insurer are related'.

In terms of education level variations have been noticed as 51.9 percent respondents having education level below matric and 75 percent respondents with education from matric and plus two expressed satisfaction with the final product received from insurer. On the other hand 76.9 percent respondents having graduation and above education level reported that they were satisfied with the final product received from the insurer (Table 6.82).These variations are found to be statistically significant at one percent level as per Chi-square test [χ^2= 30.490 (4, N = 314), p = .001]. Thus, the sub-hypothesis stands validated.

Table 6.82: Satisfaction of the Policyholders with Product of the Insurer and Variations across Education Levels

Satisfied with the policy/ product given to you by your insurer	Below Matric	Matric and Plus 2	Graduation and above	Total
Satisfied	42 (51.9)	45 (75)	133 (76.9)	220 (70.1)
Neutral	9 (11.1)	11 (18.3)	17 (9.8)	37 (11.8)
Dissatisfied	30 (37)	4 (6.7)	23 (13.3)	57 (18.2)
Total	81 (100)	60 (100)	173 (100)	314 (100)

Note: Figures in the parenthesis are percentages.

Whether income of the respondents makes a difference or not in overall satisfaction with the product/policy of the insurer was tested through sub-hypothesis, namely, 'Income of respondents and satisfaction of respondents with the product of insurer are related'.

Across income levels of respondents variations were also observed. For example, 71.1 percent respondents with below Rs.10,000 monthly income and 68.4 percent respondents having monthly income ranging between Rs. 10,000 and Rs. 30,000 expressed satisfaction with the final product received from insurer. While 71.6 percent respondents with monthly income above Rs. 30,000 stated that they were satisfied with the final product received from insurer (see Table 6.83). These variations are found to be statistically significant at five percent level as per Chi-square test as χ^2= 12.311 (4, N = 314), p= .015 and thus, above sub-hypothesis stands validated.

Table 6.83: Satisfaction of the Policyholders with Product of the Insurer and Variations across Education Levels

Satisfied with the policy/ product given to you by your insurer	Below Rs. 10000	Rs. 10000-Rs. 30000	Above Rs. 30000	Total
Satisfied	59 (71.1)	93 (68.4)	68 (71.6)	220 (70.1)
Neutral	5 (6)	25 (18.4)	7 (7.4)	37 (11.8)
Dissatisfied	19 (22.9)	18 (13.2)	20 (21.1)	57 (18.2)
Total	83 (100)	136 (100)	95 (100)	314 (100)

Note: Figures in the parenthesis are percentages.

Further the relation between place of residence (urban or rural) of the respondents and overall satisfaction with the product/policy of the insurer was tested through sub-hypothesis, namely, 'Perceptions of the urban and rural respondents and satisfaction with the product of insurer are related'.

Responses of urban and rural respondents also showed variation as 72.7 percent urban respondents and 63.2 percent rural respondents opined that they were satisfied with the product received from insurer (see Table 6.84).These variations are found to be statistically insignificant at five percent level as per Chi-square test [χ^2= 4.188 (2, N = 314), p = 0.123]. Thus the above sub-hypothesis stands rejected.

Table 6.84: Satisfaction of the Policyholders with Product of the Insurer and Variations across Rural and Urban Areas

Satisfied with the policy/ product given to you by your insurer	Urban	Rural	Total
Satisfied	165 (72.7)	55 (63.2)	220 (70.1)
Neutral	27 (11.9)	10 (11.5)	37 (11.8)
Dissatisfied	35 (15.4)	22 (25.3)	57 (18.2)
Total	227 (100)	87 (100)	314 (100)

Note: Figures in the parenthesis are percentages.

The variations between gender of the respondents and overall satisfaction with the product provided by the insurer was tested through sub-hypothesis namely, 'Gender of respondents and satisfaction of respondents with the product provided by the insurer are related'.

Variations across gender were also observed and it was found that 71.9 percent male respondents and 65.1 percent female respondents expressed overall satisfaction with the final product/policy received from insurer (Table 6.85).The variations across gender are found to be statistically insignificant at five percent level as per Chi-square test as χ^2= 1.700 (2, N = 314), p = .427. Thus the above sub-hypothesis is rejected.

Table 6.85: Satisfaction of the Policyholders with Product of the Insurer and Variations across Gender

Satisfied with the policy/ product given to you by your insurer	Male	Female	Total
Satisfied	164 (71.9)	56 (65.1)	220 (70.1)
Neutral	24 (10.5)	13 (15.1)	37 (11.8)
Dissatisfied	40 (17.5)	17 (19.8)	57 (18.2)
Total	228 (100)	86 (100)	314 (100)

Note: Figures in the parenthesis are percentages.

6.20 Efficacy of Grievance Redressal Mechanism

Along with preventive measures taken for policyholders' interest protection there is also need for curative measures which can be adopted in case the interest of policyholder is jeopardized. Thus IRDAI has designed grievance redressal mechanism in the form of grievance redressal mechanism of all the insurance companies and grievance redressal mechanism of IRDAI. In case of grievance the policyholder has to first approach grievance redressal mechanism of insurer and if he/she is not satisfied with the response he /she can lodge complaint with grievance redressal mechanisms of IRDAI. Thus ongoing discussion analyzes efficacy of grievance redressal mechanism of insurer and efficacy of grievance redressal mechanism of IRDAI separately.

6.21 Efficacy of Grievance Redressal Mechanism Of Insurer

For grievance redressal the policyholder has to follow a step-wise procedure. A aggrieved policyholder can file the written complaint with Grievance Redressal Officer of the insurer supported by necessary documents and receive a written acknowledgement of the complaint with date. The insurer has to reply back to aggrieved policyholder within 15 days.

Sub hypotheses tested in this regard is 'Insurers have effective grievance redressal mechanism for redressing grievances of policyholders'.

Field survey results revealed that out of total 314 policyholders 94 (29.9) percent policyholders had various grievances related to the insurers. Inter insurers variations were also observed and it was found that 30.2 percent respondents of LIC; 27.8 percent respondents of ICICI Prudential and 34.1 Percent respondents of Exide Life stated that they had grievances related to policy matters (Table 6.86).

Table 6.86: Policyholders Having Grievances Related to Insurer and Variations across Insurance Companies

You have any grievance related to your insurer	LIC	ICICI Prudential	Exide Life	Total
Yes	49 (30.2)	30 (27.8)	15 (34.1)	94 (29.9)
No	113 (69.8)	78 (72.2)	29 (65.9)	220 (70.1)
Total	162 (100)	108 (100)	44 (100)	314 (100)

Note: Figures in the parenthesis are percentages.

Out of these 94 respondents who had grievances, 60 (63.8 percent) respondents registered their grievances with grievance redressal mechanism of the insurer. Out of these, 57 percent respondents reported that agent imparted incomplete knowledge about the product, 26 percent respondents stated that agent did not shared knowledge regarding charges related to the product, 15 percent respondents were annoyed over claim settlement and 2percent respondents expressed that agent made wrong investment in Unit Linked Insurance Products (Figure 6.1).

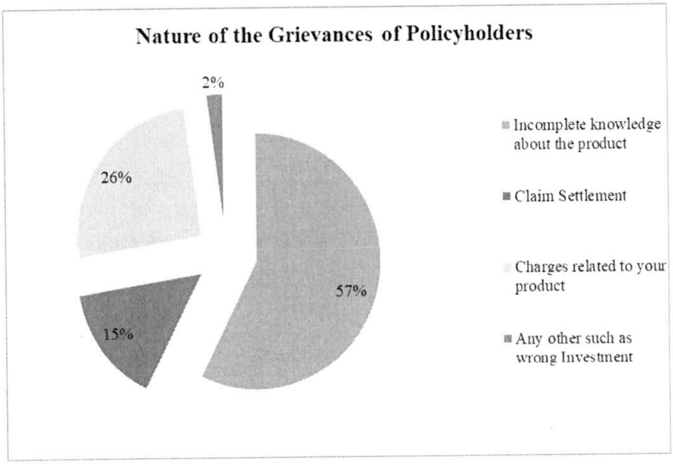

Figure 6.1

IRDAI has mandated that the insurer should reply back to the aggrieved policyholder within 15 days but amongst these respondents the turnaround time of insurance companies varies. Out of these 60 respondents who registered their complaints with grievance redressal mechanism of insurer only 25 (41.7 percent) respondents stated that the insurer reported back within 15 days. But in majority (57.3 percent) of the cases the insurers did not complied with stipulated time period of 15 days. Out of these 60 respondents who approached grievance redressal mechanism of insurance companies majority (73 percent) respondents expressed dissatisfied with the response of insurer related to their grievances while 6 (10 percent) respondents stated that they were satisfied with the response of the insurer related to their grievance. Around 17 percent respondents reported that they were neutral with the response of the insurer. Variations were noticed across insurance companies as 18.5 percent respondents of LIC and 9.1 percent respondents of Exide life expressed overall satisfaction with the response of insurer. On the other hand, none of the respondents of ICICI reported that they are satisfied with the insurer response related to their grievance (Table 6.87).

Table 6.87: Satisfaction of Policyholders with Grievance Redressal of Insurer and Variations across Insurance Companies

You were satisfied with the insurer response related to your grievance	LIC	ICICI Prudential	Exide Life	Total
Satisfied	5 (18.5)	0 (0)	1 (9.1)	6 (10.2)
Neutral	9 (33.3)	1 (4.5)	0 (0)	10 (16.9)
Dissatisfied	13 (48.1)	20 (95.2)	10 (90.9)	43 (72.9)
Total	27 (100)	21 (100)	11 (100)	59 (100)

Note: Figures in the parenthesis are percentages.

The relation between education level of the respondents and satisfaction with the grievance redressal mechanism of insurer was tested through sub-hypothesis namely, 'Education level of the respondents and satisfaction of policyholders with grievance redressal mechanism of insurer are related'.

Education level of respondents also showed variation as 8.3 percent respondents having below matric education, 12.5 percent respondents having education level between matric and plus two and 10.7 percent respondents with graduation above education level expressed overall satisfaction with the response of the insurer regarding their grievance (Table 6.88). These variations are found to be statistically insignificant at 5 percent level as per Chi-square test [χ^2= 3.362 (4, N = 59), p = .499], thus the above sub-hypothesis stands rejected.

Table 6.88: Satisfaction of Policyholders with Grievance Redressal of Insurer and Variations Education Levels

You were satisfied with the insurer response related to your grievance	Below Matric	Matric and Plus 2	Graduation and above	Total
Satisfied	2 (8.3)	1 (12.5)	3 (11.1)	6 (10.2)
Neutral	4 (16.7)	3 (37.5)	3 (11.1)	10 (16.9)
Dissatisfied	18 (75)	4 (50)	21 (77.8)	43 (72.9)
Total	24 (100)	8 (100)	27 (100)	59 (100)

Note: Figures in the parenthesis are percentages.

Whether income level of the respondents make a difference or not in satisfaction with the grievance redressal mechanism of insurer was tested through sub-hypothesis namely, 'Income level of the respondents and satisfaction of respondents with grievance redressal mechanism of insurer are related'.

Variations were also noticed across income level of respondents. It was found that 5.3 percent respondents having monthly income less than Rs. 10,000 and 17.2 percent respondents having monthly income ranging from Rs. 10,000 to Rs. 30,000 have expressed overall satisfaction with the response of insurer related to their grievance. While none of the respondents with monthly income above Rs. 30,000 was satisfied with response of insurer (Table 6.89). These variations are found to be statistically significant at five percent level as per Chi-square test [χ^2= 9.950 (4, N = 59), p= .041]. The above sub-hypothesis stands validated.

Table 6.89: Satisfaction of Policyholders with Grievance Redressal of Insurer and Variations across Income Levels

You were satisfied with the insurer response related to your grievance	Below Rs. 10000	Rs. 10000-Rs. 30000	Above Rs. 30000	Total
Satisfied	1 (5.3)	5 (17.2)	0 (0)	6 (10.2)
Neutral	2 (10.5)	8 (27.6)	0 (0)	10 (16.9)
Dissatisfied	16 (84.2)	16 (55.2)	11 (100)	43 (72.9)
Total	19 (100)	29 (100)	11 (100)	59 (100)

Note: Figures in the parenthesis are percentages.

On the other hand variations in perceptions of the urban and rural respondents and their satisfaction with the grievance redressal mechanism of insurer was tested through sub-hypothesis namely, 'Perceptions of the urban and rural respondents and satisfaction with grievance redressal mechanism of insurer are related'.

Perceptions of Urban rural respondents also showed variation as 11.1 percent urban respondents and 8.3 percent rural respondents reported that they were satisfied with the response of insurer related to their grievance (see Table 6.90 below). The variations across perceptions of urban and rural respondents are found to be statistically insignificant at five percent level as per Chi-square test as χ^2= 2.512 (2, N = 59), p= .285. The above sub-hypothesis stands rejected.

Table 6.90: Satisfaction of Policyholders with Grievance Redressal of Insurer and Variations across Rural and Urban Areas

You were satisfied with the insurer response related to your grievance	Urban	Rural	Total
satisfied	4 (11.4)	2 (8.3)	6 (10.2)
Neutral	8 (22.9)	2 (8.3)	10 (16.9)
Dis-satisfied	23 (65.7)	20 (83.3)	43 (72.9)
Total	35 (100)	24 (100)	59 (100)

Note: Figures in the parenthesis are percentages.

Whether gender of the respondents make a difference or not in satisfaction with the grievance redressal mechanism of insurer was tested through sub-hypothesis namely, 'gender of the respondents and satisfaction with grievance redressal mechanism of insurer are related'.

Perceptions of respondents varied across gender, as 10.9 percent male were satisfied with the response of insurer regarding their grievance while none of the female respondents were satisfied (Table 6.91).The variations across gender are found to be statistically insignificant at five percent level as per Chi-square test as χ^2= .624 (2, N = 59), p = .732.The above mentioned sub-hypothesis stands rejected.

Table 6.91: Satisfaction of Policyholders with Grievance Redressal of Insurer and Variations across Gender

You were satisfied with the insurer response related to your grievance	Male	Female	Total
Satisfied	6 (11.1)	0 (0)	6 (10.2)
Neutral	9 (16.7)	1 (20)	10 (16.9)
Dissatisfied	39 (72.7)	4 (80)	43 (72.9)
Total	54 (100)	5 (100)	59 (100)

Note: Figures in the parenthesis are percentages.

6.22 Perceptions of the Agents of the Insurance Firms

Agents are the main linch-pin between insurer and policyholder. In fact, the service of the agent primarily decides the sustainability and viability of the policy.

6.23 Training of the Agents

IRDAI grants license to the agents based upon their performance in the examination conducted by the Authority through NSE-IT. It is relevant to mention here that prior to exam; the person aspiring to be agent has to undergo 50 hours of mandatory training imparted by the insurer or an institute specified by IRDAI. If the person clears exam then he/she can apply for grant of license through the insurer and IRDAI grants the license on receiving the request for the same from the insurer. The license granted is valid for three years and after this duration, then again an agent has to undertake 25 hours of training for renewing his/her license.

All the agents were of view that training imparted by insurer was effective in obtaining license from the IRDAI. The training of the insurer provided opportunities for field visits and provided specific knowledge regarding various products of the company. In course of training, agents were imparted knowledge regarding importance of policy servicing for policy retention. Approximately 97 percent of the agents found the process of obtaining license from IRDAI as easy.

Policy proposal Filling process and other issues relating to Agents

Majority (83.6 percent) of the agents have stated that the customer do not fill the policy proposal themselves. In majority of the cases, the agents had themselves filled the policy proposals and prospective buyer had signed the policy document. Majority of the agents have also stated they impart all the information regarding name of the plan governing the policy, Various benefits including information regarding free-look period, date of maturity of the policy etc. But on the other hand, it is lamented stating that very few respondents have stated that - they had imparted information regarding grievance redressal cell of IRDAI and Insurance Ombudsman to the prospective policy holder at the point of sale of policy proposal. The agent deliberately concealed the information regarding free look period, IRDAI Grievance redressal cell and Insurance Ombudsman. Information regarding free look period could have impact on the commission of the agent if policyholder returns the policy on grounds of mis-dealing. Similarly, the information regarding IRDAI grievance redressal cell and Insurance Ombudsman may lead to filling the complaint against the insurer in case of grievance.

Various grievances of the policyholder, mis-selling, etc. leads to policy lapsation. Around 62 percent of the agents are of the view that, policy lapses in less than 25 percent of the cases. Main reasons for policy lapsation are inability of the policyholder to pay premium followed by target centric approach of the insurer leading to mis-selling, negligence on the part of the policyholder to pay timely premium and lastly, less commission is given to agent for policy retention.

In prevalence of this situation, majority of the agents are of the view that policy retention can be enhanced if agent provides full knowledge of the product to the prospective buyer and insurer should stop target-centric approach.

6.24 Perception of Managerial Functionaries of The Insurance Companies

Majority (79 percent) of the functionaries of the insurance firms reported that policies lapses in less than 25 percent cases. Mis-selling done by the agent at the point of sale of the policy is the main reason for policy lapsation and it could be amended by imparting full knowledge regarding policy to the prospective buyer at the point of sale of policy proposal.

6.25 Matrix Summing Up The Testing Of Hypothesis 5

Matrix 6.1: Testing of Hypothesis 5- "IRDAI has been effective in protecting the interests of policy holders by making agents of insurers to dispense full information regarding policy proposal to prospective buyer"

Sr. No.	Sub Hypothesis	Sources of Data	Analysis	Status of Sub-Hypo-thesis Accepted
1.	IRDAI has been effective in making policy proposal form policyholder-centric	Primary data	Majority (63.7 percent) of the respondents did not Fill the policy proposal themselves. Majority (65.6 percent) of the respondents found the language of policy form technical in nature. Majority (73.6 percent) of the respondents found the font size of the policy proposal illegible. Majority (83.6 percent) of the agents stated that customer do not fill policy proposal.	No
2.	IRDAI has been effective in stimulating agents to share all the necessary information regarding policy with the prospective buyer at point of sale of policy proposal'.	Primary data	Majority of the respondents stated that barring the aspects of free look period and information regarding IRDAI Grievance redressal cell of IRDAI and Insurance Ombudsman agents of the Insurers dispensed information on all other aspects related to policy proposal. Majority of the agents expressed that they did not impart information regarding IRDAI grievance redressal cell and Insurance Ombudsman. Majority of the agents and managerial functionaries are of view that misspelling is the major cause of policy lapsation.	Yes

Sr. No.	Sub Hypothesis	Sources of Data	Analysis	Status of Sub-Hypo-thesis Accepted
3.	Policyholders are satisfied with the information provided by the agent at the point of sale of policy proposal	Primary Data	Majority (61.2 percent) of the respondents are satisfied with the information provided by the agent at point of sale of policy proposal	Yes
4.	Policyholders are satisfied with the final policy of the insurance firm	Primary Data	Majority (70.1 percent) Policyholders are satisfied with the final policy they received from the insurance firm.	Yes
5.	Insurers have effective grievance redressal mechanism for redressing grievances of policyholders'	Primary Data	Majority (72.9 percent) policyholders are dissatisfied with the grievance redressal mechanism of insurer.	No

Thus, on the basis of above analysis of sub-hypotheses; the **Hypothesis 5**: "IRDAI has been effective in protecting the interests of policy holders by making agents of insurers to dispense full information regarding policy proposal to prospective buyer", **stands validated**.

II
ASSESSMENT OF IRDAI IN REDRESSING GRIEVANCES OF POLICY-HOLDERS

IRDAI has grievance redressal cell and Insurance Ombudsman for redressing grievances of the policyholders. The efficacy of the grievance redressal cell of IRDAI and Insurance Ombudsman in redressing grievances of Policyholders was done on the basis of secondary data regarding pendency of cases and primary data regarding perceptions of the policyholders.

The Hypothesis tested in this regard is "IRDAI has effective machinery in the form of Grievance Redressal cell and Insurance Ombudsman for Redressing grievances of Policy-holders".

The man hypothesis was split further in to following sub-hypothesis:

1. Pendency of cases with grievance redressal cell of IRDAI has reduced overtime.
2. IRDAI grievance redressal cell has been effective in redressing grievances of policyholders.
3. There has been reduction in complaints pendency with the insurance Ombudsman over years.
4. IRDAI has effective machinery in the form of Insurance Ombudsman for redressing grievances of policyholders

6.26 Efficacy of Grievance Redressal Cell of IRDAI

In case of failure of insurer to reply within 15 days or the policyholder is not satisfied with the response of insurer then he may approach grievance redressal cell of Consumer Affairs Department of IRDAI or make a call through toll free number 155255 (or) 1800 4254 732 or send an email to complaints@IRDAI.gov.in. The policyholder may register and monitor complaint with Integrated Grievance Management System at www.igms.IRDAI.gov.in or may download Complaint Registration form, fill it and send it by post or fax to Consumer Affairs Department of IRDAI.

Thus, sub-Hypotheses tested in this regard are 'Pendency of cases with grievance redressal cell of IRDAI has reduced overtime' and 'IRDAI grievance redressal cell has been effective in redressing grievances of policyholders'.

During year 2002-03 IRDAI received 610 grievances and resolved 252 grievances. At the year end, there were 358 grievances pending meaning thereby there was 58.68 percent pendency of cases. In year 2003-04 there were 519 cases reported and 65 cases were resolved. At the year end 454 cases were pending with high pendency of 87.47 percent. In year 2004-05, 1433 grievances were reported and 308 cases were resolved by the grievance redressal cell of IRDAI. Around 1125 cases were pending with high pendency ration of 78.51 percent at the year end with grievance redressal cell of IRDAI (Table 6.92).

Table 6.92: Status of Grievances of Life Insurance Companies with Grievance Redressal Cell of IRDAI

Insurer	2002-03			2003-04			2004-05		
	Reported during the Year	Resolved During the Year	Pending at the end of the Year	Reported during the Year	Resolved During the Year	Pending at the end of the Year	Reported during the Year	Resolved During the Year	Pending at the end of the Year
Aviva	--	--	--	3	2	1 (33.3)	16	5	11 (68.75)
Bajaj Allianz	4	3	1 (25)	4	2	2 (50)	30	4	26 (86.66)
Birla Sunlife	1	1	0 (0)	1	0	1 (100)	23	9	14 (60.86)
HDFC Standard	2	2	0 (0)	11	5	6 (54.54)	30	17	13 (43.33)
ICICI Prudential	10	9	1 (10)	8	6	2 (25)	39	22	17 (43.58)
ING Life	3	3	0 (0)	5	3	2 (40)	8	3	5 (62.5)
Kotak Mahindra	2	1	1 (50)	2	1	1 (50)	9	2	7 (77.78)
MAX Life	9	7	2 (22.2)	1	1	0 (0)	18	8	10 (55.56)
PNB Metlife	1	0	1 (100)	0	0	0 (0)	2	1	1 (50)
Reliance	--	--	--	0	0	0 (0)	1	1	0 (0)
SBILife	2	2	0 (0)	3	1	2 (66.67)	24	7	17 (70.83)
TataAIA	5	3	2 (40)	7	5	2 (28.57)	31	19	12 (38.71)
LIC	571	221	350 (61.29)	474	39	435 (91.77)	1202	210	992 (82.52)
GRAND TOTAL	610	252	358 (58.68)	519	65	454 (87.47)	1433	308	1125 (78.51)

Source: Annual Reports of IRDAI (2002-03 to 2004-05), Hyderabad

Note: Figures in the parenthesis are percentages.

During year 2005-06, 2516 grievances were reported and out of which 737 cases were resolved. At the year end, 1779 cases were pending with 70.71 percent pendency ratio with the IRDAI grievance redressal cell of IRDAI. In year 2006-07, 861 cases were reported and 562 cases were resolved and 229 cases were pending with the IRDAI grievance redressal cell. The year witnessed a sharp decrease in pendency ratio as it stood at 26.59 percent. During year 2007-08, 2057 cases were reported and 1180 cases were resolved by grievance redressal cell of IRDAI. At the year end, 877 cases were pending with pendency ratio of 42.63 percent (see Table 6.93).

Table 6.93: Status of Grievances of Life Insurance Companies with Grievance Redressal Cell of IRDAI

Insurer	2005-06			2006-07			2007-08		
	Reported during the Year	Resolved During the Year	Pending at the end of the Year	Reported during the Year	Resolved During the Year	Pending at the end of the Year	Reported during the Year	Resolved During the Year	Pending at the end of the Year
Aviva	38	11	27 (71.05)	43	33	10 (23.25)	127	110	17 (13.39)
Bajaj Allianz	114	50	64 (56.14)	145	125	20 (13.79)	403	328	75 (18.61)
BhartiAXA	--	--	--	--	--	--	0	0	0
Birla Sunlife	48	12	36 (75)	29	27	2 (6.89)	67	55	12 (17.91)
Future Generali	--	--	--	--	--	--	0	0	0
HDFC Standard	96	48	48 (50)	31	30	1 (3.23)	106	50	56 (52.83)
ICICI Prudential	122	58	64 (52.45)	84	71	13 (15.48)	233	212	21 (9.01)
ING Life	15	4	11 (73.33)	12	9	3 (25)	26	20	6 (23.08)
Kotak Mahindra	26	5	21 (80.77)	23	17	6 (26.09)	51	37	14 (27.45)
MAX Life	38	10	28 (73.68)	22	15	7 (31.82)	84	57	27 (32.14)
PNB Metlife	9	4	5 (55.56)	6	3	3 (50)	49	22	27 (55.10)
Reliance	8	4	4 (50)	10	4	6 (60)	89	77	15 (16.85)
Sahara	0	0	0	1	1	0 (0)	2	1	1 (50)
SBI Life	77	23	54 (70.13)	68	45	23 (33.82)	101	86	15 (14.85)
Shriram Life	--	--	--	1	1	0 (0)	2	0	2 (100)

TataAIA	82	41	41 (50)	32	24	8 (25)	66	39	18 (27.27)
LIC	1843	467	1373 (74.49)	354	157	197 (55.65)	651	80	571 (87.71)
Grand Total	2516	737	1779 (70.71)	861	562	229 (26.59)	2057	1180	877 (42.63)

Source: Annual Reports of IRDAI (2005-06 to 2007-08), Hyderabad

Note: Figures in the parenthesis are percentages.

In year 2008-09 1794 new cases were reported and in all 2553 cases were resolved including backlog of last year. At the yearend, 458 cases were pending with pendency ratio of 25.52 percent. During year 2009-10, 2449 cases were reported and 2152 cases were resolved and 395 cases were pending with high pendency ratio of 16.12 percent with the grievance redressal cell of IRDAI. In year 2010-11, 9656 cases were reported and 9797 cases were resolved. At the year end, only 254 cases were pending with a small pendency ratio of 2.63 percent (see Table 6.94).

Table 6.94: Status of Grievances of Life Insurance Companies with Grievance Redressal Cell of IRDAI

Insurer	2008-09			2009-10			2010-11		
	Reported during the Year	Resolved During the Year	Pending at the end of the Year	Reported during the Year	Resolved During the Year	Pending at the end of the Year	Reported during the Year	Resolved During the Year	Pending at the end of the Year
Aegon Religare	0	0	0	6	6	0 (0)	54	50	4 (7.41)
Aviva	193	197	13 (6.74)	152	142	23 (15.13)	631	654	0 (0)
Bajaj Allianz	211	251	38 (18.01)	173	195	16 (9.25)	799	811	4 (0.50)
Bharti AXA	5	5	0 (0)	38	21	17 (44.74)	267	277	7 (2.62)
Birla Sunlife	109	113	9 (8.26)	153	41	21 (13.73)	533	515	39 (7.31)
Canara HSBC	0	0	0	4	4	0 (0)	26	24	2 (7.69)
DLF Pramerica	0	0	0	0	0	0	22	17	5 (22.72)
Future Generali	5	3	2 (40)	24	24	2 (8.33)	72	63	11 (15.27)

HDFC Standard	94	65	56 (59.57)	154	171	39 (25.32)	528	562	5 (0.94)
ICICI Prudential	196	202	14 (7.14)	330	296	48 (14.54)	1294	1342	0 (0)
IDBI Federal	1	0	1 (100)	5	4	2 (40)	25	27	0 (0)
India First	--	--	--	--	---	--	0	0	0
ING Life	35	20	21 ()60	29	40	10 (34.48)	99	106	3 3.03 ()
Kotak Mahindra	95	102	10 (10.53)	151	132	29 (19.20)	779	757	51 (6.54)
MAX Life	112	105	40 (35.71)	187	227	0 (0)	525	523	2 (0.38)
PNB Metlife	46	66	9 (19.57)	75	79	5 (6.67)	246	247	4 (1.62)
Reliance	79	75	23 (29.11)	185	192	15 (8.11)	540	541	14 (2.59)
Sahara	1	1	1 (100)	2	2	1 (50)	12	12	1 (8.33)
SBI Life	62	59	19 (30.64)	80	94	5 (6.25)	293	284	14 (4.77)
Shriram Life	4	4	0	16	16	0 (0)	28	21	7 (25)
Star Union Dai Chi	0	0	0	1	1	0 (0)	16	16	0 (0)
Tata AIA	65	73	16 (24.61)	79	83	12 (15.19)	279	276	15 (5.37)
LIC	481	980	186 (38.66)	606	642	150 (24.75)	2588	2672	66 (2.55)
Grand Total	1794	2553	458 (25.52)	2449	2152	395 (16.12)	9656	9797	254 (2.63)

Source: Annual Reports of IRDAI (2008-09 to 2010-11), Hyderabad

Note: Figures in the parenthesis are percentages.

During year 2011-12, 309613 cases were reported, 308331 cases were resolved and at the year end 1282 cases were pending with pendency ratio of 0.41 percent with the grievance redressal cell of IRDAI. In year 2012-13, 341012 cases were reported while 341070 cases were resolved and at the year end; 1224 cases were pending with a very small pendency ratio of 0.35 percent with the grievance redressal cell of IRDAI (see Table 6.95).

Table 6.95: Status of Grievances of Life Insurance Companies with Grievance Redressal Cell of IRDA

Insurer	2011-12			2012-13		
	Reported during the Year	Resolved During the Year	Pending at the end of the Year	Reported during the Year	Resolved During the Year	Pending at the end of the Year
AegonReligare	3440	2774	666 (19.36)	7341	7982	25 (0.34)
Aviva	13520	13467	53 (0.39)	8948	9001	0 (0)
Bajaj Allianz	22390	22388	2 (0.01)	37092	37090	4 (0.01)
BhartiAXA	7310	7285	25 (0.34)	7402	7374	53 (0.71)
Birla Sunlife	11911	11632	279 (2.34)	30430	30577	132 (0.43)
CanaraHSBC	5258	5256	2 (0.03)	5281	5281	2 (0.03)
DLF Pramerica	621	619	2 (0.32)	1031	1000	33 (3.20)
Edelweiss Tokio	6	6	0 (0)	60	59	1 (1.66)
Future Generali	15667	15640	27 (0.17)	75081	7550	57 (0.07)
HDFC Standard	35218	35205	13 (0.03)	50947	50814	146 (0.28)
ICICI Prudential	22016	22016	0 (0)	19759	19746	13 (0.06)
IDBI Federal	502	500	2 (0.39)	823	822	3 ()0.36
India First	738	738	0 (0)	1199	1191	8 (0.66)
ING Life	10498	10497	1 (0.01)	8744	8732	13 (0.14)
Kotak Mahindra	8850	8844	6 (0.06)	8725	8719	12 (0.13)
MAX Life	10362	10360	2 (0.01)	15899	15895	6 (0.03)
PNB Metlife	2940	2940	0 (0)	3832	3825	7 (0.18)
Reliance	5807	5802	5 (0.08)	21843	21714	134 (0.61)
Sahara	29	29	0 (0)	29	28	1 (3.44)

SBI Life	18490	18482	8 (0.04)	18681	18678	11 (0.05)
Shriram Life	149	142	7 (4.69)	228	235	0 (0)
Star Union Dai Chi	284	283	1 (0.35)	432	429	4 (0.92)
Tata AIA	16307	16291	16 (0.09)	11672	11673	15 (0.12)
LIC	52300	52135	165 (0.31)	73034	72655	544 (0.74)
Grand Total	309613	308331	1282 (0.41)	341012	341070	1224 (0.35)

Source: Annual Reports of IRDAI (2011-12 to 2012-13), Hyderabad

Note: Figures in the parenthesis are percentages

The above analysis of grievance redressal cell of IRDAI reveals that over the year there has been increase in grievances received with the Cell but there had been a very sharp decrease in pendency ratio of the cases over the years. The capacity to dispose of grievances of policyholders has increased over the years pointing towards efficiency in grievance redressal mechanism of the IRDAI (Figure 6.2).

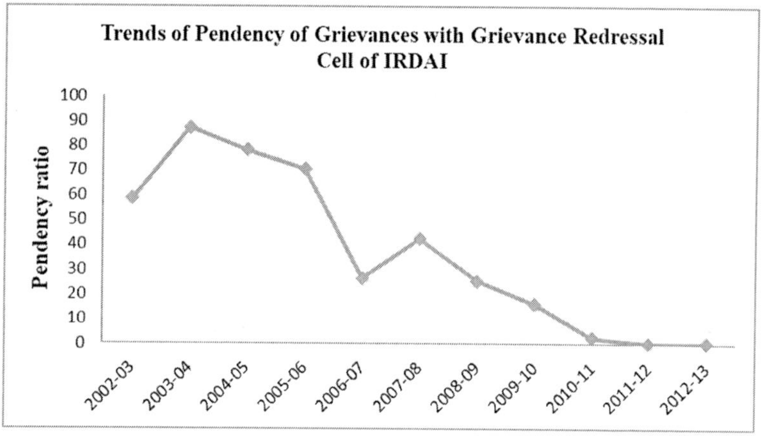

Figure 6.2

IRDAI has received majority of the cases regarding unfair business practices. In year 2012-13, around 49.5 percent of the complaints were regarding unfair business practices which increased to 56.48 percent in 2013-14 and finally witnessed a decrease and stood at 52 percent out of the total complaints in 2014-15 (see Table 6.96 and Figure 6.3).

Table 6.96: Yearly Classification of various Life Insurance Complaints

Classification of Complaints	Year		
	2012-13	2013-14	2014-15
Claims	43178 (12.69)	36685 (9.79)	31076 (11.13)
Policy Servicing	56277 (16.55)	62238 (16.61)	55869 (20.02)
Proposal Processing	38742 (11.39)	27774 (7.41)	20932 (7.50)
ULIP Related	9278 (2.72)	7127 (1.90)	4029 (1.44)
Unfair Business Practice	168482 (49.55)	211622 (56.48)	145129 (52.01)
Others	24055 (7.07)	29174 (7.78)	21957 (7.87)
Total	340012	374620	278992

Source: http://www.policyholder.gov.in/uploads/CEDocuments/Classification%20 Life%202014-15.jpg

Note: Figures in the parenthesis are percentages.

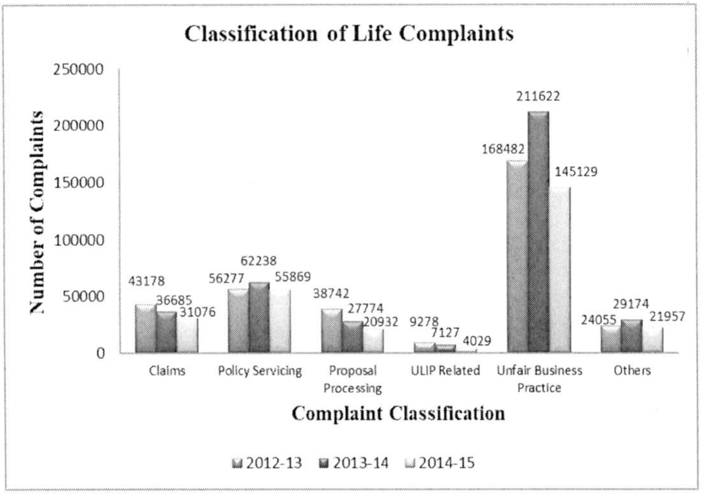

Figure 6.3

6.27 Field Survey Results

Out of 43dissatisfied respondents, only 13 (30.2 percent) respondents approached grievance redressal cell of IRDAI. Variations were observed across insurance firms. In case of LIC 23.1 percent respondents, 20 percent respondents of ICICI Prudential and 60 percent respondents of Exide Life approached grievance redressal cell of IRDAI (see Table 6.97)

Table 6.97: Policyholder Approached Grievance Redressal Cell of IRDAI and Variations across Insurance Companies

Ever approached Grievance Redressal Cell of IRDAI regarding complaint	LIC	ICICI Prudential	Exide Life	Total
Yes	3 (23.1)	4 (20)	6 (60)	13 (30.2)
No	10 (76.9)	16 (80)	4 (40)	30 (69.7)
Total	13 (100)	20 (100)	10 (100)	43 (100)

Note: Figures in the parenthesis are percentages.

It is mandated that Grievance redressal cell of IRDAI has to respond back to the policyholder within 15 days from the date of receipt of grievance. Only 8 percent respondent stated that the turn-around time for IRDAI Grievance Redressal Cell of IRDAI was 15 days while majority (92.3 percent) stated that - it took more than 15 days to respond back with regard their grievance (see Figure 6.4).

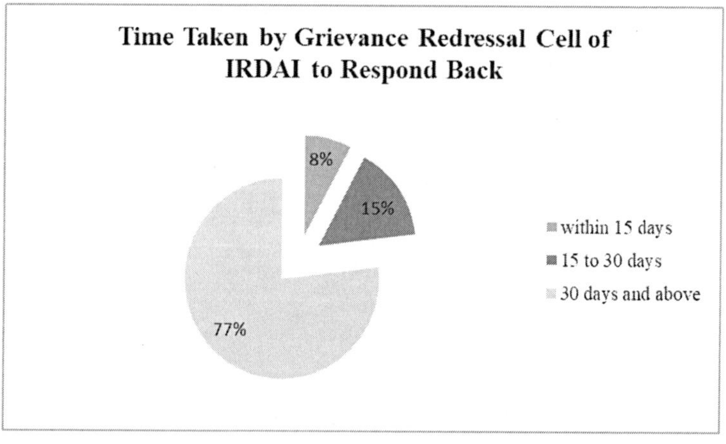

Figure 6.4

Out of 13 respondents who approached Grievance Redressal Cell of IRDAI, only 5 (38.5 percent) were satisfied while majority (61.5 percent) respondents were dissatisfied with the decision of the Grievance Redressal Cell of IRDAI. Variations were also noticed across responses of policyholders of insurance firms. For example, in case of LIC, all respondents were satisfied while none of the respondents of ICICI Prudential were satisfied. Around 33 percent respondents of Exide Life, were satisfied with response of Grievance Redressal Cell of IRDAI (see Table 6.98).

Table 6.98: Satisfaction of Policyholders with Decision of Grievance Redressal Cell of IRDAI and Variations across Insurance Companies

Satisfaction level of policyholders with the decision of the grievance redressal cell of IRDAI	LIC	ICICI Prudential	Exide Life	Total
Satisfied	3 (100)	0 (0)	2 (33.3)	5 (38.5)
Dissatisfied	0 (0)	4 (100)	4 (66.7)	8 (61.5)
Total	3 (100)	4 (100)	6 (100)	13 (100)

Note: Figures in the parenthesis are percentages.

Whether education level of the respondents make a difference or not in satisfaction with the decision of grievance redressal cell of IRDAI was tested through sub-hypothesis namely - 'Education level of the respondents and satisfaction with grievance redressal cell of IRDAI are related'.

Perception of policyholders regarding satisfaction varied across education level as all respondents with below matric education level; were satisfied while 27.3 percent respondents having education level of graduation and above were satisfied with the response of Grievance Redressal Cell of IRDAI. On the other hand, none of the respondents having education level of matric and plus two approached the cell (Table 6.98). As per Chi-square test these variations are found to be statistically significant at five percent level [χ^2= 3.928 (1, N = 13), p = .052]. Thus, the above mentioned sub-hypothesis stands validated.

Table 6.99: Satisfaction of Policyholders with Decision of Grievance Redressal Cell of IRDAI and Variations across Education Levels

Satisfaction level of policyholders with the decision of the grievance redressal cell of IRDAI	Below Matric	Matric and Plus 2	Graduation and above	Total
Satisfied	2 (100)	0 (0)	3 (27.3)	5 (38.5)
Dis-satisfied	0 (0)	0 (0)	8 (72.7)	8 (61.5)
Total	2 (100)	0 (100)	11 (100)	13 (100)

Note: Figures in the parenthesis are percentages.

The relation between income of the respondents and their satisfaction with the decision of grievance redressal cell of IRDAI was tested through sub-hypothesis namely - 'Income of the respondents and satisfaction with grievance redressal cell of IRDAI are related'.

Income level of respondents also showed variation as all the having monthly income below Rs.10,000 and around 50 percent respondents with monthly income ranging between Rs. 10,000 to Rs. 30,000 were satisfied with the decision of Grievance Redressal Cell of IRDAI. While none of the respondents with monthly income above Rs. 30,000 were satisfied with the decision of the cell (see Table 6.100).The above sub-hypothesis stands validated as variations across income levels of the respondents are found to be statistically significant at 5 percent level as per Chi-square test [χ^2= 5.998 (2, N = 13), p = .05].

Table 6.100: Satisfaction of Policyholders with Decision of Grievance Redressal Cell of IRDAI and Variations across Income Levels

Satisfaction level of policyholders with the decision of the grievance redressal cell of IRDAI	Below Rs. 10000	Rs. 10000-Rs. 30000	Above Rs. 30000	Total
Satisfied	2 (100)	3 (42.9)	0 (0)	5 (38.5)
Dis-satisfied	0 (0)	4 (57.1)	4 (100)	8 (61.5)
Total	2 (100)	7 (100)	4 (100)	13 (100)

Note: Figures in the parenthesis are percentages.

The variation in terms of perceptions of the urban and rural respondents and their satisfaction with the decision of grievance redressal cell of IRDAI was tested through sub-hypothesis, namely - 'Perceptions of the urban and rural respondents and satisfaction with grievance redressal cell of IRDAI are related'.

Perceptions of urban and rural respondents also showed variations as 37.5 percent urban respondents and 40 percent rural respondents were satisfied with the decision of Grievance Redressal cell of IRDAI (see Table 6.101). These variations are found to be statistically insignificant at 5 percent level as per Chi-square test [χ^2= .008 (1, N = 13), p = .928] and thus, the above sub-hypothesis stands rejected.

Table 6.101: Satisfaction of Policyholders with Decision of Grievance Redressal Cell of IRDAI and Variations Rural and Urban Areas

Satisfaction level of policyholders with the decision of the grievance redressal cell of IRDAI	Urban	Rural	Total
Satisfied	3 (37.5)	2 (40)	5 (38.5)
Dissatisfied	5 (62.5)	3 (60)	8 (61.5)
Total	8 (100)	5 (100)	13 (100)

Note: Figures in the parenthesis are percentages.

Whether gender of the respondents makes a difference or not in satisfaction with the decision of grievance redressal cell of IRDAI was tested through sub-hypothesis namely, 'Gender of the respondents and satisfaction with grievance redressal cell of IRDAI are related'.

Variations were also observed across gender as 33.3 percent male respondents and all the female respondents were satisfied with the satisfied with the decision of Grievance Redressal cell of IRDAI (Table 6.100).The above sub-hypothesis is rejected as variations across gender are found to be statistically insignificant at five percent level as per Chi-square test as χ^2=1.733 (1, N = 13), p = .188.

Table 6.102: Satisfaction of Policyholders with Decision of Grievance Redressal Cell of IRDAI and Variations across Gender

Satisfaction level of policyholders with the decision of the grievance redressal cell of IRDAI	Male	Female	Total
Satisfied	4 (33.3)	1 (100)	5 (38.5)
Dissatisfied	8 (66.7)	0 (0)	8 (61.5)
Total	12 (100)	1 (100)	13 (100)

Note: Figures in the parenthesis are percentages.

6.28 Efficacy of Insurance Ombudsman

IRDAI has put in place institution of Insurance Ombudsman for redressing grievances of policyholders. Insurance Ombudsman was established by the Government of India Notification dated 11thNovember, 1998 with the purpose of quick disposal of the grievances of the insured customers and to mitigate their problems involved in redressal of those grievances. The institution of Insurance Ombudsman has great importance and relevance for the protection of interest of policy-holders and also to build up their confidence in the system. This institution has helped to generate and sustain the faith and confidence amongst the consumers in insurers. In case of grievance, if a policyholder is not satisfied with the response of insurer; he/she may lodge complaint with Grievance Redressal cell of IRDAI or may directly file the complaint with insurance Ombudsman of respective jurisdiction.

To have maximum outreach twelve ombudsman have been set up across country in cities of Ahmedabad, Bhopal, Bhubaneswar, Chandigarh, Chennai, Delhi, Guwahati, Hyderabad, Kochi, Kolkata, Lucknow and Mumbai.

Insurance Ombudsman has power to deliver award on any complaint up to Rs. 20 lakhs. The insurance companies are required - to honour the awards passed by an Insurance Ombudsman within three months. The ombudsman shall pass an award within a period of three months from the receipt of the complaint. The awards are binding upon the insurance companies. If the policy holder is not satisfied with the award of the Ombudsman, he can approach other adjudicatory bodies like Consumer Forums and Courts of law for redressal of his grievances.

The sub- hypotheses tested in this regard are - 'There has been reduction in complaints pendency with the insurance Ombudsman over years' and 'IRDAI has effective machinery in the form of Insurance Ombudsman for redressing grievances of policyholders'.

For testing the above sub-hypothesis, both primary and secondary data have been used. The primary data is based on perceptions of the policyholders who approached Insurance Ombudsman. The respondents are further divided into two groups. One group contains those respondents whose complaints - have been redressed by Insurance Ombudsman and they became part of the regular sample collected from the field. The other group is of 24 respondents whose complaints are still pending with Insurance Ombudsman and researcher visited office of Insurance Ombudsman for collecting this data. These 24 respondents were not part of the regular survey carried across that city.

During Year 2000-01, total complaints received by all the Insurance Ombudsmen stood at 2839 and 2110 cases were disposed off. At the year end, 729 cases were outstanding with pendency ratio of 25.6 percent. In year 2001-02, 1967 cases were received, 1506 cases were disposed off and 461 cases with 23.43 percent pendency ratio were still outstanding. During year 2002-03, 2481 complaints were received, 1917 cases were disposed off and 564 cases were outstanding with 22.73 pendency ratio at the yearend (see Table 6.103).

Table 6.103: Performance of Ombudsman at Various Centres (Life Insurance)

Name of the Centre	2000-01*			2001-02			2002-03		
	Complaints Outstanding of the past year and received	Number of Complaints Disposed	Outstanding at the end of the Year	Complaints Outstanding of the past year and received	Number of Complaints Disposed	Outstanding at the end of the Year	Complaints Outstanding of the past year and received	Number of Complaints Disposed	Outstanding at the end of the Year
Ahmad-abad	82	22	60 (73.17)	57	27	30 (52.63)	68	51	17 (25)
Bhopal	197	132	65 (32.99)	230	209	21 (9.13)	235	154	81 (34.46)
Bhubanes-war	149	84	65 (43.62)	76	62	14 (18.42)	105	84	21 (20)
Chandi-garh	119	92	27 (22.69)	48	37	11 (22.91)	133	103	30 (22.55)
Chennai	229	215	14 (6.11)	183	181	2 (1.09)	288	262	26 (9.02)
Delhi	921	644	277 (30.07)	473	274	199 (42.07)	340	214	126 (37.05)
Guwahati	34	21	13 (38.23)	53	41	12 (22.64)	88	81	7 (7.95)
Hyderabad	208	190	18 (8.65)	77	59	18 (23.37)	137	102	35 (25.54)
Kochi	63	63	0 (0)	52	46	6 (11.53)	62	57	5 (8.06)
Kolkata	251	191	60 (23.90)	249	154	95 (38.15)	443	308	135 (30.47)
Lucknow	468	371	97 (20.72)	321	59	18 (5.60)	312	253	59 (18.91)
Mumbai	118	85	33 (27.96)	148	100	48 (32.43)	270	248	22 (8.14)
Total	2839	2110	729 (25.67)	1967	1506	461 (23.43)	2481	1917	564 (22.73)

*Figures relates for life and non-life insurance.

Source: Annual Reports of IRDAI (2000-01 to 2002-03), Hyderabad

Note: Figures in the parenthesis are percentages

In year 2003-04, 3968 complaints were received along with outstanding complaints of previous year, out of which, 3289 were disposed off and 679 complaints with pendency ratio of 17.11 were outstanding at the year end. During year 2004-

05, 5567 complaints were received along with outstanding complaints of last year out of which 5020 complaints were redressed and at the year end 547 complaints were still outstanding. In year 2005-06, 5527 complaints were received while 4926 complaints were resolved and 601 complaints were still outstanding with pendency ratio of 10.87 percent (see Table 6.104).

Table 6.104: Performance of Ombudsman at Various Centres

Name of the Centre	2003-04			2004-05			2005-06		
	Complaints Out-standing of the past year and received	Number of Complaints Disposed	Out-standing at the end of the Year	Complaints Outstanding of the past year and received	Number of Complaints Disposed	Outstanding at the end of the Year	Complaints Outstanding of the past year and received	Number of Complaints Disposed	Outstanding at the end of the Year
Ahmada-bad	77	55	22 (28.57)	105	66	39 (37.14)	171	148	23 (13.45)
Bhopal	252	151	101 (40.07)	439	419	20 (4.55)	490	486	4 (0.81)
Bhuban-eswar	133	87	46 (34.58)	181	121	60 (33.14)	316	165	151 (47.78)
Chandi-garh	238	201	37 (15.54)	500	427	73 (14.6)	514	440	74 (14.39)
Chennai	404	397	7 (1.73)	611	592	19 (3.10)	659	646	13 (1.97)
Delhi	4.19	296	123 (29.35)	557	389	168 (30.16)	451	305	146 (32.37)
Guwahati	98	88	10 (10.20)	93	78	15 (16.12)	124	90	34 (27.41)
Hydera-bad	539	482	57 (10.57)	621	599	22 (3.54)	565	554	11 (1.94)
Kochi	116	109	7 (6.03)	107	99	8 (7.47)	136	130	6 (4.41)
Kolkata	757	680	77 (10.17)	847	809	38 (4.48)	942	878	64 (6.79)
Lucknow	633	520	113 (17.85)	1121	1083	38 (3.38)	890	861	29 (3.25)
Mumbai	302	223	79 (26.15)	385	338	47 (12.20)	269	223	46 (17.10)
Total	3968	3289	679 (17.11)	5567	5020	547 (9.82)	5527	4926	601 (10.87)

Source: Annual Reports of IRDAI (2003-04 to 2005-06), Hyderabad

Note: Figures in the parenthesis are percentage.

During year 2006-07, the cumulative complaints outstanding of previous year and received in the current year stood at 6021 out of which 5418 were disposed off and 603 were still pending with pendency ratio of 10.01 percent at the yearend. In year 2007-08, 6168 complaints were received out of which 5778 were disposed off and 390 were still pending with pendency ratio of 6.32 percent. During year 2008-09, 6143 complaints were received out of which 5786 were resolved and 557 complaints with pendency ratio of 9.06 percent were outstanding with all the Insurance Ombudsmen (Table 6.105).

Table 6.105: Performance of Ombudsman at Various Centres

Name of the Centre	2006-07			2007-08			2008-09		
	Complaints Outstanding of the past year and received	Number of Complaints Disposed	Outstanding at the end of the Year	Complaints Outstanding of the past year and received	Number of Complaints Disposed	Outstanding at the end of the Year	Complaints Outstanding of the past year and received	Number of Complaints Disposed	Outstanding at the end of the Year
Ahmada-bad	182	156	26 (14.28)	157	146	11 (7.01)	166	158	8 (4.81)
Bhopal	517	515	2 (0.38)	557	544	13 (2.33)	389	323	66 (16.96)
Bhubane-swar	340	200	140 (41.17)	341	204	137 (40.17)	303	204	99 (32.67)
Chandi-garh	533	487	46 (8.63)	561	500	61 (10.87)	681	561	120 (17.62)
Chennai	694	687	7 (1.01)	712	707	5 (0.70)	782	766	16 (2.04)
Delhi	342	215	127 (37.13)	235	212	23 (9.79)	186	87	99 (53.22)
Guwahati	211	188	23 (10.90)	178	162	16 (8.99)	231	196	17 (7.35)
Hydera-bad	567	554	13 (2.29)	537	530	7 (1.30)	621	601	20 (3.22)
Kochi	172	144	28 (16.27)	263	247	16 (6.08)	300	265	35 (11.66)
Kolkata	980	893	87 (8.87)	813	749	64 (7.87)	862	807	55 (6.38)
Lucknow	925	873	52 (5.62)	1022	1006	16 (1.56)	868	868	0 (0)

Mumbai	558	506	52 (9.31)	792	771	21 (2.65)	772	750	22 (2.84)
Total	6021	5418	603 (10.01)	6168	5778	390 (6.32)	6143	5786	557 (9.06)

Source: Annual Reports of IRDAI (2006-07 to 2008-09), Hyderabad

Note: Figures in the parenthesis are percentages.

During year 2009-10, 9524 complaints were received by all the Insurance Ombudsmen across the country including outstanding complaints of previous year out of these 8636 complaints were disposed off while 888 complaints with pendency ratio of 9.32 percent were outstanding. In year 2010-11, the Insurance Ombudsman received 11905 complaints and disposed of 9551 complaints. At the year end 2354 complaints were still outstanding with increase in pendency ratio to 19.77 percent. In year 2011-12 the total complaints received by all the Insurance Ombudsmen stood at 14696 out of which 11850 were disposed off and 2846 were outstanding with pendency ratio of 19.36 percent (see Table 6.106)

Table 6.106: Performance of Ombudsman at Various Centres

Name of the Centre	2009-10			2010-11			2011-12		
	Complaints Outstanding of the past year and received	Number of Complaints Disposed	Outstanding at the end of the Year	Complaints Outstanding of the past year and received	Number of Complaints Disposed	Outstanding at the end of the Year	Complaints Outstanding of the past year and received	Number of Complaints Disposed	Outstanding at the end of the Year
Ahmada-bad	309	302	7 (2.26)	492	210	282 (57.31)	788	737	51 (6.47)
Bhopal	445	407	38 (8.54)	248	121	127 (51.21)	250	19	231 (92.4)
Bhuban-eswar	319	286	33 (10.34)	1271	227	44 (3.46)	183	128	55 (30.05)
Chandi-garh	1051	767	284 (27.02)	1552	626	926 (59.66)	2708	1367	1341 (49.51)
Chennai	957	955	2 (0.21)	935	928	7 (0.74)	893	880	13 (1.45)
Delhi	1570	1326	244 (15.54)	1689	1378	311 (18.41)	2650	2154	496 (18.71)
Guwahati	325	3107	8 (2.46)	288	223	65 (22.56)	245	226	19 (7.75)
Hydera-bad	835	822	13 (1.56)	1401	1324	77 (5.49)	1144	1082	62 (5.41)

Kochi	405	369	36 (8.89)	551	441	110 (19.96)	620	396	224 (36.12)
Kolkata	1166	971	195 (16.72)	1587	1484	103 (6.49)	1594	1457	137 (8.59)
Lucknow	1004	1004	0 (0)	1448	1188	260 (17.95)	1984	1848	136 (6.85)
Mumbai	1138	1110	28 (2.46)	1443	1401	42 (2.91)	1637	1566	81 (4.94)
Total	9524	8636	888 (9.32)	11905	9551	2354 (19.77)	14696	11850	2846 (19.36)

Source: Annual Reports of IRDAI (2009-10 to 2011-12), Hyderabad

Note: Figures in the parenthesis are percentages

In year 2012-13, all the Insurance Ombudsmen received 18557 complaints and resolved 14673 out of them. At the year end 3884, complaints were outstanding with pendency ratio at 20.93 percent (see Table 6.107).

Table 6.107: Performance of Ombudsman at Various Centres

Name of the Centre	2012-13		
	Complaints Outstanding of the past year and received	Number of Complaints Disposed	Outstanding at the end of the Year
Ahmadabad	714	704	37 (5.18)
Bhopal	411	33	378 (91.97)
Bhubaneswar	383	294	89 (23.23)
Chandigarh	4522	3162	1360 (30.07)
Chennai	1100	1047	53 (4.81)
Delhi	3095	2395	700 (22.61)
Guwahati	268	196	72 (26.86)
Hyderabad	1172	1093	79 (6.74)
Kochi	837	461	376 (44.92)
Kolkata	2011	1062	409 (20.33)
Lucknow	1684	1502	182 (10.80)
Mumbai	2333	2184	149 (6.38)
Total	18557	14673	3884 (20.93)

Source: Annual Report of IRDAI (2012-13), Hyderabad

Note: Figures in the parenthesis are percentages.

In nutshell, the pendency ratio of complaints with all the Insurance Ombudsmen across the country witnessed a declining trend from 2000-01 till 2007-08 and then it showed an increasing trend onwards. In year 2000-01, the outstanding complaints ratio stood at 25.67 percent and in year 2012-13 this ratio stood at 22.61 percent (Figure 6.5).

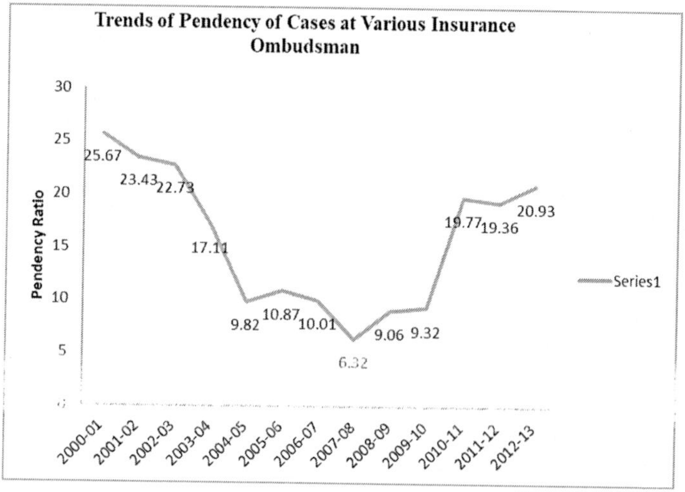

Figure 6.5

6.29 Decision Of Various Insurance Ombudsmen At National Level

The decision of Insurance Ombudsman Bhubaneswar is apt because insurer before withholding the claim must prove that life assured did not disclose material facts regarding pre-existing illness and as insurer was unable to prove the grounds for claim repudiation thus Ombudsman directed the insurer to settle the claim. In case of Insurance Ombudsman Ahmedabad the life assured disclosed all the facts about ill health which were verified by the insurer through reports and policy was issued with extra premium. Since the insurer had knowledge about the ill health of the life assured it has no right to repudiate the claim on the grounds of suppression of material facts. In case of Bhopal Ombudsman the life assured deliberately suppressed the facts regarding date of birth by submitting a proof but when it was found that the actual age of the life assured is more than as per age proof submitted the insurer repudiated the claim. Insurance Ombudsman also stated that claim repudiation by the insurer is just as life assured being a government servant deliberately, submitted the wrong age proof document and as the original age was verified to be more than the age written on policy thus the insure has right to repudiate the claim (see Table 6.108).

Table 6.108: Case Laws or Judgments of Various Ombudsman

S. No.	Ombud-sman	Reference Case No.	Brief facts of the case	Findings of the case	Decision
1.	Bhuban-eswar	21-002-0217	Insurer alleging suppression of material fact concerning health and pre-existing illnesses by the Life Assured	Insurer could not prove beyond doubt that the Life assured suffered from serious illnesses before taking the policy.	Insurer was directed to settle the claim within one month from the receipt of the consent letter.
2.	Ahme-dabad	21-001-0314	While taking the policy the life assured had informed [illegible] the state of his health and habits due to which several Special Reports were called for and the proposal was accepted with extra premium.	The life assured died within ten months from the date of proposal. The claim was repudiated on the grounds of suppression of material facts on the basis of [illegible] prescription, letters of doctors and hospital. It was observed that all the diagnosis/ treatment commenced after 7 days from the date of acceptance of risk. All the documents proved that the deceased was not aware of his ailment at the time of taking the proposal.	The respondent (the insurer) was directed to pay the full claim amount.
3.	Bhopal	L.I-1025-21/09-07/ IND	The deceased life assured had produced voter I.D Card as age proof and the agent filled up the proposal form. It was an early claim. Date of Birth mentioned was 1-1-1950. His actual Date of Birth was 1-8-1943 and was working as postman in postal department. Had he declared his correct age, the proposal would not have been accepted. He had deliberately understated his age.	The deceased was a government servant and deliberately understated his age to defraud the respondent (Insurer), in order to accept the proposal and there by misled the respondent in taking proper underwriting decision.	The decision taken by the respondent (Insurer) in repudiating the claim is just and fair and hence does not require any interference. Therefore the complaint is dismissed without any relief.

S. No.	Ombud-sman	Reference Case No.	Brief facts of the case	Findings of the case	Decision
4.	Chandi-garh	HDFC/397/ Mumbai/ Hissar/21/07	Insurer alleged that it was a case of suicide as per complaint of the father of the diseased to police; hence suicide clause applies and nothing is payable. The claim was repudiated.	The father was not present at the scene of the death. No suicide note was found. Chemical analysis did not find any poison in the body. Post Mortem report also did not find any poison in the body. The report of Panel of doctors did not confirm that death was due to consumption of poison.	Held that the sum assured of Rs. 5 lakhs along with accrued bonus if any be paid to the nominee/ complainant.
5.	Chennai	IO(CHN)/ 21.003.2264	The insurer alleging non disclosure of material fact of suffering from Acute Lymphoblastic Leukaemia (ALL) with relapse with refractory disease in the proposal form and hence the claim is repudiated.	The deceased had been undergoing treatment for ALL since 2000 and he underwent Orchidectomy for relapse in 2003. Did not disclose this in proposal form submitted in Dec 2005	There is clear medical evidence to show that the deceased was suffering from Leukaemia well before signing the application for insurance. Hence the complaint is dismissed and the decision of the insurer was upheld.
6.	Chennai	IO(CHN)/ 21.006.2420	The deceased life assured had not disclosed that he had suffered from pulmonary TB with Haemoptysis in his proposal form. The claim was repudiated by the insurer on the grounds of non-disclosure of material facts.	The life assured had suffered from TB and did not mention the same in the proposal form since he thought that TB is curable. The discharge record of K.T.V.Medical foundations clearly mentioned that the policyholder was a case of Cirrhosis of liver, old pulmonary TB with Haemoptysis.	The complaint was dismissed and the decision of the insurer in repudiating the claim was upheld.

S. No.	Ombud-sman	Reference Case No.	Brief facts of the case	Findings of the case	Decision
7.	Chennai	IO(CHN)/ 21.05.2544	The life assured (lady) lapsed her policy and it was revived with Declaration of Good Health (DGH) on 9.1.2005. The actual date of maturation was 7.12.2004 where as it was mentioned in DGH as 29.12.2004. The revival of policy was done on 10.1.2005 and the life assured died on 19.5.2005. Insurer repudiated the claim on the basis of suppression of material fact in DGH.	The life assured died within 4 months from the date of revival. Did not disclose that she had Caesarian operation in 2000. She had miscarriage during 2nd and 3rd month of second pregnancy. At the time of death she was pregnant. Had she declared the date of last menstruation as 7.12.2004, the insurer would have postponed the revival of the policy. She died of pregnancy related complications.	The complaint was dismissed since there was wrong information about her date of last menstruation and insurer was deprived of the opportunity of assessing the risk properly. Had it been declared correctly, the insurer would have postponed the revival.
8.	Chennai	IO(CHN)/ 21.03.2616	A man his wife and her brother were travelling in a two- wheeler from Kinathu Kadavu to Pollachi at night. Three people were travelling in a two-wheeler and they met with an accident. The Wife and her brother died in the accident. The insurer refused to pay the accident benefit sum assured since the accident was caused due to breach of law.	The FIR and PIR had concluded that it was breach of law since 3 people were travelling in a 2-wheeler in which only 2 are allowed to travel. Though the life assured was only pillion rider, she was travelling as one of the passengers on the Motor Cycle (as per the MV Act only two persons are permitted), which amounts to breach of law.	The complaint was dismissed on the ground that the accident happened and death occurred due to breach of law and insurer is correct in repudiating the Accident Benefit SA.
9.	Chennai	IO(CHN)/ 21.02.2648	The life assured submitted proposal on 30.3.2005. Policy commenced from 28.3.2005. The life assured died of road accident on 13.5.2005. The insurer refused to pay accident sum assured since the life assured was under the influence of alcohol at the time of accident. The claimant argued that the life assured was not driving the vehicle and hence the double accident benefit claim cannot be rejected.	The insurer contended that as per Medico-Legal-Manual if the alcohol content is 100 to 300 MG % the person would have some mental confusion, emotional instability, loss of critical judgment, impaired memory, sleeplessness, slowed reaction time, loss of muscular coordination etc. As the policy conditions of DAB, if death of the life assured is caused by intentional self injury, attempted suicide, insanity or immorality or when the life assured is under the influence of intoxicated liquor, drug or narcotic, the insurer is not liable to pay the additional sum assured.	The complaint was dismissed since the forum did not wish to interfere with the policy conditions.

S. No.	Ombud-sman	Reference Case No.	Brief facts of the case	Findings of the case	Decision
10.	Hydera-bad	L-21-009-0438-2006-07	Death claim under ULIP policy. The insurer produced the evidence, which proved that the life assured was under the treatment of High BP prior to the issue of the policy. Due to non disclosure of the material fact the SA claim was repudiated.	The life assured is suffering from Hypertension. Did not disclose in the proposal form. Life assure died within 9 months from the date of commencement of the policy. The sum assured under the claim was repudiated.	The decision of the insurer was upheld since there was suppression of material facts. Since the policy has the provision for savings, the insurer was ordered to pay the investment portion (Fund Value).

Source:http://www.policyholder.gov.in/Case_laws_or_Judgements.aspx.

6.30 Decision Of Insurance Ombudsman Chandigarh

The following discussion covers few decisions of the Insurance Ombudsman Chandigarh of life Insurance cases. The discussion deals with four types of complaints namely, death claims, maturity claims, survival benefits and miscellaneous (mis-selling).

Complaints Regarding Death Claims

Case 1:

The case 1 deals with complaint filed by Anita Devi against HDFC Life Insurance Co. ltd. vide case number HDFC/594/Mumbai/ Rohtak/22/11 and order dated on 07.11.2012.

Brief Description about the facts of the case:

Smt. Anita Devi filed a complaint about a death claim of her husband Late Shri Krishan Kumar, who expired on 15.04.2010 and had purchased a policy bearing number 11581308 on 28.01.2008, which was repudiated by the Company on the grounds of non disclosure of material facts regarding health status of the deceased.

The insurer in its reply clarified that during an investigation, it was observed that deceased life assured had a history of hypertension and diabetes mellitus disease prior to policy issue date and was admitted in PGI, Rohtak. Hence, as the deceased did not disclosed the facts about the health the claim is repudiated.

Decision of the Ombudsman

The Insurance Ombudsman stated that the Company's submission of suppression of material facts on the basis of mere history of disease is not a sufficient record to establish stringent conditions as per the Insurance Act, 1938. Moreover, the insurer has not produced any document prior to insurance to conclude that the DLA took treatment of hypertension /diabetes. In the absence of conclusive evidence to establish prior disease, repudiation of death claim was not proper and Company is directed to settle the death claim.

Critical Analysis:

The insurer should have brought forward all the documentary proofs on the basis of which it rejected the claim of the complainant. Inability of the insurer to present the evidences confirming the medical history of the deceased seems a deliberate attempt of the insurer to withhold the claim and highlights mala fide intentions of the insurer.

Case 2:

The case 2 pertains to Suman Sharma Vs HDFC Standard Life Ins. Co. Ltd. vide Case No. HDFC/760/Mumbai/Chandigarh/21/10 whose order was announced on 18.10.2012.

Brief Description about the facts of the case:

Smt. Suman Sharma filed a complaint that her husband late Shri Bal Bhushan Sharma purchased a policy bearing no. 00188388 in the year 2003. After, the death of her husband she submitted claim paper, but the company rejected the claim on the grounds that health problem of life assured was not revealed in the proposal form.

The insurer clarified the position stating that life assured did not disclose information about his adverse health history. And he was suffering from heart problem in the year 1992 before the issuance of the policy. Thus due to concealment of material facts about the medical history of the deceased, the claim was repudiated

Decision of the Ombudsman:

The Insurance Ombudsman held that contention of the insurer that the deceased had concealed material facts is not justified as the life was medically examined in detail by the company which included tread mill test. Denying claim on the basis of some ailment which reportedly happened about 11 years prior to taking policy is not justified.

Critical Analysis:

The insurer conducted the medical test of the deceased and after its satisfaction it issued policy to him. If report of the medical test was found satisfactory then only insurer issued policy or insurer at the time of policy issuance did not paid much heed to the medical statistics as business mattered most at that time.

Case 3:

The case related to Smt. Sarbjit Kaur Vs Bharti AXA Life Ins. Co. Ltd. vide Case No. Bharti/217/Mumbai/Patiala /21/11 and order of the Ombudsman was announced on 26.11.2012

Brief Description about the facts of the case:

Smt. Sarbjit Kaur filed a complaint in this office of Insurance Ombudsman about nonpayment of death claim to her mother-in-law Late Smt. Joginder Kaur in relation to policy number 5002501483 for Rs. 5.00 Lacs sum assured. The insurance company repudiated the claim on the ground that Smt. Joginder Kaur did not disclose about her previous insurance details.

The insurer clarified the position by stating that Smt. Joginder Kaur had not disclosed other company's insurance in the proposal form. Whereas she had already an insurance of Rs. 16,66,995/- with other insurance companies. Hence, the claim is not considered.

Decision of the Ombudsman:

The Insurance Ombudsman held that Smt. Joginder Kaur had taken heavy insurance without any clearly discernible insurance interest and without any relation with the income which manifests adverse moral hazard. Non-disclosure of previous insurance is non disclosure of material fact. Thus claim repudiation is justified by the insurance company. The complaint is dismissed.

Critical Analysis:

The Ombudsman aptly rejected the complaint as actions of the policyholder were detrimental to the insurance company. More over the Smt. Joginder Kaur by not disclosing the information has violated Principle of *Uberrimaefidei* (Utmost Good Faith) of insurance.

Case 4:

The case 4 is related to Shashi Kumar Vs Reliance Life Insurance Company vide Case No. Reliance/098/Mumbai/Bilaspur/21/12 whose order was announced on 31.12.2012.

Brief Description about the facts of the case:

Shri Shashi Kumar filed a complaint about nonpayment of death claim of his father Late Shri Balbir Singh under policies numbers 16376610 and 16376598. When his father died on 19.04.2010 he submitted claim papers but claim was not paid timely. He should be paid interest for delayed payment.

The insurer clarified the position by stating that death claim was not settled within 2 months because of some requirements for which 3 reminders were sent to the complainant. Finally, payment was made for Rs. 7,50,000/- on 16.04.2011.

Decision of the Ombudsman:

Insurance Ombudsman held that there inordinate delay in payment reflects the poor working of the company. The company is advised to put in place an appropriate mechanism whereby finally timely decision on admissibility or otherwise of claim is taken.

Critical Analysis:

IRDAI mandates that the agent is required to disclose all the information regarding documents required for claim settlement to the prospective buyer of the policy at the point of sale of policy proposal. The insurer had not adhered the requirements of IRDAI for protection of interest of policyholders.

Case 5:

The case 5 relates to matter of Ram Saran Vs Birla Sun Life Insurance Company vide case No. Birla/1111/Mumbai/Fatehabad/21/11 and decision of the ombudsman was announced on 23.01.2013.

Brief Description about the facts of the case:

Shri Ram Saran filed a complaint about a settlement of a death claim of his son Late Shri Laxman under a policy bearing number 002827041 dated 21.04.2009, who expired on 07.03.2010, which was repudiated by the company on suppression of material facts regarding health status of the Deceased.

The insurer in its reply clarified that during an investigation, it was observed that the deceased Life Assured was suffering from "Osteomylites" disease prior to the policy issue date and had undergone treatment at Jindal Institute of Medical Sciences, supported by laboratory reports from Nalwa Laboratories Private Limited. Hence, the claim is repudiated.

Decision of the Ombudsman:

The Insurance Ombudsman held that the company's submission of suppression of material facts does not bear any significance merely on production of Laboratory reports prior to insurance and a admission/ discharge certificate issued by Jindal Institute of Medical Sciences after commencement of insurance. The verification of death certificate done by this office from the Registrar, Birth and Death, nothing adverse was pointed out to prove any relation between cause of death and the reported disease as per letter from Civil Surgeon, Fatehabad. Keeping aside the repudiation of claim by the insurer, the company is directed to settle the death claim.

Critical Analysis:

It is relevant to state that mere existence of ill health prior to the issuance of the policy while there exist no relation between cause of death and the illness brings forth the mala fide intentions of the insurer for claim repudiation. Had the cause of death been related to the illness about which information was not disclosed the insurer would have repudiated the claim.

Complaints Regarding Maturity Claims

Case 6:

The case 6 pertains to Gurdip Singh Taneja Vs Reliance Life Insurance Company Ltd, vide Case No. Reliance/742/Mumbai/Amritsar/22/13 and Insurance Ombudsman announced the order on 16.08.2013.

Brief Description about the facts of the case:

Shri Gurdip Singh Taneja had filed a complaint against Reliance Life Insurance Company about inadequate maturity claim payment by an amount of Rs 12000/- under policy bearing number 10426355. On 11.11.2011, the company intimated about the maturity due on 31.12.2011 and an approximate fund value of Rs 102978.66 payable. But, it was conveyed that Rs 91373.04 were credited to his bank account. When he wrote several times to pay the difference, the company did not respond. Hence feeling aggrieved, he has approached this office for a refund of Rs.12000/-

The insurer clarified that the policy was a unit linked policy and fund value is dependent on volatile market situations and cannot be fixed. Fund value at maturity was Rs.102978.66 and was settled after deducting statutory deductions as per rules.

Decision of the Ombudsman:

The Insurance Ombudsman held that there is no deficiency of service as the insurer settled the maturity claim as per terms and conditions. In case of plea of insurer that the fund value is linked with market conditions was upheld.

Critical Analysis:

Policyholders are not well aware about the new products especially ULIPS and process of the claims accruing out of these instruments. The policyholder is often in dilemma when ULIPS are bought. He assumes that the claim is always fixed but the growth of fund is associated with market which is high. Thus if such instruments can yield high growth then their amount may also depreciate consequently with the market fluctuations.

Case 7:

Case 7 pertains to Shri D K Bhatnagar Mehta Vs Life Insurance Corporation of India vide Case No.LIC/545/Rohtak/Ambala/24/14 and order related to it was announced on 22.01.2014.

Brief Description about the facts of the case:

Shri D. K. Bhatnagar had filed a complaint about a nonpayment of a maturity claim of 3 policies bearing numbers 170163389, 170397993 and 171854920 despite a repeated follow up action.

The insurer in its reply clarified that all the three policies belong to salary saving scheme. Due to premium gaps and non-receipt of requisite documents maturity claim payment was not released.

Decision of the Ombudsman:

Insurance Ombudsman held that it is a case of gross deficiency in service on the part of insurer. Moreover his request for transfer of policies and change of mode was not considered. Keeping in view an award is passed to release the maturity proceeds considering policies in force after effecting deduction of unpaid premiums without charging any late payment interest and pay the maturity claim accordingly.

Critical Analysis:

IRDAI mandates that regular policy servicing should be provided to the policyholder in terms of change of address, change of nominee, etc. After the commencement of policy insurer may not deliberately provide quality policy servicing. Sometimes the agent who sold policy may leave the organization and in such cases the policy servicing also suffers but in case the onus lies on insurer to provide quality policy servicing.

Complaints Regarding Survival Benefits

Case 8:

Case 8 relates with Karuna Bhardwaj Vs Life Insurance Corporation of India vide Case No. LIC/43/Ludhiana/ Unit-I, Ludhiana/24/08 and award was announced on 13.06.07.

Brief Description about the facts of the case:

Smt. Karuna Bhardwaj purchased a policy bearing number 160294217. The payment of survival benefit of Rs.20,000/- was due on 01.09.2000. It has not been paid so far. Had she received the amount in time, she would have invested in Bima Plus policy and had gained Rs.54,980/-. Payment of second Survival Benefit of Rs.20,000/- was due on 01.09.2005 but it was paid on 22.02.2007. Had it been given in time, she would have purchased Future Plus Policy and had gained Rs.10,000/-. In all she had not received Rs.85,840/- consisting of Survival Benefit due on 01.09.2000 and the profits which would have accrued to her by purchasing the unit linked insurance policies. She urged intervention of Ombudsman in getting the compensation to the tune of Rs.85,840/-, at the earliest.

The insurer stated that Survival Benefit payment of Rs.20,000/- due on 01.09.2000 was paid to her vide Cheque No. 66724 dated 04.09.2000. The cheque was sent by Registered Post on 15.09.2000 by B.O. Unit-I, Ludhiana at her Phillaur address but it was not received and it became stale. No further action was taken in this regard as the complainant did not approach for the nonpayment of survival benefit. Regarding the other payment of Survival Benefit of Rs.20,000/- due on 01.09.2005, he informed that it was paid on 22.02.2007. An amount of Rs.2,350/- has been paid for delay from 01.09.2005 to 22.02.2007 @ 8% vide Cheque No. 405298 dated 11.05.2007. In view of the payment of both the Survival Benefits and the penal interest has been made, he has requested for closure of the complaint.

Decision of the Ombudsman:

The Insurance Ombudsman held that the contention of the complainant for non receipt of SB of Rs.20000/- due on 01.09.2000 is in order. It was ordered that an amount of Rs.20000/- be paid by the insurer to the complainant as SB installment due on 01.09.2000 along with interest @8% per annum w.e.f. 1.10.2000 till the date of payment, after obtaining an indemnity bond from the complainant to the effect that the amount will be refunded by her if it is later on revealed that she had already received the payment. Payment should be made by 30.6.2007 under intimation to this office.

Critical Analysis:

The insurer had casual attitude towards payment of survival benefits to the complainants. The Ombudsman took apt decision by obtaining an indemnity bond from the complainant so that financial interest of the insurer may also be protected. Further payment of survival benefit along with interest rate had bestowed financial gains to the complainants.

Miscellaneous Complaints:

Case 9:

The case 10 pertains to Shri Madhusudan Nair Vs HDFC Standard Life Ins. Co. Ltd. vide Case No. HDFC/122/Mumbai/Gurgaon/22/12 and order regarding it was issued on 21.02.2013

Brief Description about the facts of the case:

Shri Madhusudan Nair filed a complaint about mis-selling of a policy for Rs. 10,00,000/- in the month of February 2010 as instead of promised single premium the insurance company issued regular premium paying policy. When he requested for cancellation it was not considered.

The insurer clarified the position by stating that when the complaint was received by the company, a offer was given to Shri Madhusudan Nair to convert the policy into single premium policy which was not agreed by the complainant.

Decision of the Ombudsman:

The Insurance Ombudsman held that there are no irregularities about the service provided by the company. Moreover, Shri Madhusudan Nair had already purchased One crore policy from LIC of India and his plea about misleading into signing blank forms and not going through the policy is not justified. His request for cancellation after lapse of free look option is not reasonable. Hence, complainant is dismissed.

Critical Analysis:

The policyholder generally has a casual attitude while buying the policy document. It is onus of the policy holder to understand all the terms and conditions of the policy and on receiving the policy he/she if not satisfied with the policy may return back or buy a new product. In above case neither the policy-holder understood terms and conditions and nor he exercised the free look period on receipt of the final policy.

Case 10:

Case 10 pertains to Smt. Tejinder Kaur Vs FGI Life Ins. Co. Ltd vide Case No. FGI/1987/22/13/Mumbai/Mohali and judgement was announced on 03.01.2014.

Brief Description about the facts of the case:

Smt. Tejinder Kaur was sold an insurance policy bearing number 1027696 for a sum of Rs.13500/- in August 2012. Her application for cancellation on 05.11.2012 due to forged signature on proposal forms was not responded by the company.

The insurer clarified that the policy was issued on the basis of details furnished in the proposal forms and the policy was delivered on time, but she did not opt to return the policy within free look period. In view of a delay, request for cancellation/a refund was declined.

Decision of the Ombudsman:

The Insurance Ombudsman held that there is deficiency in service on the part of the company. In fact the signature of Smt. Tejinder Kaur prima facie does not tally with the signature on Aadhaar Card submitted by her. Moreover, her request was within reasonable time. Accordingly, an award is passed with a direction to the insurance company to refund the premium paid.

Critical Analysis:

The insurers on many occasions forge the signatures of the policyholders and also have casual attitude for policy servicing.

6.31 Decisions Of Insurance Ombudsman: A Concise View One Thing Common:

The decisions of Insurance Ombudsmen of various benches and Chandigarh bench has one thing in common that whenever the life assured as tried to suppress the material facts and it was proved by the insurer that material facts had been suppressed and claim stands repudiated the Insurance Ombudsman had justified the action of insurers. While on the other hand if insurer had repudiated the claim on the grounds of suppression of material facts and is unable to prove the same the Insurance Ombudsman had directed the insurer to settle the claim at the earliest. In cases of delay in claim settlement after the nominee or policyholder had submitted the requisite documents and poor servicing by the insurer the Ombudsman had directed to settle the claim with interest payment. One more instant is that when the policyholder had complained regarding mis-selling and his request for discontinuance of policy was not obliged by the insurer on the grounds of lapse of free-look period. Insurance Ombudsman aptly stated that before buying policy the policyholder should clearly read the instruction or understand them. Thus, due to casual attitude of the policyholder, the insurer should not suffer.

In nutshell, the prospective buyer (i) should clearly understand the terms and conditions of the policy document, (ii) should not suppress the material facts regarding health etc, (iii) should not withhold any information necessary for the document and (iv) should not furnish false information. On the other hand - the insurer should also provide quality servicing and should verify the facts with documentary proof before repudiating the claim.

6.32 Field Survey Results Of Policyholders With Disposed Of Cases

As stated earlier, out of total 59 respondents - who approached their insurer relating to their grievance - 43 were dissatisfied with the response of insurer. Out of these 43 respondents only eight (i.e. 18.6 percent) respondents; approached Insurance

Ombudsman for redressing their grievances. In term of insurance companies, 15.4 percent respondents of LIC; 15 percent respondents of ICICI Prudential and 30 percent respondents of Exide Life had approached Insurance Ombudsman (see Table 6.109).

Table 6.109: Policyholders Approached Insurance Ombudsman and Variations across Insurance Firms

Ever approached Insurance Ombudsman	LIC	ICICI Prudential	Exide Life	Total
Yes	2 (15.4)	3 (15)	3 (30)	8 (18.6)
No	11 (84.6)	17 (85)	7 (70)	35 (81.4)
Total	13 (100)	20 (100)	10 (100)	43 (100)

Note: Figures in the parenthesis are percentages.

The procedure for filling complaints with Insurance Ombudsman should be simple and policy-holder friendly, so that they do not hesitate in filling complaints. Out of total eight respondents who had filed complaints with Insurance Ombudsman seven (87.5 percent) respondents found the procedure simple while one respondent stated that the procedure for filling complaint with Insurance Ombudsman was cumbersome. Variations were also noticed across insurance companies as One respondent of LIC, all the three respondents of ICICI Prudential and all the three respondents of Exide Life found procedure for filing complaints simple (Table 6.108).

Table 6.110: Procedure of Filing Complaint with Insurance Ombudsman Variations across Insurance Companies

Procedure of Filing Complaints with Insurance Ombudsman	LIC	ICICI Prudential	Exide Life	Total
Simple	1 (50)	3 (100)	3 (100)	7 (87.5)
Cumbersome	1 (50)	0 (0)	0 (0)	1 (12.5)
Total	2 (100)	3 (100)	3 (100)	8 (100)

Note: Figures in the parenthesis are percentages.

Out of eight respondents, seven respondents were satisfied with the decision of Insurance Ombudsman. Across insurers variations were noticed in satisfaction level of respondents as one respondent of LIC, all the three each respondents of ICICI

Prudential and Exide Life were satisfied with the decision of Insurance Ombudsman regarding their grievance (Table 6.109).

Table 6.111: Satisfaction of the Policyholders with Decision of Insurance Ombudsman and Variations across Insurance Companies

Satisfaction level of the Policyholders with decision of Insurance Ombudsman	LIC	ICICI Prudential	Exide Life	Total
Satisfied	1 (50)	3 (100)	3 (100)	7 (87.5)
Dis-satisfied	1 (50)	0 (0)	0 (0)	1 (12.5)
Total	2 (100)	3 (100)	3 (100)	8 (100)

Note: Figures in the parenthesis are percentages.

In terms of education, only respondents with education level of graduation and above approached Insurance Ombudsman. Out of eight respondents, seven respondents were satisfied with the decision of insurance Ombudsman (see Table 6.112).

Table 6.112: Satisfaction of the Policyholders with Decision of Insurance Ombudsman and Variations across Education Level

Satisfaction level of the Policyholders with decision of Insurance Ombudsman	Below Matric	Matric and Plus 2	Graduation and above	Total
Satisfied	0 (0)	0 (0)	7 (87.5)	7 (87.5)
Dissatisfied	0 (0)	0 (0)	1 (12.5)	1 (12.5)
Total	0 (0)	0 (0)	8 (100)	8 (100)

Note: Figures in the parenthesis are percentages.

Whether income level of the respondents makes a difference or not in satisfaction with the decision of Insurance Ombudsman was tested through sub-hypothesis namely, 'Income of the respondents and satisfaction with decision of Insurance Ombudsman are related'.

In terms of income variations were noticed between middle and high income groups. Two respondents with monthly income ranging between Rs. 10,000 and Rs. 30,000 and all the five respondents with monthly income above Rs. 30,000 were satisfied with decision of Insurance Ombudsman (Table 7.129 and Figure 7.123). The above sub-hypothesis is rejected as variations across income levels of respondents are found to be statistically insignificant at five percent level as per Chi-square test as χ^2= 1.905 (1, N = 8), p = .168.

Table 6.113: Satisfaction of the Policyholders with Decision of Insurance Ombudsman and Variations across Income Levels

Satisfaction level of the Policyholders with decision of Insurance Ombudsman	Below Rs. 10000	Rs. 10000- Rs. 30000	Above Rs. 30000	Total
Satisfied	0 (0)	2 (66.7)	5 (100)	7 (87.5)
Dissatisfied	0 (0)	1 (33.3)	0 (0)	1 (12.5)
Total	0 (100)	3 (100)	5 (100)	8 (100)

Note: Figures in the parenthesis are percentages.

The relation between perceptions of urban and rural respondents and satisfaction with the decision of Insurance Ombudsman was tested through sub-hypothesis namely, 'perceptions of urban and rural respondents and satisfaction with decision of Insurance Ombudsman are related'.

Satisfaction level of respondents also showed variation in terms of urban and rural respondents as all the six urban respondents and one rural respondent were satisfied with the decision of Insurance Ombudsman (Table 6.112). The variations across urban and rural respondents in terms of satisfaction with the decision of insurance Ombudsman are found to be statistically insignificant at five percent level as per Chi-square test as χ^2=3.429 (1, N = 8), p = .064. Thus, the above sub-hypothesis is rejected.

Table 6.114: Satisfaction of the Policy-holders with Decision of Insurance Ombudsman and Variations across Rural and Urban Areas

Satisfaction level of the Policyholders with decision of Insurance Ombudsman	Urban	Rural	Total
Satisfied	6 (100)	1 (50)	7 (87.5)
Dissatisfied	0 (0)	1 (50)	1 (12.5)
Total	6 (100)	2 (100)	8 (100)

Note: Figures in the parenthesis are percentages.

Only male respondents had approached insurance Ombudsman. Thus, out of eight respondents - seven respondents were satisfied with decision of Insurance Ombudsman (Table 6.113).

Table 6.115: Satisfaction of the Policyholders with Decision of Insurance Ombudsman and Variations across Gender

Satisfaction level of the Policyholders with decision of Insurance Ombudsman	Male	Female	Total
Satisfied	7 (87.5)	0 (0)	7 (87.5)
Dissatisfied	1 (12.5)	0 (0)	1 (12.5)
Total	8 (100)	0 (0)	8 (100)

Note: Figures in the parenthesis are percentages.

6.33 Perceptions Of The Complainants With On-Going Cases With The Insurance Ombudsman

During visit to the office of Insurance Ombudsman 21 complainants present were interviewed whose complaints were pending with the Ombudsman. Out of these 21 respondents, 7 respondents stated that their complaint pertains to miss-selling done by the agent of the insurer during policy commencement whereas 4 respondents stated that the insurer indulged in miss-selling on the pretext of issuing new policy by surrendering the old policy. The respondents stated that after a while they realized that they have been duped as the new policy contained high premium amount which was beyond their paying capacity. Six respondents stated that they had grievance related to claim settlement and 4 expressed that agent did not imparted full information about the policy and dispute occurred during indemnity of the life assured (see Figure 6.6).

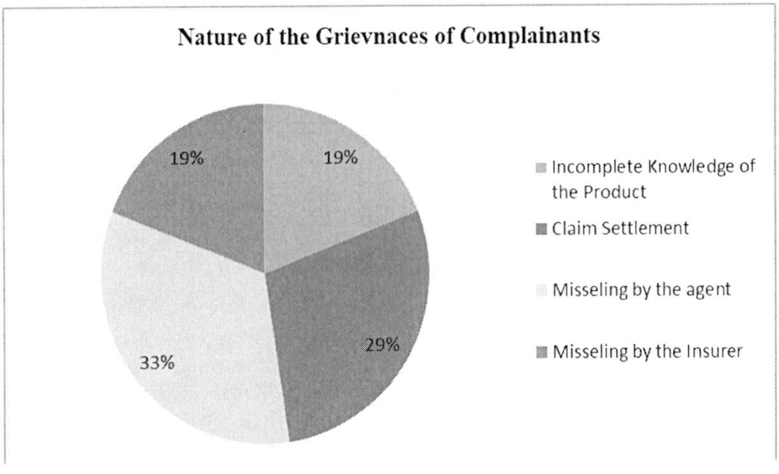

Figure 6.6

Further all the respondents stated that - they find the procedure of filling the complaint with ombudsman very simple as majority of them had sent the complaints by post and an acknowledgement was received by them on the receipt of the complaint by Insurance Ombudsman. None of the respondents had to hire a lawyer or any other legal professional for filing the complaint. All the respondents stated that they did not pay any fee for filing the case and further reiterated that they did not face any problem while filing the case with Insurance Ombudsman.

These quasi- judicial dispute adjudication mechanisms are established for the speedy disposal of the cases as justice delayed is justice denied. Out of total 21 respondents, 10 (47.6 percent) stated that their grievance is pending before the Insurance Ombudsman for more than six months. While 8 respondents (38.1 percent) expressed that their grievance is pending more than a year before the Ombudsman. On the other hand, very few respondents (14.3 percent) revealed that their grievance is pending for less than six months (see Figure 6.7).

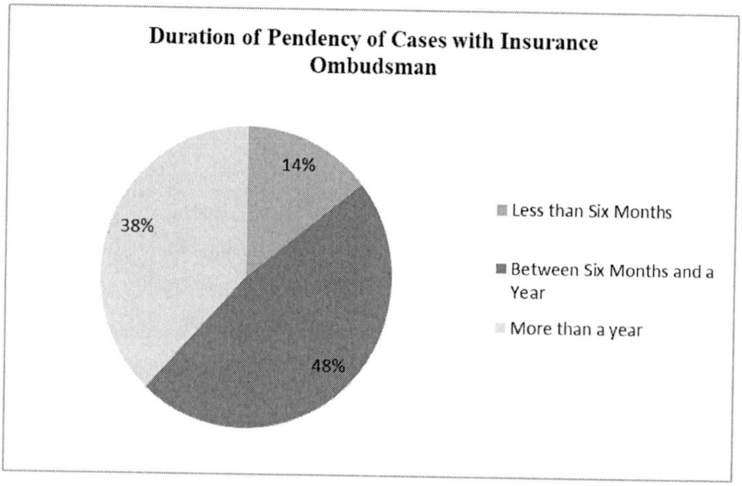

Figure 6.7

6.34 Perceptions of the Insurance Ombudsman

During interview, the Insurance Ombudsman revealed that majority of the cases pertains to the miss-selling of the products by the agents followed by claim settlement cases. The Chandigarh Ombudsman revealed that on daily basis around 35 complaints are received. Majority of the complaints are received through posts followed by e-mails and very few complaints are received in person. On receiving the complaint, the Office of Insurance Ombudsman sends an acknowledgement to the complainant along with a Performa asking for the insurer involved, amount of money involved and also seeking the consent of the complaint that the judgment of the ombudsman shall be binding on him/her. A letter is also dispatched to the concerned insurer seeking their view on the complaint received. After receiving the consent of the complainant and reviews of the insurer; a summary of the case is prepared and date for hearing is intimated to both the parties. Generally, cases regarding a insurer are heard in a single day as it is convenient for the insurance firm to represent itself in a single day. Insurance firms are represented by their legal - cell officials sent from headquarters. During hearing, Insurance Ombudsman, along with Secretary to Ombudsman and one expert from LIC; if case pertains to life insurance or one expert from GIC or other general public insurer - if the case is from non-life are present along with the two parties. It is noteworthy to mention here that all the staff of Insurance Ombudsman is on deputation either from Life Insurance Corporation or other four public general insurance companies.

Insurance Ombudsman also stated that the complainant is only represented by themselves and they do not allow the services of lawyers or legal professional to represent complainants. It also came to fore that no fee is charged from the complaint for redressing their grievances. Insurance Ombudsman office also stated that they do not suffer any shortage of funds, manpower and infrastructure. Owing to rise in number of cases being received it is suggested to hasten the process of justice delivery it is advisable to increase the number of Insurance Ombudsman specifically in those centres such as Delhi, Chandigarh, Bombay where number of complaints is more and pendency ratio of complaints is high.

6.35 Matrix Summing Up The Testing Of Hypothesis 6

Matrix 6.2: Testing of Hypothesis 6- "IRDAI has effective machinery in the form of Grievance Redressal cell and Insurance Ombudsman for Redressing grievances of Policyholders."

Sr. No.	Sub-Hypothesis	Sources of Data	Analysis	Status of Sub-Hypothesis Accepted
1.	Pendency of cases with grievance redressal cell of IRDAI has reduced overtime	Secondary Data	The pendency ration has decreased from 58.68 in 2002-03 to 0.35 in 2012-13	Yes
2.	IRDAI grievance redressal cell has been effective in redressing grievances of policyholders.	Primary Data	Majority (61.5 percent) of the Respondents who approached IRDAI Grievance Redressal cell are dissatisfied with its decision regarding their complaint.	No

Sr. No.	Sub-Hypothesis	Sources of Data	Analysis	Status of Sub-Hypothesis Accepted
3.	There has been reduction in complaints pendency with the insurance Ombudsman over years	Secondary data and Primary Data	The pendency ratio has decreased from 23.43 in 2002-03 to 20.93 in 2012-13. Insurance Ombudsman stated that there is rise in number of complaints by policyholders which may increase pendency of complaints	Yes
4.	IRDAI has effective machinery in the form of Insurance Ombudsman for redressing grievances of policyholders	Primary Data	Majority (87.5 percent) of the Respondents who approached Insurance Ombudsman are satisfied with its decision regarding their complaint.	Yes

Thus, on the basis of above analysis of sub-hypotheses, the **Hypothesis 6**: "IRDAI has effective machinery in the form of Grievance Redressal cell and Insurance Ombudsman for redressing grievances of Policy-holders", **stands Validated.**

III
ASSESSMENT OF IRDAI IN TERMS OF HAVING FEATURES OF A STRONG REGULATOR

A regulator is desired to have characteristics such as - independence from executive control, enforcement powers of authority; transparency and accountability.

Thus assessment of IRDAI is done on the basis of parameters such as independence of IRDAI, enforcement powers of IRDAI, mechanisms for ensuring transparency and accountability of IRDAI and competency of IRDAI. The main hypothesis tested in this regard is IRDAI has been - (i) independent; (ii) competent; (iii) able to enforce powers and authority; and (iv) accountable and transparent in regulating insurance business.

The main hypothesis was split into sub-hypothesis as under:

1. IRDAI is independent from executive as it has sufficient financial resources, competent manpower and infrastructure.
2. IRDAI has enforcement powers as it exercise licensing powers, penalizing powers product approval powers and lay down of standards of service.
3. IRDAI has mechanisms for ensuring transparency and accountability as it disseminates information, involves stakeholders in decision making process and its reports are audited.

6.36 Independence of IRDAI

International lending agencies and government such as of United Kingdom are of the view that independence of the regulator is most sacrosanct as it makes the regulator effective and attract private investments[1]. Independence of regulators comprises two main ideas. Firstly, the regulator should not be influenced by the regulated so as to reduce concerns of 'regulatory capture' and secondly, it should also be free from undue government intervention[2].

The Council of European Energy Regulators (CEER), have suggested that in order to be independent, a regulator should have following characteristics:

Characteristics of a Regulator:-

1. Independence from the interests of the regulated industry
2. Legal personality, separate from the ministries
3. Clear and sufficient competences
4. Financial independence from the state (revenues preferably from participant fees)
5. Board members:

a. Meritocratic and impartial appointment process

b. Fixed mandate, removal for cause only

c. No direct or indirect financial interests in the energy sector, no conflicts of interest, Sufficient highly qualified personnel and own management policy

6. Sufficient Infrastructure (budget, buildings, IT technology, etc.).

Thus, assessment of independence of IRDAI is done on the basis of parameters namely, sufficiency in financial resources, competent manpower, infrastructure and absence of regulatory capture (pressure any way) and interference from executive.

Descriptor of IRDAI Personal:

The sub-hypothesis tested in this regard is IRDAI is independent from executive as it has sufficient financial resources, competent manpower and infrastructure.

As stated earlier, the Insurance Regulatory and Development Authority of India is composed of Chairman, four whole time members and four part time members. The members are appointed by the Central Government from amongst the persons having special knowledge of life insurance and general insurance business, actuarial science, finance, economics, law, accountancy and administration. Currently, the Chairperson of the Authority is Mr. T.S. Vijayan, who has career in life insurance field spanning more than three decades and had been Chairman Life Insurance Corporation of India

---

1. Jon Stern (1997), "What Makes an Independent Regulator Independent?" *Business Strategy Review*, Volume 8, Number 2, pp. 67-74.
2. Nick Malyshev (2009), "Regulatory Reform and Building Governance Capacities" paper presented in seminaron *Building Governance Capacities in India*, by OECD and CUTS International on 3 December 2009, New Delhi, India.

for more five years. Thus, a man of acumen in field of life insurance, Mr.Nilesh Sathe is Member (life) and before joining the Authority, he was CEO and Director of LIC, Noura Mutual fund AMC and he had also served as head of Northern Zone of LIC of India as Zonal Manager. Mrs. V.R. Iyer, Member (Finance and Investments) before joining IRDAI was Chairperson and Managing Director of Bank of India. Ms. Pournima Gupte Member (Actuary), is fellow of Institute of Actuaries of India and before joining IRDAI, has worked as appointed actuary in public and private life insurance firms and had served on deputation to London Branch of LIC. Mr. D.D. Singh, member (Distribution), before joining IRDAI was Zonal manager of LIC of India south zone Chennai. The profiles of Chairperson and permanent members reflect they are experts in diverse fields such as life insurance, mutual fund, banking and actuaries.

The other feature of being an independent regulator is fixed tenure and absence of executive discretion regarding dismissal of members of the Authority. The IRDAI Act 1999, mandates that chairperson and permanent members shall hold office for term of five years or till the age of sixty five years in case of Chairperson and sixty two years in case of whole time members whichever is earlier. Further the chairperson and whole time members are eligible for re-appointment. In case of removal of members and Chairperson from office the Act mandates that they can be removed if they are adjudged solvent, had become mentally and physically incapable, had been convicted of any offence which involves moral turpitude, has acquired financial interests which are likely to affect his independent functioning and had abused his position in such member that his continuation in the office is detrimental to public interest. In case of removal from office on grounds of acquired financial interests and abused his position the member shall be provided a reasonable opportunity to be heard. Also the terms and conditions of the members cannot be varied to their disadvantage.

Debarring members and Chairperson from future employment prevents misuse of office by members by providing undue benefits in hope of future employment either in the regulated industry or other sectors. The Act mandates that, no whole-time members and Chairperson from the date on which they had relinquished their office, shall not accept any employment either under the central government or state government or in any company of insurance sector without the permission of the Central government for a period of two years. This provision helps in making interests of regulator and regulated independent from each other.

The other parameter of strong regulator is sufficiency of funds at the disposal of the regulatory authority ensuring independence from government revenues. The act mandates that IRDAI shall establish an IRDAI Fund which shall be credited with government grants, sums, fees, charges and percentage of prescribed premium income received from the insurer. The Fund shall be used for meeting expenses relating to salaries, allowances and remuneration of members, officers and other employees of the authority and other expenses of the IRDAI incurred while discharging its functions. During interaction with IRDAI official it was revealed that IRDAI fund is operational and substantive amount of revenues are generated by IRDAI itself. Although, IRDAI receive grants out of Consolidated Fund of India, but the major source of IRDAI budget are its own source revenues.

Along with funds sufficient and competent manpower is a necessity to discharge its functions effectively and efficiently. IRDAI official revealed that the Authority has sufficient and competent manpower drawn from various sectors such as insurance, legal services, financial institutions, government sector and also private sector. Moreover, in the initial years when IRDAI commenced its operations the ratio of deputation staff and permanent staff was equal but over the years the strength of deputation staff has decreased vis-à-vis permanent staff.

Finally, sufficient infrastructure facilities are also one of the pre-requisite for effective functioning authority. IRDAI official expressed that the authority has sufficient infrastructure facilities at its disposal. Currently, the Authority is operating from a state government building which is leased to it. In near future (within a year) the Authority will shift to its own new complex whose constriction work is about to complete. Thus, IRDAI will have its own building and other infrastructure facilities.

IRDAI Official also expressed that the Ministry of Finance had never interfered in the working of the Authority and IRDAI is independent from executive. Also there had never been a reported instance of regulatory capture.

6.37 Enforcement Powers of IRDAI

It is necessary for a regulatory agency to have enforcement powers, for tariff setting, laying down quality service standards, issuing licenses to the firms and regularly monitoring them and in case of non-compliance of standards penalizing the firms.

Thus, assessment of IRDAI in terms of enforcement of standards is done on the basis of parameters such as - (i) licensing power of IRDAI, (ii) product approval process of IRDAI, (iii) laying down of standards of service and (iv) penalizing powers of IRDAI in case of non-compliance with laid down standards.

The sub-hypothesis tested is - IRDAI has enforcement powers as it exercise licensing powers, penalizing powers, product approval powers and lay down of standards of service.

Registration of insurance companies is regulated by the IRDA (Registration of Indian Insurance Companies), Regulations 2000 which were subsequently, amended and latest being Insurance Regulatory and Development Authority (Registration of Indian Insurance Companies) (Sixth Amendment) Regulations, 2014. IRDAI grants, renew, modify, withdraw or cancel licenses of insurers and it also imposes penalties to insurers for non-compliance of regulations. IRDAI has granted licenses to 24 life insurers, 28 non-life insurers and 1 re-insurer to operate in India. In year 2012-13 IRDAI levied penalty on 10 life insurers and 2 non-life insurers for non compliance with various regulatory provisions. IRDAI also issued warnings, specific orders/ directions to the insurance firms who are non-complying with regulatory directions.

Various insurance intermediaries such agents, corporate agents, brokers are granted licenses to conduct the business. IRDAI specifies requisite qualifications, code of conduct and practical training for insurance intermediaries. Recently, IRDAI had exempted individual agents from its licensing process and now insurance companies can appoint agents of their own. For granting license to corporate agents IRDAI had issued IRDA (Licensing of Corporate Agents) Regulations, 2002. In 2013-14, 116 corporate agents were added and licenses of 166 were cancelled by IRDAI. Insurance brokers are licensed by IRDAI vide IRDA (Insurance Brokers) Regulations, 2013for operating in insurance market. There are 384 insurance brokers out of which 332 are direct brokers, 46 are composite brokers and 6 are re-insurance brokers. IRDAI has cancelled 51 licenses till now i.e. from 2003 to 2013-14. In year 2013-14, 38 new licenses were issued for insurance brokers.

Product Approval At a Glance:

The products of insurance firms are first approved by IRDAI and then launched by insurance firms in the market. For granting approval to products the IRDAI has constituted product approval committees of life insurance and non-life insurance products. These committees examine the viability of products submitted for approval by insurers. In 2013-14, around 780 products were received out of which 538 were approved while 141 were rejected.

Guidelines to Insurers:

IRDAI had issued guidelines to insurers for protection of interests of policy holders. It has brought out regulations regarding various do's and don'ts for insurers and intermediaries at the point of sale, point of claim. Agents of the insurance firms must disclose all the information regarding policy such as name of the plan, whether the policy includes benefits, date of maturity, free-look period, etc too the prospective buyer at point if sale of policy. IRDAI has issued regulation mandating every insurer to have in place effective grievance redressal mechanism and these mechanisms should respond back within 15 days of receipt of complaint.

IRDAI official had stated that the Authority penalizes the firms who do not follow the laid down standards.

6.38 Transparency And Accountability In Working of IRDAI

Transparency can be ensured if (i) public have access to decision-making of the regulator and (ii) provision of platform for reasoning such decisions, establishment of external auditing mechanism, and (iii) having in place an effective appeal process for agency decisions, and code of ethics to avoid conflicts of interest[3].

Thus, assessment of IRDAI in terms of ensuring transparency and accountability is undertaken on the basis of benchmarks such as - involvement of various stakeholders in decision making process, publishing about various activities of the Authority, Annual Reports and Financial reports.

The sub-hypothesis tested in this regard is - IRDAI has mechanisms for ensuring transparency and accountability as it disseminate information, involve stakeholders in decision making process and its reports are audited.

---

3. Warrick Smith (1997), "Utility Regulators: Independence Debate, Public Policy for the Private Sector", *Note No. 127*, The World Bank Group.

IRDAI disseminate information on its website and public have access to this information without any hurdle. On the website, IRDAI furnishes all the necessary information regarding acts/regulations; insurers and reinsurers, agents training institutes, appointed actuaries; surveyors, third party administrators, insurance brokers, corporate agents; insurance councils, insurance ombudsmen; Annual Report, IRDAI Journal and press releases. Annual reports provide in details all the activities undertaken by the Authority in the year.

IRDAI has launched another website named, *Bima Bemissal*, for disseminating information regarding procedure for redressing grievances of policy-holders, various mechanisms, rights of policy-holders and also grievance redressal reports.

IRDAI being a public authority also obliges to Right to Information Act, 2005. The website also contains name and designation, department and e-mail addresses of Central Public Information Officers as required to be published under Section 4(1)(b) of RTI Act 2005. IRDAI has designated appellate authority and also appointed Central Information Commissioner in consonance with terms of Chapter 3 of the Right to Information Act, 2005. The portal of RTI contains information to make application under RTI Act, 2005, whom to send this application, etc.

Stakeholders are also involved in working of IRDAI as composition of Insurance Advisory Committee has members from government and private life insurers, general insurers; insurance related institutes; Insurance Ombudsman; banks; consumer Disputes Redressal Commission and other such institutes. IRDAI has established two councils of the Insurance Association of India, namely:- the Life Insurance Council and the General Insurance Council. Members and chairmen to Executive Committee of both the councils are nominated by the IRDAI. The Executive Committees of the Councils are entrusted with the following functions such as advising and assisting insurers in setting up standards of conduct and sound practice and in the matter of rendering efficient service to policy holders; advising the Authority in the matter of controlling the expenses of insurers and informing the Authority of any insurer acting in a manner prejudicial to the interests of policy-holders.

Official of the IRDAI expressed that although stakeholders are not involved in decision making process but while formulating a policy having ramifications of larger public interest the public comments and suggestions are solicited by the Authority by publishing the matter on its website for review. Simultaneously, the opinions of Life Insurance Council, General Insurance Council and Insurance Advisory Council are also invited. Thus, the final policy decision is taken by the Authority on the basis of the views, opinions expressed by public and other stakeholders.

The accounts of IRDAI are audited annually by Comptroller and Auditor General of India and audited accounts along with audit report are forwarded to government of India and then placed in both houses of parliament.

Moreover, in the recent amendment vide The Insurance Laws (Amendment) Act, 2015 it has been incorporated that if IRDAI refuses registration to the insurer then within 30 days from the date of this decision the insurer may appeal to the

Securities Appellate Tribunal established under section 15 K of the Securities and Exchange Board of India Act, 1992. Thus, there exist appellate mechanisms which can be approached by parties in case the party is aggrieved by the decision of IRDAI. The official of IRDAI have stated that in case of grievances, the insurance firms often litigate against the authority in civil courts. Thus, the insurance firms have sufficient mechanisms to challenge the decisions of IRDAI.

6.39 Competency of IRDAI

Competency of the regulator is based on the ability of the staff to innovate, take initiatives and make decisions. Regulatory bodies may attract and retain qualified personnel by paying them higher salaries and remuneration. Competency can also be achieved by hiring outside experts whenever need arises.

Competency of IRDAI is done on the basis of its ability to attract and retain qualified staff, ability of staff to innovate and make decisions and also ability of IRDAI to hire outside experts if need arises,

The sub-hypothesis tested in this regard is, IRDAI has sufficient competency as it can attract and retain qualified personnel and hire outside experts if need arises.

The official of IRDAI revealed that manpower in IRDAI is drawn from diverse fields such as private insurers, public insurers, financial institutions, Reserve Bank of India and other banking institutions, etc. The salaries of the personnel are par with private sector which acts as an incentive for hiring and retaining the competent manpower. The service conditions are favorable for the staff.

Efficient of Quantized staff of IRDAI:

The official also stated that the staff has ability to innovate as it has designed various customer-friendly policies such as recently launching of Insurance Repository System. In this new system the policies are converted into electronic form and for submission of policy by agent, policy servicing is done electronically. It makes the policy commencement, a speedy process and reduces physical visits. Another noteworthy innovative step of IRDAI is Integrated Grievance Management System (IGMS). Grievance Redressal Cell has IGMS which receives complaints through Integrated Grievance Call centre which is a toll free number. IGMS is implemented by IRDAI which is helpful in providing information regarding status of complaints across the industry to the Authority on real time basis. IGMS is working as a repository of the industry's complaints including their status.

Another striking feature enhancing competence of a regulator is its ability to hire outside experts if need arises. The IRDAI officials expressed that there is no provision to hire outside experts. But discussions are held with outside experts if need arises and their comments on particular policy are invited. However, experts cannot be hired and put into hierarchy of IRDAI for a special need.

6.40 Matrix Summing Up The Testing of Hypothesis 7

Matrix 6.3: Testing of Hypothesis 7- "IRDAI has been independent; competent; able to enforce powers and authority; and accountable and transparent in regulating insurance business."

Sr. No.	Sub-Hypothesis	Sources of Data	Analysis	Status of Sub-Hypothesis Accepted
1.	IRDAI is independent from executive as it has sufficient financial resources, competent manpower and infrastructure.	Secondary Data and Primary Data	The members of IRDAI are drawn from diverse fields such as life insurance, non-life insurance, actuarial services making it professionally competent and independent. The fixed tenure of members and their terms of service cannot be varied to their disadvantage is also another parameter of their independence form executive. Debarring the members from future employment also alienates the members from acquiring financial interests in the regulated industry. Official of IRDAI also stated that IRDAI has sufficient finances, infrastructure and manpower to discharge its functions efficiently and effectively. Also IRDAI is independent from undue influence of executive.	Yes
2.	IRDAI has enforcement powers as it exercise licensing powers, penalizing powers product approval powers and lay down of standards of service.	Secondary Data and Primary Data	IRDAI grants licenses to the insurance firms and its intermediaries. The Authority had also cancelled the licenses and imposed fines on the firms violating norms and standards. IRDAI is the final authority for granting approval to the products of insurance firms. The official of IRDAI also stated that IRDAI penalizes the firms for violating standards of service.	Yes
3.	IRDAI has mechanisms for ensuring transparency and accountability as it disseminate information, involve stakeholders in decision making process and its reports are audited.	Secondary data and Primary Data	IRDAI discloses information of its own through its website and annual reports. IRDAI also provide the desired information as per Right to Information Act of India. The official revealed that the Authority also involves various stakeholders such as public, Insurance Advisory councils, etc by soliciting their views on a policy matter. The decision of IRDAI in case of rejection of registration may be questioned in Securities Appellate Tribunal. Thus, there exists check and balances also.	Yes

Sr. No.	Sub-Hypothesis	Sources of Data	Analysis	Status of Sub-Hypot-hesis Accepted
4	IRDAI has sufficient competency as it can attract and retain qualified personnel and hire outside experts if need arises	Secondary data and primary data	The service conditions such as high salaries act as an incentive for hiring and retaining the qualified manpower. The staff has innovative ability as visible through launching of Insurance Repository System, Integrated grievance management system. The official also opined that there is no provision for hiring an outside expert in hierarchy of IRDAI but discussions can be held with experts for specific issues.	Yes

Thus, on the basis of above analysis of sub-hypotheses; the **Hypothesis 7**: "IRDAI has been independent; competent; able to enforce powers and authority; and accountable and transparent in regulating insurance business", **stands Validated.**

6.41 Concluding Observations

The assessment of IRDAI is undertaken in terms of role of IRDAI in protecting the interests of policy holders, efficacy of Grievance Redressal Cell of IRDAI and Insurance Ombudsman in redressing grievances of policyholders and IRDAI having features of a strong regulator. In this regard, three hypotheses: namely, (i) IRDAI has been effective in protecting the interests of policy holders by making agents of insurers to dispense full information regarding policy proposal to prospective buyer; (ii) IRDAI has effective machinery in the form of Grievance Redressal Cell and Insurance Ombudsman for redressing grievances of policyholders; and - (iii) IRDAI has been independent; competent; able to enforce powers and authority; and accountable and transparent in regulating insurance business.

For testing hypotheses relating to protection of interests of policyholders the primary data was collected. The study finds that IRDAI has not been able to make policy proposal policyholder centric, it has been effective in making agents to share all the information regarding the policy to prospective buyers, majority of the policyholders are satisfied with the information imparted by the agent of the insurance firm and final product they received from the insurer and majority of the respondents expressed dissatisfaction with grievance redressal mechanism of insurer. Thus, the hypothesis, namely, IRDAI has been effective in protecting the interests of policy holders by making agents of insurers to dispense full information regarding policy proposal to prospective buyer, stands validated.

For analyzing the efficacy of IRDAI in redressing the grievances of policyholders the primary data analysis was complimented by the analysis of secondary data regarding the pendency of complaints with Grievance Redressal Cell of IRDAI and Insurance Ombudsman. The analysis found that policyholders were satisfied with these mechanisms and over the years pendency of complaints with IRDAI grievance redressal cell and Insurance Ombudsman has declined. Thus, the hypothesis, namely, IRDAI has effective machinery in the form of Grievance Redressal cell and Insurance Ombudsman for Redressing grievances of Policyholders stands validated.

For testing the hypothesis that IRDAI have features of strong regulators the parameters such as independence of IRDAI from executive, its ability to have enforcement powers and efficacy of IRDAI in ensuring accountability and transparency were used. The analysis of the secondary data revealed that IRDAI has features of strong regulator and the hypothesis namely, IRDAI has been independent; competent; able to enforce powers and authority; and accountable and transparent in regulating insurance business - stands validated.

7

Conclusions and Policy Prescriptions

Genesis: Objective

The aim of this chapter is to summarize the major findings and suggest policy prescriptions for improving the insurance regulatory framework in the Country.

Very Chapter has been organized into four parts. Part I deals with rationale of the study. Review of Literature, Scope, Objectives, Hypotheses and - Research methodology of the study are discussed in part II. Major Findings of the study are documented in part III. Policy Prescriptions are reported in part IV.

I
RATIONALE OF THE STUDY

With the ever - increasing population, development in technology, social complexity and diversification of economic activities; the role of State has witnessed a sea change from a doer of public activities to a distributor of public benefits and facilitator of change. In order to provide services to the masses the pendulum of the economy has swung from regulatory to free market, re-regulation and thus, with emerging challenges and fallacies, it adjusts its position back and forth. The doctrine of Laissez-faire propagated by Adam Smith during 17th and 18th century limits the role of government in matters relating to law and order, essential public works and defense of the country. Due to the limited role played by the state, public spending remained around 10 percent of the Gross Domestic Product in most of the industrial countries of the world.

Gradually, during the early 20th century the doctrine of Laissez-faire lost its influence. After Great Depressions (1924- 1934) the demand for government regulation and intervention in economic affairs propagated by economists such as J.M. Keynes, Paul Samuelson, Richard Musgrave, etc. grew due to market failure, welfare state concept and demand for public good. Market failure was considered as the main reason for government intervention. Thus, established regulatory bodies were expected to lessen inefficiencies engendered by the market failure. Economists were of the view that sources of market failure were natural monopoly and externalities. The Marxist and socialist thinking also stimulated the debate over income inequalities due to Laissez-faire and suggested income redistribution by state intervention. The prime focus of this era was to build a market structure which is least affected by fluctuations. This paved way for the state intervention where and when the public enterprises enhanced public employment. Furthermore, welfare schemes were launched for the poor and marginalized.

In the 1970s, state failure paved way for deregulation of economy influenced by economists such as Ludwig Von Mises, Friedrich von Hayek and Milton Friedman. During this phase instead of minimal role of state –a complementarity between market and state was advocated which Joseph Stiglitz termed as 'third way'. Thus, the state had adopted the approaches of regulation, deregulation and re-regulation with the demand of hour to discharge its functions efficiently and to overcome its earlier inadequacies.

Keeping in tune with sweeping changes in economic policies across globe, the Indian economy was deregulated in early 1990s and reforms of privatization, liberalization and globalization were introduced. In the wake of these reforms, necessary changes were carried out in economic governance by establishing regulatory commissions to streamline the economy vis-à-vis protecting interests of consumers and promotion of fair competition amongst the players.

In the wake of de-regulation of economy and introduction of liberalization, privatization and globalization reforms various sectors such as telecom, infrastructure, capital market, insurance, electricity, etc, were unshackled from government monopoly by opening it to private players and establishing sector specific regulatory bodies. Insurance sector was deregulated in 1999 with the passage of Insurance Regulatory and Development Authority Bill in December, 1999.

II
REVIEW OF LITERATURE, SCOPE, OBJECTIVES, HYPOTHESES AND RESEARCH METHODOLOGY

Review of Literature

Review of literature was broadly categorized into Regulation, Deregulation and Regulation in deregulated environment so as to make it relevant to the themes under discussion. Review of literature revealed that although regulation reduces fear, anxiety and risk factor amongst masses and promotes safety but it is often criticized for being expensive, dampening economic performance, causing delay and red-tapism. Deregulation enhances competition and accountability, which enhances domain of public's choice. It is antithetic to the capture model in which regulator and regulated dominates over public interest. Further, with establishment of IRDAI, insurance sector has witnessed a rapid growth with various players coming into the sector.

Research Gaps

Earlier studies could not depict the holistic picture of insurance sector vis-à-vis functioning of regulatory bodies like IRDAI. Studies were descriptive and lacked sound theoretical and empirical groundings. These studies focused much of their attention on urban population and have ignored the penetration of insurance in the rural sector. The studies have not tried to analyze, the role of IRDAI in promoting growth of insurance business by using rigorous methodology for policy impact analysis.

Scope of the Study

Insurance sector include life insurance, non-life insurance and re-insurance. Subject matter being complex and dynamic, was difficult to study all the facets of insurance. Thus the present study has confined to the analysis of life insurance sector.

Period of Study

IRDAI was set up in December, 1999 and more than a decade and half has passed since it came into being. With market fluctuations and emerging challenges the role of IRDAI has undergone a sea change. It has cautiously reviewed and amended the policies so as to foster accountability and equity. Major slump in market and revival also falls under the study time. Therefore the study period covers a decadal and half of IRDAI functioning i.e. from 1999 to 2014.

Objectives of Study

Insurance is an instrument of risk diversification and a way of investment. Thus, it has economic and social repercussions. It generates a sense of security among people against unforeseen calamities.

The objectives of the study are thus, classified into four categories:

A. Promotional and efficiency role of IRDAI

B. Protection of interests of policyholders and dispute adjudication

C. Regulatory role of IRDAI for funds investment of insurance companies

D. Evaluation of IRDAI in consonance with features of best regulator

A. Promotional and efficiency role of IRDAI

For studying promotional and efficiency role the major objectives are to:

1. Examine the role of IRDAI in promoting the growth of life insurance business in India.
2. Evaluate the role of IRDAI in promoting efficiency in conduct of insurance business.
3. Study the role of IRDAI in spreading the life insurance business in rural areas.

B. Protection of interests of policyholders and dispute adjudication

For evaluating the role of IRDAI in protecting interests of policyholders, the major objectives are to:

4. Analyse the effectiveness of IRDAI in protection of interests of policy holders.
5. Study the role of IRDAI in redressing grievances of Policy-holders.

C. Regulatory role of IRDAI for funds investment of insurance companies

In this regard, the major objective is to:

6. Evaluate the effectiveness of IRDAI in regulating investment of funds by insurance companies.

D. Evaluation of IRDAI as the best regulator

The major objectives examining IRDAI as best regulator are to:

7. Study the effectiveness of IRDAI for incorporating features of best regulator.
8. Suggest measures to improve the efficiency of IRDAI in regulating insurance sector.

Hypotheses of the Study

1. IRDAI has been an instrument in promoting the growth of life insurance business in India by promoting growth in number of agents, polices, single premium underwritten, total premium underwritten in comparison to pre-IRDAI period.
2. IRDAI has promoted efficiency in conduct of insurance business by making insurance firms to minimize inputs.
3. IRDAI has been effective in spreading life insurance in rural sector by fixing quota for rural sector.
4. IRDAI has been effective in regulating investment of funds by insurance companies by stipulating the percentages of investments in Government Securities, Infrastructure and Approved Investments and Other Investments.
5. IRDAI has been effective in protecting the interests of policy holders by making agents of insurers to dispense full information regarding policy proposal to prospective buyer.
6. IRDAI has effective machinery in the form of Grievance Redressal cell and Insurance Ombudsman for redressing grievances of policy-holders.
7. IRDAI has been independent; competent; able to enforce powers and authority; and accountable and transparent in regulating insurance business.

Research Methodology

The study is based on both primary and secondary data. The primary data was collected from 314 policy holders of three life insurance firms namely, Life Insurance Corporation of India, ICICI Prudential and Exide Life through a questionnaire for analyzing the role of IRDAI in protecting interests of policyholders in tricity, namely, Chandigarh, Mohali and Panchkula. These three firms are chosen as LIC - is a sole government undertaking in insurance business.

Exide Life is an Indian private firm without any foreign collaboration in life insurance and ICICI prudential has been selected as it is a firm with foreign collaboration and maximum volume of business in India.

Tricity has been chosen as the locale of the study because it has higher percentage of policy-holders per 1000 persons. Literacy rate is also higher suggesting greater awareness about policies among the customers. Per capita income is higher in the tricity indicating higher buying and sustaining policy capacity of the people. Further all the firms have their offices located in the tricity. All the three cities have rural segments which proved to be of immense importance for collecting data about rural policy holders. Second questionnaire was administered to managerial functionaries of all the three firms. Along with this the third questionnaire was administered to the agents of the three firms as agent is the linch-pin between policy holder and insurer. Interview of Insurance Ombudsman was conducted to have the holistic picture regarding efficacy of IRDAI in redressing grievances of policyholders. Finally an interview with an official of IRDAI was conducted to assess the independence, enforcement powers, competence and transparency and accountability of IRDAI.

Various secondary sources such as annual reports of IRDAI, consultation papers, research papers, newspapers, and internet were widely used to complement the findings of primary data. To analyse the role of IRDAI in promoting growth in life insurance business or to assess 'Regulatory Impact Analysis' regression analysis and counter-factual tests were employed using secondary data along with calculating compound rate of growth. Regression analysis is undertaken by employing dummy variable- an artificial numerical variable used to represent sub-groups of the sample study and it is used to distinguish different treatment groups. Regression analysis provides choice to researcher to separate information on certain variables into discreet categories by assuming 'dummy' values as 0 or 1 for each category. In the present case it is used t examine the impact of IRDAI by assigning dummy variable 0 for pre-IRDAI period and 1 for post IRDAI period. Counterfactual approach is also called as the potential outcome approach" or "Roy-Rubin model" which aims to estimate a potential outcome, or the state of the affairs that would have happened in the absence of the cause. In this study the model is used to work out contours of insurance sector in case IRDAI had not been set up. To analyse the role of IRDAI in promoting efficiency in conduct of insurance business Data Envelopment Analysis was used on secondary data. The secondary data was used to analyse the role of IRDAI in promoting insurance business in rural sector and regulating investments of life insurers.

The collected data was processed by editing, coding, classifying and tabulation. The data analysis was done by using Statistical Package for the Social Sciences (SPSS) software and simple frequencies were drawn along with graphical depiction such as bar diagrams and pie charts wherever appropriate to analyse the impact of functions of Insurance Regulatory and Development Authority of India on various issues mentioned above. Chi-square test was used to find variations across education level, income levels, urban-rural and gender of the respondents. In Chi-square test level of significance was checked at one and five percent level. In counterfactual t-test was used to check whether the difference between projected values and actual values is statistically significant or not.

III
MAJOR FINDINGS

The major findings of the study and testing of the hypothesis are presented as under:

A. Role of IRDAI in promoting growth in Life Insurance Business in India

Role of IRDAI in promoting growth of life insurance business in India have been analyzed on the basis of the indicators: namely, (i) number of insurers in life insurance, (ii) number of offices, (iii) number of individual agents, (iv) number of policies issued, (v) growth in persistency of Policies, (vi) number of products launched in market, (vii) first year (including single premium) life insurance premium, total premium underwritten in life sector, insurance penetration in life sector and insurance density in life sector. The growth of above indicators - was checked by comparing compound rate of growth in pre and post IRDAI phase, regression analysis and counter-factual analysis. On the basis of these tests, it has been found that IRDAI has been effective in promoting growth in life insurance business in India.

Buoyancy Analysis: Not Enwhrgging

On account of insurance penetration and insurance density, score card of IRDAI is not satisfactory. The Insurance penetration in India was 3.2 percent in 2012-13 which is below the world average of 4 percent. Similarly, insurance density in India was US $ 42.7 whereas the world average hovered around US $ 372.

Testing of the Hypothesis 1:

The analysis of secondary data was used to check the status of Hypothesis 1:

"IRDAI has been an instrument in promoting the growth of life insurance business in India by promoting growth in number of agents, polices, single premium underwritten, total premium underwritten in comparison to pre-IRDAI period".

Matrix Summing Up The Testing Of Hypothesis 1

Hypothesis	Sources of Data	Analysis	Status of Hypothesis Accepted
IRDAI has been an instrument in promoting the growth of life insurance business in India by promoting growth in number of agents, polices, single premium underwritten, total premium underwritten in comparison to pre-IRDAI period	Secondary data	The number of insurers had increased from one to 24 in post IRDAI phase. Growth in number of offices is higher in post IRDAI phase as the compound rate of growth was more than in pre IRDAI phase. Regression analysis and counterfactual analysis also proves that growth in number of offices was higher in post IRDAI phase. Growth in terms of agent is higher in pre IRDAI phase as compound rate of growth was more in pre IRDAI phase as compared to post-IRDAI phase. But regression analysis and counterfactual test reveal that it is more in post IRDAI phase. First year premium and total premium witnessed higher growth in post IRDAI phase as per counterfactual analysis, regression analysis and comparison of compound rate of growth. Products launched by insurance companies also witnessed higher rate of growth in post IRDAI phase as per comparisons of compound rate of growth, regression analysis and counterfactual analysis. Policies in force were more in post IRDAI phase as compared to pre-IRDAI phase as per comparison of compound rate of growth and regression analysis. But counterfactual analysis revealed that growth in policies was more in post IRDAI phase. Life insurance penetration in India had been less as compared to world average. Life insurance density in India had been consistently lower than the world average.	Yes

On the basis of above analysis the **Hypothesis 1:** "IRDAI has been an instrument in promoting the growth of life insurance business in India by promoting growth in number of agents, polices, single premium underwritten, total premium underwritten in comparison to pre-IRDAI period" **stands Validated**.

B. Promoting efficiency in Conduct of Insurance Business

Role of IRDAI in enhancing efficiency in conduct of insurance business in India was analyzed through Data Envelopment Analysis by applying BCC and CCR input-oriented model. By using MAX DEA software the efficiency scores of insurance firms were obtained and thus firms having score of one were termed as fully efficient. The scores of insurance firms were compared with average score of the year and firms were further classified as highly efficient, moderately efficient and less efficient.

The finding of study reveals that throughout the time period under life, insurance firms had been inefficient by both the models. For example, in year 2001-02, out of 13 insurance firms 8 were found to efficient by BCC model and 3 by CCR Model. In year 2012-13, out of 24 insurance firms, 9 were found to efficient by BCC model and 3 by CCR model. There is not a single year when there is no inefficient life insurance found.

Testing of the Hypothesis 2:

The analysis of secondary data was used to check the status of Hypothesis 2:

"IRDAI has promoted efficiency in conduct of insurance business by making insurance firms to minimize inputs"

Matrix Summing Up The Testing Of Hypothesis 2

Hypothesis	Sources of Data	Analysis	Status of Hypothesis Accepted
IRDAI has promoted efficiency in conduct of insurance business by making insurance firms to minimize inputs	Secon-dary data	Analysis of results revealed that in year 2001-02, out of 13 insurance firms 8 were found to efficient by BCC model and 3 by CCR Model. In year 2012-13, out of 24 insurance firms, 9 were found to efficient by BCC model and 3 by CCR model. Only one life insurance firm, namely, LIC has been proved to be efficient by both the models. Also during all the years insurance firms had been found to be inefficient by both the models.	NO

Thus, on the basis of above analysis the **Hypothesis 2**: "IRDAI has promoted efficiency in conduct of insurance business by making insurance firms to minimize inputs" **stands rejected**.

C. Effectiveness of IRDAI in Promoting Insurance Business in Rural sector

The findings of the study reveal that although IRDAI has issued guidelines for obligations of life insurance firms to mandatorily underwrite percentage of individual new policies from the rural sector but very few firms have defaulted on this account.

Testing of Hypothesis 3

The analysis of secondary data and primary data was undertaken to check the status of Hypothesis 3:

"IRDAI has been effective in spreading life insurance in rural sector by fixing quota for rural sector".

Matrix Summing Up The Testing Of Hypothesis 3

Hypothesis	Sources of Data	Analysis	Status Hypothesis Accepted
IRDAI has been effective in spreading life insurance in rural sector by fixing quota for rural sector	Secondary data and primary data	Barring for the years 2001-02, 2002-03, 2008-09 and 2010-11 all the insurers fulfilled the rural sector norms specified by the IRDAI. Managerial functionaries of the insurance firms revealed that due to lack of financial literacy in rural areas it is difficult to cater insurance products in rural markets. Rural people think insurance an instrument of investment rather than risk diversification. IRDAI officials stated that the Authority has penalized insurance firms for not complying with rural sector norms.	Yes

Thus, on the basis of above analysis, the **Hypothesis 3**: "IRDAI has been effective in spreading life insurance in rural sector by fixing quota for rural sector", **stands validated.**

D. Effectiveness of IRDAI in Regulating Investments of the Life Insurance Firms

The findings of the study reveals that although IRDAI stipulated norms for the investment pattern of life insurers in India but few firms have not followed the investment pattern specified by IRDAI.

Testing of Hypothesis 4

The analysis of secondary and primary data was undertaken to check the status of Hypothesis 4:

"IRDAI has been effective in regulating investment of funds by insurance companies by stipulating the percentages of investments in Government Securities, Infrastructure and Approved Investments and Other Investments"

Matrix Summing Up The Testing Of Hypothesis-4

Hypothesis	Sources of Data	Analysis	Status of Hypothesis Accepted
IRDAI has been effective in regulating investment of funds by insurance companies by stipulating the percentages of investments in Government Securities, infrastructure and Approved Investments and Other Investments	Secondary data and primary data	During all the years, one or another insurance firm has defaulted with the norms specified for the investment of funds by IRDAI. Moreover majority of the firms had followed the investment specifications issued by IRDAI. Around 81.2 percent of the total Management functionaries of the life insurance firms expressed their satisfaction with the IRDAI for regulating investments funds of insurance firms IRDAI official also opined that IRDAI has imposed fines on insurance firms for not adhering to investment norms specified by the authority.	Yes

Thus, on the basis of above analysis; the **Hypothesis-4:** "IRDAI has been effective in regulating investment of funds by insurance companies by stipulating the percentages of investments in Government Securities, infrastructure and Approved Investments and Other Investments" - **stands validated.**

E. Effectiveness of IRDAI in Protecting Interest of the Policyholders

The findings of the study reveal that policyholders have casual attitude at the point of purchase of policy proposal and tends to shift responsibility on agent. In majority of the cases the policy proposal form is filled by agent. The policyholder only signs the form in good faith.

The technical language and illegible font size of policy form further accentuates feeling of dis-interest in policyholder for filling the form himself/herself and the agent tends to exploit the situation at point of sale of policy and may end up providing policy proposal not compatible to customers' needs but high on agent profits. This leads to mis-selling of the product. In this case even Insurance Ombudsman may be helpless to redress the grievance because insurance firm contends that the policyholder himself/herself has signed the legal document.

Agents of the insurance firms do not disclose the information regarding free look period. Out of total respondents only 27.2 percent respondents opined that agent disclosed information regarding free look period.

Agents do not share information regarding existence of various grievance redressal mechanisms such as Grievance Redressal Cell of IRDAI and Insurance Ombudsman.

The grievance redressal mechanism of the insurer is not effective as majority of the respondents who approached it were dissatisfied with its reply.

Testing of Hypothesis 5

The status of Hypothesis 5 was tested by relying on primary data.

"IRDAI has been effective in protecting the interests of policy holders by making agents of insurers to dispense full information regarding policy proposal to prospective buyer".

MATRIX SUMMING UP THE TESTING OF HYPOTHESIS-5

Sr. No.	**Sub-Hypothesis**	**Sources of Data**	**Analysis**	**Status of Sub-Hypothesis Accepted**
1.	IRDAI has been effective in making policy proposal form policyholder-centric	Primary data	Majority (63.7 percent) of the respondents did not Fill the policy proposal themselves. Majority (65.6 percent) of the respondents found the language of policy form technical in nature. Majority (73.6 percent) of the respondents found the font size of the policy proposal illegible. Majority (83.6 percent) of the agents stated that customer do not fill policy proposal.	No
2.	IRDAI has been effective in stimulating agents to share all the necessary information regarding policy with the prospective buyer at point of sale of policy proposal'.	Primary data	Majority of the respondents stated that barring the aspects of free look period and information regarding IRDAI Grievance redressal cell of IRDAI and Insurance Ombudsman agents of the Insurers dispensed information on all other aspects related to policy proposal. Majority of the agents expressed that they did not impart information regarding IRDAI grievance redressal cell and Insurance Ombudsman. Majority of the agents and managerial functionaries are of view that misspelling is the major cause of policy lapsation.	Yes

Sr. No.	Sub-Hypothesis	Sources of Data	Analysis	Status of Sub-Hypothesis Accepted
3.	Policyholders are satisfied with the information provided by the agent at the point of sale of policy proposal	Primary Data	Majority (61.2 percent) of the respondents are satisfied with the information provided by the agent at point of sale of policy proposal	Yes
4.	Policyholders are satisfied with the final policy of the insurance firm	Primary Data	Majority (70.1 percent) Policy-holders are satisfied with the final policy they received from the insurance firm.	Yes
5.	Insurers have effective grievance redressal mechanism for redressing grievances of policyholders'	Primary Data	Majority (72.9 percent) policy-holders are dissatisfied with the grievance redressal mechanism of insurer.	No

Thus, on the basis of above analysis of sub-hypotheses, the **Hypothesis 5**: "IRDAI has been effective in protecting the interests of policy holders by making agents of insurers to dispense full information regarding policy proposal to prospective buyer", - **stands validated.**

F. Effectiveness of Grievance Redressal mechanism of IRDAI

The findings of the study reveal that overall awareness regarding grievance redressal mechanisms such as grievance redressal cell of IRDAI and Insurance Ombudsman was very low amongst the policyholders. Only 25 percent of the respondents were aware about Grievance Redressal cell of IRDAI. Around 19 percent policyholders were aware about the insurance ombudsman. Also the information regarding existence of these mechanisms is further skewed across education levels, income levels and urban and rural areas.

Pendency of cases with insurance ombudsman Chandigarh after showing a declining trend has shot up again. The field survey results reveals that pendency of cases is high as Ombudsman is overburdened with complaints. It was also found that sometimes in a single day Ombudsman has to hear around 30 cases.

Testing of Hypothesis 6

The Hypothesis 6 was tested on the basis of primary and secondary data.

"IRDAI has effective machinery in the form of Grievance Redressal cell and Insurance Ombudsman for Redressing grievances of Policyholders".

Matrix Summing Up The Testing Of Hypothesis-6

Sr. No.	Sub Hypothesis	Sources of Data	Analysis	Status of Sub-Hypothesis Accepted
1.	Pendency of cases with grievance redressal cell of IRDAI has reduced overtime	Secondary Data	The pendency ration has decreased from 58.68 in 2002-03 to 0.35 in 2012-13	Yes
2.	IRDAI grievance redressal cell has been effective in redressing grievances of policyholders.	Primary Data	Majority (61.5 percent) of the Respondents who approached IRDAI Grievance Redressal cell are dissatisfied with its decision regarding their complaint.	No
3.	There has been reduction in complaints pendency with the insurance Ombudsman over years	Secondary data and Primary Data	The pendency ratio has decreased from 23.43 in 2002-03 to 20.93 in 2012-13. Insurance Ombudsman stated that there is rise in number of complaints by policyholders which may increase pendency of complaints	Yes
4.	IRDAI has effective machinery in the form of Insurance Ombudsman for redressing grievances of policyholders	Primary Data	Majority (87.5 percent) of the Respondents who approached Insurance Ombudsman are satisfied with its decision regarding their complaint.	Yes

Analysis of above sub-hypotheses suggests that the **Hypothesis-6**: "IRDAI has effective machinery in the form of Grievance Redressal cell and Insurance Ombudsman for redressing grievances of Policyholders", **stands Validated.**

G. IRDAI as a Strong Regulator

The findings of primary and secondary data reveals that IRDAI has been independent; able to enforce powers and authority; competent; and accountable and transparent in regulating insurance business. IRDAI do not have its own personnel policy which may compromise its operational independence. Moreover, there is no provision to hire outside expert if need arises. This hampers the ability of the Authority to effectively tackle the unforeseen special challenges having complex dimensions which need outside experts support to handle.

Testing of Hypothesis 7

The analysis of primary and secondary data was carried out to check the status of Hypothesis 7.

"IRDAI has been independent; competent; able to enforce powers and authority; and accountable and transparent in regulating insurance business".

Matrix Summing Up The Testing Of Hypothesis-7

Sr. No.	Sub-Hypothesis	Sources of Data	Analysis	Status of Sub-Hypothesis Accepted
1.	IRDAI is independent from executive as it has sufficient financial resources, competent manpower and infrastructure.	Secondary Data and Primary Data	The members of IRDAI are drawn from diverse fields such as life insurance, non-life insurance, actuarial services making it professionally competent and independent. The fixed tenure of members and their terms of service cannot be varied to their disadvantage is also another parameter of their independence form executive. Debarring the members from future employment also alienates the members from acquiring financial interests in the regulated industry. Official of IRDAI also stated that IRDAI has sufficient finances, infrastructure and manpower to discharge its functions efficiently and effectively. Also IRDAI is independent from undue influence of executive.	Yes

Sr. No.	Sub-Hypothesis	Sources of Data	Analysis	Status of Sub-Hypothesis Accepted
2.	IRDAI has enforcement powers as it exercise licensing powers, penalizing powers product approval powers and lay down of standards of service.	Secondary Data and Primary Data	IRDAI grants licenses to the insurance firms and its intermediaries. The Authority had also cancelled the licenses and imposed fines on the firms violating norms and standards. IRDAI is the final authority for granting approval to the products of insurance firms. The official of IRDAI also stated that IRDAI penalizes the firms for violating standards of service.	Yes
3.	IRDAI has mechanisms for ensuring transparency and accountability as it disseminate information, involve stakeholders in decision making process and its reports are audited.	Secondary data and Primary Data	IRDAI discloses information of its own through its website and annual reports. IRDAI also provide the desired information as per Right to Information Act of India. The official revealed that the Authority also involves various stakeholders such as public, Insurance Advisory Councils, etc by soliciting their views on a policy matter. The decision of IRDAI in case of rejection of registration may be questioned in Securities Appellate Tribunal. Thus there exists check and balances also.	Yes
4	IRDAI has sufficient competency as it can attract and retain qualified personnel and hire outside experts if need arises	Secondary data and primary data	The service conditions such as high salaries act as an incentive for hiring and retaining the qualified manpower. The staff has innovative ability as visible through launching of Insurance Repository System, Integrated grievance management system. The official also opined that there is no provision for hiring an outside expert in hierarchy of IRDAI but discussions can be held with experts for specific issues.	Yes

Thus, on the basis of above analysis of sub-hypotheses, the **Hypothesis-7**: "IRDAI has been independent; competent; able to enforce powers and authority; and accountable and transparent in regulating insurance business", **stands Validated.**

IV
Policy Prescriptions

Though IRDAI has completed almost fifteen years, it still has to go a long way to reach take-off stage. In order to overcome the impediments IRDAI has to regulate the market well by resonating its role as regulator. The following policy prescriptions are put forth for making IRDAI an effective regulator.

1. **Information Dissemination Regarding IRDAI and its Role:** Information dissemination holds the key. Although IRDAI organizes insurance awareness campaigns but very few (26 percent) respondents are aware regarding these mechanisms. Out of these respondents about 5 percent respondents have stated that they had attended insurance awareness campaigns of IRDAI. Majority of the respondents (73 percent) stated that IRDAI should organize more insurance awareness campaigns. Such campaigns may educate attendees regarding insurance market and also availability of various mechanisms of grievance redressal. These information dissemination workshops/seminars will also helps in financial inclusion and may help in increasing insurance coverage. Information should be disseminated regarding IRDAI's role and existence of various mechanisms of grievance redressal by organizing more insurance awareness camps, dissemination workshops, advertise in national and regional newspapers about the services offered by it. IRDAI should conduct policyholders' surveys for improving the policy relating to consumers interest protection.

   IRDAI should increase the frequency of insurance awareness campaigns for disseminating information and increasing financial literacy of masses. IRDAI should organize more campaigns in rural areas as illiteracy and backwardness is the root cause of their elimination from insurance market.

2. **Awareness Regarding Grievance Redressal Cell of IRDAI and Insurance Ombudsman:** All the prospective policyholders should be mandatorily imparted information regarding existence of Grievance Redressal Cell of IRDAI and Insurance Ombudsman. Awareness campaigns should specifically deal with imparting information regarding existence of these mechanisms and their role and responsibilities. The information regarding their roles and responsibilities should be mandatorily disseminated so that unscrupulous elements may not dupe the policyholders in name of these institutions. IRDAI should organize concerted awareness campaigns for customer awareness on the lines of *Jago Grahak Jago* for consumer awareness and *Hum do Hamare do* for containing population and promotion of small family.

3. **Increasing Insurance Penetration in India:** Insurance penetration in India is low as compared to world average. For example, it is 3.2 percent in 2012-13 against the world average of 4 percent. It is recommended that more policies

should be underwritten and practice of recycling the policies should be discarded. Various civil society organizations should be involved for spreading information regarding benefits of insurance amongst the masses and also about the existence of safety checks. Trust of people should be enhanced with regard to insurance.

4. **Enthusing Efficiency in Working of Insurance Companies:** As per Data Envelopment Analysis (DEA) many of the insurance companies are inefficient. The policy implication of this test for these companies is to minimize their inputs such as operating expenses, commission paid to agents and net benefits paid to policyholders or these firms can maximize their output in the form of net premium revenues.

5. **Spreading Insurance in Rural Sector:** Although IRDAI mandates percentage of policies to be underwritten in rural sector but certain firms flaunt this norm. It is recommended that firms who are unable to meet the rural sector obligations should be penalized and necessary action must be taken against them. IRDAI should issue stringent rules and penalties in case of non-compliance. Along with percentage of policies for rural sector IRDAI should also mandate that certain percentage of new premium should be mandatorily from rural sector.

6. **Regulating Investment Patterns:** The IRDAI has laid down norms for investment. Few insurance firms however do not adhere to the norms of investment patterns specified by the IRDAI. It is recommended that IRDAI should strictly enforce the investment patterns. IRDAI should penalize the defaulting insurance firms.

7. **Customer Interest Protection:** The customer interest protection is one of the vital aspects of insurance regulation. A strong customer base is essential for growth of insurance business. Consumer interest protection is important for sustaining policies. Policy lapsation is also matter of concern. LIC lapsation ratio is around 25 percent whereas for private firms it is around 40 percent. One of the factors for policy lapsation is forced selling of policy by agents to meet their targets. Lapsation also impacts industry if it occurs in initial years of policy commencement as company had incurred huge cost in underwriting policy[1]. A study by IRDAI has revealed that lapse rate by number of policies has increased from 5.62 percent in 2002-03 to 7.8 percent and then it decreased to 6.64 percent in 2006-07[2]. For protecting policyholders' interests the following specific recommendations are suggested:

7.1 **Target-Centric Approach of Insurance Firms Should be Shunned:** Target-centric approach of insurance companies should be shunned and training module of agents should specifically emphasize on customer oriented services.

---

1. Kumar, Joginder (2009), "Lapsation of Life Insurance Policy", *Bimaquest,* Volume 9, Number 2.
2. Kannan, R.; Sarma, K.P.; Rao, A.V. and Sarma, S.K. (2009), "Lapsation and its impact on Indian Life Insurance Industry (2002-07)", *Occasional Paper: 1/2008*, Insurance Regulatory and Development Authority of India Development Authority, Government of India, Hyderabad.

Insurance companies should also emphasize on policy retention rather than lapsation in wake of miss-selling done by the agent to meet the target.

7.2 **Entrusting Responsibility on the Policyholder to Fill the Form Himself:** It should be onus of the policyholder to fill the form themselves. Under no circumstance agent should be allowed to fill the policy proposal form. If the person is illiterate then someone from blood relation or nominated by him/her should fill the policy proposal form. In case of educated people the policy proposal form shall be mandatorily filled by them instead of affixing signatures in good faith. Moreover policy proposals should be standardized and written in simple language with legible font size.

7.3 **Information Dissemination at the Point of Sale of Policy Proposal:** Agent should impart all the basic information regarding the policy proposal at the point of sale of policy. Agent must differentiate between the sum assured and risk cover of the policy. In case of Unit Linked Insurance Products (ULIPS) agent should impart information regarding the market fluctuation and its impact on their policy.

7.4 **Fines for Defaulters and Rewards for Performers:** Stringent fines should be imposed on erring (specially for mis-selling) insurance companies. Rewards should be announced for the best policy retaining and servicing agents by IRDAI.

7.5 **Making Grievance Redressal Mechanism of Insurer Effective:** When grievance is reported to insurer there should be auto escalation of grievance to IRDAI grievance redressal cell if it is not addressed in a time bound manner or customer is not satisfied with the reply of insurer. The complaints of insurer should also be evaluated in comparison to their customer base. If proportion of complaints is high vis-à-vis low customer base the insurer should be fined or reprimanded by the regulator.

7.6 **Reducing Pendency of the Cases with Insurance Ombudsman:** The pendency of grievances varies at Insurance Ombudsman centres in the country. Moreover with spread of information regarding available grievance redress mechanisms the pendency of complaints is bound to increase, as more people will approach such mechanism for redressing their grievances. Thus, it is suggested that the Insurance Ombudsman centres where pendency of cases is high, more than one Ombudsman should be appointed for speedy redressal of grievances of policyholders. This may result in reducing the pendency ratio and also repose trust of policyholders in insurance sector.

7.7 **Adequate Facilities at Insurance Ombudsman Centres for Complainants Suggested:** Field survey also revealed that on the day of hearing at Ombudsman Centres complainants have to wait for hours for their turn. In this regard Ombudsman should allot time slots to complainants for their hearings. In this way waiting time of respondents will be reduced. The Ombudsman Centres should have lift - as in case of Chandigarh - the centre is on second floor and it is very difficult for persons with disability and aged - to climb stairs. The Centres should have proper sitting arrangement and canteen facilities.

8. **Involvement of NGOs in Working of IRDAI:** Currently NGOs and consumer advocacy groups are not prominently involve themselves in working of IRDAI. So, IRDAI should actively involve NGOs for spreading information regarding various aspects of the insurance. Involving civil society actors and NGOs may also help in guiding policyholders in redressing their grievances. Moreover involvement of civil society actors will facilitate consumer feedback to the regulator. NGOS may provide a window to consumers for dialogue with IRDAI and their representation will also increase.

9. **Insurance Firms Should Tap New Customers:** It was reported that insurance firms tends to recycling business-meaning thereby, that when the policy of the policyholder is near maturity he/she is approached by the insurance firm for purchasing a new policy from the maturity claim. As per this practice, the agents emphasize more on existing customers and may not tap new customers. IRDAI must get an undertaking during policy processing from the insurer whether the said policyholder is a new customer or old (falling under preview of recycling business). This will improve outreach of insurance to untapped customers

10. **Frivolous Telephone Calls about Insurance Policies Should be Banned:** During field survey it was reported by many respondents that they are getting frivolous calls from IRDAI regarding disbanding the existing policy and a new policy may be issued which will bring high returns. These deceit calls may wane confidence of policyholders regarding the regulator if this practice goes undeterred. Although IRDAI has put a documentary on its website highlighting the cause of frivolous calls but again very few people visit the website of the regulator.

11. **Independent Personnel Policy of IRDAI and Insurance Ombudsman:** The regulator must have its independent personnel policy so as to ensure operational independence. During interaction with Insurance Ombudsman it was found that majority of the staff at Ombudsman office was drawn from LIC or GIC. The staff being drawn from the regulated industry compromises the impartiality of the Ombudsman. In no case, the staff of such agencies should be drawn from the regulated industry. IRDAI should have independent personnel policy and it must recruit and train staff as per its requirement and objectives.

12. **Filling up the Vacant Posts at Regional Office of IRDAI:** During interaction with IRDAI officials at Delhi it was revealed that the two posts of Joint director at Delhi office were lying vacant from past couple of months. The fact was further confirmed by official of IRDAI at Hyderabad office. The Regional office has very less staff either two or three joint directors. If out of these two vacancies are existing simultaneously; then it hampers the effective functioning of IRDAI. Thus, vacancies should be filled up on priority basis for ensuring the smooth functioning of the Authority.

13. **Capacity Building of Officials:** It was reported that officials are drawn from various sectors such as finance, insurance, law, etc. by IRDAI. Since the officials are drawn from diverse fields thus, it is recommended that their regular capacity building programmes should be undertaken. Officials should be trained to handle the responsibilities of regulatory bodies effectively and efficiently as per contingent market needs.
14. **IRDAI Should be Assessed periodically by an Independent Agency:** Regulators in India are not assessed by an external independent outside agency. In this regard it is suggested that assessment process may be patterned on Australian and United States of America style. Performance of IRDAI as a regulator should be evaluated on cost benefit analysis by external agencies. IRDAI should be subjected to regulatory impact analysis.
15. **Selection Committee for Appointment of Whole and Part Time Members:** At present Screening Committee is constituted for evaluating the qualifications of the applicants to be appointed as members of IRDAI. It is recommended that Screening Committee should be upgraded to Search cum Selection Committee for appointing members at IRDAI on the patterns of Committees dealing with selection of members of Competition Commission of India.

Concluding Observations

From above discussion, it is inferred that market failure led to state intervention in early 20th century but gradually in 1970s state intervention lost steam and deregulation of economy emerged as a new policy paradigm. Deregulation of economy led to opening up of sectors hitherto reserved for public sector. For protecting interests of consumers and promoting fair competition amongst the players regulatory authorities/commissions were established. The Indian economy underwent economic transformation by imbibing liberalization, globalization and privatization reforms in the early 1990s. In consonance with these reforms various sectors such as telecom, infrastructure, capital market, electricity and insurance were opened up for private players. Following the global trend sector specific regulatory bodies were also set-up in India.

The present study confined to insurance sector regulation which took place in 2000 with establishment of Insurance Regulatory and Development Authority of India. The scope of the present study was limited to life insurance sector. The study specifically focused on evaluating the role of Insurance Regulatory and Development Authority of India (IRDAI) on the basis of parameters such as growth of insurance sector, efficiency of insurance firms, protection of interests of policyholders and efficacy of grievance redressal mechanisms in insurance sector, spread of insurance in rural sector and investment patterns of insurance firms. The study also analyzed the working of IRDAI as a strong regulator. The study relied on primary and secondary data for analysis.

The analysis revealed that IRDAI has been effective in promoting growth in insurance sector, spreading insurance in rural sector, regulating investments of life insurance firms and protecting interests of policyholders. The findings also highlighted that IRDAI has effective grievance redressal mechanisms in place and it has features of a strong regulator. However, IRDAI has been ineffective in promoting efficiency in conduct of life insurance business in India. The other findings also revealed that score card of IRDAI in not satisfactory on account of insurance density and insurance penetration as compared with world average. The agents of insurance firms tend to conceal information to prospective buyers in matters such as free look period and existing grievance redressal mechanisms. The insurance Ombudsman centres are overburdened with complaints.

In the light of above findings, the study suggested policy prescriptions for improving the working of IRDAI. The study recommends that IRDAI should organize information dissemination workshops and campaigns for making people aware about grievance redressal mechanism for protecting their interests. NGOs and civil society should also be involved in insurance literacy and also providing feed back to the regulator. Insurance firms should tap new customers instead of indulging in recycling business for improving insurance density and penetration. They should minimize their inputs and maximize their outputs for improving efficiency. At Insurance Ombudsman Centres, where pendency of complaints is high, additional Ombudsman may be appointed. Insurance firms should shun target-centric approach and follow customer-centric approach on ethical grounds.

IRDAI should have its independent personnel policy so as to recruit and train officials and build their capacities to achieve its objectives. The next requirement is that -, IRDAI should be subjected to periodic assessment by an independent agency for social cost-benefit analysis.

Bibliography

BOOKS

Abraham, Kenneth S. (2005), *Insurance Law and Regulation*, Foundation Press.

Alexander, E. (1995), *How Organizations Act Together: Inter-organizational Coordination in Theory and Practice,* Gordon and Breach Publishers. Amsterdam.

Alter, C. and Hage, J. (1993), *Organizations Working Together,* Sage Publications, Newbury Park, CA.

Australian Government (2007), *Best Practice Regulation Handbook*, Government of Australia, Canberra.

Australian Government (2014), *Regulator Performance Framework*, Commonwealth of Australia, Canberra.

Bekke, H.; Kickert, W. and Kooiman, J. (1995), "Public Management and Governance", In Kickert and F. A. Van Vught, (Eds.) *Public Policy and Administrative Sciences in the Netherlands,* Harvester- Wheatsheaf, London.

Berger, A.N. and Humphrey, D.B. (1992), "Measurement and Efficiency Issues in Commercial Banking", In Zvi Griliches (Eds.), *Output Measurement in the Services Sector,* University of Chicago Press, Chicago.

Bergh, Van Den R. and Camesasca, P. (2001), *European Competition Law and Economics: a Comparative Perspective*, Oxford, Intersentia.

Berman, P. (1980), "Thinking About Programmed and Adaptive Implementation: Matching Strategies to Situations", In H. Ingram and D. Mann, (Eds.) W*hy Policies Succeed or Fail,* Sage, Beverly Hills, CA.

Bhatacharya, Mohit (2007), *New Horizons of Public Administration*, Jawahar Publishers, New Delhi.

Boston, J.; Martin, J.; Pallot, J.; and Walsh, P. (1996), *Public Management: The New Zealand Model*, Oxford University Press, Auckland.

Cherunilam, Francis (2000*), Business and Government*, Himalaya Publishing House, Mumbai.

Dasgupta, A. and Sengupta, N.K. (2001), *Government and Business*, Vikas Publishing House, New Delhi.

Department for Business, Innovation and Skills (2011), *Principles for Economic Regulation*, Government of United Kingdom.

Desai, Meghnad (1979), *Applied Econometrics*, Tata McGraw-Hill Publishing Company Ltd, New Delhi.

Drucker, Peter F. (1969), *The Age of Discontinuity*, Harper & Row, New York.

Ellis, H. (1990),"Government Regulation of Insurance Companies", In: Stephen Diacon, (Eds) *A Guide to Insurance Management*, Palgrave Macmillan, Basingstoke.

Government of Victoria, (2011), *Victorian Guide to Regulation*, Department of Treasury and Finance, Melbourne.

Kaur, Simrit (2003), *Privatization and Public Regulation: The Indian Experience*, Macmillian India Ltd., New Delhi.

Koutsoyiannis, A. (2003), *Theory of Econometrics: An Introductory Exposition of Econometric Methods*, Replika Press Pvt. Ltd., Kundli.

Lane, Jan Erik (2000), *The Public Sector: Concepts, Models and Approaches*, Sage Publication Ltd., London.

Law Commission of India (2003), "Consultation Paper on Revision of the Insurance Act, 1938 and the Insurance Regulatory and Development Act, 1999", Government of India, New Delhi.

Meier, Gerald M. and Rauch, James E. (2000*), Leading issues in Economic Development*, Oxford University Press, New Delhi.

Mishra, R.K. and Bhatt, K. S. (2002*), Privatization*, Vikas Publishing House Pvt. Ltd., New Delhi.

Narain, Laxmi (2005), *Public Enterprises Management and Privatization*, S. Chand & Co. Ltd., New Delhi.

Prakash, Jagdish; Rao, Nageshwar and Shukla, Mata Badal (2002), *Administration of Public Enterprises in India*, Himalaya Publishing House, Mumbai.

Rao, Potluri and Miller, Roger LeRoy (1972), *Applied Econometrics*, Prentice-Hall of India Private Limited, New Delhi.

Reddy, Y.V. (1989), "State Market and Privatization: Statement in State Action in India", In T.L. Shankar and Y.Venugopal Reddy (Eds.), *Privatisation: Diversification of Ownership of Public Enterprises*, Institute of Public Enterprise Silver Jubilee Publication, Hyderabad.

Rosenbloom, David H. (1989), *Public Administration: Understanding Management, Politics and Law in the Public Sector*, McGraw-Hill Book Company, New York.

Shafritz, Jay. M. and Russell, E. W. (1999), *Introducing Public Administration*, Longman, New York.

Stigler, Stephen M, (1986), *The History of Statistics: The Measurement of Uncertainty Before 1900*, Harvard University Press.

Tripathi, Dwijendra (2004), *The Oxford History of Indian Business*, Oxford University Press, Oxford.

Walsh, Kieron (1997), *Public Services and Market Mechanisms: Competition, Contracting and the New Management*, Hampshire, Macmillan.

JOURNALS

Ahuja, Rajiv (2004), "Insurance: Over the Transition", *Economic and Political Weekly*, Volume 39, Number 32.

Ansari, H. (2006), "Marketing Opportunities & Challenges", *IRDA Journal*, Volume IV, Number 11.

Aulich, Chris and Flynn, Janine O' (2007), "From Public to Private: The Australian Experience of Privatisation", *The Asia Pacific Journal of Public Administration*, Volume 29, Number 2.

Banker, R.D.; Charnes, A. and Cooper, W.W. (1984), "Some Models for Estimating Technical and Scale Inefficiencies in Data Envelopment Analysis", *Management Science*, Volume 30, Number 9.

Barth, James R.; Lin, Chen; Ma, Yue; Seade, Jesús and Song Frank M. (2013), "Do Bank Regulation, Supervision and Monitoring Enhance or Impede Bank Efficiency?", *Journal of Banking & Finance*, Volume 37.

Bassanini, Andrea and Brunello, Giorgio (2010), "Barriers to Entry, Deregulation and Workplace Training: A Theoretical Model with Evidence from Europe", *CESfifo Working paper NO.2945, Category 4: Labour Markets* [Online] Available from: www.ssrn.com, [Accesses on 8 August 2013].

Baumol, W.J. (1982), "Contestable Markets: an Uprising in the Theory of Market Structure", *American Economic Review*, Volume 72, Number 1.

Bawa, Sumninder Kaur and Chattha, Samiya (2013), "Financial Performance of Life Insurers in Indian Insurance Industry" *Pacific Business Review International*, Volume 6, Issue 5.

Becker, Gary (1983), "A Theory of Competition among Pressure Groups for Political Influence", *Quarterly Journal of Economics*, Volume 98.

Becker, Gary (1985), "Public Policies, Pressure Groups, and Deadweight Costs", *Journal of Public Economics*, Volume 28.

Bennett, Jonathan (1987), "Event Causation: The Counterfactual Analysis", *Philosophical Perspectives, Metaphysics*, Volume 1.

Berg, Sanford, Memon, Ali Nawaz and Skelton, Rama (2000), "Designing an Independent Regulatory Commission" *Public Utility Research Center eco. Research Papers*, Public Utility Research Center, University of Florida.

Berger, A. N. and Humphrey, D. B. (1997), "Efficiency of Financial Institutions: International Survey and Directions for Future Research", *European Journal of Operational Research*, Volume 98, Number 2.

Bertolini, Lorenzo (2004) "Regulating Utilities– Contracting out Regulatory Functions", *Public Policy for the Private Sector Note No. 269*, The World Bank Group, Washington DC.

Bhardwaj, C. L. (2009), "Asymmetry in Life Insurance Selling: Bane for Poor Business Retention", *IRDA Journal*, Volume VII, Number 11.

Bhat, Ramesh and Babbu, Sumesh K. (2004), "Health Insurance & Third Party Administrators: Issues & Challenges", *Economic and Political Weekly*, Volume 39, Number 28.

Bhatacharya, Mohit (2007), "Rolling Back of The State: Public Administration in the Age of Market Supremacy", *Indian Journal of Public Administration*, Volume LII, Number 3.

Breausc, David A.; Duncan, Christopher M.; Keller, C. Denise and Morriss, John C. (2002), "Welfare Style: Temporary Assistance for Needy families and the Search for Accountability", *Public Administration Review*, Volume 62, Number 4.

Brown, Gene (2004), *Deregulation,[Online] Available from* http://www.enotes.com/management-encyclopedia/deregulation [Accessed on 30 July 2008].

Butcher, Tony (1995), "Managing The Welfare State: The Politics of Public Sector Management", *Public Administration*, Volume. 73, Number. 3.

Chakraborty, S. P. and Anita, J. (2009), "An Overview of RBC: Life Insurance Perspectives", *IRDA Journal*, Volume VII, Number 07.

Chandersherkran, David (2009), "Marketing for Life Insurance Have Things Really Changed?",*IRDA Journal*, Volume VII, Number 05.

Chandrasekhran, David (2008), "Policy Lapsation in Life Insurance: Role of Middle Man", *IRDA Journal*, Volume VI, Number 08.

Charnes, A.; Cooper, W. W. and Rhodes, E. (1978) "Measuring the Efficiency of Decision Making Units", *European Journal of Operational Research*, Volume 2, Number 6.

Charumathi, B. (2012) "On the Determinants of Profitability of Indian Life Insurers – An Empirical Study" *Proceedings of the World Congress on Engineering*, London, U.K.

Chatterjee, Arup (2007), "Insurance Awareness: Where do We go from Here?", *IRDA Journal*, Volume V, Number 07.

Chaudhari, Sanjib (2009), "The Cost of Climate Change: Urgent Need for Action", *IRDA Journal*, Volume VII, Number 02.

Chaudhary, S. and Kiran, P., (2011) "Life Insurance Industry in India- Current Scenario" *International Journal of Management & Business Studies*, Volume 1, Issue 3.

Chenok, Dan (2015), "Regulatory Oversight: Lessons from the US and Others", presentation made at Bharti Institute of Public Policy at Expert Group Meeting on Regulating the Regulators, Mohali.

Chortareas, Georgios E.; Girardone, Claudia and Ventouri, Alexia (2012), "Bank Supervision, Regulation, and Efficiency: Evidence from the European Union", *Journal of Financial Stability*, Volume 8.

Coglianese, Cary (2012), "Measuring Regulatory Performance: Evaluating the Impact of Regulation and Regulatory Policy", *Expert Paper No. 1,* Organization for Economic Co-operation and Development.

Cohen, Steve (2001), "A Strategic Framework for Developing Responsibility and Functions from Government to the Private Sector", *Public Administration Review*, Volume 61, Number 4.

Coy, Patricia A.Mc.; Pavlov, Andrew D. and Wachter, Susan M. (2009), "Systemic Risk Through Securitization: The result of Deregulation and Regulatory Failure", *Connecticut Law Review,* Volume 41, Number 4.

Cummins, J.D.; Tennyson, S. and Weiss, M.A. (1999), "Consolidation and Efficiency in the US Life Insurance Industry", *Journal of Banking and Finance,* Volume 23, Number 2–3.

Das, Mohan and Abott, Keith (2008), "Modelling NPM in an Asian Context: Public Sector Reform in Malaysia", *The Asian Pacific Journal of Public Administration*, Volume 30, Number 1.

Davis, Lucas W. and Wolfram, Catherine (2011), "Deregulation, Consolidation, and Efficiency: Evidence From U.S. Nuclear Power", *National Bureau of Economic Research Working Paper 17341*, Massachusetts Avenue Cambridge.

Demyanyk, Yuliya (2006), "U.S. Banking Deregulation and Eelf-employment: A Differential Impact on those in Need," *Journal of Economics and Business*, Volume 60, Number 1-2.

Devas, Nick and Kelly, Roy (2001), "Regulation or Revenues? An Analysis of Local Business Licenses with a Case Study of the Single Business Permit Reform in Kenya", *Public Administration and Development*, Volume 21, Number 5.

Dutta, Anirban and Sengupta, Partha Pratim (2011), "Efficiency Measurement of Indian Life Insurance Industry in Post-Reforms Era", *Global Business Review*, Volume 12, Number 3.

Easwaran, P R (2009), "Data Driven Business: Key to Marketing Strategy", *IRDA Journal*, Volume VII, Number 05.

Editorial, Dec (1999), "Ending the Insurance Monopoly", *Economic and Political Weekly*, Volume 34, Number 49.

Eling, Martin and Luhnen, Michael (2009), "Frontier Efficiency Methodologies to Measure Performance in the Insurance Industry: Overview, Systematization, and recent, *JEL classification: D23; G22; L11*.

Eling, Martin; Klein, Robert W. and Schmit, Joan T. (2009), Insurance Regulation in the United States and the European Union: A Comparison, *Independent Policy Report*, Independent Institute, Oakland, CA.

European Insurance and Occupation Pension Authority (2013), Report on Best Practices by Insurance Intermediaries in handling complaints, *EIOPA BoS 13/171*, [Online] Available from: https://eiopa.europa.eu/Publications/ Guidelines/EIOPA-BoS-13-164_Guidelines-on-complaints-handling-by-Insurance-Intermediaries.pdf [Accessed on 30 June 2015].

Farrell, M.J. (1957), "The measurement of productive efficiency", *Journal of the Royal Statistical Society*, Series A, Volume 120, Number 3.

Fecher, F.; Kessler, D.; Perelman, S. and Pestieau, P. (1993), "Productive Performance of the French Insurance Industry", *Journal of Productivity Analysis*, Volume 4, Number 1–2.

Filipovic, Adnan (2005), "Impact of Privatization on Economic Growth", *Issues in Political Economy*, Volume 14.

Fullbirght, Norton Rose (2015), "Insurance regulation in Asia Pacific: Ten things to know about 20 countries", [Online] Available from: [Accessed on 30 July 2015].

Gangopadhyay, Shubhashis (2004), "An Alternative to Crop Insurance", *Economic and Political Weekly*, Volume 39, Number 44.

George, Alex (2007), "Critical Appraisal of Micro Health Insurance Laws", *Economic and Political Weekly*, Volume 42, Number 06.

Ghuman, B.S. (1998), "Globalization, Liberalization, Privatization: Impact on Governance", Paper presented at *Third Annual Conference of New Public Administration Society of India*, held at Department of Public Administration, Dr. B.R. Ambedkar Open University, Hyderabad.

Gopalkrishna (2009), "Healthy Expansion of Insurance: Adopting Best Method", *IRDA Journal*, Volume VII, Number 10.

Gour, B. and Gupta, M.C. (2012), "A Review on Solvency Margin in Indian Insurance Companies" *International Journal of Recent Research and Review*, Volume II.

Goyal, Kamlesh (2009), "Defining Strategies for the Future Innovations and Development in Insurance", *IRDA Journal*, Volume VII, Number 09.

Grey, Andrew and Jenkins, Bill (1995), "From Public Administration to Public Management: Reassessing a Revolution", *Public Administration*, Volume 73, Number 1.

Gruening, Gernod (2001), "Origin and Theoretical Basis of New Public Management", *International Public Management Journal*, Volume 4.

Gulati, N.C. and Jain, C. M. (2011) "Comparative Analysis of the Performance of All the Players of the Indian Life Insurance Industry" *VSRD International Journal of Business & Management Research*, Volume 1, Number 8.

Gülen, Gürcan; Makaryan, Ruzanna; Volkov, Dmitry and Foss, Michelle (?), "Improving Regulatory Agency Efficiency and Effectiveness: Best Practices, Processes and Organizational Structures", *Working Paper, Center for Energy Economics*, Bureau of Economic Geology, University of Texas at Austin.

Gupta, Aditya Kumar (2014), "Life Insurance Market: The Rural India Connect" *Management Insight*, Volume. X, Number 1.

Gupta, Indrani (2002), "Private Health Insurance & Health Cost", *Economic and Political Weekly*, Volume 37, Number 27.

Gupta, Priyanka and Aggarwal, Vani (2014), "An Analysis of Insurance Sector: Penetration Perspective in India" *Working Paper No: 14,* Centre for WTO Studies (CWS), Indian Institute of Foreign Trade, New Delhi.

Gupta,Indrani; Roy, Abhijit and Trivedi, Mayur (2004), "Third Party Administrators: Theory & Practice", *Economic and Political Weekly*, Volume 39, Number 28.

Hegde, Ashay Ravi (2015), "Increasing Insurance Penetration to Rural & Informal Sector of the Economy", *IRDAI Journal*, Volume 14, Number 6.

Hertog, Johan den (2010), Review of Economic Theories of Regulation, *Discussion Paper Series nr: 10-18,* Tjalling C. Koopmans Research Institute, Utrecht School of Economics, Utrecht University, Utrecht.

Iacobucci, Edward M.; Trebilcock, Michael J. and Ralph A. Winter (2005), "The Canadian Experience with Deregulation", *Queen's University Law & Economics Working Paper No. 2005-03,* Sauder School of Business, [Online] Available from http://ssrn.com/abstract [Accessed on 2 August 2008].

Insurance Regulatory Development Authority (2001), Annual Report 2000-2001, October, Hyderabad.

....................................(2002), Annual Report 2001-02, October, Hyderabad.

....................................(2003), Annual Report 2002-03, October, Hyderabad.

....................................(2004), Annual Report 2003-04, October, Hyderabad.

....................................(2005), Annual Report 2004-05, October, Hyderabad.

....................................(2006), Annual Report 2005-06, October, Hyderabad.

....................................(2007), Annual Report 2006-07, October, Hyderabad.

....................................(2008), Annual Report 2007-08, October, Hyderabad.

....................................(2009), Annual Report 2008-09, October, Hyderabad.

....................................(2010), Annual Report 2009-10, October, Hyderabad.

....................................(2011), Annual Report 2010-11, October, Hyderabad.

....................................(2012), Annual Report 2011-12, October, Hyderabad.

....................................(2013), "Insurance Repository a Step Towards e-world", [online] Available from: [Accessed on 18 August 2015].

......................................(2013), Annual Report 2012-13, October, Hyderabad.

......................................(2014), Annual Report 2013-14, October, Hyderabad.

Jacob, Antony (2006), "Maturing Progressively: Indian Insurance Industry", *IRDA Journal,* Volume IV, Number 11.

James, P. C. (2009), "Going from Exclusion to Inclusion: Need for Facilitating the Exercise", *IRDA Journal,* Volume VII, Number 04.

Jaswal, Malti (2010), "Understanding TPA", *IRDA Journal*, Volume VIII, Number 8.

Jong, Gjalt De and Witteloostuijn, Arjen Van (2015), "Regulatory Red Tape And Private Firm performance", *Public Administration*, Volume 93, Number 1.

Kakkar, Sunil (2008), "Asset Liability Management (ALM) in Indian Insurance Companies", *IRDA Journal*, Volume VI, Number 06.

Kapoor, Sheetal (2009), "Insurance Ombudsman" *Yojana*, Volume 53.

Kessides, Ioannis N. (2004), Reforming Infrastructure, Privatization, Regulation and Competition, *World Bank Policy Research Report,* World Bank and Oxford University Press, Washington DC.

Khandelwal, Rajesh (2008), "SRI and Relevance of ALM", *IRDA Journal*, Volume VI, Number 06.

Khandelwal, Rajesh (2009 b*)*, "Best Practises in SRI: Venturing Beyond the Bottom Line", *IRDA Journal,* Volume VII, Number 10.

Khandelwal, Rajesh (2009*)*, "Fairness and Transparency through CSR Approach", *IRDA Journal,* Volume VII, Number 03.

König, Charlotte Senftleben (2014), "Product Market Deregulation and Employment Outcomes: Evidence from the German Retail Sector", *SFB 649 Discussion Paper 2014-013*, Humboldt-Universität zu Berlin, Germany.

Krishnamurthy, Gnanasundaram (2009*)*, "Symmetry in Information: A Two Way Process", *IRDA Journal,* Volume VII, Number 11.

Kumar, Jagendra (2015), "New Insurance Regulations are more Transparent & Customer-friendly", *IRDAI Journal*, Volume 13, Number 3.

Kumari, T.H. (2013), "Performance Evaluation of Indian Life Insurance Industry in Post Liberalization", *International Journal of Social Sciences Arts and Humanities*, Volume 1, Number 1.

Loi, Massimo and Rodrigues, Margarida (2012), A note on the Impact Evaluation of Public Policies: the Counterfactual Analysis, Joint *Research Centre, Institute for the Protection and Security of the Citizen*, European Commission, Italy.

Macey, Jonathan R. and Miller, G. P. (1993) "The McCarran Ferguson Act of 1945: Re-conceiving the Federal Role in Insurance Regulation", *New York University Law Review* Volume 68, Number 14.

Mahal, Ajay (2002), "Assessing Private Health Insurance in India, Potential Impacts & Regulatory Issues", *Economic and Political Weekly*, Volume 37, Number 6.

Mahapatra, S. K. (2005), "A Healthy Ground for TPA", *IRDA Journal*, Volume III, Number 6.

Malik, H. (2011), "Determinants of Insurance Companies Profitability: An Analysis of Insurance Sector Of Pakistan" *Academic Research International,* Volume 1, Issue 3.

Malyshev, Nick (2009), "Regulatory Reform and Building Governance Capacities" paper presented in seminar on *Building Governance Capacities in India*, by OECD and CUTS International on 3 December 2009, New Delhi, India.

Mishra, K. C. (2009), "Hazards in Insurance: Essential Factors in Underwriting", *IRDA Journal*, Volume VII, Number 01.

Mishra, R.K. (2014), "Role of State-Owned Enterprises In India's Economic Development", Background material for *Workshop on State-Owned Enterprises in the Development Process*, Held on 4 April, at OECD Conference Centre, Room 4, Paris.

Mohan, S. V. Krishna (2007), "Insurance Legislation in India, Ancient yet Modern", *IRDA Journal*, Volume V, Number 11.

Mor, Nichiket and Nitsure, Rupa Rege (2002), "Organization of Regulatory Functions: A Single Regulator?", *Economic and Political Weekly*, Volume 37, Number 5.

Moss, David (2010), "Reversing the Null: Regulation, Deregulation, and the Power of Ideas", *Working Paper. 10-080*, Harvard Business School.

Murty, R. K. (2007), "Insurance Literacy in India", *IRDA Journal*, Volume V, Number 07.

Nandraj, Sunil and Khot, Anagha (2003), "Accreditation System for Health Facilities", *Economic and Political Weekly*, Volume 38, Number 50.

OECD (2014), *Regulatory Enforcement and Inspection: OECD Best Practice Principles for Regulatory Policy*, OECD Publishing.

OECD (2015), "International Comparison", in *OECD Insurance Statistics 2014*, OECD Publishing, Paris.

Office of Commissioner of Insurance (2013), *Annual Report 2013*, Hong Kong.

Pant, Niranjan (2000), "Development Agenda for Insurance Regulation", *Economic and Political Weekly*, Volume 35, Number 10.

Parasnis, Paresh (2009), "Creating Multi Prolonged Strategies in Tune With Innovations & Development", *IRDA Journal*, Volume VII, Number 09.

Parekh, Ashvin (2007), "*Regulatory* Approaches to Supervision and Inspection: A Look at Different Market", *IRDA Journal*, Volume V, Number 09.

Parekh, Ashwin (2009), "Tariff Abolition: Advantages of A calibrated Approach", *IRDA Journal*, Volume VII, Number 02.

Parsad, Parnav (2009), "Catalyst for Financial Inclusion: Insurance in the Rural & Social Sector", *IRDA Journal*, Volume VII, Number 04.

Peltzman, Sam (1989), "The Economic Theory of Regulation after a Decade of Deregulation" *Brookings Papers: Microeconomics*, University of Chicago.

Pesaran, M. Hashem and Smith, Ron P. (2012), "Counterfactual Analysis in Macro-econometrics: An Empirical Investigation into the Effects of Quantitative Easing", *Discussion Paper No. 6618*, The Institute for the Study of Labor (IZA), Bonn.

Posner, Richard A. (1974), "Theories of Economic Regulation", *The Bell Journal of Economics and Management Science*, Volume 5, Number 2.

Priyadarshi, Partik (2009), "Hazards in Health Insurance: Need for a Closer Look", *IRDA Journal*, Volume VII, Number 01.

Radhakrishna (2007), "Alternatives to Monitoring & Supervision: Difficult not Impossible", *IRDA Journal*, Volume V, Number 09.

Raju, S. S. and Chand, Ramesh (2007), "Progress & Problems in Agriculture Insurance", *Economic and Political Weekly,* Volume 42, Number 21.

Ramachandran, T. R. (2009), "Indian Banking & Insurance Industry: Treating Customers Fairly", *IRDA Journal*, Volume VII, Number 03.

Ramakrishnan, R. (2009), "Insurance Bill: Ill Conceived Changes", *The Hindu*, New Delhi, November 9, Business Review.

Ramberg, Inge and Knell, Mark (2012), Challenges measuring effects of research and innovation policy interventions in ex-post impact evaluations. A synthesis report, retrieved online from www.forskningsradet.no/servlet/Satellite?...id..., last accessed on 5 April, 2015.

Ranade, Ajit and Ahuja, Rajiv (2000), "Issues in Regulation of Insurance", *Economic and Political Weekly*, Volume 35, Number 5.

Rao, G. V. (2005), "Ensured Success for Insurance Councils: What it Takes to Make Self-Regulation Tick", *IRDA Journal*, Volume III, Number 6.

Rao, G. V. (2009), "Risk Acceptance Criteria", *IRDA Journal,* Volume VII, Number 01.

Rawson, B.L. (2001), "Data envelopment analysis of technical efficiency in the UK insurance industry", *Ph.D. Thesis series,* Nottingham University.

Rehman, Redwanur (2007), "The State, the Private Health Care Sector and Regulation in Bangladesh", *The Asia Pacific Journal of Public Administration*, Volume 24, Number 2.

Rittershaus, Annet (2009), "Integrated Risk Management Safety Back in Fashion", *IRDA Journal*, Volume VII, Number 10.

Roy, Saktinil and Kemme, David M. (2012), "Causes of Banking Crises: Deregulation, Credit Booms and Asset Bubbles, then and now", *International Review of Economics and Finance*, Volume 24.

Sastry, DVS. (2011), "Life Insurance Penetration in India" *Journal of Social and Economic Policy*, Volume 8, Number 2.

Savas, E.A. (2002), "Competition and Choice in New York City Social Services", *Public Administration Review*, Volume 62, Number 1.

Shleifer, Andrei (2005), "Understanding Regulation", *European Financial Management*, Volume 11, Number 4.

Shukla, Neha (2012), "IRDA Soft on Insurance Companies Flouting Norms" *TNN,* 12 June.

Singh, Alam (2009), "Collaborative Approaches in Implementation Risk Based Capital Regime", *IRDA Journal,* Volume VII, Number 07.

Sinha, RK; Nizammudin, MM. and Alam, I. (2012), "An Investigation of Insurance penetration and Density of India by Geography", *16th Conference of Asia-Pacific Risk and Insurance Association*, July, Seoul, South Korea.

Sinha, Tapen (2005), "An Analysis of the Evolution of Insurance in India", *Discussion Paper Series-III,* Centre for Risk and Insurance Studies, Instituto Tecnologico Autonomo de Mexico and University of Nottingham [Online] Available from: ww.nottingham.ac.uk/business/cris/papers 2005-3.pdf [Accessed on Aug.10, 2008].

Smith, Warrick (1997), "Utility Regulators: Independence Debate, Public Policy for the Private Sector", *Note No. 127*, The World Bank Group.

Sridhar, V. (2009), "IRDA against Basle II norms for Insurance Industry", *The Hindu*, November 24, New Delhi.

Stern, Jon (1997), "What Makes an Independent Regulator Independent?", *Business Strategy Review*, Volume 8, Number 2.

Stigler, George J. (1971), "The Theory of Economic Regulation", *The Bell Journal of Economics and Management Science*, Volume 2, Number 1.

Stilitz, Joseph (2003), "Globalization and the economic role of the State in the new Millennium", *Industrial and Corporate Change,* Volume 12, Number 1.

Stoker, Gerry (1995), "Intergovernmental Relations", *Public Administration*, Volume 73, Number 1.

Sud, Rajesh (2009), "Customer Relationship Your Most Important Asset", *IRDA Journal*, 2009, Volume VII, Number 04.

Tanzi, Vito (1997), "The Changing Role of the State in the Economy: A Historical Perspective", *International Monetary Fund Working Paper,* paper presented at conference on, 'Decentralization, Inter-Governmental Fiscal Relations and Macroeconomic Governance' Organized by Advanced School of Public Administration (ESAF), Ministry of Finance of Brazil and OECD Development Centre,16-17 June, Brasilia.

The Insurance Regulatory and Development Authority Act, 1999, Universal Law Publishing Co. Pvt. Ltd., Delhi 2010.

Timm, Christial (2013), "Economic regulation and State Intervention: Georgia's Move from Neo-liberalism to State Managed Capitalism", *Research Paper No. 2013/13*, Private University of Applied Science.

Venkatesan, R. (2015), "Mis-selling of Insurance Products", *IRDAI Journal*, Volume 14, Number 5.

Verma, Amitabh (2008), "Life Insurance Business: Need for Improvement", *IRDA Journal,* Volume VI, Number 08.

Vermani, Lalit (2007), "The Changing Pace of Insurance Laws: Going With Times", *IRDA Journal*, Volume V, Number 11.

Viscusi, W. Kip (1996), "Regulating the Regulatory", *The University of Chicago Law Review*, Volume 63, Number 4,

Walwei. Ulrich (2015), "From Deregulation to Re-regulation: Trend Reversal in German Labour Market Institutions and its Possible Implications", *IAB Discussion Paper Articles on labour market issues 10/2015*, Institute For Employment Research, Germany.

Williams, Anthony D. (2004), "An Economic Theory of Self-Regulation", *Working Paper prepared for The Political Economy Doctoral workshop*, Department of Government, London School of Economics and political Science.

World Bank (2003), "Regulation by Contract" *Working Paper No.14*, Washington DC.

Ziv-Av, Doron (2006), Competition versus Regulation in the Insurance Market: A Law and Economic Analysis of Policy and Institutes, *Master Thesis: European Master Program in Law and Economics*, University of Hamburg.

WEBSITES

[Online] Available from http://en.google.com.[Accessed on 22 August 2010]

[Online] Available from **http://www.enotes.com/management-encyclopedia/deregulation**. [Accessed on 15 December 2009]

[Online] Available from http://**www.irda.gov.in**. [Accessed on 26 August 2010]

[Online] Available from http://www.policyholder.gov.in/uploads/ CEDocuments/ Classification%20Life%202014-15.jpg [Accessed on 21 May 2015]

[Online] Available from **http://www.ssrn.com.[Accessed** on 19 August 2010]

[Online] Available from: http://www.nortonrosefulbright.com/files/insurance-regulation-in-asia-pacific-113885.pdf [Accessed on 30 July 2015].

[Online] Available from: www.mbcindia.com/Image/20%20insurance.pdf- The Meridian Business Consultants Pvt. Limited, [Accessed on 5 March 2015].

[Online] Available fromhttp://www.CESifo.com.[Accessed on 25 August 2010]

[Online] Available from**http://www.scribd.com**. [Accessed on 9 January 2010]

Index

D

E

J

K

L

M

N

Q

R

T

U

V

W